Science, Technology and Innovation Studies

Science, technology and innovation (STI) studies are interrelated, as are STI policies and policy studies. This series of books aims to contribute to improved understanding of these interrelations. Their importance has become more widely recognized, as the role of innovation in driving economic development and fostering societal welfare has become almost conventional wisdom. Interdisciplinary in coverage, the series focuses on the links between STI, business, and the broader economy and society. The series includes conceptual and empirical contributions, which aim to extend our theoretical grasp while offering practical relevance. Relevant topics include the economic and social impacts of STI, STI policy design and implementation, technology and innovation management, entrepreneurship (and related policies), foresight studies, and analysis of emerging technologies. The series is addressed to professionals in research and teaching, consultancies and industry, government and international organizations.

Bruce Garvey • Dowshan Humzah •
Storm Le Roux

Uncertainty Deconstructed

A Guidebook for Decision Support
Practitioners

Springer

Bruce Garvey
Croydon, UK

Dowshan Humzah
London, UK

Storm Le Roux
Ascot, UK

ISSN 2570-1509 ISSN 2570-1517 (electronic)
Science, Technology and Innovation Studies
ISBN 978-3-031-08006-7 ISBN 978-3-031-08007-4 (eBook)
https://doi.org/10.1007/978-3-031-08007-4

This Springer imprint is published by the registered company Springer Nature Switzerland AG
The registered company address is: Gewerbestrasse 11, 6330 Cham, Switzerland

Dedications are always difficult—offer too many and you risk offending someone not included—not enough, then the same sentiment can be expressed. This dedication is to the past and the future.

For the past, this book is dedicated to my late parents, Dora and Charles Garvey, who continually encouraged and supported me in seeking to broaden my horizons even though they may not always have agreed with some of my opinions at the time.

For the future, this book is also dedicated to those generations younger than I—and to those generations to come—in the hope they may seek to explore rationally both sides of an argument and not be seduced by those bad actors who seek to close off our minds to diversity of opinion.

Preface: "We Should've Seen It Coming"!

The future isn't the outcome of a single trend, working in isolation. The biggest changes often occur when multiple trends combine, altering each other in the process.—David Wood—London Futurists February 2021

Synopsis

This book argues that uncertainty is not really uncertainty at all but just demonstrates a lack of vision and willingness to think about the unthinkable—good and bad. The task of accepting that uncertainty is about exploring the possible, rather than the impossible has to be taken on board by strategists, policy developers, and political leaders, if we are to meet the challenges that an ever-changing world is throwing at us. The term "unknown–unknowns" is ubiquitous, albeit the vast majority of future uncertain events do not fall into this category. However, it has been used to absolve decision makers from criticism post event, whereas poor foresight is the prime culprit and that most future uncertainties are "known-unknowns" or "inevitable surprises". This re-positioning of uncertainties can help mitigate the impact of such risks through better foresight aware contingency planning. The enemy is not uncertainty itself but our lack of imagination when trying to visualise the future—we need to transform our behaviour. To better understand uncertainty, we have to deconstruct it and get to grips with its component parts. Three main questions are posed and practical approaches presented: What are the main structural components that make up the conditions under which uncertainty operates? What scenario lenses can be used when exploring uncertainty? What behavioural factors do we need to consider when analysing the human responses to uncertainty? Practitioners, having to deal with making better decisions under uncertainty, will find the book a useful guide.

To Whom Is This Book Targeted?

First of all, I should say that Uncertainty is a generic topic—everybody has been and will be impacted by it in some way. It is not easy to allocate it to any one discipline— every aspect of human life is affected by one form of uncertainty or the other. However, those people whose interest in the topic is more professional and academic rather than *en passant,* and who are looking for a different perspective as to how Uncertainty can be handled, include the following categories.

Practitioners and decision makers in both private and public sectors including (not exclusive):

- strategic planners
- risk analysts
- policy developers
- intelligence analysts (military and non-military)
- forecasting, foresight, and futures specialists (short, medium, and long term)
- think tank researchers
- specialist consultants in strategic development
- OR (Operational Research) specialists
- Systems analysts
- business transformation specialists

For practitioners, it provides a "strategic insurance vehicle", which can be integrated into your own custom decision-making and risk analysis processes and be adapted to the specific needs and circumstances of your own organisation.

Academic: As a generic subject, academic interest, as for the practitioner community, is broad in range. Specific academic interest for the topic is spread across the following categories:

- Faculty and post-doc Researchers
- Post and Undergraduate students
- Disciplines such as Business, Economic, Political, and Social studies (including PEP type studies), Decision Science, Strategic issue studies (such as Technology, Climate based AI, and Cybersecurity institutes), Behavioural sciences (including organisational and individual psychology and social psychology)
- Creative disciplines such as design and design engineering

Finally, the book will also be of interest to anyone who is engaged in any form of creativity and innovation and who is looking to see the world through a different lens.

Book Structure

Following an Introductory chapter, the book is divided into 4 main parts.

Part II: Theoretical Underpinnings: Structural Components of Uncertainty consists of five chapters dedicated to an understanding of the structural components of uncertainty (axis 1), two chapters relating to the role of scenarios (axis 2), and a further two chapters to behavioural factors (axis 3).

The five structural component chapters are:

- Chapter 2: Where does Uncertainty lie along the Risk/Uncertainty Spectrum?
- Chapter 3: Problem Status
- Chapter 4: Time-based Criteria
- Chapter 5: The Evidence Base
- Chapter 6: Time Horizon

Part III: Theoretical Underpinnings: Scenarios and Their Role in Dealing with Uncertainty

The two chapters relating to the role of scenarios are:

- Chapter 7: Scenario Lenses
- Chapter 8: Scenario Derivatives (Second- and Third-Order Scenarios)

Part IV: Theoretical Underpinnings: Behaviour—The Hidden Influencer in How to Deal with Uncertainty

And finally two chapters look at how behaviour influences how we deal with uncertainty such as the impact of traits such as bias and cognitive dissonance and how these traits may be mitigated.

- Chapter 9: Behavioural Factors—Cognitive Biases, Dissonance, Anomie, and Alienation
- Chapter 10: How To Mitigate the Impact of the Behavioural Minefield

Part V: Theory into Practice—Reactive and Exploratory Scenarios and Case Studies

Here we look at how the theoretical elements presented in the previous three Parts are translated into practice. Three case examples, representing reactive and exploratory scenario interpretations, are presented and illustrate how such scenarios work in an operational environment.

- Chapter 11: Reactive—the Covid-19 Pandemic.
- Chapter 12: An Exploratory Scenario Case Study—Social Mobility and Inequality.
- Chapter 13: Achieving Net Zero—The Small Island Developing States (SIDS) Initiative: An Exploratory Investment Decision Support Framework to Help Address Uncertainty.

The main section of the guidebook ends with **concluding comments**, emphasising the impact of behavioural factors when addressing uncertainty. It is here that practitioners probably need to concentrate their activity in order to affect change and transformation and where practitioners may wish, within their organisations, to intervene if uncertainty is to "tamed".

The book ends with a number of appendices (including a glossary of terms) which support previously introduced items in additional detail. *See Disclaimer*[1]

Setting the Scene: Why Should I Read This Book?

Why indeed? So much seems to be written today about uncertainty (and risk) why should you read this particular tome? The book looks at Uncertainty from a different perspective—not fatalistically, but something we can address full on—in all its different forms?

A key aim of this book is to change the perception of uncertainty as something that happens in the future but which we have no awareness or control over, to a proposition that the vast majority of future events are foreseeable when seen as "inevitable surprises" or "known-unknowns". And that a whole array of biases, impacting the individual as well as the whole of humanity in all its different parts, prevent us from making the effort to think about uncertainty as "treatable". We acquiesce to the concept it is mankind's lot to accept that our imagination is limited so we continue to be at the mercy of unknown-unknowns. This fatalism is erroneous and acts as a barrier to how we see the future and how we react to it—in all its guises.

"We should've seen it coming"? This statement is often uttered by various categories of leaders in both the public and private domains—and generally in response to having to pick up the pieces once an event, usually highly disruptive, has occurred. Such lack of foresight sees "uncertainty" as the scapegoat—the "unknown-unknown" or "black swan" event—over which, apparently we have no control—"its not our fault". The term Uncertainty has largely overtaken the concept of risk as a means to explain how we fail repeatedly to come to terms with "inevitable surprises".

This book sets out to challenge this fatalistic mindset by arguing that uncertainty, including radical and deep uncertainty, can be managed. That is, of course, if we can overcome our cognitive inhibitions, biases and better understand uncertainty's component parts so we start thinking about the unthinkable as a possibility and develop different levels of contingency to deal with such events. This argument is based on the simple supposition that "if we can think it—then it is possible",—after

---

[1] Selected portions of this book have been adapted from the author's thesis "Combining quantitative and qualitative aspects of problem structuring in computational morphological analysis—Its role in mitigating uncertainty in early stage design creativity and innovation and how best to translate it into practice" for the degree of PhD at Imperial College London, UK, successfully defended in 2016. Used with permission. This document is accessible via: https://ethos.bl.uk/Home.do;jsessionid=493F3C43FEBE93FB00A23D80F3B19881.

https://spiral.imperial.ac.uk.

all, science fiction writers have been stretching how we imagine the future for centuries.

The enemy is not uncertainty itself but our lack of imagination when trying to visualise the future—we need to transform our behaviour from having to adapt short-term survival instincts, aeons in the making, to a realisation that mankind now has it in its power to increasingly forge its own destiny. Such a transformation in the mind set of *homo sapiens* is the real challenge for mankind if we are to reduce the impact of repeatedly being "side-swiped" by an event that we erroneously call uncertain, when it really is not and "we should've seen it coming".

The task of accepting that uncertainty is about exploring the possible, rather than the impossible (however obtuse, remote, utopian, or dystopian), has to be taken on board by strategists, policy developers, management and political leaders of all shades, if we are to meet the challenges that an ever-changing world is throwing at us.

So uncertainty is not really uncertainty at all but just demonstrates a lack of vision and a willingness to think about the unthinkable—good and bad. The upside of uncertainty is that it can also provide us with opportunities to look at new and alternative ways to explore what may lie ahead.

Mankind has always been faced with uncertainty. As the saying goes there are only two certainties in life: **Death and Taxes!**

However, since the industrial revolution and subsequent advances in science, technology, medicine, knowledge of the world around us, the perceived efficacy of economics and evangelism of the rule of law, the human race, and in particular the richer North of the planet, has assumed that the odds of increased uncertainty have been reduced to the level of probabilistic risk. Or rather that anything that is perceived as taking us by surprise is real uncertainty and cannot be foreseen. This is a misguided impression and arises from confusion over the terms risk and uncertainty. This appearance of control over the factors that portray the environment we inhabit leaves mankind exposed to "anomic"[2] behaviour when confronted by a plethora of uncertainties.

The Covid pandemic has been a classic example of how a major event, capable of impacting millions of people and originally assigned a very low probability of occurrence, can challenge a global society possessing serious quantities of hubris, in the belief it can identify and control its own destiny.

Into this vacuum, "bad actors" seek to either disrupt or gain control of the means to influence society and its institutions for their own nefarious purposes. Information today is cheap but largely unchallenged as to its veracity. The Medium, more than

---

[2] Anomie—in its modern format, developed by the sociologist Emile Durkheim is a condition in which society provides little moral guidance to individuals and is characterised by a rapid change of the standards or values of societies and an associated feeling of alienation and purposelessness.

ever, has taken control of the message and has gone way beyond what Marshall McLuhan[3] first envisaged.

The fight to confront falsehoods, lies, obfuscation, selective propaganda, misinformation, and disinformation where the transmission of such information has become easier, cheaper, and subject to viral dissemination via digital means (much like a disease), is a challenge to objective thinking, free from bias confirmation and manipulation of such biases. This is not to say that we have always lived in a world of sublime objectivity, far from it—but the goal of trying to achieve an age of unbiased enlightenment should not be given away lightly. Messages are too highly dispersed across the media to make a major impact and develop into transformative opinion based on fact-checked objectivity. This dispersal of information, combined with a multiplicity of sources, makes it harder for decision makers to navigate in a world with increasing levels of uncertainty and complexity. We live on a world where a singular catastrophic risk[4] can morph into a morass of complex and interconnected situations and where simple linear responses are inadequate when confronting the danger of poorly thought through policies which generate unintended consequences.

Those events that jump up and surprise us are rarely, if ever "Black Swan" events. They can though be called "Inevitable Surprises"—an expression identified by Peter Schwartz back in 2003. In essence, it is a "known-unknown"—we know something like this can happen we just do not know when. Apart from the ongoing Covid pandemic, other examples include the expectation of another terrorist attack, the eruption of Vesuvius (long overdue), and the Grenfell tower block disaster, and, of course, the 2008 global financial crisis. In theory, the consequences of such events, being identifiable through foresight, can be mitigated by detailed contingency planning. So, let us knock this on the head, once and for all.

Nonetheless, the implications and consequences of inevitable surprises are profound and highly uncertain. It is one thing to be able to identify weak signals and outliers as being small-scale events which might not readily appear on any radar, but another to see how they can manifest themselves within any time horizon, as they may be a result of a sensitive dependency on initial conditions—what has been termed The Butterfly Effect.

But, what about once a major disruptive event has occurred? The outcomes are both multi-layered and interconnected—verging on becoming or being "a wicked problem". However, such events cannot be treated as unidimensional in that the consequences are numerous, interconnected, and complex. It is at these subsidiary or derivative levels that real dangers lurk—mankind struggles to deal with the consequences of multidimensional variables not knowing how such variables are interconnected—uncertainty running rampant.

---

[3]Marshall McLuhan was a Canadian philosopher who developed the study of media theory. He coined the expression "the medium is the message".

[4]See Chap. 8 why the term "existential risk" has not been used here.

We do have ways to broaden our vision as to what is over the horizon and perhaps mitigate the worst outcomes—we just have to select the right ones and use them. Single shot solutions will not be enough and are likely to generate negative unintended consequences in the future. Indeed, we are entering a period where humanity's ability to understand what is happening to it will be sorely tested—and that is without reference to Climate Change!

The title of this book is rather formal but in essence a good description of its content. However, using today's vernacular, and as suggested at the beginning of this preface, it could have easily been: "We should've seen it coming"? To which the answer is "of course we should have"—reading this book may get you thinking about how we can do this.

London, UK
March 2022

Bruce Garvey

Acknowledgements

This publication has been the culmination of a long process and so I would like to take this opportunity to thank a wide range of people who have encouraged me over the years to continue once I decided to write this book and who perhaps, more importantly, have contributed in helping me to keep the brain cells agitated.

I would like to thank especially Professor Peter Childs of Imperial College London, who back in 2012 took the risk of taking on board an "extra mature" student for a PhD assignment. Peter has offered and continues to offer great support not only in the realisation of my latter year academic endeavours but in encouraging me to continue writing—the outcome of which is this book.

In addition I would like to offer my sincere thanks to two topic experts who have helped majorly in contributing two of the chapters, Storm Le Roux of SCNiiC and Dowshan Humzah, both have consistently offered advice and support over the last decade.

However, none of this would have come to fruition without the support and encouragement of my colleagues and associates at Strategy Foresight Ltd, notably Dr Nasir Hussain who joined me back in 2009 in exploring the real potential of Problem Structuring Methods, Dr David Campbell, Dr Giles Russell, Jeremy Glover, Brenda King MBE, and Dr Wes Harry. In addition, a special mention has to be made to Kunal Ambasana for such sterling work in coding and solidifying the software that I developed. A special mention has to be made to Dr Tom Ritchey of the Swedish Morphological Society and who pioneered a revival in computer aided morphological analysis since the 1990s.

Other supporters who have given encouragement over recent times include David Peregrine Jones, Past Master of the Worshipful Company of Management Consultants, Keith Campbell Golding, Dr Robert Davies, and Je Hyun Kim of The Dyson School of Design Engineering Imperial College who let me showcase his trial software to combat cognitive bias. Special thanks also to Rory Sutherland at Ogilvy who has shown great enthusiasm for the behavioural aspects of my work, along with Geoff Darch and his team at Anglian Water who show what real practitioners look like. Further back I have a special mention for my "first proper boss" Barry Hamilton from whom I learned how to think differently and Keith Hubbard-Brown, whom I have known from early university days and has always been a wise advisor.

Of course, I have to mention my family who have had to put up with me over many years, my wife Golnaz (Goli), and my incredible children Sean, Patrick, and Roaya—who always said—"yes Dad, go for it". Finally, I have to thank the team at Springer, especially Dr Prashanth Mahagaonkar, who decided that what I had to say in the book was worth publishing.

London, March 2022.

Contents

About the Authors

Bruce Garvey the lead author, provides specialist support for organisations faced with high levels of uncertainty and complexity, addressing problems and issues at a strategic level. His methods are generic to all organisational types and can be deployed in areas where uncertainty and complexity abide. He has developed proprietary decision support software to help structure complex problems which has been licenced to a number of major international and national organisations.

He has published papers, presented at conferences and run workshop based courses on his specialist area and is a member of a number of working groups and networks in the Uncertainty domain.

Buttressing this specialist knowledge, he brings over 45 years' experience within the commercial arena, in staff and operational posts in the UK, Europe, and the Middle East in major corporate and SME sectors. His international experience and varied sector background makes him particularly sensitive to a wide range of behavioural and cultural issues that organisations face in an increasingly global and fast changing environment. He has a PhD from Imperial College London, an MBA from The Bayes Business School (formerly Cass), a Post-Graduate Diploma in Economic Integration from Stockholm University, Sweden, and a BSc (Hons) in Sociology from London University.

Bruce can be contacted by email at garvey@strategyforesight.org

Dowshan Humzah is an independent director and strategic advisor. He has delivered transformative business growth, industry firsts and digital innovation, having held executive roles with RSA Insurance, Virgin Media, Orange, P&G, and four start-ups. As a non-executive, he focuses on board composition and cognitive diversity. His directorships include Board Apprentice Global, Gresham College, and Overcoming MS.

Storm Le Roux is a principal of SCNiiC. He led the Aerospace and Climate Neutrality Initiative, resulting in the launch in 2018 of SCNiiC—Sustainability Climate Neutrality Impact Investment Consultancy—a specialist advisor on Net Zero Finance, Technology, and Decision-Making under deep uncertainty. He graduated in science and engineering of the University of Stellenbosch.

Part I
Introducing the Programme and Its Contents

Chapter 1
Setting the Scene and Introduction

"Unfortunately, the predilection of not wanting to think about the unthinkable will not equip us to prepare for inevitable surprises. For individuals, such a mind-set may be forgivable—for sophisticated government and supporting institutions, it is unforgivable. In this current climate, we have to strive to turn the Unthinkable—good and bad—into the Thinkable. There is no better time for all us to change our mind sets" Author's observation 2021.

Abstract There is little certainty in our world. If you ask ten experts, you can expect ten distinct responses. Nevertheless, we actually have very powerful tools for modelling uncertainty, helping to ensure that the decisions we make today do not come back to haunt us. In this chapter, we look at how to broaden our understanding of uncertainty and look at those major components which impact it. Much of the motivation for addressing the subject of uncertainty comes from identifying situations where people are involved and we will therefore also introduce the important subjects of scenarios and behavioural aspects. By way of introduction a model consisting of three criteria, Structural Components, Scenarios, and Behavioural Factors, is presented with interconnecting axes (with Methods, Tools, and Techniques—MTTs deployed within each of the criteria). These criteria form the basis of Theoretical Underpinnings in Part A. Part B looks at translating theory into practice via scenarios and case studies.

Keywords Uncertainty · Decision-making · Decision support · Complexity · Risk

This introductory chapter is broken down into two elements—**Terms of Reference**, as a way of framing the overall rationale for such a discussion on Uncertainty, and the **Introduction** itself.

© The Author(s), under exclusive license to Springer Nature Switzerland AG 2022
B. Garvey et al., *Uncertainty Deconstructed*, Science, Technology and Innovation Studies, https://doi.org/10.1007/978-3-031-08007-4_1

1.1   Terms of Reference

Uncertainty implies incomplete information where some or all of the relevant information to a problem is unavailable. Uncertainty can also be explained as being a situation where the current state of knowledge is such that:

- The order or nature of things is unknown.
- The consequences, extent or magnitude of circumstances, conditions, or events are unpredictable.
- Credible probabilities to possible outcomes cannot be assigned.
- A situation where neither the probability distribution of a variable nor its mode of occurrence is known.

It is different from Risk!

"Uncertainty" is no longer a conceptual slogan but a reality we are living through. Do we need an alternative viewpoint to help mitigate the impacts of this changing world—and do we really understand the difference between Uncertainty and Risk? Uncertainty in so many forms is ever present, and throughout history various devices have been used to reduce outcomes to the status of Risk in the Knightian[1] sense.

A key part of the ethos of this publication is to share our experience, research, and thoughts when dealing with Uncertainty. It seemed logical therefore to develop a programme providing readers with a structured approach in order to get to grips with the topic and offer a variety of ways to engage with its various constituent parts. You may think of the programme as a form of "strategic insurance vehicle", and which can be integrated into your own custom decision-making process. The aim however, is to produce a guide that users and practitioners can adapt to the specific needs and circumstances of their own organisations—or to use that ugly expression, "operationalise".

The guide acts as both a guide and toolkit for practitioners[2] looking to improve their decision-making and decision support skills when faced with high levels of uncertainty and complexity. **Uncertainty is often less about the unknown as about the identification and interpretation of objectively known but hidden data and weak signals.**

Major events that have come as a shock to many decision analysts and decision makers, such as 9/11, the 2008/9 financial crash, Brexit, the Trump presidency, and the Covid-19 outbreak, have triggered an acceleration in interest about uncertainty— the term, once rarely used is now ubiquitous. Nevertheless, it has still taken some considerable time in bringing Uncertainty to the forefront of consciousness amongst the decision and policy-making communities—whereas the term Risk has long enjoyed more exposure and frequency of use. Uncertainty was somehow seen to be vague and fuzzy and had the perceived disadvantage of being difficult to quantify.

---

[1] See Chap. 3 for a more detailed description of "Knightian" uncertainty.

[2] Practitioner being defined as one who practices something, especially an occupation, profession, or technique.

Risk, on the other hand, was more amenable to quantification (mainly via probabilities)—and decision makers like numbers. Uncertainty—"well, I don't really understand it, it's too vague, it scares us, we don't like it", "give me a metric"!

In the early twenty-first century and thanks to Messrs. Taleb and Rumsfeld—we discovered (or rather rediscovered) that there was a difference. Of course, we always knew there was one, but Frank Knight's dictum from 1921 seemed to have a life span of less than one generation before it was forgotten again and then miraculously rediscovered by the next. Now all sorts of experts, pundits, and indeed charlatans are suddenly talking about Uncertainty again to justify everything from the financial crash of 2008/9 to the Covid-19 outbreak to Climate Change. The use of the term is invariably deployed once a disruptive event has happened—one is entitled to ask, **"shouldn't they have seen it coming"?**

As the legendary Liverpool football manager Bill Shankly (Shankly & Mark, 2014) once said: *"Some people believe football is a matter of life and death, I am very disappointed with that attitude. I can assure you it is much, much more important than that"*. Well, so is Uncertainty!

Uncertainty has always confronted mankind, which has used different approaches to overcome/foresee situations in the future deemed uncertain (from goat entrails, dreams, astrology, the Oracle at Delphi, science fiction to religion). Uncertainty is certainly (yes, an oxymoron) now much more in the public domain, or rather the term is exhorted to justify (often in reaction to inadequate responses to earlier events by decision makers) poor performance in the face of that convenient expression, "Uncertainty". In other words, the term is too often applied retrospectively to an event that has already occurred so that the impossibilities of yesterday have morphed into today's challenge: *"it is one thing to be caught out by a wholly novel threat, and quite another to be toppled by something we knew about all along"* (Liu et al., 2020).

There is rarely just one event (such as an earth destroying asteroid hit), but an interconnected and non-linear complex of events which can trigger different responses especially when shaped by historical legacies, political culture and social mores, and the underlying economic structures (Liu et al., 2020). In addition, behavioural factors and *"cognitive biases also tend towards direct-causal near-term events, thereby marginalising tangential, second-order, or cumulative effects that may instead constitute an existential risk"* (Liu et al., 2020).

Since 2008/9 (remember the big financial crisis which everyone was shouting was a black swan event—but of course was not?), the use of the word Uncertainty is back with a vengeance, in terms of frequency of use by politicians, pundits, and experts alike, to justify why actions, that should have been taken in the face of a major threat, existential or otherwise, were not taken—such as the possibility of a global pandemic.

We have already identified above that "Uncertainty", in some form or other, has always been with us throughout history, albeit that it makes us uncomfortable and we try to hide from it or deflect it. However, in the twenty-first century, those Uncertain events that suddenly intrude upon our lives, appear to have grown in frequency and intensity—or is it we are just better at acknowledging and identifying them than before? We went into this century worrying about the harm that the millennium bug might cause. Then we had 9/11, and the "war on terror" and its poor decision strewn policy failures. And in a global environment it is increasingly difficult to isolate events from one another—we live in a complex and interconnected world.

Complexity and high levels of interconnectivity are fellow travellers (or cell-mates) of Uncertainty. Uncertain events are rarely discrete or independent either in their origins or their outcomes. In the 1960s, Herman Kahn (1962) of RAND and the Hudson Institute, challenged us to think about the "unthinkable" (in relation to thermonuclear war); uncomfortable yes but necessary, and it can be argued that the concept of mutually assured destruction (MAD) allowed the military and politicians of all persuasions to confront the reality and horrors of a (formal) nuclear war, then and now—and maintain a semblance of non-nuclear peace in spite of global nuclear proliferation. Note that a reduction in the "old Cold War" certainties has created a newer more uncertain world!

If I tell you that we are living in increasingly uncertain times, I do not expect you to just take my word for it. Much wiser and informed heads than mine have been flagging up the broadening impact of uncertainty—with a particular concern as to how this uncertainty is being handled by our political, business, and institutional leaders—indeed you may be one of them?

Yet people still like some form of quantification to justify such positions. At the US based National Bureau of Economic Research three academics—Baker et al. (2015) have constructed the Economic Policy Uncertainty Index (EPU) for a number of major countries around the world as well as at the global level.

Baker, Bloom, and Davis developed an index to measure policy-related economic[3] uncertainty, based on three types of underlying components—quantification of newspaper coverage of policy-related economic uncertainty, the number of federal tax code provisions set to expire in future years, with the third component using disagreement among economic forecasters as a proxy for uncertainty. Albeit US centric, they found that current levels of economic policy uncertainty are at extremely elevated levels compared to recent history. Since 2008, economic policy uncertainty has averaged about twice the level of the previous 23 years—and this observation was made initially up to 2015, before the Trump election, Brexit, and, of course, Covid-19.

The Global EPU index from January 1997 to November 2016—which does include the Brexit referendum outcome and the "just announced" US presidential election shows even further leaps in uncertainty beyond the 2015 marker as illustrated in the attached graphic (Fig. 1.1).

A recent Index, (Fig. 1.2) through to early 2020 shows that the EPU index has gone majorly beyond the 275 level of November 2016—up over 400 before reducing somewhat to 300—roughly at three times the level of the late twentieth century.

What is important to realise about this index, is that it offers only a historical (past) perspective and makes few assumptions about future levels of

---

[3] As will be discussed in Chap. 3, economic uncertainty is just one of numerous types of uncertainty.

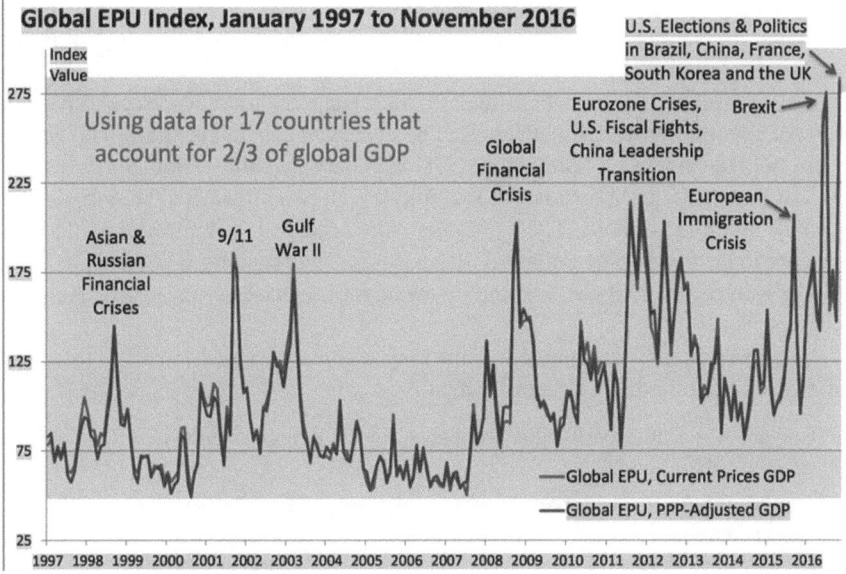

Fig. 1.1   Global EPU index January 1997—November 2016

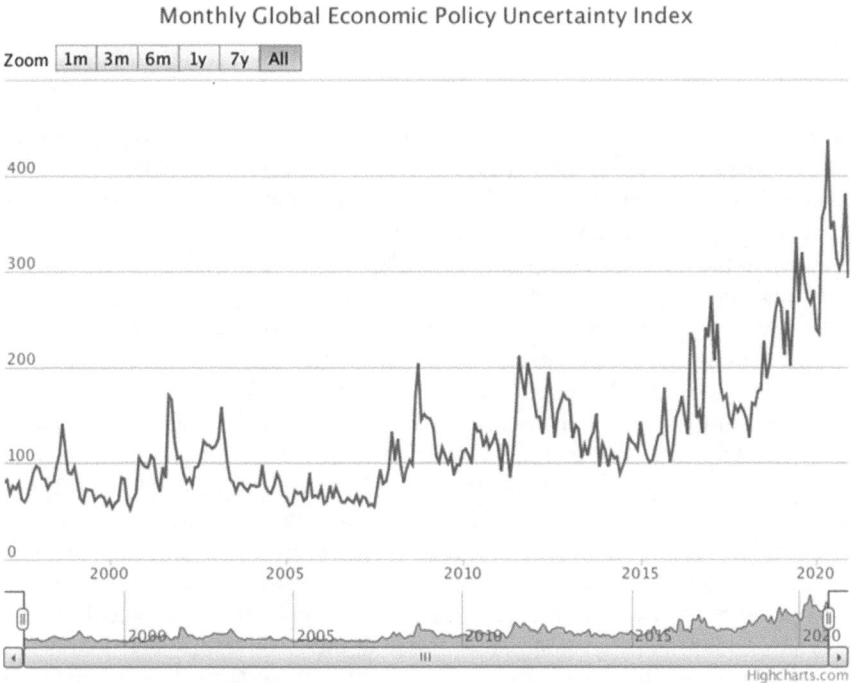

Fig. 1.2   Global EPU Index January 1997—March 2020

uncertainty to guide decision analysts and decision makers (to be fair one of their indicators did use the number of federal tax code provisions set to expire in future years as a component—albeit in a narrow field).

Another limiting factor is that the EPU index largely focuses on economic and financial uncertainty which whilst being the dominant drivers for the world we live in, are not the only ones. The nature of Uncertainty, as will be explained in more detail in Part A, is that it operates at multiple-levels, conditions, and stimuli, as well as across multiple horizons. There are many more categories of uncertainty and risk that contribute to the Uncertainty/Risk spectrum, thus making it incumbent upon analysts to broaden their outlook and be aware of any biases when approaching the topic.

A major corporate management consulting company, "PwC" (2012), articulated the problems facing decision makers thus:

- "Current risk frameworks and processes are no longer giving them the level of protection they need.
- They are seeing rapid increases both in the frequency of risk events and that such impacts are 'contagious', and can infect different categories of risk, notably 'catastrophic' risks.
- Finally, boards feel they are spending too much resources on current risk management processes, rather than moving quickly and flexibly to identify and tackle new risks. In other words, operational imperatives override strategic ones—never getting out of the loop".

The PwC paper goes on to state whilst companies have tended to concentrate on Financial and Operational risks they have tended to pay less attention to Strategic risks made up of externally derived components such as economic, political, social, technological, regulatory, and other environmental factors. In other words, the external Contextual environment within which organisations have to react to and manoeuvre, the growing awareness of the prevalence of Uncertainty, makes the task of decision-making increasingly problematical.

A major challenge confronting practitioners when faced by uncertainty during the early phases of addressing such issues, is that the amount of creativity and innovation required to support the process can be unstructured. This is highly problematical, as understanding the nature of uncertainty (as opposed to risk) is key. If not addressed early enough, these uncertainties can germinate negative unintended consequences and gestate into undesirable outcomes, which practitioners will find difficult to redress at later stages—especially where a project is subject to resource constraints (time, money, people). Early stage uncertainty can be aggravated further, as it can hide highly complex relationships between the different variables within the problem, which in turn can mutate during attempts to resolve the problem—a typical "wicked-problem" (see Chap. 3). A major requirement under such circumstances therefore requires the practitioner to be aware of these constraints and to employ a variety of methods that can help him/her structure the problem under conditions governed by uncertainty and complexity.

It can be argued by those in the "Uncertainty as Risk" camp, and who seek to quantify uncertainty, whether there is more uncertainty now? What is not without doubt is that we seem to be more aware of it. The increasing and ever exponential rate of change and impact across all forms of activity would indicate that, in spite of access to increasing analytic processes via AI and enhanced data analytics, the ability to more accurately forecast and predict the future so as to mitigate uncertainty seems as far away as ever—but with increasing consequences when a wrong decision path is selected. An assessment about the future is further compromised and/or constrained by behavioural factors such as short-termism, silo mentalities, 'not-invented here' syndrome, and a plethora of human biases, along with the over use of a whole zoo of animal metaphors and heuristics such as black swans and elephants and grey swans and rhinos.

So that is the background to this guidebook. So what—you may ask? What are we trying to address for you the reader and practitioner?

We inhabit an environment where multiple uncertainties and complexities seem to increasingly outstrip our abilities to identify problems, let alone solve them, and we are left to muddle through.

The main aim of this publication is to provide, you, the reader with a greater awareness of the components which make up Uncertainty and offer a structured pathway to navigate its complexity. This will help decision practitioners to be better prepared to meet the multiple challenges ahead—individually, socially, and organisationally. Please do not believe that getting to know a bit more about uncertainty and its implications is an easy ride—or even an easy read—it is not! But then if it were we would not be so concerned about it. Bon courage!

1.2   Introduction

Given the growing proclivity of Uncertainty, how can we ensure that we can mitigate the impact of uncertainty so that the decisions we make today do not come back to haunt us? An array of uncertainty based questions confront practitioners in the decision-making and decision support domains, such as (non-exclusive):

- How can I handle uncertainty and help mitigate strategic and operational risks?
- How do I get to grips with both internal and external operating and contextual environments impacted by high levels of uncertainty and complexity?
- What existential risks should I be aware of?
- Do I need to structure a problem before thinking about solving it?
- Are there things I have not thought about but should be aware of?
- How can I generate new yet viable solutions that will help improve my navigation in an uncertain world and improve performance?
- How do I keep my organisation on its toes in a "wicked" world?

Structural Components

Methods, Tools &
Techniques (MTTs)

Scenarios   Behavioural Factors

(Reactive or Exploratory)   (Inc. Biases and Heuristics)

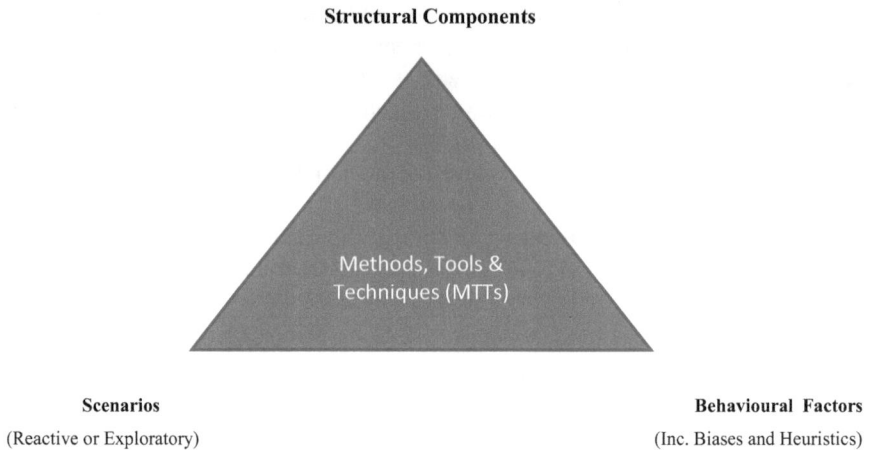

Fig. 1.3 Three axes of uncertainty

1.2.1 Looking at Uncertainty Through an Alternative Lens So as to Offer a Different Perspective?

Many of the constituent parts related to Uncertainty are all out there in the public domain—or most of them are! But information relating to Uncertainty is highly dispersed and subject to all sorts of varied inputs and interpretations. In its purest form, "Uncertainty" cannot be managed because the environment in which it inhabits is unknown. Do we then give up in face of such a problem and seek out easily understandable solutions—but which most likely will turn out to be ineffective at best or wrong at worst?

Much of the literature about uncertainty tends to look at two main areas, being:

- Various definitions of uncertainty and its relationship to risk (i.e. its structural components) and/or
- A variety of **Methods, Tools, and Techniques (MTTs)** used to help decision makers and analysts when confronted by uncertainty (and complexity).

Such aims are valid and worthwhile, but they often ignore two further criteria when attempting to determine the impact of uncertainty and which have to be taken into account to improve the quality of the decision-making process. The two additional criteria are the role of **Scenarios,** and the human role in the decision-making, defined as **Behavioural Factors.** In this schema the MTTs themselves are not seen as specific criteria in themselves but integrated into each of three core axes which allows for a better understanding of uncertainty and how to mitigate its worst impacts. This is illustrated in Fig. 1.3 above.

The Deconstructed Components of Uncertainty, Scenario, and Behavioural axes all interact with one another and together combine to make up a more realistic, if not more complex, framework as to how to approach uncertainty and is reflected in Fig. 1.3.

Axis 1: Structural Components identifies the core components and constituent parts of uncertainty and includes identifying where uncertainty lies along the risk spectrum, the nature of problems that are uncertain, the role of time, the sources and types of evidence that are available under conditions of uncertainty, and how far we need to see into the future. The first axis **deconstructs** uncertainty so as to look at the core components of its very nature, and which can be listed thus:

- Location along the risk/uncertainty spectrum
- Problem status
- Time-based criteria
- The evidence base
- Ways of seeing the future.

Axis 2: deploys **Scenarios** to identify different types of issues that analysts and decision makers have to deal with under conditions of uncertainty. The term "scenario", now in common use, is typified as being a story or narrative of alternative possible futures. They are not predictions of the future but help to explore what could happen and how to prepare for various contingencies. Stakeholder participation and collaboration is essential to the scenario activity. Scenarios need to be seen within the context of an ongoing, long-term, "closed-loop" organisational process and provide a useful tool for generating shared forward views, helping to align strategic action across an organisation on its journey into the future (Voros 2001). The main purpose of a scenario is to guide exploration of possible future states with the best scenarios describing alternative future outcomes that diverge significantly from the present (Curry & Schulz 2009).

In this programme, I shall use scenarios as seen through two but distinct lenses— the **Reactive** and the **Exploratory.**

A **reactive** scenario is defined as being how the future may roll-out based on a current problem or issue (one that has manifested itself), as the main starting point or driver—such as the Covid-19 pandemic. **Note:** the problem here is that such a scenario tends to relate to a single discrete event rather than asymmetric exponential effects based on interconnecting trends and events. The danger of such an approach is that there is a tendency to marginalise tangential, second-order, third-order, or cumulative events and effects. We can call these latter events "derivatives". Such derivatives in themselves need to be analysed by a more exploratory approach to determine possible outcomes.

An **exploratory** scenario approach, on the other hand, is much broader in scope as it seeks to identify both observable and latent drivers or trends over various future time horizons—in effect multiple futures with a much larger range of possible outcomes, impacted by weak signals and outliers. An exploratory approach comes with much fewer preconceptions and offers the analyst the freedom to investigate a much more expansive array of future (non-discrete) outcomes using a selection of methods, techniques, and tools (MTTs) to help in the investigation. We discuss here the ways in which one can imagine the multiple futures that we must foresee—

whether that future is tomorrow or months or years from now. The main challenge is how do we get decision makers et al. to listen out for and filter an array of signals which may never happen—the classic low occurrence/high impact scenario? Exploratory analysis is more open ended than the reactive approach—it is fuzzier in different ways—varying time horizons, inputs and outputs, resource commitments, etc. This makes it more difficult for decision makers to grasp the essentials, let alone identify them, when formulating policy—and where such formulation is subject to asymmetrically evolving challenges which majorly reduce the impact of traditional planning cycles.

Later in this book, we shall be exploring examples of potential uncertain outcomes from both reactive and exploratory standpoints. As highlighted above, the more challenging analysis will stem from deploying the exploratory approach, based on a number of possible futures with major levels of interconnectivity. It is here where the book seeks to offer enhanced structured insight processes for decision and policy makers as well as decision support analysts—and where current signals are weak, overlooked, or indeed ignored, inadvertently or deliberately. In effect, we are concerned less with the major event itself but with secondary (second-order), tertiary, and more layers which may be derived from any singular event. Thus, the exploration of what can be termed derivative scenarios is crucial to the process as they can manifest themselves in both the reactive and the exploratory modes.

Axis 3: The third criterion, explored in Chaps. 9 and 10, and one which is often overlooked or under-represented by method-oriented analysts, provides an overview of how **behavioural factors,** especially cognitive biases, heuristics, and cognitive dissonance, can impact, if not impede, the decision-making process from different standpoints and perspectives. These include individual, group, organisational, cultural, national, regional, etc.,—invariably negating the efficacy of any processes and analytical methods and tools used in the exercise. We could call this section "How we humans mess up when making decisions!"

I should like to point out that Methods, Tools, and Techniques (MTTs) are not forgotten. Most chapters include a number of them, albeit some are relatively unknown and under-used. Whilst acknowledging the plethora of MTTs available the book does not over rely on the "usual suspects"—and where they are identified, are re-purposed or given new slants as to their functionality.

1.2.2   Re-adjusting Our Perceptions

Since Donald Rumsfeld's famous broadcasting of the term "unknown—unknowns" during a US Defense Department press briefing in 2002, it has become ubiquitous (along with black swans), albeit the vast majority of future uncertain events do not fall into this category. However, it has been used to absolve decision makers from criticism post event, whereas poor foresight is the prime culprit. **By increasing awareness of behavioural factors on decision-making, including cognitive biases and misapplied heuristics, this book proposes most future uncertainties**

Table 1.1 The Known-Unknown matrix

	Known	Unknown
Known	Known-Known	Known-Unknowns
Unknown	Unknown-Knowns	Unknown-Unknowns

are "known-unknowns" or "inevitable surprises". This re-positioning of uncertainties can help mitigate the impact of such risks through creative awareness of broad based contingency planning.

It is this simple matrix (also called a Johari window), that I have adopted to develop a framework which encapsulates the various dimensions and interrelationships of risk and uncertainty (Table 1.1).

It is strange that in an era where our access to knowledge and information and its litany, as well as the volume of data itself, is greater than ever before, we still struggle to better identify the future or rather optional or possible futures. Perhaps there is too much information—too much noise and too few easily identifiable signals? In addition, when, in an attempt to bring order, we seek out new information technologies such as data analytics and AI methods—we need to be aware that even these "neutral" algorithmic approaches are also subject to originator bias.

There are two related challenges. First, in some cases the evidence is in front of our eyes, but we do not see it, or do not recognise the significance of what we are seeing. We are surprised by the result. Alternatively, there are occasions when the evidence is not a reliable guide to sudden shifts. In both cases, surprise manifests itself all too often and we need to ask not only whether the foresight approaches are robust enough but whether our own thought processes are robust enough.

Many of the ideas, concepts, and observations introduced in this programme are not new—in fact some have been around for decades. Many have been forgotten about or overlooked in modern times so that academic researchers (even with increasing use of modern data search techniques) end up re-inventing the wheel at best (or salami-slicing at "wurst"). References used in the programme are a healthy mix of sources from not only academic publications but from trusted practitioner sources such as McKinsey, Gartner,[4] etc., as well as from a myriad of lesser known but informed thinkers. Dealing with uncertainty should be seen as an applied discipline to be used across a variety of sectors and for improving practical decision-making.

Most chapters include a number of individual Methods, Tools, and Techniques (MTTs and Heuristics devices). These are introduced to help the reader transform the chapter topic into a practical format, with a supporting rationale as to how they can be used. Other suitable methods are identified in summary form and in some cases expanded upon via an appendix. In this way, the user is gradually introduced to a variety of MTTs which can best be deployed across the component array. The MTTs presented are in no way exclusive. There is no one method which fits all across the

---

[4]Hopefully without falling into the trap of groupthink, or following the leader (as in "no-one ever got fired for buying IBM, or hiring McKinsey").

uncertainty/risk spectrum but it is incumbent on analysts and academics alike to be at least aware of the depth and breadth of methods that can be used.

In all three sub-parts of Part A—Theoretical Underpinnings—a variety of different MTTs are presented and identified as being useful when working with each of the components. The author has been surprised over the years as to how some academics and practitioners use very narrow sets of MTTs, seemingly unaware of the wide variety of methods that do exist—a silo mentality often sets in—whereby perfectly good methods have either not been heard of (let alone being aware of how they work and can be applied) or are set aside as they do not fit precisely enough within overly specific frameworks (and some not-invented here syndromes). I would like to urge readers, in addition to those MTTs introduced here, to seek out other tools and which they are comfortable with. Remember, uncertainty has occluded boundaries—there is no one perfect method. As will be made clear in this publication Uncertainty is fuzzy—there is no single solution or indeed correct application of methods—uncertainty allows the practitioner a wide array of "leverage" as to what methods to deploy—but there are preferred ways and many of those ways are what the user is most happy to use or be comfortable with.

A major research exercise carried out by the author in 2015, as part of his PhD thesis (Garvey, 2016) used as source material 19 "aggregators" or sources, which identified 835 different Methods, Tools, and Techniques (MTTs) in the broad domain of Decision Support Methods (DSMs). It is to be noted that whilst this list can be considered as comprehensive, it is not a definitive one, and the author acknowledges there may be omissions. Since the original review subsequent analysis has not revealed any major additional MTTs of note. It was interesting however, that these 835 items were represented across 1079 identified sources. What is surprising here, is that the statistic reveals only 23% of individual items appear more than once! A schedule of the Aggregator Analysis is shown below (Table 1.2).

One of the observations made by the author in his research was that different terms were used to describe similar MTTs (salami-slicing). For example, at least 9 different terms were used to reflect the generic method "Brainstorming"—such as Brainlining, Brainmapping, Brainwriting, Brain sketching, etc. Thus, Brainstorming itself appeared across 10 aggregators, Brainlining, Brainmapping, Constrained Brainwriting, and Imaginary Brainstorming and Value Brainstorming appeared once, Dynamic Brainwriting twice, and Brainwriting 5 times. In total there were some 22 references to MTTs in the "Brain" family. No doubt each of the tool developers would specify the differences in the approach adopted by these individual techniques—but they all generically belong to the "Brainstorming" family of tools.

What is at issue here, is that, the over proliferation of terms across the Decision Support Method (DSM) domain can only confuse the practitioner community, working against a broader awareness of such MTTs.

The programme is therefore not written in an overtly academic style but more as a handbook for practitioners using both academic and practitioner source material. Many ideas and methods are too often deployed as "one-trick ponies" within epistemological silos rather than as a raft of methods which can be deployed across

Table 1.2 Aggregator analysis by contributor

Aggregator analysis

Publication title	Author (s)	Type of publication	MTT sector	MTTs identified
Rational Analysis for a Problematic World Revisited (2001)	Eds: J. Rosenhead & J Mingers	Book	Decision Support Methods (Problem Structuring)	8
The Decision Book (2011)	M Krogerus & R Tschappeler	Book	Decision Support Methods	53
Decision Support Tools—http://www.ifm.eng.cam.ac.uk/resources/tools	Institute for Manufacturing - University of Cambridge	Web-based content	Decision Support Methods	70
MCDA—Multi-Criteria Decision Analysis	Wikipedia	Web-based content	Decision Support Methods	26
Innovation by Creativity—Fifty-one Tools for Solving Problems Creatively (2011)	M Van Leeuwen & H Terhme	Book	Creativity and Innovation	50
Techniques for Creating New Product Ideas - Management Decision Vol.17 (1979)	S Sands	Paper	Creativity and Innovation	7
Module 4: Idea Evaluation Methods & Techniques—Creative Trainer Project EU Commission (2009)	M Rebernic and B Bradac	Paper	Creativity and Innovation	29
Tools for Creativity & Innovation	Creatingminds.org http://creatingminds.org	Web-based content	Creativity and Innovation	48
Creative Techniques—Classification (2006?)	Create Methodology http://www.diegm.uniud.it/create/Handbook/techniques/CreateMethod.htm	Web-based content	Creativity and Innovation	220
Product Design (1995)	M Baxter	Book	Design and Product Design	38
Engineering Design Methods (2008)	N Cross	Book	Design and Product Design	11
Key Management Models (2009)	M van Assen, G van den Berg & P Pietersma	Book	Management and OR Methods	55
Key Strategy Tools (2013)	V Evans	Book	Management and OR Methods	93
Bain Management Tools (2011 & 2013)	D K Rigby	Survey	Management and OR Methods	128

(continued)

Table 1.2 (continued)

Aggregator analysis

Publication title	Author (s)	Type of publication	MTT sector	MTTs identified
Supporting Strategy: A Survey of UK OR/MS Practitioners—Warwick Business School (2009)	F O'Brien	Survey	Management and OR Methods	40
Structured Analytical Techniques for Intelligence Analysis (2011)	R J Heuer Jr. & R H Pherson	Book	Miscellaneous	46
Technological Futures Analysis: Toward Integration of the Field and New Analysis (2004)	A L Porter	Paper	Miscellaneous	51
Miscellaneous other methods	*Added by Author*	*Various items from web*	Miscellaneous	15
Technology Forecasting—State of Art Update (2011)	M Slupinski—FORMAT Consortium	Survey	Miscellaneous	91
Total Items				1079

Note: The detailed analysis showing the full list of MTTs and their spread across the aggregator selection can be requested from the author at garvey@strategyforesight.org

the Uncertainty/Risk spectrum. There has been a dearth of approaches attempting to integrate a wide number of concepts and methods, so as to better address challenging problems about a range of futures which inherently contain numerous uncertainties. Remember that Uncertainty is fuzzy and never precise, otherwise it would not be uncertain!

As we introduce each component we introduce a number of MMTs which can be used to support the main component topic.

1.3 Conclusions

This guidebook makes the proposition that it is the role of management to be acutely aware of those individual, group, and organisational behaviours which encourage stakeholders all too easily to see uncertainty as residing as an "Unknown-known" (Q3)[5] or even as an "unknown-unknown" (Q4), often in an attempt to absolve themselves of responsibilities relative to poor decision evaluation **post event**. This encourages the relegation of Foresight methods and Foresight driven policies in the strategic planning process—when quite the opposite is required for an organisation

---

[5] See Chap. 2, Sect. 2.1.2 for a fuller description.

to survive uncertainties, no matter the status of such uncertainties as being low probability/high impact and anywhere in between. The human brain is creative enough, when challenged to think of most eventualities, however remote (as in low occurrence/high impact events). Many science fiction writers have been highly perceptive in suggesting potential future scenarios, no matter how obtuse. If we can think it—it can happen—a term we shall re-visit.

Management therefore has to put in place processes, even if it means "nudging" stakeholders, that will support decision-making to at least retreat back into Quadrant 2^6—the "Known-unknown"—the most realistic way to manage uncertainties and mitigate risks—so that such uncertainties acquire the status of, at least, "inevitable surprises". The Foresight mindset however, should not be made the responsibility of a single specialist department but rather an activity integrated and internalised across all the core functions of the organisation—with perhaps a specialist team acting as internal consultants to divisional and departmental teams.

The task of prioritising such surprises can then, at least be addressed by hierarchy based methods (e.g. Analytic Hierarchy Process, (AHP) and other Multi-Criteria Decision Analysis (MCDA) methods)—as long as those biases highlighted in quadrant 3 are addressed—otherwise too many future events will continue to be seen to reside in that quadrant characterised by "unknown-knowns".

Such an approach requires visionary leadership if management is not to be confronted with too many "Unknown-knowns" when there is really no need for this to be the case!

References

Curry, A., & Schultz, W. (May 2009). Roads less travelled: Different methods, different futures. *Journal of Futures Studies, 13*(4), 35–60.

Garvey, Bruce. Combining quantitative and qualitative aspects of problem structuring in computational morphological analysis – Its role in mitigating uncertainty in early stage design creativity and innovation and how best to translate it into practice. Chapter 5 pages 106–122. PhD thesis Imperial College London. Dyson School of Design Engineering: October 7th 2016.

Liu, H.-Y., Lauta, K., & Maas, M. (2020). Apocalypse Now? *Journal of International Humanitarian Legal Studies, 11*.

Kahn, H. (1962). *Thinking about the unthinkable*. Horizon Press.

Knight, Frank. *Risk, uncertainty, and profit*, 1921.

PWC. *Black Swans Turn Grey – the transformation of risk*, January 2012.

Scott R. Baker, Nicholas Bloom, Steven J. Davis. (2015, October). *Measuring economic policy uncertainty*. Working Paper 21633 http://www.nber.org/papers/w21633.National Bureau of Economic Research, 1050 Massachusetts Avenue Cambridge, MA 02138.

Shankly, Bill, & Mark, Yonder (eds.), The quotable shankly. Pub: Yonder Mark, Kindle Edition, August 2014.

---

[6]Ibid.

Voros, Joseph. (December 2001). A primer on futures studies, foresight and the use of scenarios, Swinburne University of Technology. Pub: The Foresight Bulletin, No 6, Swinburne University of Technology.

Part II
Theoretical Underpinnings: Structural Components of Uncertainty

Chapter 2
Locating Uncertainty Along the Risk Spectrum

"The future is uncertain . . .but this uncertainty is at the very heart of human creativity"
Ilya Prigogine

Abstract This chapter provides a better understanding of the difference between risk and uncertainty along with the impact of complexity and interconnectivity. Uncertainty and Risk lie along a spectrum, which includes, of course, Certainty. It is here where the core rationale of the book is presented as a template called the "Uncertainty Profile". The template shows how four main quadrants of Uncertainty, derived from a 2×2 matrix based on the "known" and "unknown", have been synthesised from a number of different interpretations of uncertainty. This profile acts as a *leitmotif* throughout the book leading to the argument that events need to be treated as "known-unknowns" being essentially identifiable in one form or another. Over deployment of the term "unknown-unknown", largely due to behavioural responses, encourages poor decision-making based on a lack of foresight. The chapter consists of three main components: Scoping the Risk Spectrum, the core "Uncertainty Profile", and Methods, Tools, and Techniques (MTTs) relevant to the topic.

Keywords Uncertainty · Risk · Certainty · Uncertainty profile · Complexity and interconnectivity · Cynefin · VUCA · Metaphors

2.1 Introduction

Uncertainty and Risk lie along a spectrum, which includes, of course, Certainty. This chapter consists of three main components:

- Scoping the Risk Spectrum
- Profiling Uncertainty
- Methods, Tools, and Techniques (MTTs)

The Risk Spectrum & the Uncertainty Conundrum

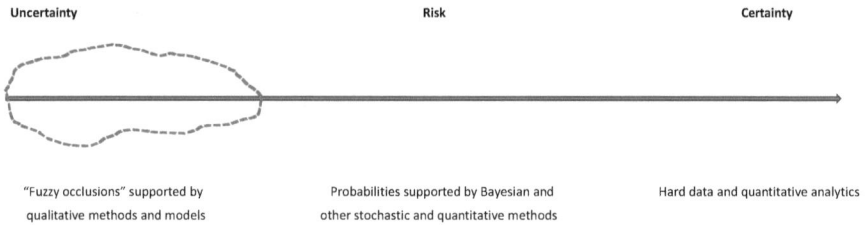

Uncertainty   Risk   Certainty

"Fuzzy occlusions" supported by   Probabilities supported by Bayesian and   Hard data and quantitative analytics
qualitative methods and models   other stochastic and quantitative methods

The main difference between uncertainty and risk is that risk can be quantified – uncertainty cannot. But you can model it!

"When high levels of uncertainty and complexity prevail, it is better to be approximately right than precisely wrong!"

Fig. 2.1 The risk/uncertainty spectrum

2.1.1 Scoping the Risk Spectrum: Positioning Uncertainty

In this first section, Uncertainty is broken down into a number of contributing elements. Figure 2.1 illustrates how Uncertainty is positioned across a broader risk spectrum.

A brief examination of the semantics involved shows that:

2.1.1.1 Certainty

Certainty occurs when it is assumed that perfect information exists and that all relevant information to a problem is known. In reality it can be argued that the complete veracity of perfect information can be challenged due to interpretative issues, and that the relevance of the information can only be assumed.

2.1.1.2 Risk

Risk, on the other hand, indicates that partial information (often involving metrics), is available and generally, is probabilistic, so that when future events or activities occur they do so with some measure of probability. Alternatively, risk can be defined as the probability or threat of a damage, injury, liability, loss or negative occurrence, caused by external or internal vulnerabilities and may be neutralised through pre-meditated action (risk management). A risk is not an uncertainty, a peril (cause of loss), or a hazard.

In essence, risk generally refers to the likelihood that some future unplanned event might occur and which can be assigned a numeric probability.

2.1.1.3 Uncertainty

Uncertainty implies incomplete information where much or all of the relevant information to a problem is unavailable. Uncertainty can also be explained as being a situation where the current state of knowledge is such that:

- The order or nature of things is unknown.
- The consequences, extent or magnitude of circumstances, conditions, or events are unpredictable.
- Credible probabilities to possible outcomes cannot be assigned.
- A situation where neither the probability distribution of a variable nor its mode of occurrence is known.

Whilst Risk can be quantified (via probabilities), Uncertainty cannot, as it is not measurable. Other structural components creating difficulties for practitioners reside at the system level and include **complexity and interconnectivity**. Indeed, understanding the characteristics and scope of the conditions of this key component is a key first stage in shaping broader analytical templates.

However, many people still confuse Risk and Uncertainty, which has led to the premature use of quantitative methods and where a more qualitative evaluation would be of greater use. This distinction is crucial, since **the appearance of precision through quantification can convey a validity that cannot always be justified.**

Uncertainty in all its imprecision needs to assert itself as a powerful condition (and yes—alongside risk), the understanding and acceptance of which can increase our foresight and preparedness in the face of the unexpected. The diversity of outcomes that might occur has to be understood in order to mitigate the impact of future events whether or not they have emanated as unintended consequences of past actions, or from situations over which we have no means of controlling.

As far back as 1921, Frank Knight in his seminal work "Risk, Uncertainty, and Profit", established the distinction between risk and uncertainty—a distinction which still is the most concise:

> ... Uncertainty must be taken in a sense radically distinct from the familiar notion of Risk, from which it has never been properly separated. ... The essential fact is that "risk" means in some cases a quantity susceptible of measurement, while at other times it is something distinctly not of this character; and there are far-reaching and crucial differences in the bearings of the phenomena depending on which of the two is really present and operating. ... It will appear that a measurable uncertainty, or "risk" proper, as we shall use the term, is so far different from an un-measurable one that it is not in effect an uncertainty at all.

The states of uncertainty and risk are not discrete—represented, as it were, by a sliding scale from Genuine Uncertainty though to Risk based on varying levels of probability and on to (near) Certainty. This is illustrated in Fig. 2.1. Quantification and measurement in turn should not be treated as existing or not in such discrete domains.

As one moves from Certainty towards the Uncertain end of the spectrum, probable outcomes are reduced to being only possible outcomes and where information, especially in its (metric) quantitative form becomes increasingly unavailable and/or not relevant. Although too much uncertainty might be seen as being undesirable, manageable uncertainty can provide the freedom to make creative decisions.

Uncertainty and Risk: A Confusion of Terms When It Comes to Measurement

Nonetheless, the confusion about the difference between Uncertainty and Risk still exists largely due to the issue of measurement. Measurement can be defined as a set of observations that reduces uncertainty where the result is expressed as a quantity. The scientific community is generally satisfied with a reduction, rather than an elimination, of uncertainty. Hubbard (2007) states: *"The fact that some amount of error is unavoidable but can still be an improvement on prior knowledge is central to how experiments, surveys, and other scientific measurements are performed"*.

Hubbard goes on to say that a measurement does not have to eliminate uncertainty but rather that:

> a mere reduction in uncertainty counts as a measurement and possibly can be worth much more than the cost of measurement.

He adds that a measurement does not have to be about a quantity. This uncertainty does not have to be quantified and that the subject of observation might not be a quantity itself but qualitative. He refers to the work of psychologist, Stanley Smith Adams, who describes different scales of measurement, including "nominal" and "ordinal": nominal measurements being set membership statements—a thing is simply in one of the possible sets. Ordinal scales allow us to say one value is "more or less" than another but not by how much and are relevant when we talk about risk mitigation and not risk elimination—which is a finite state of affairs and which in the complex world of business, economics, and politics, is nigh on impossible to guarantee.

We can but mitigate—and develop methodologies which through empirical observation and experience, allow us to offer up workable templates (rather than causal models), against which we can compare current sets of conditions and information.

Hubbard concludes by stating that:

> The commonplace notion that presumes measurements are exact quantities ignores the usefulness of simply reducing uncertainty, if eliminating uncertainty is not possible or economical. In business, decision makers make decisions under uncertainty. When that uncertainty is about big, risky decisions, then uncertainty reduction has a lot of value.

How Uncertainty is treated in terms of methods has been a moot point over the last century or so and has developed into arguments as to the relative value of qualitative as opposed to quantitative methods.

Ernest Rutherford, the Nobel Prize winning physicist claimed that—*"qualitative is nothing but poor quantitative"*. This 100-year-old dictum unfortunately still casts a long shadow in relation to the qualitative/quantitative divide present in the analytical process and subsequent decision-making. Recent dramatic increases in computing power including big data analytics have supported the view that quantitative is best. Within the financial sector much financial analysis has concentrated on risk, whereby probabilistic methods can allow decision makers to make decisions based on a belief that quantitative, and therefore measurable indicators, validate such decisions. As highlighted earlier the appearance of precision through quantification, mathematics, and excel sheets often conveys a validity that is not justified.

But how do we treat uncertainty, a situation where there is little or no measurable data and where the decision environment may not only be rapidly changing but rapidly and randomly evolving in terms of its structure? Rules of thumb do not work anymore, correlations no longer hold, or worse, sometimes they hold and sometimes not. Mathematicians such as Rene Thom (1972) the founder of "catastrophe theory" think differently, being convinced that the qualitative is a great deal more than just a mediocre form of the quantitative. When qualitative data is issued side by side with quantitative analysis, decision makers have access to more valid and more powerful information on current and potential future performance. A framework, which applies iterative monitoring of earlier judgments, has the virtue of being both more flexible and dynamic, helping practitioners and decision makers to mitigate uncertainty as well as risk.

Different Interpretations of Uncertainty: Confused Dot Com(plexity)!

In spite of all this—and it may appear to the reader that Uncertainty is highly complicated, which it is—"you ain't seen nothing yet". Uncertainty comes in different shapes and sizes and a number of academics and practitioners have attempted to differentiate its different forms—although it has to be said they all seem to be uncertain as to how many types there are! This publication will give guidance to uncertainty for decision support purposes.

Version 1

For example, Michael Goldstein (2011) at Durham University identified some 9 different sources of Uncertainty albeit qualifying such uncertainties within the domain of computer modelling, and to quote:

1. **parametric uncertainty** (each model requires a, typically high dimensional, parametric specification),
2. **conditional uncertainty** (uncertainty as to boundary conditions, initial conditions, and forcing functions),
3. **functional uncertainty** (model evaluations take a long time, so the function is unknown almost everywhere),
4. **stochastic uncertainty** (either the model is stochastic, or it should be),

5. **solution uncertainty** (as the system equations can only be solved to some necessary level of approximation).
6. **structural uncertainty** (the model only approximates the physical system),
7. **measurement uncertainty** (as the model is calibrated against system data all of which is measured with error),
8. **multi-model uncertainty** (usually we have not one but many models related to the physical system),
9. **decision uncertainty** (to use the model to influence real-world outcomes, we need to relate things in the world that we can influence to inputs to the simulator and through outputs to actual impacts. These links are uncertain.)

Wow and you thought Uncertainty was simple?

Version 2

A simpler, more practitioner based classification of uncertainty has been put forward by Courtney et al. (2000) of consulting company McKinsey & Company, in a memo entitled "Four levels of uncertainty (Strategy under Uncertainty)" namely:

- Level one: **A clear enough future** (where a single forecast that is sufficiently precise basis for defining a strategy).
- Level two: **Alternative futures** (one of a few discrete scenarios, usually with probabilities).
- Level three: **A range of futures** (A limited number of key variables define the range, but the actual outcome may lie anywhere within it. There are no natural discrete scenarios).
- Level four: **True ambiguity** (A number of dimensions of uncertainty interact to create an environment that is virtually impossible to predict at any level—it is impossible to identify a range of potential outcomes, let alone scenarios within a range. It might not even be possible to identify, much less predict, all the relevant variables that will define the future.

What Courtney, Kirkland, and Viguerie have described is less four types of uncertainty but a range of conditions across the Uncertainty/Risk spectrum. The only true uncertainty described being level four—true ambiguity. Its value though is that it does encapsulate scalable uncertainty, albeit some of the conditions are closer to risk.

Version 3

The Uncertainty Toolkit for Analysts in Government (2016) identifies three types of uncertainty:

1. **Aleatory uncertainty**—the things we know that we know (aka "known knowns") and which relates to the inherent uncertainty that is always present in

"underlying probabilistic variability". In reality it acknowledges that in practice there is no such thing as certainty!

2. **Epistemic uncertainty**—things that we know we do not know (aka known unknowns)—due to a lack of knowledge about complexity of the system assumptions are used to address gaps in the knowledge base.
3. **Ontological uncertainty**—things that we do not know we do not know (aka unknown unknowns). Based on no experience or knowledge whatsoever of an occurrence.

This interpretation is succinct and nearly fully comprehensive, in terms of cognitive variants of uncertainty. It is though somewhat academic in its use of language to describe the different types of uncertainty: aleatory, epistemic, and ontological are not everyday terms used by practitioners when communicating to real-world decision makers. It is also essentially a representation of the Rumsfeld interpretation. However, as with the Rumsfeld version it avoids identification of the fourth element of the Known Unknown axis—**"Unknown-knowns"**.

Version 4

In 2011, Swedish methodologist Tom Ritchey (2011) specified another four types of uncertainty:

- **Risk** which he defined as a type of uncertainty being based on quantitative probability. He reinforces the Knightian position by stating that if risk has well-grounded probability, then there is no uncertainty at all.
- **Genuine uncertainty** conversely embodies outcomes which cannot be ascribed probabilities.
- **Unspecified uncertainty** Ritchey positions in relation to long-term future developments and as such is "inherently ineradicable—you cannot get rid of it by trying to obtain more information about it, because the information needed to reduce it simply isn't there".
- **Agonistic uncertainty** which "refers to a network of conscious agents (e.g. individuals, organisations, institutions or nations) acting concurrently and reacting to each other", so that its development is unpredictable.

Version 5

Another interpretation of Uncertainty was put forward by the former Governor of the Bank of England, Mervyn King and Economist and FT journalist John Kay in 2020, who introduced the term **"Radical Uncertainty"**. They define "Radical Uncertainty" as being the kind of uncertainty that statistical analysis cannot deal with (as non-quantifiable risk). This interpretation is very much a hybrid, as it is akin to Ritchey's definition of "Genuine Uncertainty", Epistemic and Ontological uncertainty, and an amalgam of Goldstein's conditional, functional, solution, and decision uncertainties—but certainly Knightian!

Version 6

Yet another example of populating different types of uncertainty has been put forward in "Decision Support Tools for Complex Decisions Under Uncertainty" (French 2018) where five types of uncertainty are put forward. These are stated as follows in the publication with examples provided for each type:

- **Stochastic uncertainties** (physical randomness and variations), e.g.:

    - Will the next card be an ace?
    - What will be the height of a randomly selected child in Year 7 in Surrey?
    - What proportion of car batteries will fail in the first year of use?

- **Epistemological uncertainties** (lack of knowledge), e.g.:

    - What is happening?
    - What can we learn from the data?
    - What might our competitors do?
    - How good is our understanding of the causes of this phenomenon?

- **Analytical uncertainties** (model fit and accuracy), e.g.:

    - How well do we know the model parameters?
    - How accurate are the calculations, given approximations made for tractability?
    - How well does that model fit the world?

- **Ambiguities** (ill-defined meaning), e.g.:

    - What do we mean by "normal working conditions" for a machine?
    - What do we mean by "human error"?

- **Value uncertainties** (ill-defined objectives), e.g.:

    - What do we mean by the patient being in "good health"?
    - What weight should we put on this objective relative to others?
    - What is the right—ethical—thing to do?

Simon French (the editor) goes on to say that the stochastic, epistemological, and analytical uncertainties relate largely to questions about the external environment whilst ambiguities and value uncertainties reflect uncertainty about ourselves.

Version 7

Another term used in relation to uncertainty is "Deep Uncertainty"—a form adopted by a mixed academic-practitioner group called "The Society for Decision Making

Under Deep Uncertainty" (DMDU). The Society and publisher Springer in 2019 produced a book dedicated to the topic (Marchau et al., 2019).

The editors state that, *"Decision makers, feel decreasing confidence in their ability to anticipate correctly future technological, economic, and social developments, future changes in the system they are trying to improve, or the multiplicity and time-varying preferences of stakeholders regarding the system's outcomes"*.

They define "deep uncertainty" situations as arising from actions taken over time in response to unpredictable evolving situations—in effect such situations are non-linear and asymmetric, and where the different stakeholders are often in disagreement.

Marchau et al. see decision-making in the context of deep uncertainty and which requires a paradigm that is not based on predictions of the future (known as the "predict-then-act" paradigm). Rather the aim is to prepare and adapt, by tracking how the future evolves and allowing adaptations over time as more information or knowledge becomes available so as to implement long-term strategies. The "track and adapt" approach explicitly acknowledges the deep uncertainty surrounding decision-making for uncertain events. In other words, the deep uncertainty environment requires continual iterative and objective monitoring of future events. As we shall see later, in Chap. 7, this interpretation is very much aligned with what can be termed **Exploratory** in relation to future scenarios.

Finally we can add Rumsfeld's own classification (2002) as *Version 8* (added as a simplified alternative and is broadly understood):

- Known-knowns
- Known-unknowns
- Unknown-unknowns

So, there we have eight interpretations of Uncertainty—as I said earlier, "confusing" isn't it? Remember such interpretations are not exclusive—I have attempted to present a mix of the academic and the practitioner to demonstrate the range of opinion on the subject—no doubt you will find out others.

How do these different versions line-up against one another? And how can we portray the different types of uncertainty within a workable and meaningful structure without oversimplification of its various sub-components? In Table 2.1, we present the eight versions as described, to identify the similarities and differences of interpretation. **This combination of the different versions and interpretations of uncertainty will be synthesised into a template that will act as a core reference tool as we move through the programme.**

This exercise has I believe been worthwhile in that it has helped in:

- Identifying the various types of uncertainty being bandied about by both practitioners and academics—(so at least exposing the reader to such versions).
- Filtering the core components and version of uncertainty that we shall be using in the book.
- Creating the basis for a practical representation of the various forms of uncertainty that can be deployed when addressing various types of problem (see

Table 2.1 Interpretations of uncertainty

Different interpretations of uncertainty

Version 1	Version 2	Version 3	Version 4	Version 5	Version 6	Version 7	Version 8
Goldstein	Courtney, Kirkland, and Viguerie	Analyst uncertainty toolkit	Ritchey	King and Kay	French AU4DM	Marchau et al. DMDU	Rumsfeld
Parametric	Level 1: A clear enough future	Aleatory (known-knowns)	Risk	Radical uncertainty	Stochastic	Deep uncertainty	Known-knowns
Conditional	Level 2: Alternative futures	Epistemic (known-unknowns)	Genuine		Epistemological		Known-unknowns
Functional	Level 3: A range of futures	Ontological (unknown-unknowns	Unspecified		Analytic		Unknown-unknowns
Stochastic	Level 4: True ambiguity		Agonistic		Ambiguities		
Solution					Value		
Structural							
Measurement							
Multi-model							
Decision							

Chap. 3), and which can be used as a useful template for identifying major categories of uncertainty across the risk spectrum.

There are unfortunately two further conditions which muddy the waters of uncertainty—complexity and interconnectivity which we will address before moving onto the main reference template cited above.

2.1.1.4 Complexity and Interconnectivity

Understanding uncertainty unfortunately is not just about being able to classify its various components as to their condition of being predictable or identifiable. Into an already confusing arena the problem itself is compounded by matters of complexity. Before answering the question "what is complexity?", it is important to distinguish the difference between Complex and Complicated, and indeed "simple". Kuosa (2012) identifies that many things—such as a leaf—appear simple but on closer examination are highly complex. Just because a system made up of a large number of parts can be described in terms of its individual components, that system is best described as complicated rather than complex—such as a modern jet aircraft. Kuosa goes on to say that:

> In complexity, the interaction between the system and its environment are of such a nature that the system as a whole cannot be fully understood simply by analysing its components. Moreover, these relationships are not fixed but shift and change, often as a result of self-organization.

Thus, in summary we can state that:

- A system may be complicated, but have very low complexity.
- A large number of parts does not generally imply high complexity. It does, in general, imply a complicated system (for example, a mechanical watch or clock).
- Complexity implies capacity to surprise, to suddenly deliver unexpected behaviour.
- In order to assess the amount of complexity it is necessary to take uncertainty into account, not just the number of parts.
- The combination of complexity within a system with interconnectivity reflects the non-linearity and multidimensional interactions within the system.

What is complexity? The answer to this question is contentious. Theorists such as Mitchell (2009) states that "no single 'science of complexity' nor a single complexity theory exists yet". She does identify some common properties of complex systems, as having:

- Complex collective behaviour—it being the collective actions of vast numbers of components that give rise to hard-to-predict and changing patterns of behaviour.
- Signalling and information processing: all systems produce and use information and signals from both their internal and external environments.

- Adaptation: many complex systems adapt—i.e. change behaviour to improve their chances of survival or success—through learning or evolutionary processes.

Mitchell goes on to propose a definition of the term "complex system":

a system in which large networks of components with no central control and simple rules of operation give rise to complex collective behaviour, sophisticated information processing, and adaptation via learning or evolution.

It is to be noted that Mitchell does not specifically identify uncertainty per se but rather concentrates on the nature of a system as a network.

On the other hand, Jacek Marczyk (2009), a practitioner and theorist in the area of uncertainty and complexity management, adopts a more operationally pragmatic approach and states that complexity is a fundamental property of all systems, just like energy. He identifies complexity specifically (as opposed to Mitchell's complex system) as being a function of structure and uncertainty, where there are:

- Multiple information sources
- And which are linked (inter-dependent)
- And which are often uncertain
- An increasing number of links and in the presence of high uncertainty, it becomes impossible to comprehend a system and to manage it. This corresponds to critical complexity.

Marczyck appears to go further than Mitchell by indicating that at certain levels of uncertainty *"it becomes impossible to comprehend a system and to manage it"*. His interpretation of high levels of uncertainty brings it much closer to a number of key characteristics of a "wicked problems" (see Chap. 3), namely that:

- There is no definitive formulation of a wicked problem
- Wicked problems have no stopping rule
- There is no immediate and no ultimate test of a solution to a wicked problem.

There is one area that Marczyck can be challenged, in that he states that one can quantify the amount of structured information within a system and its "functional potential". It can be argued that under conditions of high volatility and dynamism, quantification is all but irrelevant.

Properties of Complexity

Marczyk further describes key properties of complexity as being where:

- Rapidly rising complexity is observed prior to a crisis, an extreme event, or collapse.
- Collapse is Nature's most efficient mechanism of simplification (very prominent in social systems).
- High complexity corresponds to high risk of contagion and fast stress propagation—i.e. matters can get easily out of hand by applying the wrong solutions to a

perceived problem or indeed the perception of the problem itself may be erroneous.
- Interconnectedness between system parts is dynamic and volatile, aggravated by incomplete identification of end points (c.f. the number of software bugs continually being discovered in high-profile commercial software) and indeed most software where complex coding protocols are being used.

Relevance of Complexity

No matter that Mitchell may be correct in that there is no agreed theory of complexity, the practitioner world well understands the concept of complexity and how it impacts their respective domains.

In the area of strategy development, problems of uncertainty and complexity are readily apparent. Senior executives and by implication, high-level practitioners, struggle to conceive or adapt strategies and implement them, whilst remaining relevant, and is becoming increasingly difficult to achieve. (Camillus 2008).

The real challenge is for a decision-making team to maximise the length of time it has to consider its situation before applying solutions in order to exploit opportunities, or to avoid threats, or unintended consequences.

A 2011 report published by the Economist Intelligence Unit (EIU) entitled "The Complexity Challenge" identified the growing debate about such issues and highlighted strategic management concerns and awareness. The report asked some 300 global senior executives how severely increasing complexity is affecting business. The main findings were:

- Doing business has become more complex since the 2008 global financial crisis (and now we have the 2011 financial crisis as well)
- Firms are finding it increasingly hard to cope with the rise in complexity
- The single biggest cause of business complexity is greater expectation on the part of the customer
- Complexity is exposing firms to new and more dangerous risks
- Businesses are focusing on technological solutions to tackle complexity
- A majority of firms have an organisational structure that may be adding to complexity.

Although the report is slanted mainly towards senior business executives, its findings can be ported over to apply to decision makers in general.

2.1.2   The Uncertainty Profile: From "Known-knowns" to "Unknown-unknowns"

2.1.2.1   Background: The Existential Poetry of Donald H. Rumsfeld[1]

In 2002, Donald Rumsfeld, Defence Secretary in George W. Bush's administration, the latter being a key evangelist of the Third Gulf War[2] famously said in a press conference to a largely cynical world, and in response to a question about the lack of evidence linking the government of Iraq with the supply of weapons of mass destruction to terrorist groups.

> As we know,
>   There are known knowns.
>   There are things we know we know.
>   We also know
>   There are knowns unknowns.
>   That is to say
>   We know there are some things
>   We do not know.
>   But there are also unknown unknowns,
>   The ones we don't know we don't know.[3]

There have been many references to this statement—most noticeably related to use of the term "unknown-unknowns" and indeed the recent UK's Uncertainty Toolkit for Analysts in Government referred to in the previous section uses the Rumsfeld comment as the basis for its three classifications of uncertainty almost verbatim. Yet as the combination of the two variables used in the argument (known and unknown) lends itself to a 2×2 matrix, Rumsfeld's statement (and the Uncertainty Toolkit) only addresses three of them. There is a fourth variant which is unaddressed—**the Unknown-Knowns**.

Let us first look at some of the key vocabulary, terms, and concepts that can be inserted into the "Uncertainty Profile" and which, I believe address a key element which has tended to be, if not overlooked, under-represented in these other frameworks—the "unknown-knowns".

Where are we at in having a better understand of Uncertainty and Risk? We have seen that there are a number of similar approaches and versions to visualising the various contexts and conditions in which uncertainty and risk are present.

So, let us then explain the four quadrants or permutations of this uncertainty matrix further, namely:

---

[1]This title has used that of an amusing compilation of the sayings of Donald Rumsfeld entitle "Pieces of Intelligence" by Hart Seely, The Free Press 2003.

[2]Remember the first Gulf War in modern times was the Iran-Iraq war of 1980 to 1988

[3]This statement itself a version of a technique called the Johari window—developed by psychologists Joseph Luft and Harrington Ingham back in 1955.

- Known-knowns
- Known-Unknowns
- Unknown-knowns
- Unknown-Unknowns

As seen with the presentation of the risk spectrum in Fig. 2.1, and the discussion above, there are various forms of uncertainty and risk, often with occluded boundaries. Such outcomes or events, whether they reside at the risk or uncertain end of the spectrum, can be inserted into a matrix governed by Predictability and Visibility. How can these main axes be defined?

2.1.2.2 Event Predictability

Events can be either Predictable or Unpredictable. By "predictable" is meant "to be made known beforehand" or simply, "capable of being foretold". Thus, the range of options from an event being predictable to being unpredictable can range from something which is an event that is (almost) certain—such as, "my alarm always goes off at 6.30 in the morning" to "I always know what the weather will be like tomorrow without reading the forecast". This interpretation would qualify as an Aleatory uncertainty or Ritchey's Risk.

Thus, the ability to identify how well an outcome can be predicted is dependent on how much control we have in making an event happen. Secondly what historical data (or experience if available) allows very high probability in the confirmation that an outcome can happen. To each event that may have an impact on our lives, the best we can do is to attach varying levels of probability.

2.1.2.3 Event Visibility

Can, "what type of event may occur", be identified? How different is event "Visibility" from "Predictability"? Visibility implies being able to determine what type of event may impact us as opposed to the likelihood of that event occurring—can we visualise it? This requires identification in greater detail of the kind of event or events, which can have an impact.

Before an event can be predicted it is important to identify (make visible) those events which are likely to have the greatest impact from a subjective standpoint—tempered by the probability of such an event happening.

Of course, both elements are interrelated—some events are predictable and identifiable whilst at the other extreme there exist future events that are neither identifiable nor predictable. The next section is where we present a template as a workable tool that readers can use on projects and which form part of the evolutionary use of MTTs when working with the various Uncertainty components.

Profiling uncertainty: a multi-faceted problem?

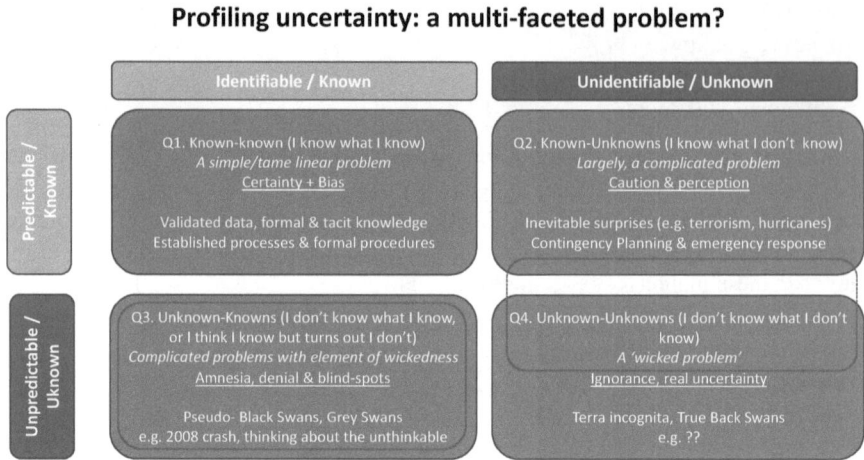

Fig. 2.2 Profiling uncertainty template

2.1.2.4 The Uncertainty Profile Template

The relationship between event visibility and event predictability can be visualised in the following matrix:

Following the presentation of an array of various interpretations of uncertainty presented in Table 2.1, the schema/template in Fig. 2.2, presented above is a synthesis that acts as a core reference tool (or *leitmotif*) as we move through the guidebook.

Those events which, any decision maker must take into account, can be positioned as follows:

2.1.2.5 Quadrant 1 (Q1): Predictable and Identifiable (Known knowns)

These events are likely to be extrapolations of events and trends that have already occurred, such as the likelihood of further regulatory and compliance measures. In this quadrant, information required to help make a decision is likely to be in formal policy documents, methods and calculations, and quantitative data previously recorded and validated.

2.1.2.6 Quadrant 2 (Q2): Identifies Predictable Events Not Yet Identifiable (Known Unknowns)

A typical example would be the July seventh Underground and bus bombings in London 2005. The public had been warned a number of times by the police and security forces that such an event would occur (i.e. it was predictable), it was just a matter of when. These events have been called, "Inevitable Surprises" by Peter Schwartz (2003): (other examples being that of a major earthquake along the San Andreas fault in California or the next overdue major eruption of Vesuvius). Such events, being predictable but not yet visible can be addressed by advanced, foresight-based contingency planning or emergency response so that when they do happen the consequences can be mitigated to some degree. (Is Covid-19 an inevitable surprise?). It is worth stating that identifying an event as an inevitable surprise and the putting in place of contingency plans offers little certainty that substantial mitigation to out-comes will occur and that responses to such events can still go very wrong. These plans have to be robust to address a wide range of event "surprises" as they challenge our ability to visualise the unthinkable.

Two recent tragic events indicate that operational foresight weaknesses still occur even when such events might have been seen as "an inevitable surprise". The Grenfell House fire with its prior warnings of the flammability of the cladding combined with the lack of a high-rise fire ladder to reach fire sources in high-rise buildings is just one example—the second being the Manchester Arena bombing where paramedic and emergency response teams were delayed in gaining access to the injured inside the Arena due to procedural safety measures, based on the possibility of secondary explosive devices, being imposed.

We now jump to quadrant 4—the third section of Rumsfeld's statement.

2.1.2.7 Quadrant 4 (Q4): Unpredictable and Not Identifiable (Unknown Unknowns)

Events here move into the realm of unknown territory "Terra Incognita". At the most extreme these are Rumsfeld's "unknown unknowns",—the ones we do not know we do not know. Such events have also been called "Black Swans". As defined by Taleb (2007) the term is a true unknown unknown. However, the reference to an event being "a Black Swan"[4] has been hi-jacked and used to justify what, in essence, is a straightforward lack of foresight and proper due diligence. Post the 2008 financial crisis commentators, bankers, and financiers alike were using the term "Black Swan event" as a reason as to why the crisis could not have been foreseen. This is a misrepresentation of the term as the event **was** foreseen by numerous but unfash-ionable commentators such as Nouriel Roubini (2010) and Raghuram Rajan (2005), who were just ignored. 2008 was not a true "black swan event" nor is the Covid-19 pandemic (We will see later in this section how Animal Metaphors have been frequently used to explain problematic situations).

These events can be described though as being **"pseudo black swans"**. I t can be argued that if we can think it—it is possible, and if we cannot then it is an "unknown unknown" or "true black swan" event and thus time should not be spent on worrying about the latter. On the other hand, one reason for not thinking about "IT" maybe just

---

[4] See the appended note at the end of this section referring to Animal Metaphors.

lack of vision and imagination so that its rightful place is in quadrant 3! Anything else, no matter how improbable, does qualify for consideration, and methods should be adopted which might in some way allow us to recognise such an eventuality and to develop (robust) contingency plans to mitigate their impact.

The cataclysmic nature of such events makes for uncomfortable reading.[5] In addition to the maintenance of entrenched paradigms by various vested interests, decision makers are required to enter the "zone of uncomfortable debate", the ZOUD (Bowman, 1995), which many organisations, policy makers, designers, and practitioners, find difficult to confront—again see the section at the end of this chapter on Animal Metaphors.

2.1.2.8 Quadrant 3 (Q3): Unpredictable and Identifiable (Unknown Knowns)

In many cases this cell is a flipped version of its Predictable/Identifiable (Quadrant 2) partner except that the level of probability is far less certain. The level of certainty is reduced not only by how far in the future an event might occur but exacerbated by the numerous permutations influencing the outcome of an event in the intervening period. An example in the sphere of international relations might be that confronting analysts as to what will happen in the Middle East over the coming 12 months in a post Trump world. We can identify the areas of concern—Iran/Saudi tensions, Yemen, Libya, and Syria and the impact of the Taliban taking charge in Afghanistan, but the outcomes are highly unpredictable due to the variety of different stakeholders with interests in the region—each with their own agenda (the countries themselves, USA, Russia, UK, France, China, Turkey, UN). Now in early 2022, it is the Ukraine where attention is heavily focussed by a variety of actors.

These **Unknown Knowns** can be interpreted as meaning **"I don't know what I know"** and hence lead to analysts missing weak signals, and/or **"I think I know but turns out that I don't"**—a form of hubris. Either way weak signals can be manifest but often due to a variety of behavioural factors and biases, ignored. Behavioural factors are to the fore in this quadrant with actors suffering from amnesia, denial, blind spots, silo thinking, and hubris—sometimes all or a combination of such behaviours—any of which can distort judgement. Event indicators in this quadrant are also asymmetric and non-linear which makes it difficult to ascertain the relative importance of both individual and clustered signals. This is a challenge to the inclination to weight the variables too early. The dictum that **policy driven evidence should be challenged by evidence based policy** is pertinent to this quadrant.

As a result, this is the most insidious, nay pernicious, of the quadrants, largely due to a number of behavioural factors as identified above—we think we know what or

---

[5]Kahn H in 1963 who wrote his famous study on "Thinking about the Unthinkable" (1963), and his earlier 1960 book entitled "on Thermonuclear War" which articulated the need to confront the impact of cataclysmic events which could theoretically happen.

where the problem is or might occur, but can we handle the inherent complexities or do we even have the tools, let alone the desire to deploy them, to address such complexity based uncertainty?

Groupthink and dogma based policy are the real enemies here and the issue is whether the stakeholders themselves are prepared to explore outcomes which may produce uncomfortable truths a theme expounded by Nik Gowing and Chris Langdon (2017). In other words, **weak signal identification is as much challenged by individual and group willingness to accept such signals through bias intervention, as by the strength of the signal itself.**

Quadrants 3 and 2 and to some extent even Quadrant 4 require an open-mindedness not always present in organisations. In addition to the maintenance of entrenched paradigms by various vested interests, decision makers are required to enter the "zone of uncomfortable debate", the ZOUD, which many organisations, policy makers, designers, and practitioners find difficult to confront (similar to the animal metaphors). The disruptive and often cataclysmic nature of such events makes for uncomfortable reading—thinking about the unthinkable, which is why, when they occur, they are too readily deemed to belong to Quadrant 4: in the vast majority of cases they are not and just demonstrate a lack of foresight.

Similarly, it should be pointed that events such as the "Kodak moment"[6] is not a black swan event—it could be foreseen and demonstrates poor judgement by management.

Weak signals, **which by definition may have already become manifest in some way,** tend to be allocated to the third quadrant of Unknown/Knowns (as per the major area bordered by a thin red line). Also by definition it can be argued that they cannot exist in the unknown/unknown quadrant because they are already manifest as a weak signal. In turn there is a strong justification that weak signals actually reside in Q2 but requiring vision if their impacts are to be acknowledged as possible.

In the end, management has to accept reality and realise that in order to avoid inevitable, outcomes, it has to be more readily amenable to acknowledging that precision and the future are incompatible terms. Thus, those events which, as a minimum, any decision maker must take into account, are represented in the top left-hand quadrant.

Mapping "wicked problems" and messes (see next chapter) against the above schematic is not precise as the boundaries of a problem can be fuzzy. It can be argued that all problems identified as having characteristics of Q4—"Terra Incognita", can automatically be classified as "wicked" type problems. Yet due to situations where some elements of the problem data (both hard and soft) are lost or misplaced, then degrees of "wickedness" can manifest themselves in Q3 and to an even lesser extent in Q2.

---

[6]The term is used as an example of lack of commercial foresight. Kodak did much of the early work in digital photography but failed to see its significance as it sought to protect its core product base which was film-based. Such lack of vision caused its demise.

It will be this schema that will act as a major heuristic device as we develop the knowledge base when looking at the deconstructed components of Uncertainty. The importance of the schema presented in Fig. 2.2 will become apparent as we explore the other components in Part A and beyond.

2.1.3 Methods, Tools, and Techniques (MTTs)

2.1.3.1 Other Templates

In addition to the main "Uncertainty Profile" template presented in Fig. 2.2, there are of course numerous other such templates which have been devised over the years. Below are presented two such examples, "Cynefin" and "VUCA" which the user may wish to work with alongside the Uncertainty Profile introduced above. Already in the text there has been reference to a number of animal metaphors used to explain various states of knowledge or lack thereof in an organisational setting—such as Black and Grey Swans. To end this chapter, a number of such animal metaphors are highlighted with explanations as to how they have been deployed.

2.1.3.2 Cynefin[7]

In 1999, David Snowden, when working at IBM, produced a different conceptual framework for categorising uncertainty called Cynefin, a Welsh word for habitat and used here to describe five different decision-making contexts and is represented below.
The central cross-over of the axes represents the fifth context "disorder" and confusion.

These contexts or domains have been changed by Snowdon and colleagues over the years and the main titles used here reflect largely the latest nomenclature. In the *Known Space*, also called *Obvious*, relationships between cause and effect are well understood, so we will know what will happen if we take a specific action. All systems and behaviours can be fully modelled so that the consequences of any course of action can be predicted with near certainty. In such contexts, decision-making tends to take the form of recognising patterns and responding to them with well-rehearsed actions often in the form of established policy documents and laws derived from familiarity. This implies that we have some certainty or at least high probability about what will happen as a result of any action. There will be little

---

[7]Much of the description of Cynefin used here has been adapted from a useful summary written by Simon French in "Decision Support Tools for Complex Decisions Under Uncertainty" edited by Simon French: published by the Analysis Under Uncertainty for Decision Makers Network (AU4DM). 2018.

ambiguity or value uncertainty in such contexts. This could also be described as a "known known"?

In the *Knowable Space*, earlier called *Complicated*, cause and effect relationships are generally understood, but for any specific decision further data is needed before the consequences of any action can be predicted with certainty. The decision makers will face epistemological (knowledge), stochastic (probabilistic), and analytical uncertainties too as per the types of uncertainty outlined previously. Decision analysis and support will include the fitting and use of models to forecast the potential outcomes of actions with appropriate levels of uncertainty. As decision makers will have experienced such situations before they can mitigate the uncertainties by detailed contingency planning. One may use the term "known-unknowns" for this element or "inevitable surprise".

In the *Complex Space*, decision-making faces many poorly understood, interacting causes and effects. Knowledge is at best qualitative: there are simply too many potential interactions to disentangle particular causes and effects. There are no precise quantitative models to predict system behaviours such as in the Known and Knowable spaces. Decision analysis is still possible, but its style will be broader, with less emphasis on details, and more focus on exploring judgement and issues, and on developing broad strategies that are flexible enough to accommodate changes as the situation evolves. Analysis may begin and, perhaps, end with much more informal qualitative models. Issues are close to being not just complex problems but have elements of "wickedness" as well (see the next chapter for more details on this).

Contexts in the *Chaotic Space* involve events and behaviours beyond our current experience and there are no obvious candidates for cause and effect in effect "unknown-unknowns". Decision-making cannot be based upon analysis because there are no concepts of how to separate entities and predict their interactions. These are fully "wicked problems". Decision makers will need to take probing actions and see what happens, until they can make some sort of sense of the situation, gradually drawing the context back into one of the other spaces (if this is possible).

The central cross over the axes intersection in Fig. 2.3 below is sometimes called the Disordered Space. It simply refers to those contexts that we have not had time to categorise. The Disordered Space and the Chaotic Space are far from the same. Contexts in the former may well lie in the Known, Knowable, or Complex Spaces; we just need to recognise that they do. Those in the latter will be completely novel. Using this interpretation of "disorder" then one could state that they are "unknown-knowns".

2.1.3.3   VUCA

Another common approach for visualising various types of uncertainty is VUCA. This is an acronym dating from 1987 developed by Bennis and Nanus from their original 1985 publication on leadership, and stands for Volatility, Uncertainty, Complexity, and Ambiguity. Following the collapse of the Soviet Union in the early 1990s, the world became more unpredictable and a new way of identifying and

Fig. 2.3 The Cynefin
model

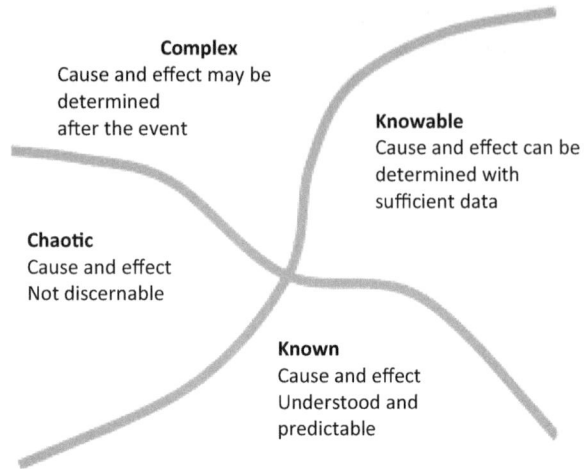

reacting to potential threats was required and the adoption of the VUCA template appeared to fit well with the new political landscape. As a set, the four elements themselves characterise potential organisational uncertainty in terms of both systemic and behavioural failures. Thus:

- V = Volatility signifies both the nature and dynamics of change, **and** the nature and speed of change forces and catalysts.
- U = Uncertainty reflects the lack of predictability and the prospects for surprise.
- C = Complexity indicates the multiplicity of interconnectivities present with a particular system.
- A = Ambiguity highlights the fuzziness of reality, the potential for misreads, and the mixed meanings of conditions.

These elements illustrate the context in which organisations envisage their current and future state in an asymmetric world and encourage management to challenge assumptions that the (immediate) future will resemble the recent past. For most organisations—business, government, education, health, military, and others—VUCA is a simple acronym to prompt organisational preparedness, anticipation, evolution, and intervention.

Bennett and Lemoine (2014) in the Harvard Business Review (HBR) produced a useful guide where each of the VUCA elements is explained in terms of its characteristic and approach. In addition, an example is provided for each element as well (Fig. 2.4).

Of course, the 4 elements within the VUCA acronym can be used in a variety of combinations. The table shows some 13 different combinatory options in addition to the full VUCA acronym (Table 2.2).

complexity

Characteristics: The situation has many interconnected parts and variables. Some information is available or can be predicted, but the volume or nature of it can be overwhelming to process.

Example: You are doing business in many countries, all with unique regulatory environments, tariffs, and cultural values.

Approach: Restructure, bring on or develop specialists, and build up resources adequate to address the complexity.

volatility

Characteristics: The challenge is unexpected or unstable and may be of unknown duration, but it's not necessarily hard to understand; knowledge about it is often available.

Example: Prices fluctuate after a natural disaster takes a supplier off-line.

Approach: Build in slack and devote resources to preparedness—for instance, stockpile inventory or overbuy talent. These steps are typically expensive; your investment should match the risk.

ambiguity

Characteristics: Causal relationships are completely unclear. No precedents exist; you face "unknown unknowns."

Example: You decide to move into immature or emerging markets or to launch products outside your core competencies.

Approach: Experiment. Understanding cause and effect requires generating hypotheses and testing them. Design your experiments so that lessons learned can be broadly applied.

uncertainty

Characteristics: Despite a lack of other information, the event's basic cause and effect are known. Change is possible but not a given.

Example: A competitor's pending product launch muddies the future of the business and the market.

Approach: Invest in information—collect, interpret, and share it. This works best in conjunction with structural changes, such as adding information analysis networks, that can reduce ongoing uncertainty.

(Vertical label, left side:) HOW WELL CAN YOU PREDICT THE RESULTS OF YOUR ACTIONS?

(Bottom label:) HOW MUCH DO YOU KNOW ABOUT THE SITUATION?

Fig. 2.4 The VUCA matrix

Table 2.2 Different options emanating from the VUCA matrix

Volatile	Uncertain	Complex	Ambiguous
Volatile	Uncertain	Complex	Ambiguous
Volatile and Uncertain	Uncertain and Complex	Complex and Ambiguous	
Volatile and Complex	Uncertain and Ambiguous		
Volatile and Ambiguous	Uncertain, Complex, and Ambiguous		
Volatile, Uncertain, and Complex			
Volatile, Uncertain, Complex, and Ambiguous			

2.1.3.4 Animal Metaphors

Although not strictly a MTT, the use of metaphor is regularly used as an aid to introduce or simplify a concept. A number of metaphors can be used in the explanation of uncertainty—here are a few that are in regular use. Animal metaphors generally highlight human and organisational frailties and limitations.

Which Metaphor to Use?

In recent times, there has been a proliferation of animal based metaphors to describe both situations and organisational behaviour in the broader domain of uncertainty. Two animals have been noticeably used—Elephants and Swans. In this note I have outlined the most common types and their variants. Whilst metaphors can be a useful shorthand to describe a situation, the danger is not only overuse but misinterpretation and misuse.

The first "beast" is the elephant and common metaphorical expressions include:

- *The Elephant in the room*: This idiom is used to describe a major issue especially a controversial one that is obvious (elephantine in size) but no-one wants to discuss as it arouses behavioural responses which makes people feel uncomfortable or is embarrassing, even inflammatory, or dangerous. A typical example could be where management is discussing staff diversity but where there are no women and/or people from an ethnic background and/or staff from a different social background in the management group itself.
- *Black Elephants*: a more recent addition to the business metaphor library (after Thomas Friedman, 2014; Peter Ho, 2017), this is a cross between a black swan and "the elephant in the room" (a problem that is visible to everyone, yet no one still wants to deal with it so they pretend it is not there). When a problem blows up a common reaction is one of shock and surprise, and is treated as though it was a black swan. In reality, it should not have come as a surprise.
- Another big beast metaphor similar in size and habitat as the elephant is the rhino. Michele Wucker (2016) recently introduced the term *"Grey Rhino"*, defined as being a highly probable, high impact yet neglected threat. Although similar to elephants in the room and black swans, grey rhinos are not random surprises, but occur after a series of warnings and visible evidence. Interestingly enough Wucker states that the 2008 financial crash was not a black swan event but a grey rhino—it was evident in advance but was selectively ignored in spite of the growing evidence. This is almost identical to an Unknown-known as described in the quadrant 3 profile of Fig. 2.2 earlier.

The second high-profile animal used in metaphors is the **swan** largely thanks to Nassim Nicholas Taleb's 2007 book "The Black Swan".

- *Black Swan*: Taleb's metaphor has majorly entered the management lexicon but has been frequently misused. A black swan is an extremely rare event with severe consequences. It is strictly an Unknown-Unknown but increasingly used to describe low probability/high impact events which are highly unpredictable. Unfortunately, the term has been misused to describe an event which could or should have been predicted beforehand such as the 2008 financial crash (which of course was predicted but ignored). Is this also just a grey rhino?

- *Grey Swans*: this variant of the swan metaphor was introduced around 2012 by a team at management consultants PwC (2012). The paper states that although black swan events should only occur at unpredictable (and rare) intervals *"recent experience suggests events that fit the definition of black swans are happening more and more frequently. So, are black swans actually turning grey? Rather than being infrequent 'outlier' events, are they now just part of a faster-changing and more uncertain world"?* PwC observe that organisations can have blind spots from which high impact risks emerge.

Whilst there has been a profusion of metaphors—particularly since Taleb's 2007 book—in essence elephants, swans, and rhinos are all quite similar in trying to use metaphor when describing the occurrence of uncertain events, or more specifically our (behavioural) responses to them.

I see the elephant and rhino metaphors as reflecting largely behavioural responses, individually and organisationally, in dealing with unpleasant yet highly visible circumstances—if the parties are prepared to look harder and overcome prejudice and bias.

On the other hand, the black swan metaphors seem much more allied to identification, or lack, of risk and uncertainty. The main area of misrepresentation appears to be a lack of understanding as to the real nature of uncertainty in the term "black swan"—which should be defined as an "unknown-unknown". In numerous instances, the term has been hi-jacked to justify the failure to act to an event even when evidence was present, even as a weak signal. My preferred term, rather than grey rhino or grey swan is to call such event profiles, **"pseudo-black swans"**—a more pejorative description for a paucity of foresight especially when accompanied by behavioural failures such as bias, group think, silo mentality, etc.

So, in conclusion, I recommend we use elephant metaphors for behaviourally driven responses in decision-making and the two swan metaphors when faced with different levels of uncertainty. You choose!

2.2 Summary

This chapter has set out to introduce a better understanding of the difference between risk and uncertainty. In spite of numerous forms of uncertainty, we have synthesised these into four main variants presented as the "Uncertainty" matrix. This can be used as a template for a variety of scenarios, so as to offer the analyst or decision maker a starting point for the further exploration of a problem with varying levels of uncertainty. However, understanding of the nature of the problem itself is also critical to narrowing down those variables to be used when developing such scenarios. This is the topic of the following chapter.

References

Bennett, N., & Lemoine, G. L. (Jan–Feb 2014). What VUCA really means for you. *Harvard Business Review Magazine.*

Bennis, W., & Nanus, B. (1985). *Leaders: The strategies for taking charge.* Harper & Row.

Bowman, C. (1995). Strategy workshops and top-team commitment to strategic change. *Journal of Managerial Psychology, 10*(8), 4–12.

Camillus, J. (May 2008). Strategy as a wicked problem. *Harvard Business Review.*

Courtney, H. G., Kirkland, J., & Viguerie, S. P. (2000). *Four levels of uncertainty (Strategy under Uncertainty).* McKinsey & Company.

EIU. (2011). The complexity challenge – How businesses are bearing up, the economist intelligence unit.

French, Simon, (Ed.). (2018). Decision support tools for complex decisions under uncertainty: published by the Analysis Under Uncertainty for Decision Makers Network (AU4DM).

Friedman, T. (2014). Stampeding black elephants. *New York Times*, November 22nd 2014.

Goldstein, Michael. (2011). *Uncertainty analysis for computer models.* Durham University.

Gowing, N., & Langdon, C. (2017). *Thinking the Unthinkable – A new imperative for leadership in the digital age*: An interim report – Published by CIMA London.

Ho, P. (2017). *Hunting black swans & taming black elephants: Governance in a complex world.* IPS-Nathan Lectures, Singapore, April 7 2017.

Hubbard, D. W. (2007). *How to measure anything – Finding the value of intangibles in business.* Wiley.

King, M., & Kay, J. (2020). *Radical uncertainty – Decision-making for an unknowable future.* The Bridge Press.

Knight, Frank. (1921). *Risk, uncertainty, and profit.*

Kuosa, T. (2012). *The evolution of strategic foresight.* Gower.

Marchau, V., Walker, W., Bloeman, P., & Popper, S. (Eds.). (2019). *Decision making under deep uncertainty – From theory to practice.* Springer.

Marczyk, J. (2009). *A new theory of risk and rating.* Editrice UNI Service.

Mitchell, M. (2009). *Complexity: A guided tour.* Oxford University Press.

Mohammad, A., & Sykes, R. (2012). *Black swans turn grey – The transformation of risk.* PWC.

Rajan, R. (2005). Address to Conference at Jackson Hole Wyoming.

Ritchey, T. (2011). *Wicked problems and social messes: Decision support modelling with morphological analysis.* Springer.

Roubini, N. (2010). *Crisis economics.* Penguin Group.

Rumsfeld, D., February 12th 2002. *Department of defense news briefing.*

Schwartx, P. (2003). *Inevitable surprises – Thinking ahead in a time of turbulence.* Gotham Books (Penguin Group – USA).

Taleb, N. N. (2007). *The Black Swan.* Allen Lane.

Thom, R. (1972). *Structural stability and morphogenesis.* W.A. Benjamin.

Uncertainty Toolkit for Analysts in Government. (2016). https://analystsuncertaintytoolkit.github.io/UncertaintyWeb/index.html

Wucker, M. (2016). *The Grey Rhino.* St Martin's Press.

Chapter 3
Problem Status

> "Earlier, I didn't understand why I got no answer to my
> question, today I don't understand how I presumed to ask a
> question. But then I didn't presume, I only asked" Franz
> Kafka—the Zurau Aphorisms.

Abstract A major problem for researchers, analysts, forecasters and, indeed, investors is to identify how, when, and where new events and trends will play out. In essence most problems have multiple numbers of variables, and where each variable has a number of conditions or dimensions. So, how can we address the outcomes of futures governed by such complexity? This chapter introduces the notion that problems come in various shapes and sizes which can be best addressed via a set of techniques known as Problem Structuring Methods (PSMs). Once the problem characteristic has been identified (is it a puzzle, a causal problem, or a wicked problem?), then the problem can be positioned within the Uncertainty matrix so the most appropriate PSM can be applied. This positioning also allows the analyst to explore issues such as decision stakes and systems uncertainties. The chapter ends by introducing Rosenhead's Robustness Analysis method as an appropriate MTT for addressing the early stages of problem identification.

Keywords Puzzle · Causal problem · Wicked problem · Mess · Tame problem · Unintended consequences · Problem structuring method · Post normal · Robustness analysis

3.1 Introduction: What Is the Problem?

Problems can come in different shapes and sizes. Analysts and decision makers are often too impatient with trying to solve the problem—without understanding the problem's true nature So, how can we clarify this true nature as failure to do so can lead us down sub-optimum paths possessing any number of unintended consequences?

> ...the most demanding and troubling task in formative decision situations is to decide what
> the problem is. There are too many factors; many of the relationships between them are

© The Author(s), under exclusive license to Springer Nature Switzerland AG 2022
B. Garvey et al., *Uncertainty Deconstructed*, Science, Technology and Innovation
Studies, https://doi.org/10.1007/978-3-031-08007-4_3

unclear or in dispute; the most important do not reduce naturally to quantified form; different stakeholders have different priorities (Rosenhead & Mingers, 2001).

The space which the problem occupies is called, naturally enough, a **problem space**—the latter being a mental representation of the mix of variables and their respective conditions relating to a particular problem. Problem spaces do not necessarily contain any details of the solution of what is important, as one must not make any assumptions about a solution too early and thus eliminate viable possibilities. And, as we shall see in Chap. 9, we need to allow for a whole array of biases to play out, particularly at an early stage when the problem is still being articulated.

Apart from identifying and tracking different groups of variables, an additional concern is to ascertain where specific topics (e.g. technologies), might be in relation to a time horizon—now, next year, within 5 years, 20 years, the distant future, or even never—the When or Temporal driver (more on this in Chap. 4). This chapter lays out the main boundaries to help different stakeholders address the range and scope of the problem and its current and new event impacts.

Of additional concern however, is the sheer scale of what different events might occur. More crucially is the requirement to identify not only core sectors but their rate of development, what are the visible trends as well as hidden, outlier trends.

One category of Decision Support Methods (DSMs), **Problem Structuring Methods (PSMs)** is particularly applicable to supporting decision-making under uncertainty. In the latter part of this chapter—the section on methods, tools, and techniques (MTTs), a more detailed description of PSMs is presented, particularly by its main advocates Jonathan Rosenhead and John Mingers. The chapter ends with a run-through of a little-known method developed by Rosenhead, "Robustness Analysis", which I urge readers to explore further.

Simon (1977) states that the Decision-Making process can be broken down into three main stages:

- Intelligence: Fact finding, problem and opportunity sensing, analysis, and exploration.
- Design: Formulation of solutions, generation of alternatives, modelling and simulation.
- Choice: Goal maximisation, alternative selection, decision-making, and implementation.

Decision Support Methods (DSMs) thus fit well within the first of Simon's three stages and are represented by a body of models, tools, and processes which help to mitigate risk and provide greater clarity under conditions of uncertainty and where the intelligence ingredients may be rapidly changing and not easily specified in advance. PSMs are largely used where a problem is poorly defined or unstructured. Such methods were developed independently from the mid-1960s onwards by academics such as Stafford Beer (1984), Rittel and Webber (1973), Kunz and Rittel (1970), Ackoff (1961, 1974), and Nelson (1974). The area of thinking covered matters concerning systems thinking, including systems dynamics (Simon's second stage).

The very nature of unstructured problems would indicate that, such are the uncertainties inherent therein; no single methodology is likely to "solve" such a problem. Indeed, such a condition of initial ambiguity as to a defined outcome creates fuzziness, encouraging the introduction of assessing problems with more than one methodology—"multi-methodology".

The inherent complexity of integrating current models and methods should not act as a deterrent since such complexity, although a challenge for practitioners, outweighs the dangers of using overly discrete methods to solve problems in the areas of uncertainty and risk. It may be that concepts such as "Fuzzy Management", which recognises that we live in an occluded world, can help smooth the route from theory into performance enhancing practice (Grint, 1997). **It is often better to be approximately right than precisely wrong!**

Such complexity is a problem for practitioners of all shades. The problem is that no one method or tool is sufficiently robust to help the decision-making process when faced with uncertainty (and risk). Some of these methods are relatively easy to grasp, leading to wide adoption by numerous practitioners. Unfortunately, many of them only address part of the problem. When applied discretely they can appear to be over simplistic and not address the high levels of complexity, interconnectivity, and uncertainty inherent in the problem space. The situation is exacerbated exponentially when multiple criteria and parameters have to be addressed.

3.2 Problem Types: Not All Problems Are the Same

By understanding better, the nature of the problem, practitioners can improve their selection of the most appropriate method to help in their decision-making. If the problem is ill-defined or understood, then how can an appropriate method be selected and used to help overcome the problem?

Treverton (2010) notes that (analytic) problems vary from the simple to the highly complicated such that:

- *A Puzzle*—is a well-defined and well-structured problem with clearly defined boundaries with one correct answer for a specific solution.
- A *Problem* (or tame problem)—has a defined form or structure; it is dimensioned; it has variables but it does not have any one, single, clear-cut solution and does have known probabilities, e.g. computer hacking, management of pricing and costs.
- *A "Wicked Problem" or Mess*—is a complex issue with no defined boundaries. Such problems are highly unstructured (even unsolvable) with multiple actors and stakeholders, multiple perspectives, incommensurable and/or conflicting interests, and numerous intangibles. They do not have a single correct solution or even any solution as they do not provide any way of knowing when a solution has been reached.

This is very similar to the identification of problem type initially highlighted by the likes of Ackoff, Rittel, and Webber, Nelson, and Conklin. As ever the re-invention of the wheel.

It is this third category of problem that we shall be concentrating on in this chapter as such problems have their origins in heightened levels of uncertainty. However, before embarking on a more detailed explanation of Wicked Problems and Messes, it may be worth spending a little time expanding on understanding what is a standard or tame problem.

3.2.1 A Note About Tame Problems

Conklin (2006) identifies a "tame problem" as being one for which the traditional linear process is sufficient to produce a workable solution in an acceptable time frame. A tame problem:

- Has a well-defined and stable problem statement,
- Has a definite stopping point, i.e. when the solution is reached,
- Has a solution which can be objectively evaluated as right or wrong,
- Belongs to a class of similar problems which are all solved in the same similar way,
- Has solutions which can be easily tried and abandoned,
- Comes with a limited set of alternative solutions.

Conklin provides examples of tame problems such as finding the square root of 7358, finding the shortest route from A to B on a map, repairing a computer, raising money, and selecting a new doctor when moving to a new town. All these are tame, if complex and difficult, problems. Note that the concept "Tame", does not necessarily mean simplicity. In summary, for any given tame problem, an exhaustive formulation can be stated containing all the information the problem-solver needs for understanding and solving the problem.

3.2.2 Wicked Problems and Messes

In 1973, Horst Rittel and Melvin Webber in an article titled "Dilemmas in a General Theory of Planning" observed that there is a whole realm of social planning problems that cannot be successfully treated with traditional linear, analytical approaches. They called these **"wicked problems"** (in contrast to tame problems).

A year later in 1974, Russell Ackoff (1974), then at the LSE, in a book entitled "Re-designing the Future", independently came up with a similar concept which he called "a mess", later to become a "social mess".

Rittel and Weber identified 10 characteristics of a wicked problem.

- There is no definitive formulation of a wicked problem—You do not understand the problem until you have developed a solution. In order to describe a wicked problem in sufficient detail, one has to develop an exhaustive inventory of all conceivable solutions ahead of time. Therefore, in order to anticipate all questions (in order to anticipate all information required for resolution ahead of time), knowledge of all conceivable solutions is required. The formulation of a wicked problem is the problem!
- Wicked problems have no stopping rule—No stopping rule; since as there is no definitive "Problem", there is also no definitive "Solution".
- Solutions to wicked problems are not true-or-false, but good-or-bad—Solutions to wicked problems are not right or wrong but better or worse.
- There is no immediate and no ultimate test of a solution to a wicked problem— any solution, after being implemented, will generate waves of consequences over an extended—virtually an unbounded—period of time.
- Every solution to a wicked problem is a "one-shot operation"; because there is no opportunity to learn by trial-and-error, every attempt counts significantly (every implemented solution is consequential. It leaves "traces" that cannot be undone)—as per Rittel and Webber.
- Wicked problems do not have an enumerable (or an exhaustively describable) set of potential solutions, nor is there a well-described set of permissible operations that may be incorporated into the plan.
- Every wicked problem is essentially unique—Every wicked problem is essentially unique and novel.
- Every wicked problem can be considered to be a symptom of another problem.
- The existence of a discrepancy representing a wicked problem can be explained in numerous ways. The choice of explanation determines the nature of the problem's resolution—Wicked problems have no given alternative solutions.
- The planner has no right to be wrong.

As identified above, in the year following Rittel's and Webber's treatise, Russell Ackoff developed a very similar interpretation of a wicked problem, within a framework encompassing an explanation of two other categories of problem (as opposed to just tame problems).

As per the initial three problem categories Ackoff's first version of a problem he calls a "puzzle". A puzzle is a well-defined and well-structured problem with a specific solution that can be worked out.

The next level Ackoff called a "problem" per se. This is an issue that does have a defined form or structure; it can have certain dimensions however and will contain a number of variables about which some information is available in addition as to how they may interact. Nonetheless there may not be a single easily identifiable solution. Indeed, there may be a variety of alternative solutions subject to different types of input such as what resources might be available, access to certain technologies, or what the political landscape might look like after an election. As we may not know these things yet, we have to leave the problem's solution open to different hypotheses about how the future might turn out (Ritchey, 2002).

Table 3.1 Comparing wicked and tame problems

Wicked problems vs tame problems	
Wicked problems	Tame problems
• There are many apparent causes of the problem that are inextricably tangled (in effect there is a high level of complexity).	• Has a well-defined and stable problem statement
• To describe a wicked problem in sufficient detail, requires one to develop an exhaustive inventory of all possible solutions ahead of time. The formulation of a wicked problem is the problem!	• Has a definite stopping point, i.e. when the solution is reached
• It is impossible to be sure when you have the correct or best solution.	• Has a solution which can be objectively evaluated as right or wrong
• Solutions to wicked problems are not right or wrong but better or worse.	• Belongs to a class of similar problems which are all solved in a similar way
• Any solution, after being implemented, will generate waves of consequences over an extended period of time.	• Has solutions which can be easily tried and abandoned
• There are multiple stakeholders with conflicting values and priorities.	• Comes with a limited set of alternative solutions.

Ackoff's equivalent of a "wicked" problem he defined as a "mess". A mess is a complex issue, which does not yet have a well-defined form or structure. When you have a mess, you do not even know with any certainty, what the problem is yet.

There is a tendency to treat problem structuring and problem resolution in isolation, as puzzles. The relationship between messes, problems, and puzzles is summed up succinctly by Michael Pidd (1996), stating:

> One of the greatest mistakes that can be made when dealing with a mess is to carve off part of the mess, treat it as a problem and then solve it as a puzzle—ignoring its links with other aspects of the mess.

Finally, Table 3.1 above illustrates the comparison between Wicked and Tame problems.

An empirical and visual approach to problem solving is presented by Conklin (2006) who compares traditional, linear (or "top down") approaches to problem solving with non-linear and dynamic situations. Conklin states that in the linear approach one begins by understanding the problem which can include gathering and analysing users' requirements. Once the problem has been specified and the requirements analysed, the designer or analyst is ready to formulate a solution, leading to implementation of that solution. He illustrates this pattern of problem solving as the "waterfall" approach (Fig. 3.1).

Yet this is an oversimplification of any problem-solving and design activity. Conklin states that even late into a creative process analysts and designers may have to return to problem definition and re-evaluate their understanding of said problem:

> Our experience in observing individuals and groups working on design and planning problems is that, indeed, their understanding of the problem continues to evolve—forever!

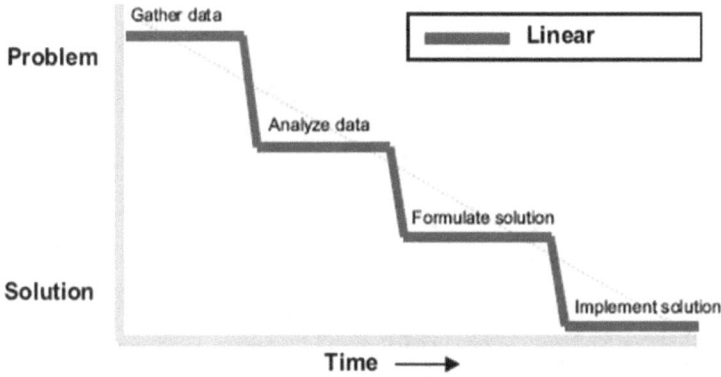

Fig. 3.1 Traditional wisdom for solving complex problems "the waterfall". (Conklin, 2006, p. 5)

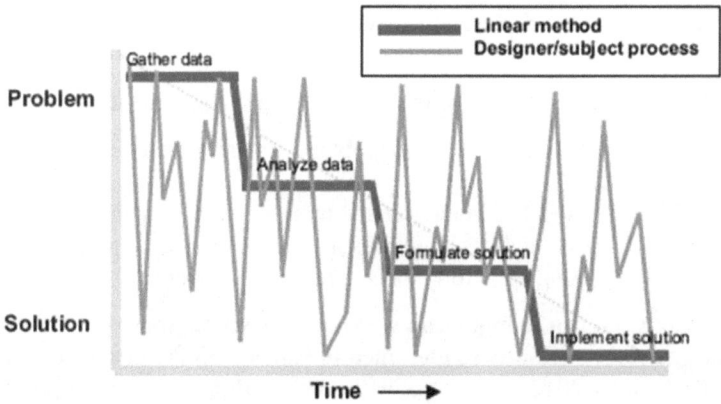

Fig. 3.2 Evolution of the problem

> Even well into the implementation of the design or plan, the understanding of the problem, the 'real issue,' is changing and growing.

Figure 3.2 this shows the observation that problem understanding continues to evolve until the very end of the experiment or project. Linearity provides little help in the way of guideline the practitioner through an iterative process

Finally, Conklin illustrates how even the highly irregular cognitive paths identified in Fig. 3.2, can be rendered more chaotic by the inclusion of an additional designer or, indeed any new stakeholder or stakeholders (as in Fig. 3.3)—as it can reflect, "a deeper order in the cognitive process" and where:

> The non-linear pattern of activity that expert designers go through gives us fresh insight into what is happening when we are working on a complex and novel problem. It reveals that the feeling that we are 'wandering all over' is not a mark of stupidity or lack of training. This non-linear process is not a defect, but rather the mark of an intelligent and creative learning process Conklin (2006) p. 1.

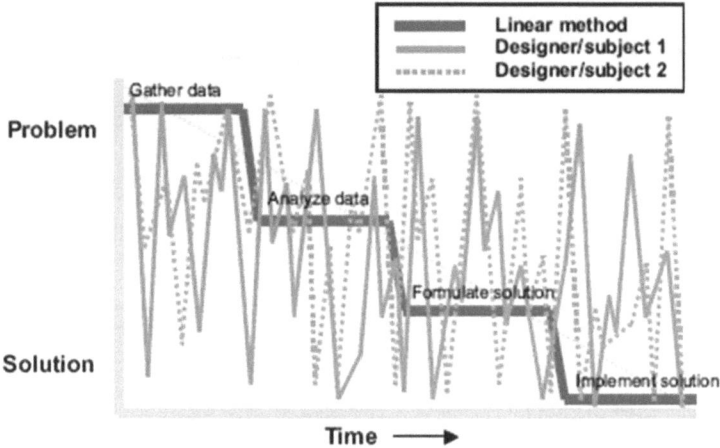

Fig. 3.3 A wicked project with a second designer working on the problem. (Conklin, 2006, p. 12)

Conklin (2006) summarises the problem to be faced as consisting of:

- Strong fragmenting forces of wicked problems, social complexity, combined with technical complexity.
- The confusion, chaos, and blame created by failing to distinguish these forces.
- The lack of tools and techniques for "defragmenting" project dynamics (or alternatively using the wrong tools to address the problem).

BUT Just when you thought that we knew everything there is to know about problems, another variant was identified to "spice" up the discussion. In 2007, Levin et al. (and 2012) came up with the addition of the "super wicked problem"!

Levin's original reference point was global climate change and they defined "super wicked problems" as having the following additional characteristics:

1. Time is running out.
2. No central authority.
3. *Those seeking to solve the problem are also causing it.*
4. Policies discount the future irrationally.

I particularly like number 3 on the list—it is always us humans that mess things up!

I am sure that readers are able to come up with their own "super wicked problems" beyond that of just climate change—the situations in Afghanistan and Syria come to mind and the rest!

It is thus important to ask "Is your problem"

- A puzzle?
- A "causal" problem?
- "Wicked" or a "Mess"?

Or is it a problem with elements of "wickedness"?

3.2.3   Problems and the Uncertainty Profile

The table below allocates each of the problem types identified to the Uncertainty profile as presented earlier in Table 3.2 below.

3.3   Post Normal

Why have I included this as a topic? It is based on the link between **Wicked Problems and Systems Uncertainties.**

Post-normal science (PNS) represents a novel approach for the use of science on issues where *"facts are uncertain, values in dispute, stakes high and decisions urgent"*. Developed in the 1990s by Funtowicz and Ravetz (1994), drawing upon earlier dialogues between schools of thought developed by Popper (1959) and Kuhn (1962), which discussed the uses and abuses of the scientific method and its ability to address "uncertainties" and where the use of evidence is contested due to different norms and values.

Funtowicz and Ravetz focused on the quality of the scientific inputs to the policy process as being problematic with no-one willing to claim "truth" for his or her results, stating:

> Nor can uncertainty be banished, but good quality can be achieved by its proper management. The interaction of systems uncertainties and decision stakes can be used to provide guidance for the choice of appropriate problem solving strategies. When either of both are high, then mission-oriented applied science and client- serving professional consultancy are not adequate in themselves, and an issue-driven post-normal science is necessary. Just as in cases with ethical complexities (as in biomedical science) there must be an "extended peer community", including all stakeholders in the dialogue, for evaluating quality of scientific information in the policy process (Funtowicz & Ravetz, 1994, p. 1881). They go on to say that "systems uncertainties" can be interpreted as meaning a problem is less concerned with the;

Table 3.2 Matching problem type to the Uncertainty profile

	Identifiable/known	Unidentifiable/unknown
Predictable/ known	Q1. Known-known (I know what I know) Puzzle A problem	Q2. Known-unknown (I know what I do not know) A problem (with elements of wickedness)
Unpredictable/ unknown	Q3. Unknown-known (I do not know what I know or I think I know but turns out I do not) Wicked problem (and often a super wicked problem)	Q4. Unknown-unknown (I do not know what I do not know) Super wicked problem (but probably a Q3 issue)

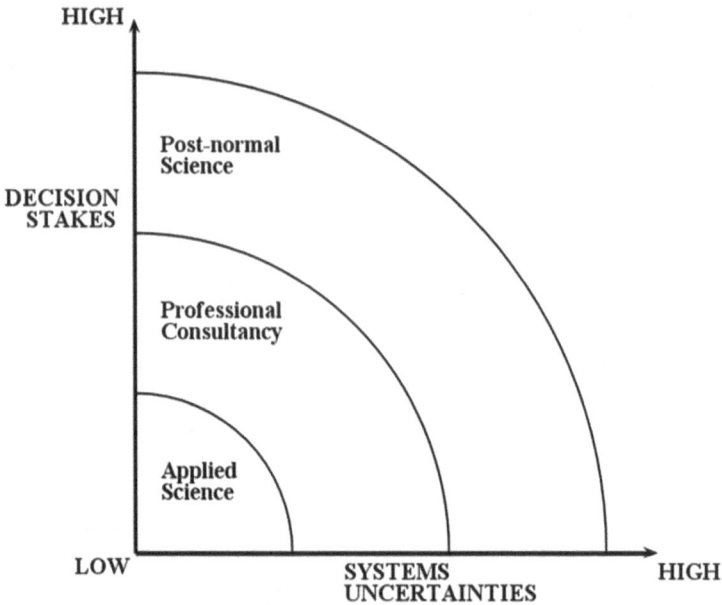

Fig. 3.4 Decision Stakes vs Systems Uncertainties (after Funtowicz and Ravetz)

"discovery of a particular fact (as in traditional research), but with the comprehension or management of a reality that has irreducible complexities or uncertainties" (Funtowicz & Ravetz, 1994, p. 1882).

On the other hand, their term "decision stakes" refers to:

all the various cost, benefits, and value commitments that are involved in the issue through the various stakeholders (Funtowicz & Ravetz, 1994, p. 1882).

The real commonality of the Funtowicz/Ravetz and the Rittel/Webber/Ackoff strands, is their plea against an over reliance on causal, usually quantitative, methods and their identification of the intangible and stakeholder-driven nature of numerous problems. It is important to drive home this difference between causal and non-causal approaches to problem identification. This standpoint acts as a warning against the over use of quantitative methods where dealing with the future and its inherent uncertainties—and to re-iterate Funtowicz and Ravetz's original proposition that *"facts are uncertain, values in dispute, stakes high and decisions urgent"*. Graphically the Funtowicz and Ravetz argument can be represented as in Fig. 3.4.

3.4   Methods, Tools, and Techniques (MMTs)

3.4.1   Problem Structuring Methods (PSMs)

PSMs have been developed to structure issues, problems, and decisions, rather than solving them. Prior to their development, it was seen that traditional Operational Research (OR) methods tended to restrict themselves to well-structured problems yielding finite answers which could be accurately monitored. In addition, traditional OR addressed systems which were complicated, often had a large number of parts. However, as identified via the Complexity and Interconnectivity section in Chap. 3, whilst such problems can be deemed to be complicated this does not imply that such systems have high complexity—the latter being a function of multiple information sources or inputs which are linked and interdependent and are often uncertain or intangible. In other words, there were a whole category of problems where traditional OR methods could not justify such a causal approach (Garvey, 2016; Garvey & Childs, 2013).

PSMs have a vital role in "mitigating" and formulating, rather than "solving" problems. They are especially suited in developing scenarios where behavioural factors impact perceived physical/causal considerations, particularly at the early stages of analysis, by reducing the number of "blind alleys" the analyst or decision maker may be induced to follow. Ormerod (2001) notes that the value of "soft OR", an alternative term used to accommodate PSMs, need not be judged solely on whether outcomes to the problem are successful or not, but that the processes carried out supported greater understanding, not necessarily resolution of higher complex problems. In response to a paper by Connell (2001), whereby a successful problem structuring exercise led to an apparently unsuccessful implementation, Ormerod argued that the use of PSM or soft OR processes allowed for greater understanding of highly complex problems particularly when key but varied stakeholders were engaged. The fact that implementation might be compromised due to a number of external factors (such as timing, budgets, engagement of teams not originally part of the initial programme) should not detract from the value provided initially by the PSM process—a process characterised by an acceptance of non-linearity as opposed to a linear approach to problem-solving—the latter methods often failing to understand the complexity generated by organisational and individual behaviours of participants within the problem space.

In the UK, Rosenhead and Mingers, leading exponents and academics, clustered a number of academic/practitioner generated methods under the title "Problem Structuring Methods (PSMs)". Their interpretation has tended to define the subject in fairly narrow terms based principally on British sourced methods such as:

- Soft Systems Methodology (SSM).
- Strategic Choice Approach (SCA).
- Strategic Options & Development Analysis (SODA).
- Robustness Analysis (RA).
- Drama Theory & Confrontation Analysis.

- Viable Systems Model (VSM).
- Systems Dynamics.
- Decision Analysis.

Other methods that could also be included but not addressed by Rosenhead and Mingers include "Rich Pictures", "Mind Mapping", and "Morphological Analysis", the latter two items being introduced in more detail in Chaps. 7 and 12.

Rosenhead and Mingers synthesise the function of PSMs as follows:

> (PSMs) provide a more radical response to the poor fit of the traditional OR approach for wicked problems. These conditions suggest that decision makers are more likely to use a method and find it helpful if it **accommodates multiple alternative perspectives, can facilitate negotiating a joint agenda, functions through interaction and iteration, and generates ownership of the problem formulation and its action implications through transparency of representation.** These social requirements in turn have various technical implications. Representing the problem complex graphically (rather than algebraically or in tables of numerical results) will aid participation. The existence of multiple perspectives invalidates the search for an optimum; the need is rather for systematic exploration of the solution space (author's bold font).

Rosenhead's substantive contribution is that he defines the nature of problematic situations for which PSMs aim to provide analytic assistance; in effect, he re-enforces those criteria identified by Rittel and Webber, Ackoff and Conklin, cited earlier, as being "wicked problems", and:

> in all cases, there is a meta-characteristic, that of complexity, arising out of the need to comprehend a tangle of issues without being able to start from a presumed consensual formulation.

Thus, in summary the situations referred to be Rosenhead are characterised as having:

- Multiple actors.
- Differing perspectives.
- Partially conflicting interests.
- Significant intangibles.
- Perplexing uncertainties.

In effect the same general characteristics as a "wicked problem".

As Rittel, Webber, and Conklin describe the converse "tame problems" so does Rosenhead compare PSM criteria with that of traditional Operational Research (OT) analysis:

- The client organisation is structured as a tight hierarchy.
- Few of its members are analytically sophisticated.
- The organisation or relevant unit performs a well-defined repetitive task generating reliable data.
- There is general consensus on priorities.

Rosenhead concludes that; *"in orthodox OR, the consultant is an analyst committed to extracting from perhaps recalcitrant data usable knowledge about the content of the problem confronting clients. When operating with PSMs, the consultant is a facilitator, attempting to manage the complexities and uncertainties of problem content while simultaneously managing the interpersonal processes and dynamic of the client group".*

The consultant role identified by Rosenhead is very similar to that expressed by Funtowicz and Ravetz (see Fig. 3.4 above), when describing the criteria of systems uncertainties. Ritchey (2006) also identified that many of Rosenhead's criteria apply to morphological analysis (MA) and thus should qualify as a PSM, albeit that the method is not specifically mentioned by Rosenhead. Ritchey reinforces the latter's argument about the role of facilitation along with there being additional criteria applicable to both established PSMs and MA, namely that such methods should be enhanced by being:

- Facilitated by a graphical (visual) representation for the systematic, group exploration of a solution space.
- Focusing on relationships between discrete alternatives rather than continuous variables.
- Concentrating on possibility rather than probability.

It is to be noted that Rosenhead also suggested that a wider acceptance and exploitation of PSMs is important if the potential of soft OR is to be realised in practice and that the unique characteristics of problem structuring in complex organisational settings require a holistic approach based not only on theory, but also practical and easy to use in the field. This view was corroborated by the author's own empirical action programme, where iterative methods helped to improve performance effectiveness and eradicated operational barriers to user understanding and uptake.

The criteria for describing the nature of a problem and its position in the decision-making process are extensive and can be used to qualify methods beyond those 8 methods presented by Rosenhead and Mingers. Such criteria are highly relevant to a much broader spectrum of problems than that originally postulated as being a PSM and can be expanded to embrace additional conditions such as volatility, interconnectivity, ambiguity, and complexity.

3.4.2   Robustness Analysis

One of the methods developed by Rosenhead is a hidden gem of a decision support method but has received insufficient attention and is called Robustness Analysis (RA)—not to be confused with Robust Decision-Making (RDM) as practiced by exponents at the Society of Decision Making under Deep Uncertainty (MDU) which is of more recent provenance (Marchau et al., 2019).

Traditional (linear) forms of operational research aim to eliminate uncertainty about the future through the identification of a single, preferred future and then plot a course towards this. Robustness analysis, on the other hand, embraces future uncertainty. Decisions made now are **robust** if they leave your options open. The method allows for the evaluation of initial decisions under conditions of uncertainty, but where subsequent decisions are likely to be introduced and implemented at some time in the future. The robustness amounts to the degree of flexibility which that initial decision or commitment allows for in future decision choice. This relationship is expressed as a ratio of the total number of acceptable options at a particular pint in the future or even multi-futures. In essence robustness provides options as to the relative flexibility of alternatives—leaving your options open.

Marsh (2011) offers an example of the use of robustness analysis within the domain of a military research programme such that:

> Decisions are made now about the research programme for the next few years. A decision might be to research further into robotic vision, or build a demonstrator of a robot able to move itself across rough ground. Products are planned, ultimate results of the research, e.g. new equipment or improvements in current equipment. Given the uncertainty of research, and of later procurement decisions, these products might or might not get implemented. Scenarios represent circumstances when the products will be of use. A single scenario is only one part of a 'possible future', since more than of them may 'occur' in the timeframe of interest.

Marsh states that the value of a product in a scenario can be expressed in terms of how well the products help the military achieve their objectives. Being a judgemental technique, Robustness Analysis is best suited to identifying "fuzzy" or coarse scale outcomes such as high, medium low, or not applicable.

3.4.3 Rosenhead's Summary

Rosenhead's own description of the method (apart from the more detailed descriptions and process in Chap. 8 of the 2001 book "Rational Analysis for a Problematic World Revisited) was best summarised in a EWG-MCDA Newsletter dated Autumn 2002. An edited version is presented in Appendix 1.

3.5 Summary

This chapter has introduced to the reader that problems come in various shapes and sizes. Once the problem characteristic has been identified (is it a puzzle or a wicked problem?), then the problem can be positioned within the Uncertainty matrix so the correct PSM can be applied. The chapter ends by introducing Rosenhead's Robustness Analysis method as an appropriate MTT for addressing the early stages of problem identification.

References

Ackoff, R. (1961). *Progress in operations research*. Wiley.

Ackoff, R. L. (1974). *Redesigning the future*. Wiley-Interscience.

Beer, S. (1984). The viable system model: Its provenance, development, methodology and pathology. *Journal of the Operational Research Society, 35*, 7–26.

Conklin, J. (2006). *Dialogue mapping: Building shared understanding of wicked problems*. Wiley.

Connell, N. (2001). Evaluating soft OR: Some reflections on an apparently "unsuccessful" implementation using Soft Systems Methodology (SSM).

Funtowicz, S. O., & Ravetz, J. R. (May 1994). Uncertainty, complexity and post-normal science. In *The annual review of environmental toxicology and chemistry*, Vol 13, No 12. Pergamon.

Garvey, B. (October 2016). *Combining qualitative and qualitative aspects of problem structuring in computational morphological analysis*. PhD thesis. Dyson School of Design Engineering, Imperial College London.

Garvey, B., & Childs, P. R. N. (2013). Applying problem structuring methods to the design process for safety helmets. *Proceedings of the 1st International Conference on Helmet Performance and Design, London*, February 15, 2013.

Grint, K. (1997). *Fuzzy management: Contemporary ideas and practices at work*. Oxford University Press.

Kuhn, T. (1962). *The structure of scientific revolutions*. University of Chicago Press.

Kunz, W., & Rittel, H. (1970). Issues as elements of information systems. Working Paper No. 131, Heidelberg-Berkeley.

Levin, K., Cashore, B., Auld, G., & Bernstein, S. (2012). Introduced the distinction between "wicked problems" and "super wicked problems" in a 2007 conference paper, followed by a 2012 journal article in *Policy Sciences*. Problems.

Marchau, A., Walker, W., Bloeman, & Popper, S. (Eds.). (2019). *Decision making under deep uncertainty, Chapters 2, 7*. Springer.

Marsh, D. (2011). *A robust approach to military research programme planning*. Smith System Engineering Ltd.

Nelson, R. R. (1974). Intellectualizing about the Moon-Ghetto Metaphor. *Policy Sciences, 5*, 375–414. Elsevier Scientific Publishing, Amsterdam.

Ormerod, R. (2001). Viewpoint: The success and failure of methodologies – A comment on Connell (2001): Evaluating soft OR. *The Journal of Operational Research Society*, Palgrave, October 2001.

Pidd, M. (1996). *Tools for thinking* (p. 40). Wiley.

Popper, K. (1959). *The logic of scientific discovery*. Springer and Hutchinson.

Ritchey, T. (2002). *Modelling complex socio-technical systems using morphological analysis*. Adapted from address to the Swedish Parliamentary IT Commission, Stockholm, December 2002.

Ritchey, T. (2006). Problem structuring using computer-aided morphological analysis. Published by *Journal of the Operational Research Society, 57*.

Rittel, H., & Webber, M. (1973). Dilemmas in a general theory of planning. *Policy Sciences*, Vol. 4, pp 155–169. Elsevier Scientific Publishing Company: Amsterdam.

Rosenhead, J., & Mingers, J. (2001). *A new paradigm of analysis in rational analysis for a problematic world revisited* (2nd ed.). Wiley.

Simon, A. H. (1977). *The new science of management decision*. Prentice-Hall.

Treverton, G. (2010). Addressing complexities in homeland security. In L. K. Johnson (Ed.), *The Oxford handbook of national security intelligence*. Oxford University Press.

Chapter 4
Time-Based Criteria

Does anyone know where the love of God goes when the
waves turn minutes to hours?
Gordon Lightfoot—The Wreck of the Edmund Fitzgerald.
1975

Abstract When we think about uncertainty we tend to think about future uncertainty. In essence the degree of uncertainty makes it difficult to forecast or predict the future. This perception may be erroneous. Many forecasting and foresight processes use the past, especially the recent past, as a starting point, for their projections. That being said there is nothing to say that our assessment of the past is free from uncertainty, and more importantly bias, or that data from the past should be blindly accepted as being true. How should we treat time. Different criteria for addressing time are examined including time frames, time paths ranging from the linear to exponential, manifestations of underlying influences such as cycles and trends, and finally visibility, including weak signals and outliers.

Keywords Times frames · Time paths · Linear · Non-linear · Exponential · Cycles · Trends · Megatrends · Emerging issues · Weak signals · Outliers

4.1 Introduction

Part of the conundrum when dealing with time is that time is flexible and often seen in subjective terms. Thus, for a financial markets analyst, 6 months may be a long time whereas for an astrophysicist or an archaeologist 6 months is almost not worth bothering about as a period of interest or investigation. How should we treat time and, to mix metaphors, how long is a piece of string?

4.2   Time Frames

Indeed, the further away the time horizon in which we have to assess uncertainty consists of a spectrum made up of three flexible time frames, *past time, now, and future time*, further complicated by reference to the more commonly used subjective expressions short term, medium term, and long term. In turn each of these categories can be broken down into a myriad of sub-periods or time frames.

4.2.1   Past Time

Past time (or history) can be divided into a number of different time frames such as (for example):

- Very recent—usually less than 1 year and relating to events that took place yesterday, last week, last month, earlier months in the last 12-month year.
- Individual years over the previous 2–10 years
- Previous nine decades
- Previous ten centuries
- Previous millennia and beyond

And as identified above, time frames are highly subjective from the standpoint of the person trying to determine how long a time frame should be in relation to forming a projection.

4.2.2   Now

Now—is where we are at this instance but this "instance" can be stretched to possibly mean today, this week or month, or longer—again depending on the perspective of the subject—it still is all rather beautifully (or annoyingly) fuzzy.

4.2.3   Future Time

How long do you want your string to be? Again, very subjective but here are some common time frames.

- *Short term:* usually less than 1 year and relating to events that are forecast to happen tomorrow, next week, next month, next quarter, rest of year (remaining three quarters for a rolling forecast)? For the purposes of this chapter "short term" is defined as being within the usual annual planning cycle of 12 months with by far the greater emphasis on the forthcoming quarter. Such forecasts will often include a quarterly breakdown for the second year of the plan.

- *Long term:* This expression is a somewhat movable feast. Many organisations use the term to cover the 3- to 5-year period, others up to 10 years, a few to 20 or even 30 years out. Perceptions of what exactly is the long term are very often dictated by the nature of the business sector. The financial sector largely operates within a much shorter time horizon with anecdotal evidence claiming that 1–3 months is short term and anything beyond that is long term. On the other hand, in sectors such as the life sciences, extractive industries, and aerospace/defence, characterised by long product discovery and development times, short to medium term is seen as extending up to 5 years out with the long term defined as any period beyond this. "Confusing, isn't it?"
- Years 2 through to 5 (sometimes called medium term)[1]
- Years 6–10 (often referred to as long term)
- Next 20–50 years (also long term)
- Far future—50 to 200 years and beyond and for science-fiction writers can be millennia or even aeons into the future.

Other frameworks of classifying different time horizons exist of course. One example developed by a team at Imperial College London (ICL) produced a table of Disruptive Technologies (2018) broken down into four main futures categories namely:

- Horizon 1—happening now,
- Horizon 2—near future 10–20 years hence
- Horizon 3—distant future 20 years +
- Ghost Technologies—fringe science and technology, defined as improbable but not actually impossible and worth watching according to the ICL team.

Uncertainty is present to a lesser or greater extent across the whole of the time spectrum. Many people assume that there is little uncertainty relating to events which have already occurred. This may not be strictly so. The past or our knowledge of the past is no guarantor that everything is known and there are no hidden uncertainties.

By way of a summary in which to frame time periods, Table 4.1 below offers a possible schema for allocating different periods in relation to time-related terminology. Please note that such boundaries are not set in stone—which of course is part of the challenge when dealing with time in relation to uncertainty. It is then up to you, the individual reader, to define your own or your organisation's time frame boundaries.

The author would advise that the reader select their own time reference as long as you can justify your interpretation and provide a logical rationale for the time frames.

---

[1] In fact, medium term can be stretched to mean anything from 1 year to 5 years depending on your perspective.

Table 4.1 Time period alternatives

	Past	Future
Short term	Less than 1 year/less than 5 years	Next 12 months/next 3 years
Medium term	Last 2–10 years/last 25 years	Years 1–3/4–10 years
Long term	Last 50 years–last century	4–10 years/10–30 years
Very long term	Last millennia and beyond	10 years plus/30 years plus

4.3   Time Paths

The time frames identified in Table 4.1, however, do not give any indications as to how time "wends its way". It can follow various paths or patterns and it is these routes which we shall now explore.

In this section, I'll be summarising ways in which we look at time. The approach will be to assess a number of time concepts as they relate to planning as well as to uncertainty. I should warn readers in advance don't expect an in-depth treatise into TIME let alone into parallel universes. If that is what interests you then might I suggest you read books such as *A Brief History of Time* by Stephen Hawking or Carlo Ravelli's *The Order of Time*. And, if you are really into heavy duty physics— then take your pick from any number of learned books and papers by eminent physicists and astro-physicists of the last century. In Einstein's general theory of relativity, there's no conceptual distinction between the past and the future, let alone an objective line of "now". But we mere mortals have to deal with the everyday constraints of yesterday, today, and tomorrow—as if "uncertainty" about the future were not problematic enough!

4.3.1   Linear

This is the time path that most of us can relate to and live by—whereby we move from the past into the future in a straight line in a sequence that moves in one direction—the daily routine of life. A linear mind-set allows us to "hope" that the future, essentially the immediate or short-term future, will be a continuation of the recent past, and with a reasonable level of certainty. Unfortunately, future events can be knocked off a linear path by a host of external stimuli. With such a mind-set, taking 30 linear steps (1 m a step) one after the other (1.2.3.4, etc.) our brains have an easy time understanding that we would arrive 30 m away at the end of that sequence. Moreover, as human beings, we believe the past cannot be changed, let alone visit it, as we live according to linear future time.

4.3.2   Non-linear and Asymmetric

Non-linear is a deviation from linearity and in statistical terms is used to describe a situation where there no direct relationship between an independent variable and a dependent variable—and cannot be represented therefore as a straight line. In a non-linear relationship, changes in the output do not change in direct proportion to changes in any of the inputs. Thus, it can be argued that non-linearity can be represented by any number of lines, not just one. More importantly, these lines are interconnected with different pasts leading to alternative presents and futures. In reality non-linearity is a reflection of how most of mankind has to deal with the future, making life difficult to navigate—albeit exciting at times. Acknowledging non-linearity is an essential cognitive state that needs to be adopted if we are able to confront the future and embrace its uncertainties.

Asymmetry
Asymmetry means that something (physical objects, ideas, or concepts) is not identical and has two halves, sides, or parts that are not exactly the same. It should not be confused with non-linearity. Something which follows a non-linear path can be symmetric or asymmetric—or start in a state of symmetry and change into a state of asymmetry and even back again. An example of how the concept of asymmetry works has been in the term "asymmetric warfare".

> Asymmetric warfare can describe a conflict in which the resources of two belligerents differ in essence and, in the struggle, interact and attempt to exploit each other's characteristic weaknesses. Such struggles often involve strategies and tactics of unconventional warfare, the weaker combatants attempting to use strategy to offset deficiencies in quantity or quality of their forces and equipment. Wikipedia.

Asymmetric warfare such as guerrilla style engagement or using low-cost new technology such as drones is waged against traditionally structured and equipped opposition. Modern examples include the war fought in Vietnam by the Viet Cong against the USA in the 1960s and 1970s, by the Taliban and other guerrilla formations in Afghanistan against Soviet and then Western-based forces from the 1989s onwards and in post-Saddam Iraq. In business terms, we tend to use the more polite term "disruptive". Even more recently cyber warfare has added a new dimension as to our understanding of asymmetric warfare. Perhaps, asymmetry can be best expressed when the actions required to achieve an objective in one period of time (say a year) are out of kilter with actions developed in a different time period.

4.3.3   Exponential

In mathematical terminology "exponential" means an equation having one or more unknown variables in one or more exponents rising or expanding at a steady rate. For us more simpler souls, the term is most familiar when speaking about "Moore's law"

Fig. 4.1 Exponential
versus linear growth

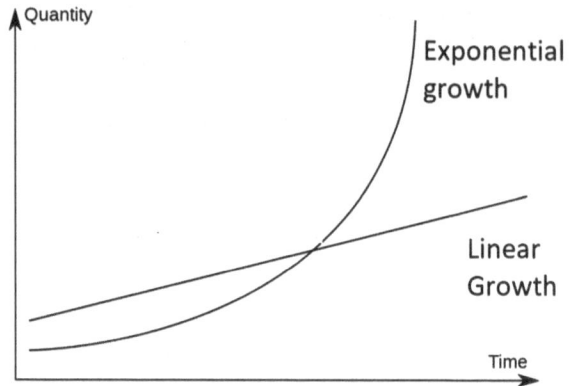

whereby the eponymous scientist in 1958 observed that the number of transistors per square inch on integrated circuits doubled every 2 years since they were invented and where he predicted that this trend would continue into the foreseeable future.

Another way of describing exponentiality is by taking our original 30 steps example referred to in the section on linearity. If we now double each of the 30 steps taken (1, 2, 4, 8, 16, and so on) in an exponential fashion, this would lengthen to 26 times around planet Earth! Another example supplied by the "Singularity University" is that *"when you fold a piece of paper roughly 0.005 cm thick (5/1000th of 1 centimetre), the paper will be just over 1 cm thick after the 8th folding. After only 42 folds, that piece of paper is thick enough to reach the moon! And after just one more fold, the 43rd doubling, it reaches all the way to the moon and back"*.

Humans are not equipped to process exponential growth, particularly as futurist Ray Kurzweil states that *exponentials* only become dramatic over long timescales, and the initial doublings can be almost imperceptible. Exponential growth is deceptive as the doubling of small numbers inevitably leads to numbers that outpace our brain's intuitive sense.

Our intuition is to use our assessment of how much change we've seen in the past to predict how much change we'll see in the future. Moreover, we tend to overestimate what can be achieved in the short term but majorly underestimate what we can do in the long term whilst assuming a constant rate of change. It is the gap between *linear* and *exponential* that is at the heart of why the future is so uncertain and the present is so unbelievably surprising—it is even more difficult to grasp when adding in non-linearity—is it random, part of a pattern or trend, or exponential (or exponentially random!)? (Fig. 4.1 above).

4.3.4   The Law of Accelerating Returns

Influenced largely by the impact of technology on mankind, Ray Kurzweil, in 1999, introduced what he called the Law of Accelerating Returns (1999) in which he addresses the accelerating rate at which technological progress occurs in the world and exponential effects of such progress. According to Kurzweil, the law states that:

- The rate of progress in any evolutionary learning environment (a system that learns via trial and error over time) increases exponentially.
- The more advanced a system that improves through iterative learning becomes, the faster it can progress.
- Advances breed faster advances and that what people anticipated to come in 50 years will be around in 5 years.

His proposition is that according to the law, machine intelligence is getting to a completely new level of advancement and that in a few decades to come artificial intelligence will overtake human intelligence. His predictions depend on existing developments, making them, in essence, reactive as opposed to exploratory scenarios (*see Chap. 7 for a detailed description of these two scenario lenses*).

4.3.5 How to Predict Exponential Growth

There are a number of examples that futurists such as Kurzweil and Diamandis at the Singularity University mention such as:

1. How in the early 1980s the consulting firm McKinsey was asked by US telecoms giant AT&T to forecast how many mobile phones would be in use by the year 2000. McKinsey forecast a global market of 900,000 units—yet by 1999 some 900 k people were signing up for mobiles every 3 days!
2. In the more up-to-date situation regarding battery technology for cars a US federal agency, the Energy Information Alliance, predicted in 2015 that the total number of electric vehicles with a range of 200 miles per charge would not exceed 1000—by the year 2040. A few months later, Tesla announced a car with a battery range of 215 miles per charge, and receiving over 300,000 pre-orders in a week!
3. Similarly, exponential growth from initial low estimates of development has been seen in relation to DNA sequencing by the Human Genome Project.

The future is notoriously difficult to predict. Failure to see, let alone extrapolate the exponential trends that will shape our world in the coming century, is likely to cause high levels of social anomie, social alienation, and "future shock"—the later concept originally coined by Alvin Toffler back in 1970.

The rate of change does appear to be increasing. Society (individuals, businesses and governments) will need to dramatically modify its predictive models to adapt to this changing reality when faced with the profound implications of disruptive technologies such as those illustrated in Imperial College's "Table of Disruptive Technologies" (2018) and in particular genetic modification, augmented and virtual reality, artificial intelligence, and other exponentially growing sectors that will manifest themselves in our lifetimes. I should also like to refer the reader to a recently published book by Azeem Azhar called *Exponential* (2021)—which addresses how accelerating technology is leaving us humans behind.

Note: The original Imperial TechForesight graphic is not suitable for transfer to either the book or e-version formats of this publication due to its original size and dense background colour. The author recommends that for those readers who wish to explore the table in greater detail that they access the Table and download the original image. This can be accessed via: https://imperialtechforesight.com/visions/table-of-disruptive-technologies-2/

An Odd Thought

So what might happen if something continues extrapolating. I looked at some elementary wave theory to introduce a "wacky" idea which you may wish to spend a few minutes to think about.

Scientists have concluded that waves break when their amplitude reaches a critical level which causes large amounts of wave energy to be transformed into turbulent kinetic energy, like a ball rolling down the hill. In other words, when waves reach shallow waters—usually near coastlines—they increase in height, and their crests meet the Law of Gravitation. The waves break.

Nevertheless, ocean floor topography will critically decide how wave energy will transform into whitewater. As waves reach the shore, the energy in front of the wave slows down due to friction with the shallow bottom.

Meanwhile, the energy behind the wave moves at full speed and is channelled upwards, climbing the back of the bulging wave. The wave breaks, and it usually does so in water depth that is 1.3 times the wave height.

Imagine that a technology life cycle accelerates exponentially so much that before it is able to transform into a typical S-curve that the rate of exponential growth is so fast that it collapses under its own weight—with dramatic effect as in a breaking wave. Or what if it turns back on itself once it reaches its peak such that it not only collapses but goes back on itself? Marczyk (2009) states that collapse is Nature's most efficient mechanism of simplification. Does this indicate that exponentiality has its limits or that if it doesn't, we cannot imagine what it is, what it might look like or be in a different dimension—or maybe a real "unknown-unknown"? *BUT* No doubt a mathematician and/or physicist has the "theoretical" answer!

We can now represent the various elements of the time path categories in the following schema (Table 4.2):

As an exercise for the reader you may wish to populate each of the cells with possible events which match each of the six cells from your or your team's perspective—quite an introductory ice-breaker thinking game.

Table 4.2 Time path alternatives		Linear	Non-linear	Exponential
	Symmetric			
	Asymmetric			

At the end of this chapter, we shall merge (or integrate) this matrix with the time period matrix introduced earlier, before combining it with a further matrix illustrating the relationships between manifestations and visibility.

4.4   Time Path Overlays (Manifestations of Underlying Influences)

Hidden within the various time periods and time paths are other time-related phenomena, which I call "manifestations" and which play out across both time frames and time paths, these being:

- Cycles
- Trends
- Megatrends

4.4.1   Cycles (and Waves)

A cycle can be defined as an interval of time within which a set of actions is completed or a process that returns to its beginning and repeats itself in the same sequence. In relation to time a cycle can also be interpreted as a wave, albeit that the peaks and troughs of the wave may be asymmetric. For example, long economic cycles as hypothesised by Kondratiev (2002) have been called supercycles and such phenomena are similar to technology life cycles.

Kondratiev's long wave theory is contentious within broader economic circles, including that it may involve recognising patterns that may not exist. The Kondratiev wave—also known as supercycles, K-waves, surges, and long waves—refers to cycles, lasting about 40–60 years, experienced by capitalist economies and indicated by periods of evolution and self-correction, brought about by technological innovation that results in a long period of prosperity.

4.4.2   Trends

Trends on the other hand can be defined as an inclination in a particular direction and in analytic terms can be interpreted as a line drawn on a graph that approximates the trend of a number of disparate points.

It is more accurate to argue that a trend describes *history, or rather a* historical change over time. Changes in a trend are particularly identifiable where certain variables have been identified as being important, so that data relating to the variable having been collected are seen to alter direction of the trend—such as how households have changed their purchasing habits over the Covid pandemic lock-down: from physical purchase of goods from physical retail stores to online pur-chases. The trouble is that there is a tendency to imply that when talking about a trend we are imputing something about the future—this is not accurate as such an activity turns a trend into a forecast (see Chap. 6 for more discussions on forecast-ing). In the case of post-pandemic purchasing habits, to what extent will buyer behaviour revert to pre-pandemic patterns—or will there be a hybrid behaviour? A similar question may be asked of real and virtual office work patterns.

Nevertheless, futures studies experts do refer to trends as key precursors to exploring the future. Kuosa and Stucki (2020) state that *"A trend has a recognisable development path that is supported by multiple credible sources. It is a flow of transformations that is not redirected easily. In general, trends can be verified by collecting enough data to form statistics that prove their existence."*

Kuosa and Stucki also point out that: *"Trends usually are identified either by using time-series analyses or by experts who are well aware of the latest changes within their fields . . . . Trends and their behaviour become more challenging to predict over a more extended period."*

A large number of trends are "in process" at any one time—easily identifiable examples include the Internet of Things, and rising populism in Europe and other formerly politically democratic countries.

The Future Today Institute (2020) goes on to state that strategic trends share a set of four laws called the Four Laws of Tech Trends (2020).

1. *Trends are driven by basic human needs*
2. *Trends are timely, but they persist*
3. *Trends are the convergence of weak signals over time*
4. *Trends evolve as they emerge*

One method cited by Kuosa and Stucki to explore trends is Trend Impact Analysis (TIA), first introduced by Theodore Gordon in the early 1970s, when forecasting used mainly quantitative methods based on historical data and via trend extrapolation but tended to ignore the impacts of future unexpected events. The focus is on identifying the sub-trends of a larger trend and analyses the impact of each of these separately or combined with the primary trend. The TIA method, although using quantitative methods, tries to improve the basic forecast by using expert opinion approaches such as the Delphi method about probable events in the future—an early-stage hybrid approach. TIA has been used not just for forecasting but contingency planning and strategic planning. It has also been used for scenario writing but as identified in Chap. 8, due to its inflections off past trends, is largely deployed in *reactive* scenario mode.

Kuosa and Stucki point out that trend extrapolation, at its heart, is pure forecast-ing—directly extrapolating the development shown in a past or present time series into the future answering the question of "What if this development continues to the future without any changes?" Yet this approach assumes that whilst a trend can be extrapolated all other things are to be treated equal *"meaning that only one trend and its impacts are at the focus, and all other impacting factors and trends are left out of the calculation"*. In essence TIA ignores "future noises" and relies more on probabilities rather than the in-depth exploration of, yes, "uncertainty".

Yet trend analysis does have its uses, as long as the analyst is aware of its limitations, so it can help the analyst understand what other interactions (or collisions) the trend may have with other trends.

The Future Today Institute (FTI) in its 2020 Tech Trends Report states that a trend should not be confused with trendy. *"Trends driven by demographics, the economy, technology, politics and social movements and are formed over a number of years and are not necessarily linear. Trendy on the other hand are much more transient or ephemeral (fads), briefly capturing out attention before burning out"*.

Trends are constantly changing and mutating—some increase in prominence—others decline—somewhat similar to a football league table. With reference to the Future Today Institute, cited above, its 2020 Tech Trends Report was published in January 2020—and contained no reference to the impact of a pandemic—as it was in the future and not visible as a trend (or was hidden or disguised enough to be not identified as being a trend). Yes, trends have their uses but other uncertainties need to be assessed when looking to even the near future.

For those readers wanting to review what other experts in the domain of trend identification have come up with, there are numerous professional sources—however at a personal level may I point out those trends dynamically represented by organisations[2] such as:

- The Futures Platform: https://www.futuresplatform.com/ (Finland)
- Shaping Tomorrow: https://www.shapingtomorrow.com (UK)
- The Future Institute: https://thefuturesinstitute.org (USA)
- The Future Today Institute: https://futuretodayinstitute.com/foresight-tools-2/ (USA)
- SITRA: https://www.sitra.fi/en/ (Finland)

Many countries carry out foresight activities. A report published by the European Union Institute for Strategic Studies (2014) called "Foresight in Government—Practices and trends around the world" carries a review of countries which carry out foresight activities including Australia, Brazil, Canada, China, Finland, France, Germany, India, Indonesia, Italy, Japan, Mexico, the Netherlands, Norway, Russia, Singapore, South Africa, South Korea, Sweden, Switzerland, the UK (UK), and the USA. https://espas.secure.europarl.europa.eu/orbis/document/foresight-govern ment-practices-and-trends-around-world

---

[2]There are numerous other sites where the reader can access trend data including:

- The Future Today Institute: https://futuretodayinstitute.com/foresight-tools-2/
- European Data Protection Agency: https://edps.europa.eu/press-publications/press-news/blog/foresight-essential-element-analyse-tech-trends_en
- European Commission Knowledge for Policy.: https://knowledge4policy.ec.europa.eu/foresight/megatrends-implications-assessment-tool_en

There are of course many other organisations providing trend evaluations from *The Economist* to the *Financial Times* as well as all the main global consulting companies such as McKinsey, PwC, Kearney, Gartner, etc. along with a plethora of output from national and international NGOs.

4.4.3 Megatrends

Now then, what is the difference between a trend and a megatrend? Megatrends are seen as major, global, long-term change developments that impact the broader environment in which we live—economic, social, cultural, etc. Often, they are combinations of multiple trends and issues with heightened levels of interconnectivity and can help shape, once identified, strategic directions for organisations of all types as well as social movements.

Megatrends can be the foundation for foresight analysis. They contain opportunities and risks—invariably both—and when the latter happens the analyst and decision-maker has to be aware of unintended consequences—as such megatrends may be precursors of, or have hidden in their complexity—"wicked problem" outcomes.

Megatrends usually reflect observable phenomena over longer periods of time than just simple trends (years and decades). This allows the analyst greater confidence when projecting or extrapolating the path of the trend. The danger, however, is that the stronger the duration of a trend the greater the temptation to ignore signals which may alter the trend line—and therefore the analyst must be aware of weak signals that could bring about unexpected and dramatic change to the trend (see the next section).

Reader Aware Notice *Trends and Megatrends. Many organisations profess to be the experts at identifying trends and megatrends. One has to challenge them as whilst they may be good at identifying current trends, how good are they at identifying how that trend might pan out or mutate and at what rate? How many of the trend specialists identified the Covid-19 pandemic—or Putin's invasion of Ukraine?—very few!*

4.5 Visibility (and Its Relationship with Time)

One of the main issues with data, whether in quantitative or qualitative form, is how visible such data are—even if some data are visible, have they been properly interpreted and/or do they hide information which can have an impact on the future? Let's look at some aspects of data in both their visible and less visible manifestations. Visibility as discussed in Chap. 2 is a key component of the uncertainty profile matrix (Fig. 2.2).

4.5.1   Current

Current—it's what data we have today—that is, we have access to some data that does exist and from which we can assign degrees of confidence as to the veracity and/or accuracy (see next chapter on the Evidence base), and from which the analyst can develop rationales and assumptions—subject to . . . . The fact that current data is visible does not guarantee such data is accurate or true—but does provide some form of (if only a temporary) anchor to develop further hypotheses until more data can be obtained. Propaganda sourced information is eminently visible but rarely true.

4.5.2   Emerging Issues

Emerging Issues—Although regularly used by analysts and decision-makers when attempting to address the future, a *"trend is just one of the key "building blocks" that analysts use when forecasting alternative futures"* (Lum, 2016). Lum qualifies this statement by saying the phrase, "trends and emerging issues" are often used as meaning the same thing albeit they are distinct components in the foresight process. He points out that the analyst needs to be aware of emerging issues as a trend-based forecast:

- May not have all the relevant variables.
- May not reflect correctly all the relationships between the variables used in the forecast.
- The historical relationships of the selected variables may have changed without the analyst being aware of it—hidden or lost in the noise.
- The subject of the forecast may inherently produce unpredictable outcomes with low visibility due to the early stage of emergence.

With a trend, it is presumed that various data points related to key previously defined variables can be tracked and used for extrapolation purposes. With emerging issues a different mind-set has to be deployed as the analyst is looking at *new* things that *may* become important in the future. In essence a more exploratory viewpoint is required as opposed to a more a reactive, backward looking one (see Chap. 9). Emerging issues reflect technology, concepts, and policy which are not yet mature or properly formulated but could emerge into the mainstream under certain conditions, whether they be known today or unknown.

Some emerging issues may be considered so weak that they are overlooked, ignored, or discarded. This leads us into a discussion about "weak signals" themselves.

4.5.3 Weak Signals

What are weak signals, and when and where do they exist? Again, it is important not to confuse them with a trend (as per emerging issues above). It is argued that with weak signals being seen as phenomena which may play out in the future, it is important to distinguish between prediction methods relating to forecasting and foresight—the former relying on historical and current data which can be predicted with high degrees of confidence or probability, the latter much less so—this will be discussed further in Chap. 7.

If not strictly by definition, one can say that "weak signals" reside within the domain of the uncertain. Decision- and policy-makers are continually seeking alternative, if not new, approaches to make better, more informed decisions and to mitigate risks of making bad decisions under various states of uncertainty (and complexity) (Camillus, 2008; PWC, 2012).

One of the earliest references to weak signals was by Igor Ansoff (1975) (of *Corporate Strategy* fame) in 1975. He used the term within the context of a *Strategic Early Warning System (SEWS)*, developed to help organisations deal with discontinuities and strategic surprises. A SEWS assumes that discontinuities do not emerge without warning. As an early warning system, it identifies behavioural factors such as "blind spots" which in turn hinder identification of weak signals.

Yritys (2014) states that *"Weak signals are first symptoms or early signals of a change telling about a strengthening trend and bringing information that is not yet seen . . .and can reveal threats and opportunities for an organisation. They could also be defined wild cards that change the development and are unpredictable when turning up. Weak signals are events below the surface, overlooked, but that may be signs of big evolution."*

Looking for weak signals can be seen as one of the foundations for strategic foresight; however, be aware that non-rationality of humans make accurate prediction difficult if not impossible. The challenge of course is how can such signals be identified amid all the noise generated by high levels of interconnectivity and complexity in a rapidly changing environment.

The *uncertainty profile matrix*, introduced in Chap. 2, can be used as a guide in positioning where weak signals are most likely to occur within the risk spectrum and why the barriers to detection are as much behavioural as methodological.

Digging Deeper to Find Weak Signals
Maybe the best place to start is to ask what they are not. Pedbury (2019) claims that weak signals have to be isolated from the notion of "trends" (discussed in the previous section) since:

> **Trends** describe the expected future, the high probability, high impact developments we need to address. Focusing exclusively on the trends risks being blindsided by surprises. Trends are based on data. All data is in the past. It may be unreliable if the underlying system is changing in fundamental ways.

Pedbury re-enforces his position by stating that surprises come from places people are not looking and that *"Scanning identifies **weak signals** with unknown probability but potentially significant impact that are often ignored."* His argument is that many organisations are focused too much on predicting the expected future, those high probability, high impact developments that could disrupt their operations. Conversely those issues seen to have low or unknown probability and potentially high impact are often discounted or ignored with weak signals being lost in the general noise of issues to be addressed (Harrysson et al., 2014). Voigt et al. (2011) highlight the dilemma of analysts when challenged to identify where and how to weak signals reside:

> Generally speaking, incorporating weak signals in strategic discussions is a known dilemma because on one side the vast variety of potential signals requires us to select which signals to process and which to ignore and on the other side the very concept of 'weak signals' disqualifies the selection rules we would usually apply, such as selecting signals that stand out or signals that have been helpful in the past.

In addition, cultures exist within organisations that militate against addressing new challenges to current policy, acting as barriers to foresight. In effect analysts lack (or have not identified) those tools and methods which might allow them to narrow down weak signals in terms of not just inevitable surprises, but the differing shades of uncertainty and in particular genuine uncertainty (confirming the standpoint of Camillus and PwC noted earlier).

Although weak signals often have no history, and thus no basis on which to build a pattern, one has to consider that there may be "Sleepers"—overlooked, forgotten, dormant potential indicators waiting for some "techno-analyst prince charming" to awaken it. Such signals will tend to be qualitative in nature as there is little hard data to enable signal strengthening. This problem is compounded by the non-linearity of issues development, with some changing slowly, much like the "slowly boiling frog" analogy, whilst others change fast and very radically.

In addition, whilst information exists in the environment, individually of little consequence or impact, but when clustered together with other weak phenomena can reveal interesting information or signal strengthening options—what can be termed "symbiotic clustering". Both symbiosis and serendipity have useful roles in resurrecting and transforming "interesting" but neglected signals and new clusters, e.g. biomimicry.

Note Not every point in the cluster has to be weak but a combination of the unknown, semi-known, and even known. And, as Yritys rightly points out, weak signals are a continuous or non-stop process and that consequently weak signal search should not be seen as a discrete activity.

Sources of Weak Signals and Where Do They Abide?
Current methods and tools used to identify weak signals include think-tank groups, brainstorming, Delphi method, or a pattern management framework, which means collecting signs of weak signals from published documents including magazines,

academic papers—and of course social media along with data analytic "trawlers". Note that the danger exists of spurious correlation!

Hiltunen (2008) differentiated between texts, online resources, and human sources. However, much of the former are static in that they cannot elaborate on the signals they contain, whereas human sources engaged in face-to-face debates, virtual chats, or email exchanges can provide further contextual information if needed (e.g. reasons, assumptions, examples). Hiltunen's study did reveal that the most frequently used sources of weak signals are researchers, future studies experts, and colleagues. For a more expansive view of methods in the broader futures domain, Poli (2018) discusses how future-related methods should be classified. Perhaps, more important is how much influence such practitioners have over policy- and final decision-makers?

There has been a recent tendency to think of weak signals as mainly manifesting themselves in the new technology/product area—partly due to the seemingly exponential rate of technological change and the urgency attached to identifying future development opportunities. However, weak signals should not be seen as just "eureka" moments which can only be identified by the analyst or indeed brainstorming-sourced inspiration processes—and mistakenly being classified as "unknown/unknowns" (aka black swan events). Weak signals are also present within the domain of socio-economic and political—identification of which is key to developing ongoing strategic awareness via scenarios so that policy (commercial and political) can be continually challenged and re-assessed.

There is one final category of phenomena which can influence the future and is often overlooked—outliers and wild cards and which we shall briefly introduce.

4.5.4   Outliers/Wilds Cards

If you thought weak signals were difficult to spot, how about these two little fellas?

An outlier is basically data which does not "fit in" with the other data being analysed. It doesn't really matter if it is part of a group as long as it is a valid data point, i.e. possible. The conundrum for analysts is that it may be just a discrete random piece of noise. One shouldn't become obsessive about looking for outliers, which may or may not be real, but recognition that they may exist should be enough to put into place processes which allow "fringe" ideas to be considered—the "unthinkables" of this world. It is also possible that outliers may morph into weak signals or into emerging issues. Just be aware that there is some "weird stuff" out there—so do not develop a mind-set which is antipathetic to considering such eventualities.

Both the "manifestation" and "visibility" criteria can be combined into a matrix framework (Table 4.3), populated with examples of each paired cell. Readers can populate the empty cells according to their specific problem issue.

Table 4.3 Time frames manifested and visibility

Visibility	Manifestation		
	Cycles	Trends	Megatrends
Current			
Emerging issue			
Weak signal			
Outlier/wild card			

4.6   Integrating Time-Based Criteria (MTTs)

In this chapter, we have introduced four basic criteria for classifying time and discussed how they play a role across the uncertainty/risk spectrum, being: times frames, time paths, manifestation, and visibility. From these four criteria three frameworks were developed: times frames, time path, and combined manifestation/visibility matrices. These three frameworks were individually presented in matrix format. At the conclusion of this chapter the task is to integrate, or merge, the three matrices into a combined framework which analysts can use as a template when looking at time-based variables for individual futures projects.

These frameworks when combined into an integrated table yields some 960^3 different configurations for time-related criteria as shown in Table 4.4. What this section has identified is that when time-based criteria are included as part of the exercise to better understand uncertainty, the analyst has to consider a large number of different parameters. The tables presented in this chapter will help the analyst to:

(a) Comprehend better the importance and characteristics of time-based criteria when addressing uncertainty
(b) Isolate particular relationships within each of the three time-based matrices presented
(c) Understand the combinatory influence of these time-based criteria
(d) Prevent oversimplification of time-based influences when dealing with uncertainty; this helps improve the quality of the analytical process.

User Exercise
It is now time, for you the reader, to populate these templates according to those boundaries of the problem that is facing you or your organisation. In Table 4.5, please feel free to amend any of the time period in each of the cells—such that your interpretation of "short term" could be the previous 3 months or "long term" defined as being up to 10 years.

---

[3] The reader may wish to carry out a pair-wise analysis exercise, identifying inconsistence pairs thus reducing the total number of viable configurations to be evaluated. For example, it can be argued that a short-term time period within the last 5 years is likely to be inconsistent with a long-term future time frame over, say, the next 25 years—the gap between something that happened 3 years ago is unlikely (but not impossible) to be linked to something which will manifest itself in 25 years' time.

Table 4.4 Integrated time criteria

Time frame past	Time frame future	Time paths	Manifestation/ visibility
S-T < 1 year/5 years	S-T next 12 months/ next 3 years	Linear symmetric	Cycle—current
M-T 2–10 years/last 25 years	M-T years 1–3/4–10 years	Linear asymmetric	Cycle—emerging issue
L-T last 50 years/last century	L-T 4–10 years/10–30 years	Non-linear symmetric	Cycle—weak signal
Very L-T—last millenium & beyond	Very L-T up to next 500 years	Non-linear asymmetric	Cycle—outlier/wild card
		Exponential symmetric	Trend—current
			Trend—emerging issue
			Trend—weak signal
			Trend—outlier/wild card
			Megatrend—current
			Megatrend—emerging issue
			Megatrend—weak signal
			Megatrend—outlier/ wild card

Table 4.5 Time frame alternatives

	Past	Future
Short term	Less than 1 year/less than 5 years	Next 12 months/next 3 years
Medium term	Last 2–10 years/last 25 years	Years 1–3/4–10 years
Long term	Last 50 years–last century	4–10 years/10–30 years
Very long term	Last millennium and beyond	Up to +250 years

Top-Down/Bottom-Up Approaches

Another level of analysis can be achieved by changing the order within which each of the matrices is introduced. Thus, for example you may deem that a more exploratory approach needs to be carried out by allocating different scenario options to the "time frame" table as a first phase followed by refining the possible event (s) the manifestation/visibility. Alternatively one could begin with the manifestation/ visibility criteria and then work backwards to allocating the event to a particular time frame. I would recommend that both routes are explored as such an exercise can identify gaps within the analysis—the examination of which can yield interesting sets of differing rationales (Tables 4.6 and 4.7).

Table 4.6 Time paths

	Linear	Non-linear	Exponential
Symmetric			
Asymmetric			

Table 4.7 Manifestation and visibility

	Manifestation		
Visibility	Cycles	Trends	Megatrends
Current			
Emerging issue			
Weak signal			
Outlier/wild Card			

When you have populated each of the three matrices you can then combine them into the "integrated time criteria" template (Table 4.4)—you may be surprised at some of the outcomes of such an exercise.

References

Alexander, M. A. (2002). *The Kondratiev cycle*. Writers Club Press.

Ansoff, H. I. (1975, Winter). Managing strategic surprise by response to weak signals. *California Management Review, XVIII*, 2.

Azhar, A. (2021). *Exponential*. Random House.

Camillus, J. (2008). Strategy as a wicked problem. *Harvard Business Review*.

European Union Institute for Strategic Studies. (2014). *Foresight in Government – Practices and trends around the world*. https://espas.secure.europarl.europa.eu/orbis/document/foresight-government-practices-and-trends-around-world

Future Today Institute. (2020, January). *2020 Tech trends report* (13th ed.). The Future Today Institute.

Harrysson, M., Metayer, E., & Sarrazin, H. (2014, February). *The strength of 'weak signals'*. McKinsey Quarterly.

Hiltunen. (2008, May). Good sources of weak signals: A global study of where futurists look for weak signals, Journal of Futures Studies, *12*(4), 21–44.

Imperial College TechForesight. (2018). *Table of disruptive technologies*. Imperial College. https://imperialtechforesight.com/visions/table-of-disruptive-technologies-2/

Kuosa, T., & Stucki, M. (2020, December). Trends – They are everywhere. *The Futures Platform*.

Kurzweil, R. (1999). *The age of spiritual machines – How we will live, work and think in the new age of intelligent machines*. Texere.

Lum, R. (2016, March). *4 steps to the future: A quick and clean guide to creating foresight*. Vision Foresight Strategy.

Marczyk, J. (2009). *A New Theory of Risk and Rating*. Editrice UNI Service.

Pedbury, P. (2019). *An overview of the horizons foresight method using system based-scenarios and the "inner game" of foresight*. Chief Futurist, Policy Horizons, Government of Canada.

Poli, R. (2018). A note on the classification of future-related methods. *European Journal of Futures Research, 6*, 15.

PWC. (2012, January). *Black swans turn grey – The transformation of risk*.

Toffler, A. (1970). *Future shock*. The Bodley Head.

Voigt, C., Unnterfrauner, E., & Kieslinger, B. (2011). Identifying weak signals in expert discussions of technology enhanced learning. In P. Cunningham & M. Cunningham (Eds.), *eChallenges e-2011 conference proceedings*. IIMC International Information Management Corporation. ISBN: 978-1-905824-27-4.

Yritys, A.-M. (2014, October 18). Identifying weak signals before they become strong trends. *Change Management, Futurology, Global Economics*.

Chapter 5
The Evidence Base

*If everybody always lies to you, the consequence is not that
you believe the lies, but rather that nobody believes anything
any longer . . . . And a people that nobody can believe
anything cannot make up its mind. It is deprived not only of its
capacity to act but also its capacity to think and to judge. And
with such people you can then do what you please.*
Hannah Arendt

Abstract The chapter explores how decision-makers and analysts need to validate
and be aware of the veracity of the data that they are confronted with, both
qualitative and quantitative. History examines the impact of past events. Yet,
proximity to an event having occurred in relation to a contemporary standpoint is
no guarantee that an objective interpretation can be made. It can be argued that the
more recent the event, the less likely researchers will have access to all the "facts".
The issue of data evaluation is illustrated via a template indicating how we understand and action data. The concept of "dark data" in its various forms is discussed as
a precursor to a section on the veracity of information and how delinquent forms
such as misinformation, disinformation, and malinformation increasingly attack the
ability to form objective judgements. Finally, another template is presented
highlighting the different forms of bad actors to be aware of.

Keywords Evidence status · Dark data · Veracity · Fake news · Misinformation ·
Disinformation · Malinformation · Social media bubbles

5.1 Introduction: Beware of the Past—What History Do You Believe in or Want to Believe in?

Time-related data, past present and future, are the building material with which
analysts develop both qualitative and quantitative judgements. Such data needs to be
validated if such judgements are be both efficacious and objective—which is not
always the case.

The concept of historical recency can be misused, misunderstood, and exploited by stakeholders. It can be argued that the more recent the event, the less likely researchers will have access to all the "facts"—as witnessed by the imposition of 30-year rules (and even longer restrictions for certain "sensitive" historical material). Indeed, it can be argued that the more recent the event, the less likely that researchers will have access to all the facts. The full effects of many events do not become apparent until much later (months, years, decades, and longer), impacted by lengthy gestation periods before unforeseen and unintended consequences manifest themselves. This of course allows for the proliferation of so-called revisionist versions of events—an interpretive process which can still be distorted by the subjectivity of the history researcher. The evidence base can also be "contaminated" by "the loss of history"—data that is deemed to be not worthy of recording, physically misplaced, re-written, deleted, or classified. This reduces not only the ability to improve the evidence base but the ability to develop reliable forecasting coefficients (Ceeney, 2010).

Then there is the seeding of "fake" data, not to mention "sensitive dependence on initial conditions"—the actual interpretation of what is also known as chaos theory (Lorenz, 1993). And, of course, the dictum that "history is written by the victor" is there to continually remind us to challenge accumulated myths ever present in historical observations—modern and ancient. Yes real "facts" are certainly hard to find and validate.

5.2 Evidence Status

5.2.1 The Availability of Data

Challenged by accuracy of interpretation of even recent events—how can we expect to extrapolate with any certainty or accuracy into the future, short or long term?

As will be introduced in Chap. 6, "Futures" exercises often begin with all the participants relating their memories of the recent past to generate alternative futures, as people have very different versions of history. Short-term "endemic myopia" occurs as many stakeholders are still able to influence not only the interpretation of recent past events but subjectively influence how their motives and actions are interpreted in relation to the "foreseeable" future. If historical distortion can occur in the short term then planning and the forecasts upon which it is based can be as error-prone as long-term forecasts. Again we refer to the so-called butterfly effect where small differences (sensitive dependencies) to initial conditions can make large differences to final outcomes.

When faced with future uncertainty and its inherent dearth of data, we tend to grab hold of any information available—which invariable is from the past. History is about the impact of events which have happened in the past—though it can prove equally difficult to determine what actually took place (including before and after a specific event)—as numerous interpretations of historical events assail us.

In addition, there is still a school of thought that believes there is no such thing as "modern history"—as the impacts of past events need a lengthy gestation period to reveal their full implications. The main premise here is that a whole range of unintended consequences of past actions and events need time to play out—witness Modern Africa which is still living with problems caused by "straight-line border demarcation" imposed by the former colonial rulers.

On the other hand, distant history (which can be thought of as being between the time frame outside living memory to ancient history going back to several millennia BC or BCE) tends to have an increasing dearth of contemporaneous documentary material the further into the past we go and therefore deductive assumptions proliferate the further back the period studied goes. This filling in the gaps is again subject to a variety of inflections, including biased interpretation, by the historical researcher.

If we struggle to achieve accuracy in the interpretation of events that have already happened—how can we expect to extrapolate with any certainty or accuracy into the future. Whilst it is understandable that the "event" forecast error rate will grow exponentially the further we look into the future, this does not mean that we are more likely to make accurate forecasts in the short term (up to 5 years). This is for similar reasons that recent historical viewpoints and analyses have to be re-written in subsequent periods. Very often the historical time frame upon which these stakeholders make their forecast is too short, and thus does not embrace enough information as to the range of possible events which could impact their forecast. Through ignorance and/or hubris they believe that in the short term they themselves can influence events so that "they" as actors are seen to give a good performance.

5.2.2 Understanding and Actioning Data (How Can We React to Evidential Data?)

How we and, indeed, any organisation relate to data has become a hot topic in the age of fake news, data analytics, policy wonks, and of course the assumed ever present black swans.

To get a better handle on how to assess the validity and efficacy of data (and indeed information in general) in a world where we are all bombarded and overwhelmed by "stuff" it may be of some use to try and categorise not just data but how we action and respond to such data.

The good old 2 × 2 matrix allows us to explore and unearth underlying tensions between the presence of data and how we respond to such data whether actionable or not actionable. The two primary axes of this data matrix are how such data are acted upon or actioned, and how they are understood by data analysts and decision-makers. Each of the primary axes is then divided into two sub-categories:

Our understanding of data axis

Table 5.1 Data options matrix

	Data understood	Data not understood
Data actioned	Understood and actioned	Not understood/actioned
Data not actioned	Understood/not actioned	Not understood/not actioned

Table 5.2 Populating the data matrix

	Data understood	Data not understood
Data	Q1. Understood and actioned **Strategic confidence based on evidence** *The ideal but requires successful monitored implementation (not common)*	Q2. Not understood/actioned **Knee-jerk reaction** *Short-term solutions to complex issues with unintended consequences down the line*
Data not actioned	Q3. Understood/not actioned **Ideologically or policy constrained** *Hubris, tunnel vision, group think, deliberate obfuscation, and grey rhinos*	Q4. Not understood/not actioned **Lack of vision** *Oh dear, but all too common. Often a combination of quadrants 2 and 3 plus stupidity of course!*

- Data which is understood
- Data which is not understood (and/or misinterpreted)

  The action axis

- Data which is actioned upon
- Data which is not actioned upon

In its basic form the data and their interpretation and consequences can be represented in Table 5.1 thus:

Let us populate each of the four cells within the matrix—(bold type shows the prime interpretation—lower case italics supporting interpretations) (Table 5.2).

To be somewhat polemical, I suspect that many organisations and their decision-makers demonstrate a propensity to occupy quadrants 2 & 3! Occupying quadrant 1—where data (and of course the awareness of a lack of data) are best understood and, where available, acted upon—is the holy grail. The challenge for organisations of course is to select and use those foresight methods which mitigate the consequences of making inferior decisions where there is a paucity of data. The next chapter addresses this issue.

5.2.3   Beware of the Dark: Dark Data

David Hand, emeritus professor of mathematics at Imperial College London, recently published a revelatory book on dark data (Hand, 2020). Hand's argument is that with all the talk of "big data", we have been seduced into thinking that all the data we need is close at hand. He counters that the data we have are never complete, and what we do have is only the tip of the iceberg. He compares the observation that whilst much of the universe is composed of dark matter, "invisible to us but nonetheless present, the universe of information is full of dark data that we overlook at our peril".

One issue of overuse of the term "big data" is to assume that organisations can access most of the data that is out there—that we can reduce the search time and use what is now available on vast databases. This is erroneous when one considers that much data, especially in relation to advanced technology, is produced by large and small specialist companies who actively protect their proprietary data for commercial purposes—the pharmaceutical industry is a prime example where protection of such data is rigorously applied—creating vast volumes of dark data which rarely see the light of day. It could be hypothesised that like the universe, the amount of dark data is actually expanding. Gartner (2021) sees dark data as comprising most organisations' universe of information assets which are often retained for compliance purposes only.

Hand explores numerous ways in which we can be blind to missing data which can lead us to conclusions and actions that are mistaken, and dangerous. Examining a wealth of real-life examples, from the Challenger shuttle explosion to complex financial frauds, Hand gives us a practical taxonomy of the types of dark data that exist and the situations in which they can arise, so that we can learn to recognise and control them. In doing so, he teaches us not only to be alert to the problems presented by the things we don't know, but also shows how dark data can be used to our advantage, leading to greater understanding and better decisions.

He identifies 15 types of dark data (Hand, 2020), as follows:

- DD-Type 1: Data we know are missing (known-unknowns)
- DD-Type 2 Data we don't know are missing (unknown-unknowns)
- DD-Type 3: Choosing just some cases
- DD-Type 4: Self-selection
- DD-Type 5: Missing what matters
- DD-Type 6: Data which might have been
- DD-Type 7: Changes with time
- DD-Type 8: Definitions of data
- DD-Type 9: Summaries of data
- DD-Type 10: Measurement error and uncertainty
- DD-Type 11: Feedback and gaming
- DD-Type 12: Information asymmetry
- DD-Type 13: Intentionally darkened data
- DD-Type 14: Fabricated and synthetic data
- DD-Type 15: Extrapolating beyond your data

This is a pretty comprehensive list, making us aware of the data challenge and helping us to reduce the risk of making poor decisions especially when faced by more deliberate attempts to manipulate data in the form of disinformation. Such disinformation is now addressed.

Recognition of there being dark data opens a Pandora's box of such data being used for nefarious purposes and which decision-makers need to be aware of in the face of uncertainty—especially Hand's types DD-Type 13: intentionally darkened data and DD-Type 14: fabricated and synthetic data. This leads neatly into the next section about information veracity.

5.3 Veracity (or Lies, Damned Lies, and "Fake News")

5.3.1 Validated Evidence (Basically Truthful)

Validation is the process of establishing documentary evidence demonstrating that a procedure, process, or activity maintains the desired level of compliance at all stages. For example, in the pharmaceutical industry, it is very important that in addition to final testing and compliance of products, it is also assured that the process will consistently produce the expected results. The desired results are established in terms of specifications for the process outcome. Qualification of systems and equipment is therefore a part of the process of validation. Validation is a requirement of food, drug, and pharmaceutical regulating agencies such as the FDA (Food and Drug Administration) in the USA, the General Medical Council (GMC), and MHRA (Medicines and Healthcare products Regulatory Agency) in the UK.

Data validation is intended to provide certain well-defined guarantees for fitness and consistency of data in an application or automated system. Data validation rules can be defined and designed using various methodologies, and be deployed in various contexts.

Note that the guarantee of data validation does not necessarily include accuracy, and it is possible for data entry errors such as misspellings to be accepted as valid. Other clerical and/or computer controls may be applied to reduce inaccuracy within a system.

5.3.2 Misinformation, Disinformation, Malinformation (and of Course Fake News)

Back in January 2017 Amol Rajan, the BBC Media Editor, in an article entitled "Fake News: Too important to ignore" (Rajan, 2017) stated that:

> Fake news is nothing new but it has become a cancer in the body politic, growing from an isolated but malignant tumour into a raging, mortal threat. Fake news is an assault on truth. Therefore, it behoves all right-thinking journalists to combat fake news.

To broaden the constituency one could substitute people for journalists, or at least those of us concerned as to the veracity and validity of what we read, see, and hear.

Later in that same year (September) two researchers, Wardle and Derakhshan (2017), produced a report published by the Council of Europe called "Information Disorder".

Combining the Rajan and Wardle/Derakshan viewpoints, four types of false information can be identified. Both contributors identify three kinds of false information, two of which are common to both, namely:

Misinformation—information usually in the form of unintentional mistakes such as inaccurate captions or sloppy use of statistics. Although such information is false it is not created or disseminated to cause harm but stems from poor validation of source material.

Disinformation—which is false information deliberately made up with the intent to harm a person, social group, organisation, or even country as well as advancing a particular standpoint in favour of those with different positions. As Rajan states "this kind of fake news—deliberate lies—has been energised by the viral power of social media".

Each of the quoted commentators allows for the addition of a third type of false information, both valid and can be added to the two common kinds identified above.

Malinformation—which according to Wardle and Derakshan, is the deliberate publication of private information as well as deliberate manipulation of genuine content based on reality but intended to harm a specific target and their reputations (person, persons, ideas, and views). A typical example being how Trump sought to establish that Obama was not born in the USA—so negating his right to become President—the so-called birther row.

We'll return a little later in this chapter to explore the Wardle and Derakshan position further.

Finally, *Inconvenient truths*—Rajan claims this isn't really fake news at all—it's simply news that some people (often those in positions of power or status) don't like and wish to silence and de-legitimise by branding it "fake news". Such de-legitimising is often a trigger for individuals or groups supporting the target of such inconvenient truths to embark upon campaigns of disinformation—again by active use of social media.

Wardle and Derakshan also warn that the term "fake news" has been used by *"politicians around the world to describe news organisations whose coverage they find disagreeable. In this way, it's becoming a mechanism by which the powerful can clamp down upon, restrict, undermine and circumvent the free press"*. Both contributors therefore seem to agree that disinformation or real "fake news" is the most dangerous of these categories—as it seeks to silence scrutiny.

The term "information disorder" is an apt way to describe what has been going on, especially when exploiting technology, stating:

> While the historical impact of rumours and fabricated content have been well documented, we argue that contemporary social technology means that we are witnessing something new: information pollution at a global scale; a complex web of motivations for creating, disseminating and consuming these 'polluted' messages; a myriad of content types and techniques

for amplifying content; innumerable platforms hosting and reproducing this content; and breakneck speeds of communication between trusted peers. (Wardle & Derakshan, 2017).

Rajan's piece was also very much a call to action—and in the intervening period since then and now, is as relevant as ever—if not more so. Truth is highly vulnerable and for a number of reasons.

- Firstly, it is being majorly impacted by the power of social media to instantaneously disseminate information.
- Secondly, due to the explosion of information readers and contributors alike are encouraged to "headline skim" and/or generate headline grabbing sound bites.
- Thirdly, the above two factors combine to constrain tight enough validation of content. The need for news and other information outlets to excite their viewers by rolling news stories and the continual need to initiate "breaking news" militate against validating the accuracy of such content.
- Finally, and always lurking in the background are an array of cognitive biases (such as confirmation bias), misapplied heuristics, such as satisficing and group-think, as well as intuitive traps such as ignoring inconsistent evidence, confusing causality with correlation, and assuming a single solution. Part 3 explores these behavioural considerations in more detail.

Rajan makes the point that *"the truth is hard, expensive and boring. Whereas lies are easy, cheap and thrilling"*. Finding out the real story not only takes time and effort but verification also takes time and effort—all of which cost money!

5.3.3   What to Do?

Wardle and Derakshan identify that the purveyors of disinformation tap into our biases, conscious or otherwise, and our deep-seated fears. Truth therefore needs to be more resonant if it is not to be drowned out. They identify research that shows false information, if it is to be challenged effectively, requires our brains to replace such falsehoods with an alternative narrative.

As seen above social media and its supporting technologies have allowed dissemination of information to be cheap and rapidly presented. Bad actors of various guises have fully grasped how to exploit such methods to bring nefarious messaging to the fore. The trouble is that such bad actors are no longer waiting in the wings but taking centre stage. It is time to fight back.

A policy of *"Tous Azimuts"* needs to pro-actively evangelise "Truth-based Propaganda" (a wonderful oxymoron)—against the tsunami of false information from all sides of the political, economic, and social spectrum whilst being acutely aware of being "hacked" or "hijacked" by highly competent bad actors. The key challenge here is, "How do you bite-size truth"?—a wicked problem facing ethical journalists and thought leaders alike.

In their conclusions, Wardle and Darakshan identify a number of major stake-holders to be tasked with mounting a counter-insurgency against fake news and disinformation in particular. These include technology companies, national governments, media organisations, civil society, education ministries, and grant-making foundations. The dilemma here is that bad actors can hide amongst these groups—are the tech companies really onside, are media organisations themselves paragons of truth and free speech?

It would appear that much greater resources, neutrally funded, be made available to fact-checking organisations—since as has been identified earlier "fact-checking" costs money whereas lies are cheap. The cost of mounting a "counter-insurgency campaign" against the increasing hegemony of fake news will be a high one, requiring massive amounts of creativity and innovation—but failure to do so will surely lead to us becoming emasculated observers of an Orwellian "Ministry of Truth". Is this what we really want?

In Chap. 10, a variety of approaches to challenge entrenched mind-sets are reviewed to help mitigate the worst of human biases.

5.4 The Danger of Losing Control: A Fragmented Internet and Social Media Bubbles

With social media platforms tailoring information flows to individuals at increasingly personalised and granular levels, biases are continually being re-enforced so that competing, maybe more objective, positions are isolated and discarded. More pernicious still is the dangerous tendency when a user broadcasts an alternative viewpoint from that of other users within the filter bubble, to trash or "troll" that individual, sometimes in a most threatening manner. In this way, social media can not only accentuate an erroneous point of view but scare competing views—the evidence base thus becoming highly contaminated through intimidation and bullying.

Sandal (2021), a futurist based in Finland, states that *"Fragmentation of the internet is not limited to filter bubbles, either. Known as the splinternet or digital balkanisation, the internet is increasingly divided both geographically and politically."*

Sandal identifies other trends that impact the evidence base and manipulate reality such as

- Online misinformation—which has become the most active channel for disseminating this form of information.
- Political polarisation—targeted to re-enforce biases of individuals and like-minded groups.
- De-platforming—often for violent web communi
- s but can drive such groups underground or to niche media platforms (an increasing trend).

• Deepfakes and AI-enabled synthetic media—AI-generated videos, images, and speech of human beings are becoming more and more common (such as Pope Francis appearing to endorse Donald Trump for the US presidency).

Sandal also pointedly warns that:

> As it has been the case with social media, the fast evolution and adoption of these new technologies may mean that they will have wide-reaching social implications before regulations can catch up. Thus, an ongoing conversation around the potential future impacts of these emerging technologies and ethical frameworks for designing them will be needed to ensure that their use will not cause harm or disconnect people from the world of facts entirely.

The challenge for those individuals, groups, organisations, and even nations wishing to maintain and secure the veracity of their evidence bases will be to continually seek out and deploy technology-driven strategies that will counteract "bad actors"—a complex, daunting, and, probably, never-ending task. Failure to do so will jeopardise trust by those entities seeking to distribute validated evidence and allow these bad actors to disseminate information as alternate realities (now referred to as "alternative facts"), so that they become indistinguishable from reality.

This proliferation of data minefields increases the need for new initiatives that help consumers find, synthesise, and fact-check relevant knowledge amidst the digital noise growing exponentially. In addition to governmental regulations, this may translate into new business models such as fact-checking-as-a-service (itself open to infiltration and abuse). Another recent and nasty new trend in the netherworld of false information has been the emergence of what has become known as *black or dark PR*—essentially highly organised mercenary firms selling negative propaganda against a target to the highest bidder—the term "disinformation-for-hire" services being increasingly used to promote such businesses (although "malinformation" is probably a better expression). Tech-driven propaganda (usually negative) is now a reality. The now defunct Cambridge Analytica and the associated scandal comes to mind, whilst an Israeli black PR firm the Archimedes Group remains very active in this area. Other prominent players include "mainstream" PR firms such as Bell Pottinger, whilst nation-state actors in particular Russia, China, Iran, and Israel, but no doubt most developed economies, deploy such techniques on an industrial scale.

Uncertainty makes the future by its very nature, open to numerous points of view—the greater the uncertainty and the greater the quest for certainty as a "comforter" the greater the opportunity for promoting stories which cannot be quantified—anything is possible. Increasing uncertainty and the awareness of such uncertainty opens up a Pandora's box for bad actors to exploit—some ideas cannot be disproved easily as "facts are uncertain" or it takes time to accumulate counter-evidence and arguments. The near instantaneous distribution of information, from any source, using social media technology indicates a constant battle to hold the ground of validated data, information, and assumptions to support the evidence base, re-enforcing Rajan's earlier statement that "the truth is hard, expensive and boring. Whereas lies are easy, cheap and thrilling".

Table 5.3 Profiling information disorder

Information disorder					
Misinformation	Disinformation	Malinformation	Phases	Agent	Medium
False connection	False context	(Some) leaks	Creation	Governments	Newspapers (hard)
Misleading content	Imposter content	(Some) harassment	Production	Psy-ops	Newsheets (soft)
	Manipulated content	(Some) hate speech	Distribution	Political parties	Advertorials
	Fabricated content		Re-production	Entrepreneurs	Websites
				PR firms	Email
				Individuals	Social media text feeds
				Media	Videos (inc. YouTube)
				"Dark agent"	Word of mouth

Thus, if scenario supported foresight is not only to be meaningful but seen to be meaningful, then the task of validating data (both qualitative and quantitative in the form of rationales and assumptions) whilst negating false information has to be a core activity of practitioners engaged in mitigating the risks of uncertainty.

5.5   MTT Support Template: Spotting the Bad Actors

The schedule below amalgamates the various components which make up "information disorder". Such a template can be used as a checklist by readers when gathering data and can be a useful tool when formulating scenarios and their narratives. The various forms of "information disorder" can be summarised in Table 5.3 above:

Much of the impetus for information disorder is driven by a variety of behavioural factors and biases which are presented in more detail in Chap. 9.

References

Ceeney, N. (2010, February). The National Archives – *Challenges and opportunities going forward for information and knowledge management across government* at The Future of Evidence. Foresight Horizon Scanning Centre – Government Office for Science.
Gartner Glossary. (2021). *Dark Data.*
Hand, D. J. (2020). *Dark data – Why what you don't know matters.* Princeton University Press.
Lorenz, E. (1993). *The essence of chaos.* University of Washington.
Rajan, A. (2017, January). *Fake news: Too important to ignore.* BBC News item.
Sandal, G. (2021, February 16). *Future of truth in the information age?* The Futures Platform.
Wardle, C., & Derakshan, H. (2017, September). *Information disorder: Toward an interdisciplinary framework for research and policy making.* Council of Europe.

Chapter 6
Ways of Seeing the Future

The relation between what we see and what we know is never settled. Each evening we see the sun set. We know that the earth is turning away from it. Yet the knowledge, the explanation, never quite fits the sight.
John Berger: "Ways of Seeing"—1972

Abstract This chapter examines how the way we see things is affected by what we know or what we believe. Initially how we look at the past (history) before examining different types of futures is reviewed. The differences between forecasting and foresight principles are identified and how the use of the disciplines influences strategic planning. The "futures cone" is introduced as a tool to help identify the different forms and interpretations of the future along with a discussion of the role of science fiction when looking at outlier scenarios. Of the two terms, we shall see that "foresight" is a more meaningful concept when applied to uncertainty and this relationship is demonstrated when allied with the uncertainty profile template. The chapter ends with a more detailed description of one particular method, causal layered analysis (CLA) which is particularly suited in helping to contextualise the future.

Keywords History · Futures · Forecasting · Foresight · Strategic foresight · Market intelligence · Science fiction · Causal layered analysis

6.1 Introduction

The way we see things is affected by what we know or what we believe.

Four basic approaches when exploring how we look into the future are explored. Of course, looking into the future also means we have to look at the past so as to identify what factors in this past—our history—help in a better understanding of the future. The *first two* elements, "history" and "futures", operate at a broad generic level without reference to any specific methodological approach, whereas *the second set of elements* "forecasting" and "foresight" can be represented by a range of specific methodological approaches. Again, there is often some confusion between "forecasting" and the less used term "foresight". Of the two terms, we shall see that the latter term "foresight" is a more useful concept when combined with the issue of uncertainty. What we are trying to do in this chapter then is to take the reader from a broad understanding of how we see time and the future through to an introduction of the type of methodological approaches one can use to improve the quality of decision-making and which allows us to better develop insights into how we can frame the future for decision-making purposes. The chapter ends with a more detailed description of one particular method, causal layered analysis which is particularly suited to helping us contextualise the future.

6.2   History

Be under no illusion, forecasting and foresight analysis are difficult disciplines to grasp when seeking to differentiate them.

Risk and uncertainty are central to forecasting and prediction although in far too many instances practitioners confuse the two terms. But as has been highlighted in Chap. 2, it's not that difficult—"risk" you can quantify, "uncertainty" you cannot—but both can be modelled.

A number of strategists have come to accept that we can only analyse the past and that, even in the present, information is not immediately available. Analysis of the future is impossible as it is unknowable; we do not have access to "facts" which have not yet happened. Moreover, the future is never exactly like the past as there are always new and unforeseen events, which cannot be predicted beforehand and that further increase future uncertainty—and based on our current mind-sets.

The integration of historical data into how we determine the future should not mean we should blindly accept what has happened in the past as being totally factual either. Indeed, it has been an overriding area of concern that all too often too much credence has been given to the accuracy, if not veracity of past events and their derived "facts". Historians often seek recourse to only using the "facts". But what really is "a fact"?

There are countless incidences of facts being found out not to be so in later time periods and where the subject concerned is open to renewed scrutiny in the light of new evidence. Much of the information being evaluated cannot be defined as located at one discrete point but rather as a range of possibilities around that point—and with it less certainty. This is important to bear in mind when using historical time series data as a basis for prediction. Previous small-scale events which might not appear on any radar can manifest themselves within any time horizon as they may be a result of sensitive dependence on initial (i.e., the past) conditions. Acting upon the "wrong" short-term forecast can seriously damage your long-term decision-making health.

This short-term "myopia" occurs due to many of the stakeholders still being able to influence not only the *interpretation* of recent past events but of subjectively *influencing* how their motives and actions are recorded and interpreted in relation to events in the "foreseeable" future. And then there is access to hidden data. Very often the historical time frame upon which these stakeholders make their forecast is too short, and thus does not embrace enough information as to the range of possible events which could impact their forecast, or through ignorance and/or hubris they believe that in the short term they themselves can influence events. It is a frame of mind that is too commonly prevalent within quadrant 3 of the uncertainty profile matrix—the "unknown-known". The previous chapter on the evidence base covered much of the issues relating to our understanding of history.

6.3 Futures

"Futures" exercises generally begin with all the participants relating their memories of the recent past to generate alternative futures, albeit that people have very different versions (or experiences) of history. Short-term "endemic myopia" occurs as many stakeholders are still able to influence not only the interpretation of recent past events but subjectively influence how their motives and actions are interpreted in relation to the "foreseeable" future. If historical distortion can occur in the short term, then planning and the forecasts upon which it is based can be as error-prone as long-term forecasts and predictions and where small differences to initial steering conditions can make large differences to final outcomes.

The two states that govern how we might start to construct a forecast or a prediction, the past and the future, each require analysts and decision-makers to make different assumptions about what approaches, and how information sources, should be used, including checking thoroughly the evidence base. These various sets of information sources challenge the futures analyst and forecaster to ascertain how accurate the forecast or projection can be. This involves not just quantifying future projections but qualifying them as well. Forecasters and futures analysts must also ascertain the veracity of any historical data that may be used as a basis for the projection. As highlighted in the previous chapter on the evidence base, too often numerical data used as input, especially when sourced externally, is treated as "gospel". The limits of accuracy will also be challenged by acknowledging what can be quantified and what cannot—and by understanding the difference between risk and uncertainty.

A considerable body of work on futures has been published by Australia-based academic Joseph Voros, and much of the content in this section is based upon his research.

Voros (2001) proposes *three "laws" of futures.*

The future is not predetermined "*At the most fundamental level of nature, the physical processes of the universe are inherently indeterminate (the Heisenberg Uncertainty Principle). Therefore, there is no, and cannot be, any single predetermined future; rather there are considered to be infinitely many potential alternative futures.*" This is a prime consideration as better practice looks not at a single future scenario, but at alternative, often diverse, ones.

The future is not predictable   *"Even if the future were predetermined, we could never collect enough information about it to an arbitrary degree of accuracy to construct a complete model of how it would develop. At some point, the errors introduced by not having infinitely-precise information would cause the model to deviate from "reality "(whatever that is). And because the future is not predetermined, predictability is doubly impossible; we are therefore able, and forced, to make choices among the many potential alternative futures."* (Voros, 2001)

Future outcomes can be influenced by our choices in the present   *"Even though we can't determine which future of an infinite possible variety will eventuate, nevertheless we can influence, by the shape of the future, which does eventuate by the choices we make regarding our actions (or inaction) in the present (inaction is also a choice). These choices have consequences and so they need to be made as wisely as we know how."* (Voros, 2001)

Having introduced the concept of alternative futures, how might these alternative and potential futures be characterised.

6.3.1   Types of Potential Futures

Back in 1978 Canadian futurist Norman Henchey (1978) offered up an earlier classification of types of futures, namely:

1. Possible futures—representing what may happen, including events with a very low probability of occurrence, but which cause major changes.
2. Plausible futures—one that could happen as a natural consequence of what we know today.
3. Probable futures—represents what will likely happen and are usually futures derived from forecasts.
4. Preferred futures—what we want to happen often described as normative forecasting. These are imposed futures that did not exist until the start of the foresight exercise. started. Can be overly subjective due to bias preference.
5. Alternative futures—are futures that are probabilistically invisible and remain invisible after the foresight exercise. Close to being "unknown-unknowns" but not quite as there can be outlier signals which go unobserved.

We shall be expanding Henchey's initial classification later in the chapter when addressing the concept of foresight in more detail. But let us examine the roles of forecasting itself and the difference between forecasting and foresight.

6.3.2   The Prediction Challenge: Forecasting or Foresight, and Where Does Strategic Planning Fit in?

A number of issues arise when working with traditional short-term planning and forecasting processes, and include:

- The cumbersome nature of the annual planning cycle
- Processes not being sufficiently adaptive to the demands of rapidly changing environments
- Forcing the fit of fragmented and insufficient data into probabilistic distributions
- How fixed periodic planning cycles can inhibit adapting to short-term threats
- The lack of flexibility in traditional decision-making mechanisms when refinement is required
- Insufficient scenario planning integration
- The tendency for "knee-jerk" reactions without reference to the underlying causes of greater than expected variances, in turn exposing the organisation to the effects of unintended consequences

An alternative combination of methods and processes is proposed, so that plans can be developed, modified, and iterated faster, help speed up analytical feedback, allow for greater emphasis on both qualitative and quantitative frameworks, and examine recent time series data from both contextual and strategic standpoints—leading to more dynamic and plausible outcomes.

On the basis that "weak signals" will only manifest themselves, in terms of situational impact, at some time in the future (albeit that they may already exist, but unidentified, in the present), their very "fuzziness" challenges us to differentiate between the type of methodology to draw them out. Padbury (2019) points out that the discipline to identify weak signals resides within the foresight domain rather than that of forecasting, stating:

> Foresight is often confused with forecasting. **Forecasting does** try to predict the future. It takes data from the past and extrapolates it into the future using a variety of tools, from statistics to simulations. Forecasting helps users understand the present and the most likely future (often with upper and lower limits). However, at a time when the underlying systems are changing in fundamental ways, users of forecasting should take care to confirm that the supporting assumptions are still accurate.

Foresight's function is to prepare strategies and shape policies that are robust enough across a number of plausible futures, particularly where the underlying systems are evolving (often asymmetrically). Thus, when surprises occur they can be highly disruptive to the incumbent system. In effect, it can be said foresight is a form of "strategic options analysis".

Earlier, Ansoff (1975), in a similar vein, saw the difference between strategic planning and strategic issue analysis stating that strategic *planning* has been used *"to convert environmental information about strategic discontinuities into concrete action plans"* but had had little success in dealing with surprises. He identified that a major reason was that *"strategic planning is overly demanding for input information"*.

He identifies that when a potential surprise originates simple extrapolation will not suffice, leading to *"discontinuous departures from past growth trends or, at least, sharp changes in the curvature of past growth curves"*. This is part of the nature of uncertainty and that *"planners can have longer range forecasts from the forecasters, but they must be willing to put up with content that becomes increasingly vague as the time horizon is extended"*. This in turn would appear to confirm that under such circumstances qualitative assumptions are of more interest and relevance than quantitative ones. The lack of data is itself a challenge to the efficacy of developing quantitative assumptions when high levels of uncertainty and complexity prevail.

Central to his argument is that: *"there is an apparent paradox: if the firm waits until information is adequate for strategic planning, it will be increasingly surprised by crises; if it accepts vague information, the content will not be specific enough for thorough strategic planning"*. This sentiment is close to that of Voigt's highlighted in the section on weak signals earlier.

The premise here is that it is reasonable to expect that historical knowledge and data can help identify future threats and/or opportunities as they arise from familiar prior experience. However, when the threat or opportunity is discontinuous (or disruptive in modern parlance), then in the early stages, the nature, impact, and possible responses are unclear. Frequently it is not even clear whether the discontinuity (disruption) will develop into a threat or an opportunity and fits neatly into quadrant 3 of the uncertainty profile matrix.

6.3.3   What Is Strategic Foresight?

Strategic foresight (sometimes also used interchangeably with, for instance, "futures studies" or "futures research") is a discipline by which organisations gather and process information about their future operating environment (such as trends and developments shaping the organisation's political, economic, social, technological, legal, and environmental context). Strategic foresight is relatively new to businesses and public organisations. Consequently, the terminology that is used to describe the activity of making sense of the future opportunities and threats has not cemented itself quite yet.

The purpose of the foresight activity is to ensure informed decision-making that is based on carefully analysed views on the alternative future scenarios.

6.3.4   From Market Intelligence to Foresight

Better known and more established than foresight activity is its "sister discipline" market or competitive intelligence (MI or CI, respectively). To make the distinction clear between traditional market and competitive intelligence activities and foresight, we'll need to look at the time horizon and the analysis methods used. Strategic foresight looks into the future with a minimum time horizon of 2–3 years with the maximum range extending much further beyond that. Many developments that will greatly shape people's behaviour in 5 years' time can be anticipated, and alternative evolutionary paths of the demanded products and services can be mapped. This is also where specific foresight-related methodologies such as horizon scanning, backcasting, or the Delphi method come into play.

Finnish foresight specialists Kuosa and Stucki (2020) expand upon the concept of "futures intelligence". Whilst they state that such forms of intelligence will largely depend on the organisation's specific needs and context, they do identify a number of common themes, namely:

- *Early warning*: alerting the organisation about threats and opportunities
- *Informing and future-proofing decisions, plans, and strategies*: ensuring that no important future changes are overlooked when future success is at stake
- *Thought leadership*: communicating informed views about future yields benefits
- *Innovation*: understanding or creating future market needs
- *Risk analysis*: understanding potential and emerging risk related to the plans, strategies, and objectives

6.3.5   Benefits of Systematically Organised Foresight Activity

Foresight activity is seen to be critical for organisations for two main reasons:

1. *The current pace of change* in technologies, business models, the overall environment, and society at large is so rapid that organisations need to pull together and spend time on making sense of the developments and plan their operations accordingly.
2. There's no shortage of future-related information. However, so much of the information is unstructured and comes from a variety of sources that merely *bringing order and structure to the chaos can add value*. When analysis work is done with professional methods of a structured knowledge base, the odds of successful outcomes for the organisation are greatly improved.

However, foresight leaders still often find it challenging to clearly communicate the hard and soft benefits that the investment in an organisational foresight capability is expected to yield, especially at times when budgets are tight and where extrapolations based on traditional forecasting approaches tend to override the more holistic approach of foresight-based methods.

Typical outcomes of systematic foresight activities in an organisation include:

- Increased organisational awareness of future trends and phenomena that are relevant for the organisation's future success
- Holistic and contextualised mapping of key future developments ("foresight radar"): Making sense of the otherwise random themes in the context of one's own organisation and mapping the developments into a logically structured picture
- Early warnings: Continuous horizon scanning to alert the organisation about opportunities and threats that are relevant in the organisation's context
- Future-proof plans and decisions: Future-oriented deep dives into specific topics to ensure strategic plans and investment decisions are aligned with future changes
- Thought leadership: Having educated views of the future developments puts the organisation in a natural thought leader's position. This is useful in marketing but also in leading insightful discussions with customers and other interest groups

Never before has the pace of change been this rapid on so many fronts in parallel: in technology, business models, ecological environment, and entire societies. As will be expanded upon in Chaps. 9 and 10, the challenge of new threats, and indeed, opportunities, is aggravated by the behavioural reactions of organisations and the individuals and groups within organisations to these threats—it being a daunting prospect to accept that the old methods are no longer offering sufficient support to decision-makers. A joint Cass Business School/Airmic study (2011), "Roads to Ruin—A Study of Major Risk" Events, highlighted that the increasing interconnectivity of today's world weakens decision-makers' ability to identify weak signals or even develop the willingness to identify such signals and is all part of the behavioural barriers facing organisations.

6.3.6   So How Can the Differences Between Forecasting vs Foresight Be Summarised?

- Forecasting does try to predict the future. It takes data from the past and extrapolates it into the future using a variety of tools, from statistics to simulations. However, at a time when the underlying systems are changing in fundamental ways, users of forecasting should take care to confirm that the supporting assumptions are still accurate.
- Foresight's function is to prepare strategies and shape policies that are robust enough across a number of plausible futures, particularly where the underlying systems are evolving (often asymmetrically). Thus, when surprises occur they can be highly disruptive to the incumbent system. Here foresight carries out the function of "strategic options analysis".
- The premise here is that it is reasonable to expect that historical knowledge and data can help identify future threats and/or opportunities as they arise from

familiar prior experience. However, when the threat or opportunity is discontinuous (or disruptive in modern parlance), then in the early stages, the nature, impact, and possible responses are unclear. Frequently, it is not even clear whether the discontinuity (disruption)) will develop into a threat or an opportunity.

Foresight can be considered as being a part of strategic thinking, and helps to reveal an expanded range of perceptions of the strategic options that might be available.

A Note on Scenarios
In Chaps. 7 and 8, we shall be discussing the role of scenarios when addressing uncertainty in more detail. However, as a taster it will be useful to discuss in outline the role of scenarios in the overall foresight process. *Scenarios* are descriptions of alternative development paths. They are either plots in the form of narratives or quantitative forecasts in the form of curves. They are not predictions of the future but help to explore what could happen and how to prepare for various contingencies. Voros identifies scenarios as being key to foresight work but that creating scenarios should come *"at the end of a careful and detailed process of wide information gathering, careful analysis and critical interpretation . . . . . . and that scenarios are a valuable part of foresight work—they are just not the only part—and need to be seen within the context of an on-going, long-term, "closed-loop "organisational foresight process. With this understanding of their place in foresight work, they are a useful tool for generating shared forward views, helping to align strategic action across an organisation on its journey into the future."*

As will be presented shortly foresight concepts such as the "futures cone" act as useful devices in helping to visualise, generate, select, and position scenarios.

6.4 Foresight: Challenging Uncertainty So We Can Move from the "Unknown-Known" Quadrant (3) to the "Known-Unknown" Quadrant (2)

6.4.1 Alternative Outcomes and the Futures Cone: An Aid to Foresight

Moving on from Henchey's earlier work (see above reference), Voros (2001) identifies seven types of alternative futures or outcomes. He calls these "subjective judgements" about the future that are based on the present moment adding that every future is a potential future, "including those we cannot even imagine", the unknown-unknown. He identifies these categories as follows:

- *Potential*—everything beyond the present moment is a potential future. This comes from the assumption that the future is undetermined and "open" not inevitable or "fixed".

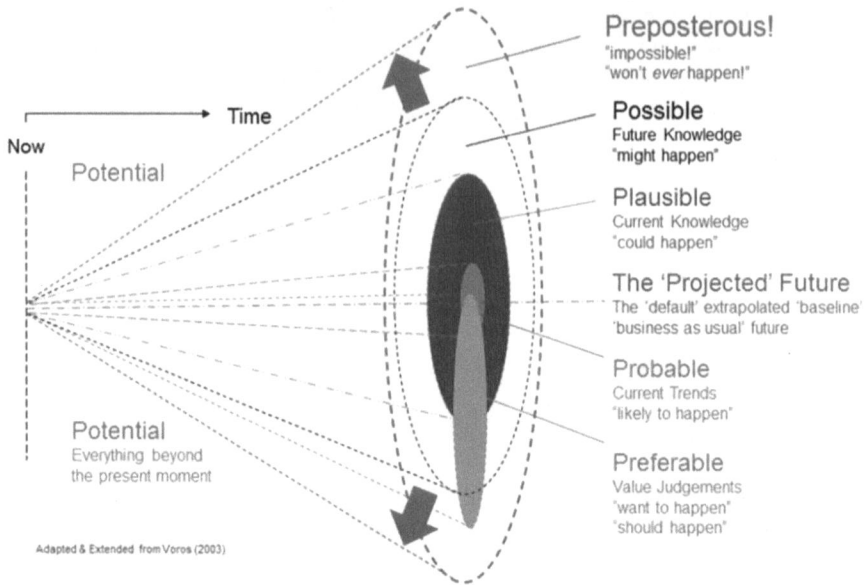

Fig. 6.1 Futures cone (after Voros, 2017)

- *Preposterous*—these are the futures we judge to be "ridiculous", "impossible", or that will "never" happen.
- *Possible*—these are those futures that we think "might" happen, based on some future knowledge we do not yet possess, but which we might possess someday (e.g. warp drive).
- *Plausible*—those we think "could" happen based on our current understanding of how the world works (physical laws, social processes, etc.).
- *Probable*—those we think are "likely to" happen, usually based on (in many cases, quantitative) current trends.
- *Preferable*—those we think "should" or "ought to" happen: normative value judgements as opposed to the mostly cognitive, above. There is also of course the associated converse class—the un-preferred futures—(e.g. global climate change scenarios come to mind).
- *Projected*—the (singular) default, business as usual, "baseline", extrapolated "continuation of the past through the present" future. This single future could also be considered as being "the most probable" of the probable futures.

He also mentions an eighth category *"predicted"*—as a specific singular future that someone claims "will" happen (or at least with a very high probability of occurring). Whilst Voros's list is comprehensive it does mix the more objective versus subjective descriptions—such that "preposterous" or preferable (as well as undesirable) should be seen as being more subjective. Voros illustrates the various future outcomes using the oft deployed "futures cone" (Voros, 2017), in the Fig. 6.1, above.

Voros (2017) also introduces *wildcards to the set*—by definition low probability/ high impact *events* (which he refers to as being similar to "mini-scenarios)". *"Since they are considered 'low probability' (i.e., outside the Probable zone), any member of any class of future outside the range of probable futures could be considered by definition a wildcard"*. He does qualify this statement by saying such usage is not common as the tendency is to seek out "high impact" events.

Marchau et al. (2019), editors of a publication about decision-making under deep uncertainty (see Chap. 3 for an earlier reference to this team's work and Chap. 13), state that complete certainty, also known as complete determinism, is—almost never attainable—but acts as a limiting characteristic at one end of the spectrum. The editorial team also identify various levels of uncertainty, namely:

Level 1 uncertainty—there is a clear enough future usually related to short-term decisions and where historical data (which of course may not always be accurate) can be used as predictors for the future. (Services are predictable, e.g. mail delivery.) One could call these low-level uncertainties).

Level 2 uncertainties probabilistically "where there are a few alternative futures that can be predicted well enough".

Level 3 uncertainties relate to situations with a few plausible futures but where probabilities cannot be assigned. Nonetheless "the future can be predicted well enough to identify policies in a few specific plausible future worlds"—classic scenario methods can be deployed here.

Level 4 uncertainty represents the deepest (most radical?) form of uncertainty. Here Marchau et al. make a distinction between those situations which contain many plausible future and situations which we acknowledge that we don't know (aka black swans).

Finally, we have *"total ignorance"* which is the other extreme from determinism. Marchau et al. include this state as it acts as a limiting characteristic at the opposite end of the uncertainty spectrum.

Marchau's schema below presents in graphic form the concerns confronting decision-makers confronted by high level (or as they say "deep") uncertainty and can be used alongside the futures cone to broaden one's understanding of how foresight terminology can be classified.

As a framework it offers a useful yet simple perspective about evolutionary levels of uncertainty, the variants of which can be introduced as to allow for different forms of outcome that scenarios can investigate: See Fig. 6.2 below.

6.4.2 The Role of Science Fiction

Tuomo Kuosa (2012), a Finnish strategic foresight and futures specialist, also deploys the futures cone model, using three main classes of futures—the probable, plausible, and the possible with the probable being shown to manifest itself within a shorter time frame and the possible within a longer one. However, he develops the

	Complete determinism	Level 1	Level 2	Level 3	Level 4 (deep uncertainty)		Total ignorance
					Level 4a	Level 4b	
Context (X)		A clear enough future	Alternate futures (with probabilities)	A few plausible futures	Many plausible futures	Unknown future	
System model (R)		A single (deterministic) system model	A single (stochastic) system model	A few alternative system models	Many alternative system models	Unknown system model; know we don't know	
System outcomes (O)		A point estimate for each outcome	A confidence interval for each outcome	A limited range of outcomes	A wide range of outcomes	Unknown outcomes; know we don't know	
Weights (W)		A single set of weights	Several sets of weights, with a probability attached to each set	A limited range weights	A wide range of weights	Unknown weights; know we don't know	

Fig. 6.2 Progressive transition of levels of uncertainty (Marchau et al., 2019)

basic cone by introducing two other identifiable components—wild cards (also known as outliers)—as per Voros, and *science fiction*. Wild cards when used in conjunction with the "not desirable" and "preferable" conditional categories generate two further scenario outcomes—highly unlikely dystopias and highly unlikely utopias, respectively. Kuosa presents four variants of science fiction:

- Possible "as we know the technology already exists"
- Possible in science fiction (e.g. warp drive)
- Possible in science fiction but not according to our current knowledge
- Possible at least in imagination and therefore theory

Science fiction allows for scenarios that reflect fringe possibilities or "out of the box narratives" and its introduction within the overall foresight discipline is presented in a separate box within this chapter shortly.

The introduction of science fiction (SF) in future scenarios is an interesting feature. Much of the average SF literature has concentrated on purely technological aspects of the future. The best SF will highlight a much broader spectrum of scenarios such as changes and their implications in the spheres of social, cultural, environmental, political, economic, ethical, or scientific advances as well as human–technology interactions.

One key advantage of including SF based narratives in scenario development is that it frees the writer from the strait-jacket of academic rigour when exploring new, often bizarre horizons. Where the future is subject to high levels of uncertainty and complexity, no one has hegemony over what will and what could happen.

It is important in scenario development to encourage thinking about the "unthinkable"—not just dystopian but utopian—although as identified above, much of SF reflects the concerns of the author in the age in which they are written. Some of the "prophecies" or visions come true—even if eventually—some not (or at least not yet). It is remiss of scenario developers to allow themselves to be constrained by the strait-jacket of conformity to linear projections.

A Note on Science Fiction

Ota and Maki-Teeri (2021) state that SF:

> ...provides out-of-the-box and visionary narratives that may become self-realising predictions and prove useful when generating new concepts, schemes, products, and services.

In addition, they observe that SF prototyping in the form of an imaginative narrative based explicitly on science fact allows foresight practitioners to explore a wide range of scenarios and can majorly influence technological innovation and scientific research. SF is also a useful vehicle to introduce weak signal, wild card, and outlier phenomenon into scenario narratives and where such narratives are wonderfully exploratory.

A number of high tech corporates have already introduced SF as part of their innovation strategy processes, such as Apple, Google and Microsoft.

A recent book by Ethan Siegel called *Star Trek Treknology—the Science of Star Trek from Tricorders to Warp Drive* (2017) takes an amusing look at the various advanced technologies in the Star Trek series and the likelihood of them being realised. This approach fits nicely into Kuosa's categories *possible in science fiction, or possible in science fiction but not according to our current knowledge*—"It's life Jim, but not as we know it."

Other literary examples of how SF may reflect the future, both utopian and dystopian, include George Orwell's *1984*, its precursor Yevgeny Zamyatin's 1921 *We*, Arthur Koestler's *Ghost in the Machine*, Huxley's *Brave New World*, and the visionary works of Arthur C Clark and Isaac Azimov and more recently Neal Stephenson's *Snow Crash*. Nor should we forget the impacts of social breakdown following unexpected events such as *Day of the Triffids* and *The Kraken Wakes* by John Wyndham, *The Road* by Cormac McCarthy, and more recently John Lanchester's *The Wall* and climate change issues addressed specifically in the novels of Kim Stanley Robinson—*New York 2140* and the more recent *The Ministry for the Future* and *The Every* by Dave Eggers.

Much of science fiction projects current social and environmental concerns. Climate change and its impact in the relatively near future provides the background of two books cited above by Kim Stanley Robinson. *New York 2140* (which has become a Venice like metropolis) addresses the issue of climate impacted by rising sea levels) whilst his 2020 publication *Ministry for the Future* explores mankind's reaction to global warming (set within a shorter time horizon of around 30 years) introducing the concept of a crypto-type currency called a "carbon coin" as a means of encouraging society to reduce its carbon usage. Importantly, he also addresses the cognitive barriers to bringing about change when the problem is seen as distant or is currently not affecting them—a major challenge for climate change policy-makers. In one section (p. 349), he highlights that following a heat wave in the southern USA (a major one had already happened in India killing thousands)

> —although in the months that followed, peoples biases emerged. It was the South where it happened. It was mostly poor people, in particular poor people of colour. It couldn't happen in the North. It couldn't happen to prosperous white people. . . . .

This was yet another manifestation of racism and contempt for the South, yes, but also of a universal cognitive disability, in that people had a very hard time imagining that catastrophe could happen to them, until it did. So, until the climate was actually killing them, people had a tendency to deny it could happen. To other, yes, to them, no. This was cognitive error that, like most cognitive errors, kept happening even when you knew of its existence and prevalence.

Science fiction, when applied to scenarios, has a close relative in "thinking about the unthinkable". Chapter 2 has already highlighted the potential "reality" of unthinkable events. As we have seen in the uncertainty profile matrix presented in Chap. 2 "unthinkables" should not automatically be confined to quadrant 4—unknown-unknowns. Unfortunately, a mind-set which equates unthinkable with "preposterous" risks at some time in the future (tomorrow or the next millennium or longer—to being unnecessarily surprised and having to fall back on protestations that such events are black swan events, when they are not)—can only lead to the likelihood of future dystopias!

6.5   Methods, Tools, and Techniques (MTTs)

The most accessible and frequently used template for assisting foresight work is the futures cone, shown in Fig. 6.1 above—and apart from Voros's version a number of variants are also used. However, for a more in-depth analysis there is one method that seems to encapsulate a fuller time horizon when exploring the future—causal layered analysis (or CLA)—as it attempts to "layer" both the past and the future, offering a more in-depth appreciation of the dynamics which make up the foresight discipline.

6.5.1   Causal Layered Analysis

Causal layered analysis (CLA) was developed by the Australia-based futurist Sohail Inayatullah in the 1980s as a way of integrating different futures perspectives and is less concerned with predicting a particular future and more with opening up the present and past to create alternative futures.

Inayatullah's own interpretation is thus:

CLA broadens our understanding of issues by creating deeper scenarios. We can explore deep myths and new litanies based on the points of view of different stakeholders and then see how they construct problems and solutions.

CLA is used for implementing new strategies to address issues. Does the new strategy ensure systemic changes (incentives and fines)? Does it lead to worldview-cultural change? Is there a new metaphor, a narrative for the new strategy? And, most importantly, does the new vision have a new litany, a new way to ensure that the strategies reinforce the new future and are not chained to the past?

CLA thus can be used to deepen our understanding of strategy. Mapping reality from the viewpoint of multiple stakeholders enables us to develop more-robust scenarios. It helps us to understand current reality, and, by giving us a tool to dig deeper and more broadly, it allows us to create an alternative future that is robust in its implementation.

In practice, the method is not yet widely known, certainly outside of the southern hemisphere. Although there is a developing literature, it warrants entering the mainstream of foresight methods (Curry & Schultz, 2009). Using the same approach as in Chap. 3 where we deployed Jonathan Rosenheads' own words to describe robustness analysis we shall use the same format by allowing Inayatullah to speak straight from "the horse's mouth" as it were. The following text is taken from a paper produced by Sohail Inayatullah where he defines CLA.

CLA is based on the assumption that the way in which one frames a problem changes the policy solution and the actors responsible for creating transformation.

*The **first level is the problem itself defined as the "litany"** or the official public description of the issue—quantitative trends, problems, often exaggerated, often used for political purposes—(e.g. overpopulation) usually presented by the news media. Events, issues, and trends are not connected and appear discontinuous. The result is often either a feeling of helplessness (what can I do?) or apathy (nothing can be done!) or projected action (why don't they do something about it?). This is the conventional level of futures research which can readily create a politics of fear. This is the futurist as fearmonger who warns: "the end is near". However, by believing in the prophecy and acting appropriately, the end can be averted. The litany level is the most visible and obvious, requiring little analytic capabilities. It is believed, rarely questioned.*

*The **second level is concerned with causes in the form of social science analysis based on short-term historical facts**. These are represented by social causes, including economic, cultural, political and historical factors (e.g. rising birthrates, lack of family planning). Interpretation is given to quantitative data. This type of analysis is usually articulated by policy institutes and published as editorial pieces in newspapers or in not-quite academic journals. If one is fortunate then the precipitating action is sometimes analysed (e.g. population growth and advances in medicine/health). This level excels at technical explanations as well as academic analysis. The role of the state and other actors and interests is often explored at this level. The data is often questioned; however, the language of questioning does not contest the paradigm in which the issue is framed. It remains obedient to it.*

*The **third deeper level adopts a worldview concerned with structure and the discourse analysis that supports and legitimates it**—examples include population growth and civilisational perspectives of family; lack of women's power; lack of social security; the population/consumption debate. The task is to find deeper social, linguistic, cultural structures that are actor-invariant (not dependent on who are the actors). Discerning deeper assumptions behind the issue is crucial here as are efforts to revise the problem. At this stage, one can explore how different discourses (the economic, the religious, the cultural, for example) do more than cause or mediate the issue but constitute it and how the discourse we use to understand is complicit in our framing of the issue. Based on the varied discourses, discrete* *alternative scenarios can be derived here. For example, a scenario of the future of population based on religious perspectives of population ("go forth and multiply") versus cultural scenario focused on how women's groups imagine construct birthing and childraising as well as their roles in patriarchy and the world division of labor. These scenarios add a horizontal dimension to our layered analysis. The foundations for how the litany has been presented and the variables used to understand the litany are questioned at this level.*

*The **fourth layer of analysis is at the level of metaphor or myth**. These are the deep stories, the collective archetypes, the unconscious, of often emotive, dimensions of the problem, or the paradox (e.g. seeing population as non-statistical, as community, or seeing people as creative resources). This level provides a gut/emotional level experience to the worldview under inquiry. The language used is less specific, more concerned with evoking visual images, with touching the heart instead of reading the head. This is the root level of questioning; however, questioning itself finds its limits since the frame of questioning must enter other frameworks of understanding—the mythical, for example.*

CLA thus goes beyond conventional framing of issues. It is argued that normal academic analysis tends to stay at the second layer (causes) with occasional forays into the third (worldview), with little reference to the fourth layer (myth and metaphor). CLA does not treat the different levels in hierarchical terms but treat each level equally. This is seen to increase its flexibility and analytical richness.

Different scenarios can be developed at each level. Litany type scenarios reflect current popular trends and thinking; social level (cause analysis) scenarios are more policy oriented, with worldview scenarios tending to capture basic differences. Myth/metaphor type scenarios articulate these differences through a more cultural reference base (poem, story, image).

Inayatullah also proposes that problem-solving actors are different at each level so that *"at the litany level it is usually others—the government or corporations. At the social level, it is often some partnership between different groups. At the worldview level, it is people or voluntary associations, and at the myth/metaphor it is leaders or artists"*.

A major observation is *"that coming to the CLA process from other scenario-building approaches, it was sometimes necessary to remind oneself during the analysis phase of the layers that one is deepening one's understanding of a current existing view of the future, and that the scenario development process (and the development of alternative futures) does not begin until after the worldview and/or metaphor layers have been first constructed and then inflected to disrupt the prevailing view"*.

6.5.2 Summary of Benefits and Disadvantages of CLA

Finally, Inayatullah provides a useful summary of the benefits and disadvantages of the method as well as a guide to using the process itself, thus:

Uses of the Method
- Questions conventional future thinking
- Uncovers why things are not working today and develops potential and shared solutions
- Explores issues from qualitative perspectives to strengthen understanding of the issue
- Develops shared organisational strategy
- Facilitates multicultural dialogue and understanding
- Gains a better understanding of one's own worldview and ways of making sense of the world
- Develops different sorts of products and services and revised policies

Benefits
- Expands the range and richness of scenarios
- Collaborative and appealing to a wide range of participants
- Integrative with other foresight methods
- Supports the development of powerful and richer future scenarios
- Useful check that constructed scenarios are robust across diverse perspectives
- Develops shared visions of a preferred organisational future
- Potential for issue transformation
- Links short-, medium-, and long-term strategic thinking

Disadvantages
- Needs a clearly expressed question to be prepared
- Requires participants to be willing to share their perspectives and challenge their assumptions about how the organisation operates
- Requires acceptance of the basic CLA theory by the participants
- Needs to be connected with other foresight methods to generate future scenarios
- May constrain action through "analysis/paralysis"
- May reduce individual creativity
- Needs time and patience
- Requires experienced facilitator

The method process extracted from Inayatullah's own notes is provided in Appendix 2.

For readers who wish to delve in depth into the CLA method I would suggest that they read

The Causal Layered Analysis (CLA) Reader
Theory and Case Studies of an Integrative and Transformative Methodology

Edited by Sohail Inayatullah—Published by Tamkang University Press Graduate Institute of Futures Studies, Taipei, Taiwan 251 2004. (Document can be downloaded from the web as a Pdf).

Summary

Can you see a developing theme here? All of these more "way out" ideas have actually been thought about—they are not "unknown-unknowns". They tend to be shovelled into either quadrants 4 or 3 in the risk/uncertainty matrix, when in fact there is no reason why they shouldn't reside in quadrant 2 (known-unknowns). As has been said earlier—"if we can think it—it can happen". The prime reasons for treating them as Q3 and 4 issues is largely down to a variety of cognitive barriers in individuals, organisations, and broader culture. Chapters 9 and 10, covering behavioural factors—the impact of human influences, address these concerns in depth.

References

Ansoff, H. I. (1975). Managing strategic surprise by response to weak signals. *California Management Review, XVIII*(2).

Cass/Airmic. (2011). *Roads to ruin – A study of major risk events*. Cass Business School/Airmic.

Curry, A., & Schultz, W. (2009). Roads less travelled: Different methods, different futures. *Journal of Futures Studies*.

Henchey, N. (1978). Making sense of future studies. *Alternatives, 7*, 104–111.

Inayatullah, S. (Ed.). (2004). *The causal layered analysis (CLA) reader – Theory and case studies of an integrative and transformative methodology* (Vol. 251). Tamkang University Press. (Document can be downloaded from the web as a Pdf).

Kuosa, T., & Stucki, M. (2020). Futures intelligence: Types of futures knowledge. *Futures Platform*.

Kuosa, T. (2012). The evolution of strategic foresight. In *Alternative futures Finland*. Gower.

Marchau, V. A. W. J., Walker, W. E., Bloeman, P. J. T. M., & Popper, S. W. (Eds.). (2019). *Chapter 1: Decision making under deep uncertainty*. Springer.

Ota, S., & Maki-Teeri, M. (2021). Science fiction. In *Futures platform – Wild cards and science fiction: Free imagination*.

Padbury, P. (2019). *An overview of the horizons foresight method: Using system based-scenarios and the "inner game" of foresight*. Chief Futurist, Policy Horizons, Government of Canada.

Siegel, E. (2017). *Star Trek treknology – The science of Star Trek from tricorders to warp drive*. Voyageur Press.

Stanley Robinson, K. (2020). *The ministry for the future*. Orbit.

Voros, J. (2001). A primer on futures studies, foresight and the use of scenarios. *Prospect – The Foresight Bulletin*, No. 6.

Voros, J. (2017). *The futures cone, use and history*. (Source: Adapted from Voros (2003, 2017), which was based on Hancock and Bezold (1994).)

Part III

**Theoretical Underpinnings: Scenarios
and Their Role in Dealing with Uncertainty**

Chapter 7
Scenarios: What Are They, Why Are They Useful and How Can We Best Use Them?

When good or bad come, why give thanks, and why complain? Since what is written won't remain or stay like this.
Hafez—Persian poet

Abstract *Scenarios* are descriptions of alternative development paths of an issue and help to explore what could happen and how to prepare for various contingencies. Scenarios explore the space of uncertainties in defining possible futures whilst forecasts tend to be used more for anticipating timing in relation to specific stimuli such as technology. Two categories, or lenses, of scenarios are introduced—the reactive—where alternative futures are explored based on a major disruptive event which has already happened, and the exploratory—"what-if" events which contain latent characteristics or trends over various future time horizons and can be influenced by weak signals. Under the broader term of strategic options analysis two methods supporting decision-making are reviewed—morphological analysis and morphological distance analysis. The chapter also shows how preferable and undesirable scenarios can be identified and allocated to the uncertainty profile matrix including doomsday scenarios which can be represented as catastrophic or existential risks.

Keywords Scenario lenses · Reactive · Exploratory · Strategic options analysis · Contextual · Morphological analysis · Morphological distance · Catastrophic risk · Existential risk

7.1 Introduction

Having identified and deconstructed the major analytical components of uncertainty in Chaps. 2–6, we need to find a suitable vehicle which enables us to explore uncertain environments. Scenarios provide such a vehicle.

The term *"scenario"*, now in common use, is typified as stories or narratives of alternative possible futures. Kahn and Wiener, in their 1967 book *The Year 2000*, provided one of the earliest formal definitions of scenarios, *"...a hypothetical sequence of events constructed for the purpose of focusing attention on causal events and decision points."* In the corporate world, the use of scenarios has been used by the petroleum giant Shell (2005) since the mid-1960s under the guidance of pioneers such as Pierre Wack and Kees van der Heijden (1996). This led to a broader definition whereby scenarios were seen as being *"...descriptions of possible futures that reflect different perspectives on the past, present, and future."* (Van Notten et al., 2003).

Scenarios are descriptions of alternative development paths of an issue. They are not predictions of the future per se but help to explore what could happen and how to prepare for various contingencies (Kuosa & Stucki, 2020). Stakeholder participation and collaboration is essential to the scenario activity. Ringland et al. (2012) make a distinction between scenarios and forecasting in that *"scenarios explore the space of* **uncertainties** *in defining possible futures"*, whilst forecasts tend to be used more for anticipating timing in relation to specific stimuli such as technology. Ringland does point out though that there is no reason not to integrate more specific forecasts within a broader scenario-based horizon.

As was flagged in the previous chapter, scenarios need to be seen within the context of an ongoing, long-term, "closed-loop" organisational process and provide a useful tool for generating shared forward views, helping to align strategic action across an organisation on its journey into the future. The main purpose of a scenario is to guide exploration of possible future states with the best scenarios describing alternative future outcomes that diverge significantly from the present (Curry & Schultz, 2009) and thus avoid falling into the trap that the future will generally resemble the past. Scenarios can help us look out for surprises!

Like Ringland, Curry and Schultz also emphasise the collaborative, cross-functional nature of carrying out scenario activities, stating that it *"means creating participatory processes: scenarios create new behaviour only insofar as they create new patterns of thinking across a significant population within an organisation"*. As will be indicated in Chaps. 9 and 10, behavioural considerations are a major component when confronted with decision-making governed by an uncertain landscape.

One critique of certain scenario practices and their output (List, 2004) is that too much consists of "snapshot" scenarios, *"which merely describe the future conditions without explaining how they evolved"*. In other words, such scenarios lack comprehensive enough but all important accompanying narratives. We saw in Chap. 6 how methods such as causal layered analysis and being aware of the history and its litanies are crucial in establishing the deep roots of a problem. This theme will be picked up later in the next section when introducing reactive and exploratory scenario approaches.

Voros states that the creation of scenarios requires an in-depth process of information gathering and careful analysis. He goes on to add that *"scenarios based solely on trends and forecasts will generate a very narrow range of alternative potential futures"* and that where decision-makers assume too much credibility due to hard/quantitative data, such organisations fall into the trap of the dictum identified in Chap. 3 where *"the appearance of precision through quantification can convey a validity that cannot always be justified"*. In this guidebook, the primary resource for such a strategic foresight exercise has been presented in Chaps. 2–6, "Uncertainty Deconstructed", which is why it is recommended that elements within the template are used to prepare the groundwork for scenario development.

7.2 Lenses

In this chapter, I shall be using scenarios as seen through two but distinct lenses—the reactive and the exploratory (plus a hybrid).

7.2.1 Reactive

A *reactive* scenario is defined as being how the future may roll out based on a current problem or issue (one that has manifested itself), as the main starting point or driver. For example, the Global Risks Report 2021, recently published by the World Economic Forum, looks at the future impact of the COVID-19 outbreak based on three horizons: short term up to 2 years, medium term 3–5 years, and long-term 5–10 years. Note, the problem here is that such a scenario relates to a single discrete event rather than potential asymmetric exponential effects based on interconnecting trends and events. To re-iterate, the WEF report offers scenarios in reaction to a specific event that has already manifested itself. The additional danger of such an approach is that there is a tendency to marginalise tangential, second-order, third-order, or cumulative events and effects in the scenario chain.

Reactive scenarios are problem-oriented as they seek to explore how society and organisations may respond to, usually, shorter-term challenges. Voros (2001) claims it is where most futures work takes place and "often touches upon the" big-picture "problems". The event has happened and the main response is to ask "how do we deal with it?" (e.g. the COVID-19 pandemic).

7.2.2 Exploratory

An *exploratory* scenario, on the other hand, is much broader in scope as it seeks to identify both observable and latent drivers or trends over various future time horizons—in effect multiple futures with a much larger range of possible outcomes, impacted by weak signals and outliers. Peter Schwartz (2003) said it simply: *"What has not been imagined will not be foreseen. . .in time."* An exploratory approach comes with much fewer preconceptions about what are the main drivers when exploring the future or rather future uncertainties. Indeed, some of these drivers or indicators may not have been sighted or even emerged. It offers the analyst the freedom to investigate a more expansive array of future (non-discrete) outcomes using an array of methods, techniques, and tools to help in the investigation.

Exploratory analysis is much more engaged with issues of foresight rather than in response to one specific main driver (reactive). It involves ways in which one can imagine multiple futures that we must foresee—whether that future is tomorrow or months, years, or decades from now. The main challenge here is how do we get decision-makers and others to listen out for and filter an array of signals which may never happen—the classic low occurrence/high impact scenario? Whilst exploratory analysis is more open ended than the reactive approach—it is fuzzier—with varying time horizons, inputs and outputs, resource commitments, etc. and where second and subsequent order occurrences can be non-linear. This makes it more difficult for decision-makers to grasp the essentials, let alone identify them, when formulating policy—and where such formulation is subject to asymmetrically evolving challenges which majorly reduce the efficacy of traditional planning cycles and methods and upon which management still relies too heavily.

The exploratory approach requires that an organisation be more prepared to formalise the foresight process as a continuing strategic AND operational activity in its own right rather than in reactive mode. It should be highlighted nonetheless that such a mind-set should not be siphoned off just to one department or division (or sub-contracted out to consultants) but be integral to all functions, strategic and operational, within the organisation.

This more challenging form of analysis with its range of possible futures (as represented in the futures cone) is based on major levels of interconnectivity. It is here where the programme seeks to offer enhanced structured insight processes for decision- and policy-makers as well as decision support analysts—and where current signals are weak, overlooked, or indeed ignored, inadvertently or deliberately. We are concerned less with the major event itself but with secondary (second order), tertiary, and more layers which may be *derived* from any singular event and which in turn may generate their own causal and non-causal effects. Moreover, these derivative triggers are often asymmetric and non-linear in impact adding to the difficulties of carrying out foresight exercises. Linear forecasting approaches are not realistic in such circumstances and therefore the futures analysis must be a continuous activity unconstrained by formal planning cycles—after all a pandemic doesn't recognise planning cycles nor does climate change. Thus, the exploration of what can be termed *derivative* scenarios is crucial to the process as they can manifest themselves not just in exploratory mode but in reactive mode as well.

It is strange that in an era where our access to knowledge and information and its litany, as well as the volume of data itself, is greater than ever before, we still struggle to better identify the future or rather optional or possible futures. Perhaps there is too much information—too much noise and too few easily identifiable signals? In addition, when, in an attempt to bring order, we seek out new information technologies such as data analytics and AI methods—we need to be aware that even these "neutral" algorithmic approaches are subject to originator bias—and has been discussed by a number of commentators (O'Neil, 2016; Wachter-Boettcher, 2017; Mau, 2019).

There are three additional challenges which are related and need to be considered. First, in some cases the evidence is in front of our eyes, but we do not see it, or do not recognise the significance of what we are seeing. We are surprised by the result. Alternatively, there are occasions when the evidence is not a reliable guide to sudden shifts. In both cases, surprise manifests itself all too often and we need to ask not only whether the foresight approaches are robust enough but whether our own thought processes are robust enough. Finally, there is the danger of just relying on reactive scenarios so that decision- and policy-makers spend too much time in respond mode and reduce their chances to explore "potential" future events—whether such events be low occurrence/high impact or not.

I'd like to clarify a further point in relation to the reactive and exploratory variants. As mentioned, a reactive scenario uses an actual event occurrence as its starting point. It will then use foresight methods when exploring subsequent potential future developments in specific response to such an event—e.g. COVID-19—irrespective of whether we should have seen it coming. It has already been stated that the exploratory approach is more open-ended, and by definition exploratory, and is less constrained in its vision of the future both in terms of ideas generated and the length of the time horizon. On the other hand, there is no reason why the exploratory approach should not be used to examine an initial single identifiable issue as its starting point as long as that issue may have been identified somewhere before the horizon is arrived at—possibly in the form of a weak signal or outlier—or as a recognised ongoing problem which has not been fully addressed or resolved. Topics such as social mobility and social inequality come to mind as examples and, of course, climate change.

By offering a structured and holistic approach to the topic—the main advantage is that future projections, having passed through a particular time horizon, can then be audited against actuals. Variances can be identified and rationales for such variances articulated so that the inputs into the structure can be improved over time and future errors mitigated—offering *the insurance of iteration as a learning and feed-back process.*

Within both the reactive and exploratory scenarios the role of the social and behavioural sciences must not be overlooked, as many of the issues being addressed which make up the dynamics of a scenario have socially based inputs and outputs. Part A3 will highlight such behavioural factors as being a critical indicator of how problems are created and how, or how not, they may be identified and resolved.

An alternative approach for conducting exploratory scenarios, and worth reviewing, was developed in the 1970s by Jim Dator of the Hawai'i Research Centre for Futures Studies (2002), and which uses a workshop-based forecasting technique called "incasting" (Curry & Schultz, 2009). Participants are presented with roughly defined scenarios to explore and are then required to add details to the scenarios, using their creative imaginations. This is almost akin to a form of script writing that a science fiction author might employ and in Chap. 6 we saw what S-F could offer in scenario formulation. *"With organisations, participants may be asked to consider how they would redefine, reinvent, or otherwise transform their mission, activities, services, or products to succeed in the conditions of each scenario"* (Curry &

Schultz, 2009). This tool aims to increase the flexibility when planning futures and increasing creativity and exploring what strengths and weaknesses might emerge during the changes taking place in the scenario.

7.2.3   Scenarios as a Design Process

Scenario development can be defined as a design activity which at inception is unstructured and faced with an array of uncertainties. If not addressed early enough these uncertainties can gestate into undesirable outcomes which the design team will find difficult to redress at later stages in project (Garvey & Childs, 2016)—especially where the project is constrained by resources (time, money, people). In order to militate against such circumstances occurring the design team has to understand both the nature of the problem facing it and the nature of the uncertainties contained with the problem space.

7.2.4   So, What Is the Design Process?

Nelson and Stolterman (2012) state that *"Design is the ability to imagine that-which-does-not-yet exist, to make it appear in concrete form as a new, purposeful addition to the real world"*. In other words, it can be argued that early-stage design, whether for products, services, or concepts, contains numerous uncertainties.

What can be said is that, at the beginning of a new design project (and this can also be interpreted as identifying a scenario), a problem exists for the designer or the design team caused by uncertainty of outcome (and for designer we can substitute analyst). Indeed, the further away a design concept is from realisation as a finished item, the more it is prone to varying conditions of uncertainty and asymmetric inflexions.

Garvey and Childs (2016) identify further areas of specificity by stating, *"Physical design methods and the behavioural responses to such design (many of which are not quantifiable), are highly complex, exacerbated by high levels of interconnectivity. This is not just due to the variety of components that have to be considered in the design process (physical complexity), but to intangible factors inherent within the nature of individual and group behaviour in response to designed objects"*.

Sounds familiar, doesn't it?

7.2.5   Strategic Options Analysis or "What If" Scenarios: An Exploratory Approach

We shall see in Chaps. 9 and 10 how behavioural biases at all levels (individual, group, organisational) can constrain the generation, and hinder the manifestation, of ideas under conditions of uncertainty. The exploratory mind-set which encourages us to ask the question "what if?" is paramount if scenarios can truly provide a variety of "stretched" alternatives which might happen. In Chap. 3, we were introduced to the importance of the ability to structure a problem prior to actually attempting to solve it (that is if the problem concerned is "solvable"—and unfortunately not all problems are).

One of the key questions I've always tried to answer is "who decides what the inputs are when constructing a scenario?" and is perhaps more crucial than picking a scenario in the first place whether looked through a reactive or exploratory lens. There are a number of methods the reader may have heard of such as "brainstorming" (and its variants) and mind maps. The common weakness of such methods is that groups engaged in the process can be overly influenced by a dominant member or suffer from groupthink, hubris, and/or adherence to rigid ideological positions, often put forward by the dominant participant themselves.

I often recall the old story of the American tourist who gets lost trying to look for the correct route to Limerick in Ireland, and on finding the local Garda (police) officer asks how to get there—to which the policeman replied, *"well if I were you Sir, I wouldn't be starting from here"*. Whilst seen as an example of Irish quirky humour, the response is actually correct—too often people ask the wrong question from where they are standing.

A method expanded upon in the MTT section of this chapter is eminently suitable in helping decision-makers and analysts to address the issue of defining the boundaries of any one scenario. Unfortunately, it has a rather scary title of morphological analysis (MA) but may be better understood using the term *"strategic options analysis"* (see Sect. 7.5.1 below).

7.3   Types of Outcome: A Work Through of a Tentative Options Analysis Process

Setting the Scene

So, what types of outcome should we anticipate as potential future scenarios? Various categories of outcome can be identified. Whilst it is generally assumed that the further one looks into the future the greater the uncertainty, we should not take this as a given. There are black swan events but not as many as we are often told there are—and I refer here to those characteristics of quadrant 3 in the uncertainty profile introduced in Chap. 2—or "pseudo-black swans".

Outcomes which the scenario process allows us to explore come in a variety of forms, albeit that like uncertainty, numerous different interpretations have been put forward. For the purposes of this document, a number of different viewpoints by academics and researchers are reviewed. From this review, a hybrid schema of types of outcome has been developed. Following a further editing process (as will be explained), the key components will be positioned into their respective quadrants in the uncertainty profile model.

7.3.1   Towards a Synthesis of Scenario Options

We have introduced a number of different but overlapping interpretations as to how we can represent scenario-based outcomes. We shall now bring together the various strands so as to provide the user with a template for classifying different types of scenarios with varying levels of certainty/uncertainty and over a range of time periods. This is followed by allocating the various types of scenario outcome options to the four quadrants within the risk/uncertainty profile matrix. The objective here will be to provide guidance to practitioners as to the range of pathways expressed in the form of narratives that they may follow when confronted by uncertainty and in relation to reactive and/or exploratory responses.

7.3.2   Strategic Options Analysis for Different Scenarios

Synthesising the various scenario options by researchers we have earlier referred to experts such as Voros, Marchau, and Kuosa, I shall now present different but often overlapping interpretations in the form of a problem space or options landscape.
   Four main variables or parameters selected are:

- *Contextual:* where is a particular event or issue positioned along the risk/uncertainty spectrum?
- *Conditional:* defined as being how we might visualise and feel about a future event or issue.
- *Occurrence impact:* a range of "stretched" possible outcomes from the expected to outliers, wild cards, and fringe possibilities. This variable refines each contextual condition in terms of some form of expectation.
- *Time horizon:* Readers may have noted that the futures cone presented in Chap. 7 is usually shown with a "time" axis. As was discussed in that chapter time periods are flexible. This main variable is thus flexible as to how the scenario analyst wishes to define the future and will change from scenario objective to scenario objective. In one scenario a time horizon of, say 10 years, may be broken down into three periods: short term may cover up to the first 2 years, medium term up to

5 years, etc. On the other hand, scenarios may define short term as being the next 10 years and medium term up to 20 years.

Note: It is a common error to believe that the (usually) more undesirable impacts will occur further into the future than the more preferable ones. As humans, we have a tendency to procrastinate and defer unpleasantness until it is clearly visible and close at hand (ref: the Kim Stanley Robinson quote on the section on science fiction in the previous chapter). Uncertainty has no time determined horizon—the COVID-19 outbreak manifested itself and spread rapidly and globally within a relatively short time period which caught most countries unaware. An earthquake can also occur with very little, if any, warning.

Each of the four main variables is then populated with various conditions extracted from those identified in Chap. 6; thus:

Contextual future conditions are:

Predicted future—this condition reflects both the Marchau level 1 uncertainty and Voros interpretations. There is a clear enough future for short-term decisions and where historical data (which of course may not always be accurate) can be used as predictors for the future usually for a singular event with a very high probability of occurring. Forecasting methods rather than foresight ones are deployed here

Probable—something with few alternative futures and likely to happen—it is probable. Quantitative data and stochastic methods are generally used here to support a prediction.

Possible—Voros defines this condition as being something which might happen. Possible events are seen to be reasonable and unreasonable—they could happen, even if undesirable.

Plausible—on the other hand, "plausible" refers to possibilities that are reasonable and it excludes possibilities that are unreasonable. Marchau calls this category a level 3 uncertainty which relates to situations with a few plausible futures but where probabilities cannot be assigned. He expands this interpretation by stating "the future can be predicted well enough to identify policies in a few specific plausible future worlds".

In semantic terms, *"The main difference between "plausible" and "possible" is that "plausible" means you could make a reasonably valid case for something, while "possible" means something is capable of becoming true, though it's not always reasonable".*

Highly unlikely—here we are starting to stretch the boundaries of both plausibility and possibility, also called radical uncertainty or deep uncertainty and conforms to Marchau's level 4 uncertainty. He makes a distinction between those situations which contain many plausible futures and situations that we are not sure about. The term "wild card or outlier" is often used here—there is a hint of possibility of something occurring we are just unsure as to when and how it might manifest itself. However, it should be stated that such is the weakness of a signal for a wild card event that it can occur even under possible and plausible conditions.

Unthinkable—is a condition and is included as it is on the outer fringes of both possibility and imagination. Such event realisation or even visibility is heavily constrained by behavioural factors and boundaries as per Gowing and Langdon's (2017) interpretations.

Conditional conditions are:

- Preferable (or desirable)
- Undesirable (not preferable)
- Not sure (agnostic)

All three conditions tend to be subjective with values attached. Both the preferable and undesirable conditions offer the decision-maker the choice of determining which future event is more preferable than the other so that policies to encourage or mitigate such occurrences can be developed in advance. Of course, the greater the uncertainty of something, the more an agnostic or non-action standpoint is likely to be adopted. For example, the argument surrounding the future of artificial intelligence as being a force for good or evil—many arguments have been put forward for both visions but the jury is still out.

Occurrence/impact (or impact probability) states are:

- High occurrence/low impact—in the predicted zone, e.g. seasonal flu
- High occurrence/high impact—as above e.g. hurricanes, tornadoes, annual monsoon
- Low occurrence/low impact—"mast" years for acorns (every few/7? years)
- Low occurrence/high impact—UK hurricanes, pandemics, earthquakes, climate change
- Possible in science fiction—as per Kuosa and Ota and Maki-Teeri—AI, robotics, genetic engineering
- Possible in S-F but not according to current knowledge (e.g. warp drive)—as above
- Possible in imagination and therefore in theory—dystopias and utopias.

For this category, it should be noted that uncertainties, by definition, ought to preclude those two states with high occurrence or probability. However, as we have shown earlier in Chaps. 2 and 6 the apparently obvious—from known-knowns to known-unknowns—are often ignored and end up in quadrant 3—an unknown-known or even an unknown-unknown. For this reason, these two states are initially included within the options outcome model.

Time horizon—Time frames are open to variation (as mentioned in Chap. 4) as these are dependent on the boundaries defined by the scenario authors. For the model used in this chapter I've selected seven different time futures.

- Less than 1 year
- Less than 3 years
- Less than 5 years
- 5–10 years
- 11–20 years
- 21–30 years
- 31 years +

Contextual	Conditional	Occurrence/Impact	Time Horizon
Predicted	Preferable	High Occurrence/Low Impact	< 1 year
Probable	Undersirable	High Occurrence/High Impact	< 3 years
Possible	Not Sure (Agnostic)	Low Occurrence/Low Impact	<5 years
Plausible		Low Occurrence/High Impact	5-10 years
Highly Unlikely		Possible in Science Fiction	11-20 years
Unthinkable		Possible in S-F but w/o current knowledge	21-30 years
		Possible in Imagination & Theory	31 years +

Fig. 7.1 A problem space

		Contextual						Conditional		
		Predicted	Probable	Possible	Plausible	Highly Unlikely	Unthinkable	Preferable	Undesirable	Not sure (agnostic)
Conditional	Preferable	-	-	-	-	-	X			
	Undesirable	-	-	-	-	-	-			
	Not sure (agnostic)	X	-	-	-	-	X			
Impact Probability (inc Fringe)	High Probability/Low Impact	-	-	-	X	X	X	-	-	-
	High Probability/High Impact	-	-	-	X	X	X	-	-	-
	Low Probability/Low Impact	X	X	-	-	-	X	-	-	-
	Low Probability/High Impact	X	X	-	-	-	X	-	-	-
	Possible in Science Fiction	-	-	-	-	X	X	-	-	-
	Possible in S-F but w/o current knowledge	X	X	X	-	-	-	-	-	-
	Possible in Imagination & Theory	X	X	X	X	-	-	X	-	-

Fig. 7.2 Pair-wise analysis table (partial view)

The *scenario options analysis problem space* is presented as Fig. 7.1 above:

This schedule indicates that there are 882 different configurations of the 4 variables and their states (6 contextual × 3 conditional × 7 occurrences/impact × 7 Time). Within these configurations, we can assume that there will be a number of inconsistence pairs. Pair-wise analysis (as illustrated in Fig. 7.2—partial) allows us to strip out those configurations within the problem space with inconsistent pairs. There are 752 configurations with inconsistent pairs, leaving 130 consistent configurations which can work. It should be pointed out that the pair-wise evaluation can be subject to subjectivity, but by identifying inconsistent pairs within any of the configurations generated by the problem space, the process mitigates against the worst of such inconsistencies. Readers should also be aware that this representation is mainly for demonstration purposes only and different pairing outcomes may occur depending on the specific problem being addressed. In Fig. 7.2, inconsistent pairs are identified by an "X" in a red cell.

Total Solutions = 882.		Total Viable Solutions = 130		Selected Solutions 4	
Solution Number	Contextual	Conditional	Occurrence/Impact	Time Horizon	
1	**Predicted**	Preferable	High Occurrence/Low Impact	< 1 year	
8	Probable	Undesirable	High Occurrence/High Impact	< 3 years	
50	Possible	Not Sure (Agnostic)	Low Occurrence/Low Impact	< 5 years	
57	Plausible		Low Occurrence/High Impact	5-10 years	
	Highly Unlikely		Possible in S-F	11-20 years	
	Unthinkable		Possible in S-F but w/o current knowledge	21-30 years	
			Possible in Imagination & Theory	31 years +	

Fig. 7.3 Input variable (predicted)

Total Solutions = 882.		Total Viable Solutions = 130		Selected Solutions 54	
Solution Number	Contextual	Conditional	Occurrence/Impact	Time Horizon	
1	Predicted	Preferable	High Occurrence/Low Impact	< 1 year	
8	Probable	Undesirable	High Occurrence/High Impact	< 3 years	
50	Possible	Not Sure (Agnostic)	Low Occurrence/Low Impact	< 5 years	
57	Plausible		**Low Occurrence/High Impact**	5-10 years	
	Highly Unlikely		Possible in Science Fiction	11-20 years	
	Unthinkable		Possible in S-F but w/o current knowledge	21-30 years	
			Possible in Imagination & Theory	31 years +	

Fig. 7.4 Low occurrence/high impact as input

Total Solutions = 882.		Total Viable Solutions = 130		Selected Solutions 9	
Solution Number	Contextual	Conditional	Occurrence/Impact	Time Horizon	
	Predicted	Preferable	High Occurrence/Low Impact	< 1 year	
	Probable	Undesirable	High Occurrence/High Impact	< 3 years	
	Possible	Not Sure (Agnostic)	Low Occurrence/Low Impact	**< 5 years**	
	Plausible		Low Occurrence/High Impact	5-10 years	
	Highly Unlikely		Possible in Science Fiction	11-20 years	
	Unthinkable		Possible in S-F but w/o current knowledge	21-30 years	

Fig. 7.5 Less than 5 years as main input driver

Total Solutions = 882.		Total Viable Solutions = 130		Selected Solutions 16	
Solution Number	Contextual	Conditional	Occurrence/Impact	Time Horizon	
	Predicted	Preferable	High Occurrence/Low Impact	< 1 year	
	Probable	Undesirable	High Occurrence/High Impact	< 3 years	
	Possible	Not Sure (Agnostic)	Low Occurrence/Low Impact	< 5 years	
	Plausible		Low Occurrence/High Impact	**5-10 years**	
	Highly Unlikely		Possible in Science Fiction	11-20 years	
	Unthinkable		Possible in S-F but w/o current knowledge	21-30 years	
			Possible in Imagination & Theory	31 years +	

Fig. 7.6 5–10 years as input option

In Fig. 7.3 above, within the set of solutions and using the six different states within the contextual variable as the main driver, we can see that for *predicted* scenarios there are four options:

Note: In Figs. 7.3, 7.4, 7.5, and 7.6, the following images are in black and white only for visualisation purposes. In the matrix itself (below the variable headings), *the input variable is shown in **bold text** (**e.g. predicted**) and the output options are the shaded cells.*

Further viable (i.e. solutions) mini-scenarios are detailed in Appendix 3.

***Note for Reader: Due to the amount of detail provided in Appendix 3 and Appendices 4 through 7 referred to below, the information is best referenced by a link to the author's website at* https://www.strategyforesight.co.uk/general-5**

Alternatively once on the landing page called "Insights"—scroll down page to section "On-line resources" and follow instructions to access appendices.

Using a decision support method called morphological analysis (or MA), which is explained in more detail in the MTT section below, it has been identified that any state within any of the main variables can be an input or an output. In the example below, if we wish to identify potential scenario characteristics using "low occurrence/high impact" as the main input driver we see that there are 54 options:

Using the time horizon as a main input/driver we see that within 5 years there are nine viable options:

Whilst in the 5–10 year horizon there are 16 options to explore:

As indicated previously the original solution set following pair-wise analysis was reduced from 882 to 130 different scenario profiles. All the configurations which make up this set of 130 are presented in Appendix 4 and as mentioned above can be accessed at https://www.strategyforesight.co.uk/general-5

However, the prime objective of this exercise is really to identify not just the usual suspects which appear in the list of scenarios which work (the known-knowns), but those scenarios *excluding* these usual suspects. In this case, we can therefore afford to ignore those scenario configurations which are less challenging or do not yield any great insight beyond what we already know. Thus, for this exercise we have chosen to discard any scenario configuration which:

(a) Has a high level of occurrence and a low impact (yellow)
(b) Has a low level of occurrence and with a low impact (red)

We are looking for those scenario configurations which are the most impactful.

These configurations are identified in Appendix 5 (yellow and red rows) also at https://www.strategyforesight.co.uk/general-5

From our original 130 scenarios, there are 34 configurations identified as being in these categories. This reduces the key scenarios to 96 out of the original 882 or just 11% of the original problem space set.

From a subjective policy point of view, there are two distinct drivers present in the model and they abide within the conditional variable—

• The preferable (or desirable)
• The undesirable

If a future scenario is to be preferred or desired, specific pro-active policies need to be pursued or actioned in order to create and bring about the realisation of such an outcome. On the other hand, if potential scenarios are deemed undesirable, avoidance and/or mitigation strategies need to developed and deployed.

Under the same conditional variable there is a third state—not sure (or agnostic). To some extent, such a condition is the worst of the three states as the level of uncertainty relating to any action is highest.

Of the remaining 96 scenario solutions 31 are deemed to be preferable or desirable, whereas 33 are undesirable. The balance of the 96 leaves 32 agnostic scenarios. If we exclude the agnostic scenarios, then there remains 64 preferable or undesirable scenarios which are shown in Appendix 6—https://www. strategyforesight.co.uk/general-5

Incidentally, Voros (2017) pointed out that the predicted (expected) is often left out as the probability of an event not happening is deemed to be very small. In our solutions set there are two scenarios which appear in the predicted category. I wouldn't totally assume that what we expect will happen will actually happen— there are always surprises to take us off guard—indeed have we not been rigorous enough in seeking outliers and wild cards? My inclination in this instance is to leave this group as a form of insurance—it can be audited in the future.

7.4 Allocation of Viable Scenarios to the Uncertainty Profile Template

Preamble
The final phase in the process is to allocate each of the 64 preferable and undesirable scenario configurations to one of four quadrants in the uncertainty profile template (Chap. 2).

The reader will notice that some of the scenarios appear in more than one quadrant. For example, whilst all the scenarios in the possible category can be allocated to quadrant 2—the known-unknown, it is not unrealistic that some of these scenarios manifest themselves in quadrant 3—the unknown-known—namely scenarios 8 and 10—preferable but with low probability and high impact and scenarios 17 and 18— undesirable with low probability and high impact (within 1 and 3 years).

Examples of a scenario 17 or 19 situation include the Grenfell high-rise fire and the Manchester Arena bombing. In both cases, such events would normally reside in Q2—the known-unknown (or Schwarz's inevitable surprise) and appropriate contingency plans put in place for such an eventuality. Poor fire evacuation guidelines and inadequate testing of the building materials made the Grenfell fire to be many times worse had such foresight been up to the mark. In the case of the Manchester Arena bombing it has been argued that a number of deaths could have been avoided if emergency response crews had been allowed in the first instance to treat the injured rather than being held back for fear of secondary devices. In both cases, inadequate mitigation and emergency response planning fell short of the type of vision required for them to have been addressed by quadrant 2 foresight.

Similarly, we see in quadrant 4 scenarios 45, 46 and 54, 55 in the highly unlikely category also appear in quadrant 3: (scenario 45 is highly unlikely but preferable with low probability/high impact whereas scenario 54 is also highly unlikely but is undesirable with low probability/high impact). The events being unpredictable could appear any time—even within 3 years. Such is the high level of uncertainty pertaining to this category of scenario that depending on the rate of change of awareness within an outlier event, an occurrence may morph from a Q4 black swan into a Q3 grey swan without the analyst or decision-maker being aware of what is happening. A detailed breakdown is shown in Appendix 7.

https://www.strategyforesight.co.uk/general-5

7.4.1   So, How Does This All Work and What Does It All Mean: A Process Summary?

The final part of this section describes a summarised version of the above process and allows the readers to view the whole path and rationale for deploying such a methodology.

1. *Phase 1:* Analysis of various types of scenario outcomes (sources include Vuosa, Marchau et al. (DMDU), Kuosa, Curry, & Schultz, Gowing & Langdon).
2. *Phase 2:* Establishment of a problem space (PS) for scenario options based on four core variables:

   (a) Contextual (with six different states)
   (b) Conditional (with three states)
   (c) Occurrence/impact (seven states)
   (d) Time horizon (seven states)

   PS matrix generates 882 different configuration scenarios as follows (Fig. 7.7):

   – Pair-wise analysis reduces the PS to a solution space of 130 viable/consistent solutions.
   – A second reductive iteration discards an additional 34 configurations (high occurrence/high impact and high occurrence/low impact options) as being scenarios which we know about and thus of little exploratory interest.
   – A third iteration reduces the set to 64 scenarios based on those configurations which are either preferable or undesirable.

3. *Phase 3:* Allocate the 64 solution options to the four quadrants within the uncertainty/risk profile matrix (from Chap. 2) as in Table 7.1 below.
4. *Phase 4:* Allocate scenario to options list and location within uncertainty profile matrix detailed in Appendix 7—https://www.strategyforesight.co.uk/general-5

What this process allows us to do is to help decision-makers and their analysts to narrow down the options faced by scenario strategists and planners. Importantly, it helps identify what are the challenges faced by them in order to elicit responses which will lead to action. Quadrants 2 and especially 3 present the greatest

Contextual	Conditional	Occurrence/Impact	Time Horizon
Predicted	Preferable	High Occurrence/Low Impact	< 1 year
Probable	Undersirable	High Occurrence/High Impact	< 3 years
Possible	Not Sure (Agnostic)	Low Occurrence/Low Impact	<5 years
Plausible		Low Occurrence/High Impact	5-10 years
Highly Unlikely		Possible in Science Fiction	11-20 years
Unthinkable		Possible in S-F but w/o current knowledge	21-30 years
		Possible in Imagination & Theory	31 years +

Fig. 7.7 Generation of configurations from the problem space

Table 7.1 Allocation of preferable and undesirable scenarios to the uncertainty profile

	Identifiable/known	Unidentifiable/unknown
Predictable/ known	Q1. Known-known (I know what I know) Scenarios 1–2 predicted Scenarios 3–6 probable	Q2. Known-unknown (I know what I don't know) Scenarios 3–6 probable Scenarios 7–24 possible
Unpredictable/ unknown	Q3. Unknown-known (I don't know what I know or I think I know but turns out I don't) Scenarios 8, 10 and 17, 19 possible Scenarios 25–44 plausible Scenarios 45, 46 and 54, 55 highly unlikely	Q4. Unknown-unknown (I don't know what I don't know) Scenarios 45–62 highly unlikely Scenarios 63, 64 unthinkable

challenges as the boundaries between the various scenario categories become increasingly blurred—a situation which makes decision-makers constrained by key resources such as time and money particularly leads them to concentrate more on shorter time frames. This, of course, yields ground to a position of decreased preparedness for low probability/high impact events and the intendant consequences.

7.5   Methods, Tools, and Techniques

In this extended final section, I'll be introducing two decision support methods (DSM) along with a case example. One of the DSMs has already been used in the first parts of this chapter to help identify viable scenario categories.

7.5.1   Morphological Analysis (MA)

Unfortunately, this first DSM has the rather scary title of morphological analysis (MA) but may be better understood using the term *"strategic options analysis"*

(SOA) which is how I have described it in earlier sections. To date its exposure to the uncertainty and futures community has been limited and overlooked, partly through it being seen as rather time-consuming combined, more importantly, with the "combinatorial explosion" that the method generates so that it can appear unmanageable—unless computer assisted. Such computer software has been around for the last couple of decades but not been easy to access. Encouraged by the intervention of a neutral facilitator along with a preference for cross-functional and cross-disciplinary teams, it can prove invaluable as a decision support tool under conditionals of high levels of uncertainty where hard data is in short supply.

What really is MA? Morphological analysis (MA) belongs to a broader set of methods in the decision support area known as problem structuring methods (PSMs)—methods which were highlighted in Chap. 3. As we know PSMs are a set of methodologies to support groups confronted with problems involving multiple actors, conflicting perspectives, and key uncertainties. PSMs enable the structuring and analysis of complex problems which:

- Are inherently non-quantifiable
- Are stakeholder orientated with strong socio-political, cultural, and technical positions
- Contain non-resolvable uncertainties
- Cannot be modelled easily or simulated
- Require a judgemental approach to be placed on a sound methodological basis

Morphological analysis (MA) itself is an extension of the morphological method, and was developed in its more generalised form in the period 1940–70 by the astrophysicist Fritz Zwicky (1947, 1948, 1962, 1967, 1969). Heuer and Pherson (2011) offer a broad definition of MA which encapsulates its generic status as a PSM:

> ...is a method for systematically structuring and examining all the possible relationships in a multidimensional, highly complex, usually non-quantifiable problem space. The basic idea is to identify a set of variables and then look at all the possible combinations of these variables......and reduces the chance that events will play out in a way that the analyst has not previously imagined and considered.

Zwicky and later Jantsch (1967) and Ayres (1969) initially applied morphological analysis to explore potential technological breakthroughs for engineering design purposes. In the 1980s, Majaro (1988) advocated its value as a creativity and ideation method. In the 1990s, MA was applied more to the futures and socio-economic fields and in the 2000s into a more general methodology (Ritchey, 2006, 2011) targeting the broader aspect of "wicked problems", with inherent high levels of "systems uncertainties" (Funtowicz & Ravetz, 1994). As a generic method, MA can be used in any one or combination of the following core streams:

1. Ideation and technology forecasting
2. Futures and scenario planning
3. Systems uncertainties (aka "wicked" problems)

In a morphological model, there is no pre-defined driver or independent variable (or parameter). Any variable—or set of variables or discrete conditions within the main variable—can be designated as a driver. It is this ability to define any combination of conditions as an input or output that gives morphological models such flexibility. Thus, given a certain set of conditions—what is inferred with respect to other conditions in the model? This "what-if" functionality makes MA an extremely powerful tool, and when combined with software, allows researchers to explore viable alternatives in real time from very large configurations of variables and conditions (also known as the problem space). In essence MA can be introduced to help shape and identify possible paths for analysts of all types (be they designers, forecasters, creatives, and policy framework initiators). This flexibility in determining what the main variables and parameters to a problem are makes MA a particularly useful tool for developing exploratory scenarios whilst encouraging high levels of objectivity. For reactive scenarios, a MA model can be used to interrogate second and third order scenario options as well.

MA fits our criteria for modelling uncertainty, especially when dealing with large amounts of intangible data, and can be updated and modified in real time, especially where it incorporates strong facilitation with "stretched" teams of multi-disciplinary experts.

This form of morphological analysis straddles the fence between "hard" and "soft" scientific modelling. It is built upon the basic scientific method of going through cycles of analysis and synthesis and parameterising a problem space. It defines structured variables, and thus creates a real, dynamic model, i.e. a linked variable space in which inputs can be given, outputs obtained, and hypotheses ("what-if" assertions) made.

MA can help us discover new relationships or configurations, which may not be so evident, or that might have been overlooked by other, less structured, methods. It can also be used to highlight potential weak signals and outliers using the concept of "morphological distance" (Ayres, 1969). Importantly, it encourages the identification and investigation of boundary conditions, i.e. the limits and extremes of different contexts and problem variables. It provides a structured environment within which to handle uncertainty (and even deep or radical uncertainty) and is an exploratory method par excellence.

In its most basic form MA can be broken into three core processes.

- Generation of the problem space
- Pair-wise analysis
- Compilation of the solution space
- Recently developed and available software and processes (Garvey, 2016) have now overcome a traditional criticism of MA, in that it creates so many potential configurations or outcomes in the problem space as to be unmanageable. The combinatorial explosion of options created by MA can now be majorly reduced (typically over 95%), leaving the analyst to review a much smaller set of viable, internally consistent solutions. A summary of the overall MA process is illustrated in three definite phases as below (Table 7.2).

Table 7.2 MA three phase process

Phase 1 *Generate the entire problem space (steps 1–6)*	• Identification of the main problem being addressed • Selecting an expert team representing the key stake-holders • Determining a focus question which encapsulates the problem • Facilitating the expert team to generate a problem space made up of the key parameters of the problem and then the states/dimensions within each of the parameters • *The first steps here may require external facilitation and stakeholder management to finely structure the problem—before programming the software to generate the problem space which reflects the total number of possible configurations to be addressed*
Phase 2 *Perform cross-consistency assessment (steps 7–8)*	This phase involves a form of cross-impact or pair-wise analysis where the problem space is transposed[a] and each state within a parameter is assessed for consistency against every other state within the other parameters (i.e. can these two states logically co-exist). If they cannot, then every configuration where such an inconsistent pair exists is discarded
Phase 3 *Generate the solution space for decision support (steps 9–10)*	Supporting software compiles those configurations only where all pairs within a configuration are consistent with each other. This process can eliminate over 95% of the original problem space to produce a set of viable, internally consistent solutions. These solutions are presented as "what-if" scenarios where any dimension in a parameter can be an input or an output

[a]Transposition software converts the problem space into the cross-consistency matrix (cross-impact and assessment). Once this latter matrix has been completed (or assessed), then the software goes into compile mode, discarding those configurations which contain any one or more pairs of inconsistent arguments as determined by the expert team. The remaining fully consistent configurations are then presented as a solution space

As highlighted earlier in a morphological model, there is no automatically designated driver or independent variable. Any variable (parameter)—or set of conditions within a variable—can be designated as such. Thus, anything can be an input and anything an output. For instance, instead of simply letting a scenario stakeholder define a relevant strategy, one can reverse the process and let chosen states within a proposed strategy configuration designate relevant scenarios. This is the basis of an inference model: given a certain set of conditions, what is inferred with respect to other conditions in the model?

The "what-if" functionality makes the model an extremely powerful tool, for not only looking at a wide array of possible outcomes, but through computerisation enables management and researchers to examine alternatives in real time.

Operating at the fuzzier end of the uncertainty/risk spectrum, a central feature of morphological analysis is the flexibility it provides to parameterise a problem complex, acting as scene setter for other decision support methods. In this case, the results of a morphological model can provide input for the development of other (possibly more complex) models such as Bayesian belief networks (BBNs) and multi-criteria decision analysis (MCDA) methods such as AHP—the analytic hierarchy method. Here, possible outcomes derived via a MA exercise can be compared according to a hierarchy of goals and goal criteria, providing validated inputs for scenario planning exercises.

When supported by pair-wise analysis, where pairs of sub-variables within all the variables are assessed for viability or consistency (i.e. can the pairs live with each other), MA is a method for rigorously structuring and investigating the internal properties of inherently non-quantifiable problem complexes and empowers practitioners to explore a wide variety of contrasting configurations and policy solutions. As a method for identifying and investigating the total set of possible relationships or "configurations" contained in a given problem complex MA's primary task is to generate ideas with the aim of generating as many opportunities as possible. Such functionality makes it ideal for not only generating new scenarios but qualifying them as well.[1]

Yes, but...!

Whilst an excellent concept for generating (thousands or even millions of) ideas or scenarios/configurations derived from multiple variables, it does create a practical problem of how to analyse all the configurations generated by the model's initial problem space.

The solution is to reduce this vast number to examining "*. . . the internal relationships between the field parameters and to reduce the field by identifying, and weeding out, all mutually contradictory conditions*" (Ritchey, 2011). This is carried out for each matrix by an exercise called pair-wise analysis or cross-consistency assessment (CCA), where all of the parameter values or main variables in the matrix field are compared with one another on a pair-wise basis—similar to a cross-impact matrix. As each pair of conditions is explored a judgement is made to see if the pair can co-exist. Note: It is important to understand there is no reference to causality—only to mutual consistency. Via this process, a typical morphological field can be reduced by well over 95% internally consistent configurations. Actual exercises carried out by the author show that the larger the problem space in terms of configurations generated, the greater the tendency there is to increase the 95% reduction, highlighted above, to much higher levels. Conversely where a problem space has just a few thousand configurations or even a few hundred then lower percentage reductions are to be expected.

The graphic below shows an example of a completed pair-wise matrix, post-problem space creation but prior to compilation of the viable solutions. The original problem space consisting of seven main variables yielded 80,640 configurations. After the pair-wise analysis (as shown in the matrix), a solution space of 5671 of potentially viable solutions was generated—a reduction of 93% (Fig. 7.8).

---

[1] On Strategy Foresight Ltd.'s website a number of video presentations are available and involve a number of examples as to its operational working.

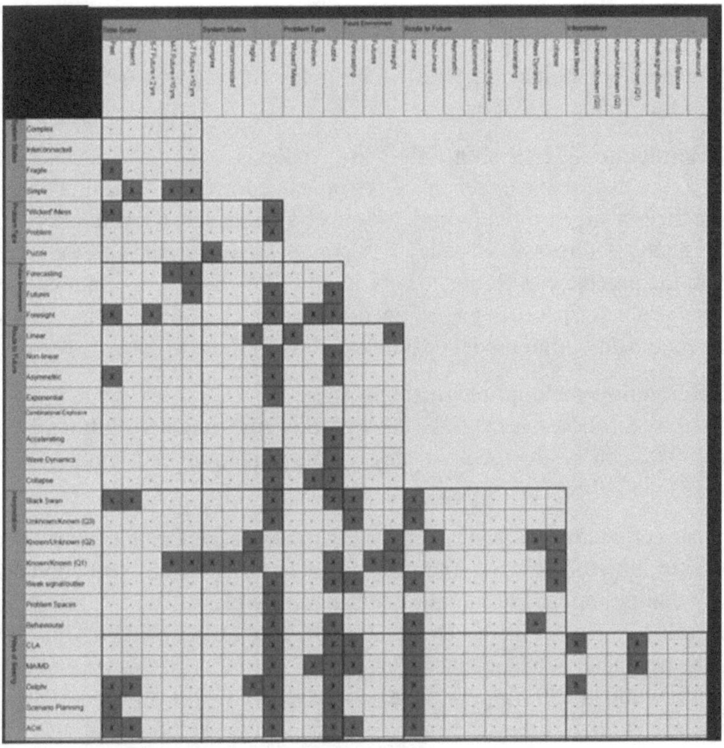

Fig. 7.8 Pair-wise analysis table

Compilation, whereby inconsistent pairs as presented in the matrix are eliminated, allows the original problem space to be converted into a solution space—the latter operating as an interactive inference model where any parameter or state can be selected as an input and any other as an output.

7.6   A New Approach to Identifying Weak Signals for Scenario Development Using MA: Distance Analysis

7.6.1   Using MA as a Tool to Draw Out Weak Signals

Whilst the combinatorial explosion of options created by MA can now be majorly reduced (typically over 95%), leaving the analyst to review a much smaller set of viable, internally consistent solutions. The question still exists as to "what can we do with the viable options identified"?

Those concerns that manifest themselves in quadrant 3 in the uncertainty profile matrix (unknown/knowns) can be mitigated by the deployment of two mutually supporting methodological methods—morphological analysis (MA) and morphological distance analysis (MD).

Level 1 Reduction—MA Using Pair-Wise Analysis

Suffice it to say that we have seen in the previous section on MA the first phase of the process reduces a large problem space to a much smaller set of viable solutions using pair-wise analysis (cross-consistency assessment—CCA). And, as we have seen, this part of the process can eliminate very large volumes of configurations present in the original problem space. Even so how does one analyse the often large number of solutions produced by the model in order to classify them in some way?

Level 2 Reduction—Morphological Distance

When used as a follow-on from the MA process once viable solutions have been generated, MD can be deployed to classify the remaining configurations (Garvey et al., 2013) via a triage process (Ayres, 1969).

By resurrecting Robert Ayres' concept of *morphological distance (MD)*, and using it as a follow-on process, once the pair-wise analysis has been conducted, the remaining configurations can be more meaningfully classified via a triage process. Ayres identifies three forms of classification (or triage): occupied territory (state of the art), the perimeter zone, and "terra incognita", the latter two criteria consisting of those configurations differing from state of the art whilst still remaining viable solutions. Given the distance from identified viable solutions in the occupied territory, terra incognita solutions are likely to be truly creative and "off radar". Such configurations can thus be assumed to be very similar in nature to a weak signal as they will be at the periphery of the analyst's vision. Ayres' triage approach can be said to introduce a form of disintermediation into the distance determining process.

Ayres defines morphological distance (MD) as being the distance between two points in the (problem) space and is:

> the number of parameters wherein the two configurations differ from one another. Two configurations differing in only a single parameter are morphologically close together, while two configurations differing in many parameters are morphologically far apart.

Note: It is important to clarify firstly that Ayres' use of the term parameter is really a discrete state within the selected parameter and that a configuration consists of a selected individual state in each of the parameters which make up the overall problem space. Secondly, it should be noted that the areas and boundaries of each sector will be subjective according to the particular technology or design being evaluated, and to the consensual subjectivity of a team of experts introduced to assist in determining the problem parameters and states of the morphological space.

The three sectors Ayres specifies are:

1. Known or occupied territory (OT)—composed of those configurations identified as representing "existing art" or (state of the art—SoA). This is the area where minimal innovation is likely to occur because it is already known.

2. The perimeter zone (PZ)—those configurations which contain between, say, 2 and 3 parameter/states different from state of the art (SoA). Configurations with just a two parameter/state distance are closest to the SoA or occupied territory sector and thus will have limited innovative potential. In essence they can be said to represent some form of basic product development: the low-risk option. On the other hand, those configurations with a parameter/state distance of 3 show a heightened level of innovation being further away from OT at the outer fringes of the perimeter zone. Event indicators in this quadrant are asymmetric which makes it difficult to ascertain the relative importance of signals.

3. "Terra incognita" or unknown territory (TI) is composed of those configurations characterised by a distance factor of 4 or more parameter/states from SoA. According to Ayres, these configurations are so different from SoA that *they are likely to embrace configurations containing something which has not previously been considered, thus increasing the probability of some form of technological breakthrough.* Possible configurations appearing in this sector are as likely to be truly creative as well as innovative or in the case of scenarios offer wild card options as true outliers. Within scenarios they may reflect unintended consequences—good or bad, but nonetheless possible and worth identification and examination. Conversely where refinements/improvements occur which are similar to an "existing art" configuration (differing up to 1 parameter/state cell), there is little chance of a breakthrough.

Specifically, Ayres mentions that:

> The probability of a breakthrough in a technological area, per unit of time, is a decreasing function of its morphological distance from existing art, other things being equal.

Such configurations, allocated to the terra incognita (TI) zone, and being significantly different from SoA options, are more likely to offer analysts the probability of a technological or alternative scenario breakthrough as given the distance from identified viable solutions in the OT territory, outlier solutions are likely to be truly creative and "off radar". *Such configurations can thus be assumed to be very similar in nature to a weak signal as they will be at the periphery of the analyst's vision.*

The combined MA and MD process can be represented as follows (Fig. 7.9):

7.6.2   Issue of Determining What Is Current Knowledge (State of the Art)

It is apparent that the determination of distance begs the question, "distance from what"? Within the viable solution sets, those configurations deemed to reflect SoA (in occupied territory) act as the base set of configurations from which more distance sets in the PZ or TI zones can be determined. It is thus crucial that identifying the parameter profile of OT solutions be made easily and as objectively as possible. As a manual exercise this may take some time, bearing in mind that OT selection should

Isolating Weak Signals

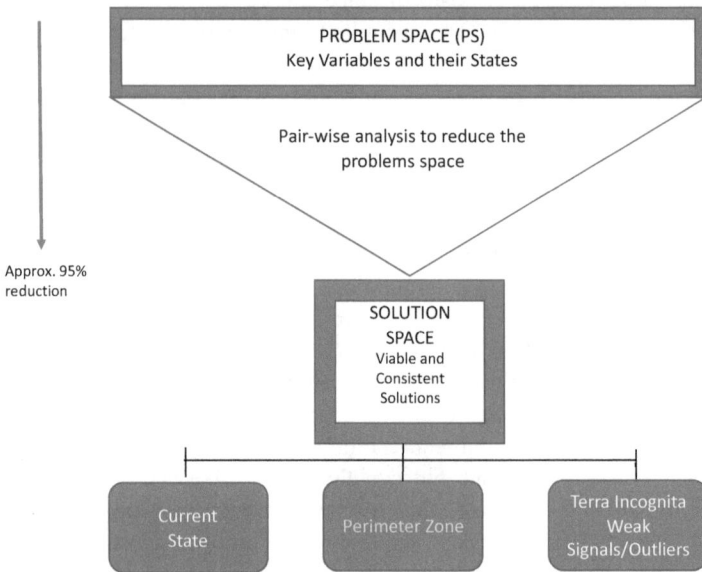

Fig. 7.9 Process for isolating weak signals

be carried by the team who generated the original problem space and CCA exercise. In the future, it may be of value to see how data mining might short-circuit the process. By way of comparison the Delphi method process is somewhat cumbersome and iterative. The above form of process would undoubtedly reduce the risk of introducing highly levels of subjectivity introduced by using weighting factors too early.

In the graphic (Fig. 7.10) one of the outlier scenarios is shown (configuration with red cells), which is at the maximum distance from the anchor scenario (purple cells)—i.e. the selected scene has passed muster as a solution, but is very much an outlier in relation to current knowledge or policy—across all six of the variables.

For ease of presentation, it is assumed that following a CCA exercise the original problem space of 5184 configurations has been reduced to some 38 internally consistent scenes.

More recent researchers have attempted to introduce distance concepts in relation to morphological spaces. Gallasch et al. (2017) talk about the degree of overlap and degrees of divergence when comparing configurations in a morphological space. Overlap and divergence are terms very similar to Ayres' concept of difference mentioned earlier and repeated here for context:

> the number of parameters wherein the two configurations differ from one another. Two configurations differing in only a single parameter are morphologically close together, while two configurations differing in many parameters are morphologically far apart.

How to identify outliers and weak signals from reduced sets

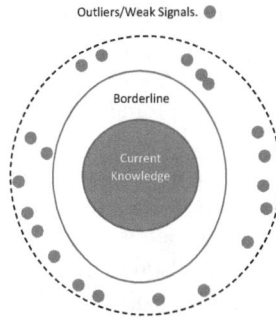

Fig. 7.10 Identifying outliers

However, Gallasch et al. then go on to try and weight factors within a sector as well as weighting the sectors themselves (within the morphological space). The issue of weighting has arisen before by observers of the morphological method. The authors' view is that the introduction of weighting too early in the process can introduce a quantitative-based bias into a space which in turn can degrade the inherent objectivity of the morphological process. MA itself is a method which is highly suitable for representing highly uncertain and "fuzzy" situations which allows for the integration of both qualitative and quantitative factors. By introducing weighting metrics too early may introduce subjective bias (as to the weighting criteria themselves) and/or attempt to quantify the unquantifiable in terms of the qualitative inputs into the morphological problem space and the cross-consistency assessment analysis phases.

The author recognises nonetheless that the status of configurations within the occupied territory zone is crucial to the parametric distance process as the OT configurations themselves provide the base from which the parameter distances are determined. However, the Gallasch weighting approach may be a useful way of placing into a hierarchy those configurations identified as being in the TI zone.

7.7   Catastrophic and Existential Risks

"Doomed—we're all doomed" Private Frazer—a stalwart of "Dad's Army"

This section looks at those risks which are truly external—and by external, I mean those events which occur beyond the control of an individual, group, organisation, or even a nation or nations—and in the case of catastrophic risks they are generally global in scale and impact.

These risks are typically low probability/high impact (LP/HI) events and fall into the category of highly unlikely or unthinkable—in most cases they are not pleasant. The challenge of such events for decision- and policy-makers is how much resources and scaled-up contingency planning should be committed for events which may not occur in the foreseeable future—which prompts the question what is the foreseeable future?

In reaction to a LP/HI event such as a global pandemic (e.g. COVID-19), reactive scenarios are based on an event which has already happened—although it can be argued that the pandemic was not such a low probability event. Climate change, on the other hand, was originally seen as a LP/HI event but has morphed in character so that it can no longer be seen as a low probability event. There is too much evidence that climate change is happening, albeit the ongoing changes are spread over lengthy time periods which may reduce the sense of urgency by humans (and policy-makers). Although it is happening and indeed accelerating, no one can forecast with any accuracy what the outcomes will be over short-, medium-, and long-term time horizons—multiple variables which are also dynamic in nature create a highly uncertain set of future circumstances.

Two terms are used for this category of risks (or levels of uncertainty)—*catastrophic* and *existential*. But what is a catastrophic risk compared to an existential one?

They are different but like those two terms, risk and uncertainty, they are often used interchangeably so that the terms global catastrophic risk and existential risk are misinterpreted as being the same and used interchangeably.

Much of the reference source material in this chapter has been extracted from two eminent experts in catastrophic and existential risk—Nick Bostrom at Oxford and Toby Ord (2020) at Cambridge. Bostrom is the founding director of the Future of Humanity Institute at Oxford University. Ord is senior research fellow at the same institute. Other work carried out in a similar vein is at Cambridge University's Centre for the Study of Existential Risk (CSER), and studies possible extinction-level threats posed by present or future technology.

Back in 2008 Bostrom and Cirkovic (2008) defined the term *"global catastrophic risks"* as

> a risk that might have a potential to inflict serious damage to human well-being on a global scale.

They acknowledged that such a definition was very broad which embraced events ranging from

> volcanic eruptions to pandemic infections, nuclear accidents to worldwide tyrannies, out-of-control scientific experiments to climate changes and cosmic hazards to economic collapse.

Bostrom and Cirkovic go on to suggest that a sub-set of global catastrophic risk is existential risks and where:

An existential risk is one that threatens to cause the extinction of Earth-originating intelligent life or to reduce its quality of life permanently and drastically.

They identify that specific to an existential risk is the feature that:

as it is not possible to recover from existential risks we cannot allow even one existential disaster to happen; there would be no opportunity to learn from the experience.

Interestingly, they qualify this interpretation by stating that managing such risks must be pro-active—there is no opportunity to be reactive. This would seem to place scenario development primarily in the domain of the exploratory—negating automatically a reactive response.

This interpretation claims that whilst a global catastrophic risk may kill the vast majority of life on earth, humanity could still potentially recover. On the other hand, an existential risk either destroys humanity entirely or prevents any chance of civilisation's recovery. It is strange therefore that the term "existential" tends to be used more by observers, pundits, and politicians alike rather than the term "catastrophic". Numerous commentators during the COVID-19 pandemic have described it as being an "existential" threat. It isn't, because although severe at the global level it is unlikely to wipe out all human life—but it is catastrophic! Remember that in Medieval Europe the Black Death wiped out roughly one-third of the population yet European mankind survived without suffering anything close to a collapse of civilisation (although by bringing about a shortage of manual labour due to the high death rate it did help bring about the demise of feudalism in much of Europe).

In brief then, *"a global catastrophic risk may kill the vast majority of life on earth, humanity could still potentially recover. An existential risk, on the other hand, is one that either destroys humanity entirely or prevents any chance of civilization's recovery"*[2]—the latter is definitely nastier!

7.7.1   Welcome to the Anthropocene

The Anthropocene era has been postulated as reflecting the influence and impact of human behaviour and action (and indeed inaction) on the Earth's geology, ecosystems, and atmosphere in recent times. This influence is seen as being so significant as to constitute a new geological epoch.

The term was popularised in 2000 by chemist Paul Crutzen, and there are a number of different opinions as to when it began. One view is that it started as soon as humans became established on the planet, another being the start of the industrial revolution whilst a more recent argument is that it was the Trinity explosion—the testing of the first atomic bomb in July 1945. The latter position is based on the ease with which mankind could destroy itself through its own technological

---

[2] Wikipedia definition.

Table 7.3 Different interpretations summarised

Ord	Bostrom and Cirkovic
Natural risks, asteroids and comets, supervolcanic eruptions, stellar explosions, other natural risks	*Risks from nature*, supervolcanism, asteroids and comets, gamma ray bursts, solar flares, etc.
Anthropogenic risk nuclear weapons, climate change, environmental damage	*Risks from unintended consequences*, climate change, pandemics, AI, runaway tech, social collapse
Future risks pandemics, unaligned AI, dystopian scenarios, runaway nanotech, alien invasion	*Risks from hostile acts*, nuclear war, nuclear/bioterrorism, biotech and biosecurity, nano-tech, totalitarian risk

inventiveness. Whatever the specific date of origin, Anthropogenic risks are *caused by humans or their activities*.

Bostrom, Cirkovic, and Ord's interpretation of global catastrophic and existential risk, along with examples, can be summarised as follows (Table 7.3):

As we can see there are a number of ways to cut the catastrophic/existential risk "cake".

Both Ord and Bostrom agree on natural risks (risks from nature). Ord specifically includes Anthropogenic risks, whereas the closest Bostrom comes to anthropogenic influence is in the identification of risks from hostile acts (i.e. by people). Ord is a little more expansive in his categories which he classifies as future risks such as pandemics, AI, and alien invasion, whereas Bostrom sees pandemics and climate change as unintended consequences (which of course do take place in the future).

Can Global Catastrophic Risks Turn into Existential Risks?

The other consideration is whether global catastrophic risks can morph into existential ones. Well, of course, they can—for example, a pandemic virus can move from being classified as a catastrophic/anthropogenic risk to an existential/bad actor risk via deliberate genetic manipulation by a bad actor and where the virus runs out of control through untreatable (in time) virulence.

7.7.2   MTT: Support Tool

In order to identify both catastrophic and existential risks as separate categories, the following schema allocates different types of such risks to three event groups.

- Natural risks
- Anthropogenic risks
- Hostile/bad actor risks

Each cell is populated with risks according to the catastrophic/existential and the natural/anthropogenic/bad actor axes. It is to be noted that the separate events are not

Table 7.4 Risk type categorisation

	Natural risks	Anthropogenic risks	Hostile/bad actor risks
Global catastrophic	Gamma ray bursts, solar flares, shifts in Earth's magnetic field	Nuclear war, climate change, environmental damage, pandemics, over-population, social collapse	Nuclear/bioterrorism, tech-based intrusions (hacking, denial of service), cyber warfare, increasing totalitarianism (government or corporate)
Existential	Asteroids, comets, supervolcanic eruptions, stellar explosions	Unaligned AI, runaway nanotech	Hostile extra-terrestrial invasion. Deliberate release of doomsday weapons

exclusive but are just indications of how different events can be categorised (Table 7.4).

7.7.3 Allocating the Risks to the Uncertainty Profile

Each of the cells contains identifiable risks. Uncertainty resides in when, if, and how such events will take place. Recognition of these events, no matter how unthinkable and unpleasant, is a basic step so that contingency scenarios can be developed. Planners and analysts should therefore attempt to allocate different scenario options identified in the previous chapter to each of the items listed in the catastrophe/risk matrix above. If they can remove themselves from being in an unthinkable mode of thought then at least some provision will have been made to avoid a future situation whereby *"we didn't see it coming"*. The main judgement call, however, will relate to the time horizons that analysts and decision-makers might base selected scenarios on.

The key take-away though is to treat this category of uncertainty as worthy of an exploratory approach. Scenarios need to reflect here: the development of strategies and actions which are less mitigation but set up to avoid such events or at least avoiding the worst effects should they occur in one form or another. Such is the severity of the impacts of each of the above that they need to be treated as more existential impacts whether catastrophic or existential, as the likelihood of learning from the experience is majorly reduced, i.e. let's scare people.

As highlighted earlier we can treat exploratory scenarios as initially primary events—as long as the analysts are aware of second and third order and more events. On this assumption, then of the six cells identified above, planners should concentrate on those events which a technologically enhanced political society "could" influence in some way. The two prime areas are thus defined as being anthropogenic risks and bad actor risks along the global catastrophic risks axis—the bad actor group itself being anthropogenic in the ways such risks manifest themselves. Across the existential axis, how mankind reacts to the development of technologies such as

AI and nanotechnology, both potentially capable of becoming runaway and uncontrollable, places them firmly in the anthropogenic camp—humans generated such technologies. Similarly, the deliberate release of doomsday weapons by bad actors also requires "manual" intervention and thus inception of such devices needs to be closely observed and monitored.

From this analysis, it does appear that the major threats will be generated by our own species—as a result these should not be thought of as Q4 unknown-unknowns but as Q2 known-unknowns. Unfortunately, mitigation responses are likely to be limited by mankind continuing to manifest Q3 behaviour, treating the risk as a Q4 and failing to think about the unthinkable—unable or unwilling to stop treating the risk as an unknown-known. This is the true challenge for analyst and decision-makers—bringing uncertainty in from the cold!

7.8   Case Examples

In this section, a summary is given which validates the MA/MD approach in generating identifiable outlier and weak signals.

The case study (Garvey et al., 2013) addressed the focus question: "What possible configurations can the design of an apartment block take, which ensures cross-ventilation and sufficient daylight". Admittedly this is not a futures exercise *per se* but it does highlight the concept of morphological distance and configuration reduction.

The question was chosen so that it could be easily translated in parametric geometry terms and to show that additional focus questions (e.g. energy usage or glare analysis) could be used applying the same methodological approach. The methodology helped to design new options for apartment typology. A ten-parameter problem space, composed of 155,520 configurations, was initially reduced by deploying morphological analysis (and CCA) then reduced further using morphological distance triage principles. The two-stage process generated a 99.9% reduction of the initial (155k configuration) problem space, to a mere 213 internally consistent options classified as being in the terra incognita zone. Such was the remoteness from current state of the art that these 213 options qualify as representing weak signal configurations.

The final 213 solutions, post-morphological distance, were found to be distanced 4–5 parameters away from existing, state-of-the-art, solutions (from a ten-parameter configuration set). Finally, these terra incognita solutions were processed by a visual algorithmic editor and output as tri-dimensional CAD models which in turn could be easily evaluated and analysed by the designer. A more detailed description is provided in Appendices 8 and 9.

7.8.1 A Scenario Based Example

The chapter ends with a simplified and theoretical case example as to how the process plays out at a geo-economic level.

This basic example looks at the impact of a major volcanic eruption in the Northern European Hemisphere. As such an event has not occurred in the last 5 years the scenario can be termed an exploratory one and not a reactive one, albeit that it is based on one major anticipated event.

The most recent impactful volcanic eruption in Northern Europe occurred in 2010 with the Eyjafjallajökull eruption in Iceland. We are fortunate in that past eruptions can provide major insights into the impact of such events and thus it is worth reviewing what actually happened with that eruption and what were the impacts. The following sub-set, taken mainly from Wikipedia, outlines some of the historical data and features of the event.

Although comparatively small for volcanic eruptions, the Eyjafjallajökull eruption caused enormous disruption to air travel across western and northern Europe in April of that year as ash from the eruption covered large areas of Northern Europe. About 20 countries closed their airspace to commercial jet traffic affecting around 10 million travellers—the highest level of air travel disruption since WW2. The volcanic activity impacted air travel due to a number of factors:

- The volcano is directly under the jet stream.
- The direction of the jet stream was unusually stable at the time of the eruption's second phase, continuously southeast.
- The second eruptive phase happened under 200 m (660 ft) of glacial ice. The resulting meltwater flowed back into the erupting volcano, which created two specific phenomena:

  - The rapidly vaporising water significantly increased the eruption's explosive power.
  - The erupting lava cooled very fast, which created a cloud of highly abrasive, glass-rich ash.

- The volcano's explosive power was enough to inject ash directly into the jet stream.
- Volcanic ash is a major hazard to aircraft. Smoke and ash from eruptions reduce visibility for visual navigation, and microscopic debris in the ash can sandblast windscreens and melt in the heat of aircraft turbine engines, damaging engines and making them shut down.

The eruption was not large enough to have an effect on global temperatures like that of Mount Pinatubo in 1991 which resulted in worldwide abnormal weather and decrease in global temperature over the next few years.

Its short-term economic effects were sharp and profound, but it was the combination of factors—each with its own level of probability, which exacerbated the problem—so again applying the dictum "if it can happen—it will happen".

To begin with let us try and identify how such scenarios can be categorised—how are they configured? From the risk/uncertainty profile matrix, such an event will be located in quadrant 2 as a known-unknown. We know such an eruption will happen—we just don't know when and where precisely.

Within Q2 there are two scenario categories "probable" and "possible". Based on historical records it can be stated that the event is "probable", being at a higher order of probability than "possible". Any new eruption on a scale similar to or greater than Eyjafjallajökull can be characterised as having the following configuration "probable—undesirable—high occurrence/high impact within 1 year or 3 years". Beyond 3 years we might add scenarios characterised as being "possible—undesirable—low occurrence/high impact within 5 or 10 years".

One may ask why add the extra "possible" scenario? The argument here is that one needs to challenge or stretch the policy-makers' thought processes across an array of viable alternatives. The danger of not using the possible longer term horizon scenarios is that mitigating actions might be delayed, thus endangering the efficacy of contingency planning should the event occur sooner rather than later. Whilst accepting that in the longer term some scenarios will require a longer lead time for the development of such contingency plans. Using this argument, it would be logical therefore for decision-makers to request the detailed development of multiple scenarios.

However, there is the additional danger that by using the Icelandic eruption as the main historical model, the analysts might erroneously assume that any future eruption in Northern Europe would be of the same intensity as that of Eyjafjallajökull—identified as a Category 4 on the VEI index (Volcanic Explosivity Index). What if the eruption were to be a VEI 5 category (similar to Mount St Helens in 1980) or a VEI 6 (similar to Mount Pinatubo of 1991)—there are eight VEI categories in total. In Italy, Vesuvius is the only volcano on the European mainland to have erupted within the last 100 years (Etna is on an island), and regarded as one of the most dangerous volcanoes in the world because of the population of 3,000,000 people living nearby as well as its tendency towards violent, explosive eruptions of the Plinian type (as was Mount St Helens). And Vesuvius is overdue a major eruption!

So, whilst a model based on the original Icelandic explosion might yield a variety of scenario development options, it would be remiss of policy-makers and planners not to include additional scenarios in quadrant 3—the dangerous "unknown-known" sector such as "possible-undesirable-low occurrence/high impact within 1 or 3 years" and "plausible-undesirable-low occurrence/high impact with 1 or 3 years". Yet by doing so we can elevate the event for a quadrant 3 (where post-event excuses can be made) to a quadrant 2 type event and where contingency plans can be prepared.

By including these additional four narratives the decision-makers, faced with lower probability occurrences within shorter time frames, would be acting with major foresight by seeking out these outliers as a form of insurance. In other words, by just altering one variable description of an event, it is shown how important it is to adjust, if not increase, the number of scenarios requiring review in a controlled and responsible manner.

The example being addressed has concentrated on exploring the impact of a major first order event. It is also necessary to look at second order events emanating from this first event apart from the immediate damage to the surrounding area and risk to life (described as derivative scenarios). As an example, we saw that the particular height and nature of the Icelandic eruption created severe disruption to air traffic as the plume was spread by the jet stream. Depending on the severity of the eruption—such as that of Mount Pinatubo—other conditions such as the ejection of a very large number of particulates into the atmosphere causing climate change effects can be anticipated. Derivative effects, some causal and some asymmetric, could be severe economic and social disruption and health service breakdown especially amongst large urban populations close to the eruption—as in the case of Vesuvius—apart from more geographic dispersion of the physical effects. And with climate change already a critical concern, additional stimuli could accelerate such change further at a very climatically sensitive time. Each of these second and third order events need to be examined according to a separate set of profile configurations—hence the usefulness of the scenario outcome options index (see Sect. 8.3) albeit that different configurations might be selected from the index.

7.9   A Concluding Set of Questions

At a more general level of enquiry one can compile a short list of questions to be asked by the scenario writer as a starting point and in relation to an event identified via this exploratory process such as:

- What time horizon should we be looking at for another major eruption?
- What type and severity of eruption should be considered?
- What locations are the most active and need to be considered?
- What primary impacts should be expected?
- What second and third order impact might we expect?
- What climate impact should we expect—short, medium, long?
- How long will such impacts affect us?
- What uncertainties have not been analysed or considered? (Maybe the unthinkable?)
- What scenario options do we need to identify and prioritise?
- How quickly should we carry out the scenarios and implement their findings?
- What resources do we have? Do we need to access more within the time frame?

This is by no means an exhaustive list and I'm sure you can add to them—think of these as a part of a starter pack.

Summary

The presence of high levels of uncertainty makes the task of identifying weak signals and outliers, which can mutate rapidly or conversely very slowly, problematical for analysts and decision-makers. Corporate and individual behaviours can act as additional barriers to weak signal identification. We have shown how, by combining two problem structuring methods, viable and internally consistent outlier scenarios can be identified at the periphery of the analyst's vision: scenarios which might have been overlooked or ignored using more traditional forecasting approaches. Such is the distance of these scenarios from current knowledge that they offer real insights into options that are difficult to identify in multi-variable and highly complex problem spaces.

The next chapter continues exploring different examples of scenario in both reactive and exploratory forms. In addition, we shall be looking at second and third order scenarios where the first order or prime scenario allows for spin-off or derivative options to manifest themselves.

References

Ayres, R. U. (1969). Ch. 5: Morphological analysis. In *Technological forecasting and long range planning* (pp. 72–93). McGraw-Hill.

Bostrom, N., & Cirkovic, M. M. (2008). *Global catastrophic risks*. Oxford University Press.

Curry, A., & Schultz, W. (2009). Roads less travelled: Different methods, different futures. *Journal of Futures Studies, 13*(4), 35–60.

Dator, J. A. (2002). *Advancing futures*. Praeger.

Funtowicz, S. O., & Ravetz, J. R. (1994). Uncertainty, complexity and post-normal science. *Annual Review of Environmental Toxicology and Chemistry, 13*(12) Pergamon.

Gallasch, G., Jordans, J., & Ivanova, K. (2017). Application of field anomaly relaxation to battlefield casualties and treatment: A formal approach to consolidating large morphological spaces. In *Data and decision sciences in action*. Springer.

Garvey, B. (2016). Combining quantitative and qualitative aspects of problem structuring in computational morphological analysis. *Its role in mitigating uncertainty in early stage design creativity and innovation and how best to translate it into practice*. PhD thesis, Imperial College London. This document is accessible via: https://ethos.bl.uk/Home.do;jsessionid=493F3C43 FEBE93FB00A23D80F3B19881; https://spiral.imperial.ac.uk

Garvey, B., Childs, P. R. N., & Varnarvides, G. (2013). *Using morphological distance to refine morphological analysis solutions*. Unpublished paper. London.

Garvey, B., & Childs, P. R. N. (2016). Design as an unstructured problem: New methods to help reduce uncertainty – A practitioner perspective. In *Impact of design research on industrial practice*. Springer.

Gowing, N., & Langdon, C. (2017). *Thinking the unthinkable – A new imperative for leadership in the digital age: An interim report*. CIMA.

Heuer, R. J., Jr., & Pherson, R. H. (2011). *Structured analytic techniques for intelligence analysis*. CQ Press.

Jantsch, E. (1967). *Technological forecasting in perspective* (pp. 29–34). OECD.

Kahn, H., & Wiener, A. J. (1967). *The year 2000 – A framework for speculation on the next thirty-three years*. Macmillan.

Kuosa, T., & Stucki, M. (2020). Futures intelligence: Types of futures knowledge. *Futures Platform*.

List, D. (2004). Multiple pasts, converging presents, and alternative futures. *Futures, 36*. Elsevier.

Majaro, S. (1988). *The creative gap: Managing ideas for profit*. Longman.

Mau, S. (2019). *The metric society*. Politu Press.

Nelson, H. G., & Stolterman, E. (2012). In H. G. Nelson & E. Stolterman (Eds.), *The design way* (2nd ed.). MIT Press.

O'Neil, C. (2016). *Weapons of math destruction*. Allen Lane.

Ord, T. (2020). *The precipice – Existential risk and the future of humanity*. Bloomsbury.

Ringland, G., Lustig, P., Phaal, R., Duckworth, M., & Yapp, C. (Eds.). (2012). *Here be dragons*. The Choir Press.

Ritchey, T. (2006). Problem structuring using computer-aided morphological analysis. *Journal of the Operational Research Society, 57*, 792–801.

Ritchey, T. (2011). *Wicked problems and social messes: Decision support modelling with morphological analysis*. Springer.

Schwartz, P. (2003). *Inevitable surprises – Thinking ahead in a time of turbulence*. Gotham Books (Penguin Group).

Shell. (2005). *Shell global scenarios to 2025*. Shell.

The Global Risks Report 2021, 16th Edition, is published by the World Economic Forum. Strategic Partners Marsh McLennan SK Group Zurich Insurance Group.

van der Heijden, K. (1996). *Scenarios – The art of strategic conversation*. Wiley.

van Notten, P., Philip, W., Rotmans, J., van Asselt, M., & Rothman, D. (2003). An updated scenario typology. *Futures, 35*. Pergamon/Elsevier.

Voros, J. (2001). A primer on futures studies, foresight and the use of scenarios. *The Foresight Bulletin, 6*. Swinburne University of Technology.

Voros, J. (2017). *The futures cone, use and history*. (Source: Adapted from Voros (2003, 2017), which was based on Hancock and Bezold (1994)).

Wachter-Boettcher, S. (2017). *Technically wrong*. Norton.

Zwicky, F. (1969). *Discovery, invention, research: Through the morphological approach*. Macmillan.

Zwicky, F. (1948). Morphological astronomy. *The Observatory, 68*(845), 121–143.

Zwicky, F. (1947). Morphology and nomenclature of jet engines. *Aeronautical Engineering Review, 6*(6), 49–50.

Zwicky, F. (1962). *Morphology of propulsive power*. Society of Morphological Research.

Zwicky, F. (1967). *The morphological approach to discovery, invention, research and construction from new methods of thought and procedure*. Springer. Contributions to the Symposium of Methodologies.

Chapter 8
Scenario Derivatives First, Second, and Third Order Scenarios: Generic (Landscape) Variables

As I write, our much vaunted windmills aren't turning because it isn't very windy, and we can't rely on coal-fired power stations because they're all being closed down. And we haven't been able to build any new nuclear reactors because of some newts. Which makes us reliant on gas. And that's a problem because a burly Russian with a beef about something or other is standing on the hose that delivers natural gas from the Urals to Europe. And to make matters worse for our energy needs, the cable that brings electricity from France to Britain was damaged by a fire, and it won't be mended for the best part of a year . . . .
Jeremy Clarkson—Motoring Journalist and Farmer—Sunday Times October 2021.

Abstract It is rare for scenarios to be stand-alone and discrete: rather they contain any number of linked downstream sub-scenarios called derivatives. The bigger the initial primary event the more likely that it will have multiple ramifications generating spin-offs of varying degrees of intensity and visibility. Yet, the subsidiary status of derivative scenarios makes them more dangerous as they are often overlooked due to the dominance of the primary event and where the impact of unintended and uncertain consequences of initial actions generated by the first order scenario can play out. A number of MTTs are introduced which help the analyst determine what, when, and where these derivative scenarios can occur. A variety of qualitative and quantitative methods such as horizon scanning, mind maps, PESTLE and dynamic PESTLE, hypothesis generation and analysis, the analytic hierarchy process (AHP), and Bayesian belief networks (BBNs) are highlighted. The chapter thus posits that only constant scanning can mitigate unconsidered surprises hidden within derivative scenarios.

Keywords Scenario derivative · Horizon scanning · Mind maps · PESTLE and dynamic PESTLE · Hypothesis generation and analysis · The analytic hierarchy process (AHP) and Bayesian belief networks

8.1   Introduction

In Chap. 7 two different scenarios lenses were identified—the reactive and the exploratory. However, whilst initial main scenarios, or first order scenarios, can be classified in this way, it is very rare for such scenarios to be stand-alone and discrete but impact other areas of the contextual environment. Such conditions can generate additional inputs varying in degree of intensity and, indeed, visibility which in turn can feed back and impact the first order scenario—a classic "wicked problem" situation.

With each first order scenario invariably producing second, third, or more levels of scenario type events we can call such additional outcomes "derivative" scenarios. It is within these derivatives that the impact of unintended and uncertain consequences of initial actions as generated by the first order scenario (good and bad) can play out, for the main actors and stakeholders concerned. We have seen such an example of how the responses, or lack of them, to an initial event such as the COVID pandemic are not limited to the prime objective of developing an effective vaccine against the virus. Other areas have been impacted as well—some of which have been aggravated by poorly thought-out responses to the impact of the virus spread—such as the impact on the education of children and students as a result of lockdown, mental health issues from extended social isolation, the impact on specific business sectors especially hit hard by lockdown and travel restrictions such the commercial aviation and the hospitality sector, and so it goes on. Chapter 11 in Part B will specifically look at the reactive response to the COVID-19 pandemic.

When trying to identify derivative scenarios the analyst has to take into account the issues such as the following (non-exclusive):

(a) Are secondary, tertiary, and further scenarios easily identifiable?
(b) At each level what different states present themselves as possible options?
(c) The further removed the derivative scenario is from the first level or core scenario, the weaker the likelihood of such a chain of sequences will occur although they may of course actually occur at some unspecified time in the future.
(d) Derivative scenarios identified at "time t" can change significantly at "time t + 1" and, more importantly, how far away is "t + 1"?
(e) The challenge for the analyst is that traditional planning cycles such as weekly, monthly, quarterly, or annually do little to address the dynamic nature of events so that such scenario option identification has to be performed in real time.
(f) Both reactive and exploratory type scenarios need to incorporate secondary and tertiary impacts as potential downstream outcomes. This requires continuous scanning as in e.) above.

Having identified that most scenarios generate downstream second, tertiary, and more possible outcomes, this chapter introduces the reader to a variety of methods (MTTs) which can be deployed to address such derivative scenarios. Be aware though that such methods are only support tools to bring about awareness of the existence of such derivative outcomes. In themselves they are essentially scanning devices.

Whilst the following section introduces a number of MTTs, it is important to recognise that derivative scenarios cannot be assumed to follow linear or overtly causal paths. Foresight approaches rather than trend extrapolating forecasting methods need to be used (as per Chap. 6). Therefore:

- Do not assume linear causality
- Do not rely on fixed observation cycles (weeks, months, etc.)
- Seek rough preferences or options rather than fixed probabilities. Bayesian approaches have a role here as long as they are used as rough guides to decision-making.
- Apply adaptive planning principles to help define:

  - Regular defined intervals (weekly, monthly, quarterly, or annually)
  - Ad hoc—response mode
  - Continuous monitoring activity

The key take-away from this introductory part of the chapter is not so much the use of particular methods to identify derivative scenarios as the awareness that such derivatives exist. Thus, analysis doesn't end once a core scenario has been identified or selected.

So what MTTs might help us in seeking our derivative type scenarios?

8.2 Methods, Tools, and Techniques (MTTs)

The MTTs introduced in this chapter are:

- Horizon scanning
- Mind maps
- PESTLE and dynamic PESTLE
- Hypothesis generation–analysis of competing hypotheses (ACH, inconsistency finder, quadrant crunching
- Analytic hierarchy process (AHP)
- Bayesian neural networks (BNNs)

8.2.1 Horizon Scanning

At a basic level awareness of derivative scenarios can be described as "horizon scanning", and as such makes management aware of the need to look beyond a single specific scenario itself.

According to "horizonscan.org" the activity is:

a systematic process focusing on detecting the early signs of any potential developments. It helps researchers confirm or discredit existing phenomena as well as identify emerging trends that are on the margin of current thinking. In today's fast-paced world, things can become obsolete as quickly as they emerge. Horizon scanning aims to detect patterns or signals of coming disruptions that could have a transforming impact on our cities, the way we work, our communities, and our habits. The result of horizon scanning will help decision makers plan on how to exploit or mitigate these changes and secure the most positive outcome for their organization.

In November 2017, the UK's Government Office for Science published "The Futures Toolkit" in which it highlighted horizon scanning defining it as *"the process of looking for early warning signs of change in the policy and strategy environment"*.

8.2.1.1   The Process

Horizon scanning combines desk research and some workshop discussion and, whilst it tends to look towards a long termer term horizon, is not focused exclusively on it. Many of the further out, downstream developments are the long-term outcome of a range of factors, some of which may be apparent already.

Horizon scanning is an open-ended process involving participants who are both internal and external to the organisation and with no limit as to the number of participants. The "futures toolkit" suggests that in order to keep the process manageable the early stages of an exercise should involve around 10 people and be expanded at a later date if specific expertise is sought. The participants are in essence authors, and it is suggested they each should produce roughly one scan a week over a 6 week period—although this is only a guideline.

Although this can offer an in-depth view of the horizon in a short period of time it does not address the open-ended nature of changing circumstances which can impact downstream outcomes. The author would suggest a more permanent ongoing process to address this issue and develop an in-house team dedicated to the activity. Another risk is that certain key stakeholders may not be included resulting in missed content and hence lower credibility in the scan. One interesting point made in the "toolkit" is that whilst horizon scanning is relatively straightforward it does rely on intuition and insight:

which can feel counterintuitive to those who are more practiced in evidence based strategic thinking. The hardest part for many authors is knowing whether something they have read is interesting or different enough to include in the scan. Scanners should always err on the side of being irrelevant. (The Futures Toolkit, 2017)

8.2.2   Mind Maps

Mind maps have been used to "kick off" discussions relating to a complex problem with numerous levels of complexity and interconnectivity. Many readers may have seen such maps already; a typical example is shown in the example below (Farrand et al., 2002) (Fig. 8.1).

As you can see it is a very visual approach and as such encourages participants to engage directly with the map's construction. A mind map is a powerful graphic technique which helps the brain to include a variety of cognitive factors such as word, image, number, logic, rhythm, colour, and spatial awareness—in a single format.

Mind maps provide an effective method of taking notes as they show not only facts but also the overall structure of a subject and the relative importance of individual parts of it. Key to the format is that the map helps individuals to associate ideas and make connections they might not otherwise make. Mind maps hold information in a format that your mind will find easy to remember and quick to review. In fact, they abandon the list format of conventional note taking, doing this in favour of a two-dimensional structure. The maps support representation and creativity because they let participants and the reader have an overall point of view of the topic by a single observation of that topic context or structure. .

Maps can be constructed offline by individual team members who then are brought together to discuss the various versions in order to help develop a map enhanced by group consensus. Whilst often created around a single subject or concept a mind map does allow the user to see how ideas can be connected to the central concept from which other ideas can branch out.

In summary, five main characteristics of mind mapping can be identified:

1. The main idea, subject, or focus is crystallised as a central image.
2. The main themes radiate from the central image as "branches".
3. The branches comprise a key word (or even a key image) attached to its associated line.
4. Topics of lesser importance are represented as "twigs" of the relevant branch.
5. The branches form a connected nodal structure.

The case example presented as part of Chap. 12 uses mind mapping as an initial stage in the process which is then integrated with an additional method for further analysis.

8.2.3   PESTLE and Dynamic PESTLE

Another methodical approach looking at how the analyst and decision-maker can begin to visualise and identify and address linked issues includes the presentation of a simple contextual tool to identify some of the main variables and their different

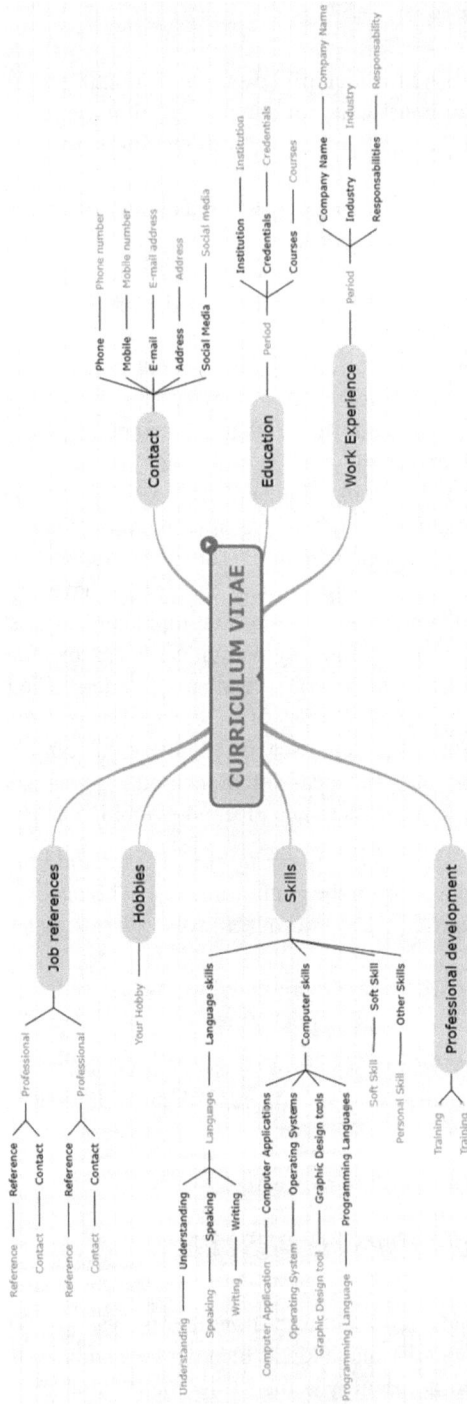

Fig. 8.1 Mind map example. *Ref.* mindomo.com

dimensions which in turn will help visualise derivative scenarios. The term "contextual" implies external rather than internal drivers.

The impact of second/third/nth order derivatives: Because we are now able to "identify" or rather select the various components of a scenario beyond its initial prime modus operandi, such potential outcomes can be elevated from quadrants 3 and 4 (unknown-unknowns or unknown-knowns) in the uncertainty profile template, to quadrant 2—"known-unknowns". Re-defining an uncertainty event in this category will allow the analyst to allocate a rough hierarchy of probable outcomes— but be aware these probability-derived numbers should not be seen as a rigid hierarchical classification but act as a rough guide for decision-makers (see BNNs later in this chapter).

8.2.3.1   A Basic Contextual Framework Using PESTLE

PESTLE is an acronym for political, economic, social, technological, legal, and environmental variables or factors. The "E" is often used to reflect "ethical" considerations but such is the prevalence of environmental (including climate change) issues that it probably outweighs ethical standpoints. In any case, ethical and regulatory factors can be nested under the legal heading. It's often used in conjunction with another acronym, SWOT—which mainly relates to internal/micro factors. There are a number of other acronymic variations such as STEEPLE—the main variables just changed or STEMPLES social, technical, economic, military, political, legal, and environmental and security plus demographic, religious, psychological, or other factors) (50 minutes.com, 2015).

A key starting point in the process to identify the main scenario drivers is to begin at the macro level—that is an overall perspective of the key contextual factors which determine strategic decision-making. The PESTLE strategic framework thus helps environmental scanning and enables management to track key external and macro factors impacting their organisation.

In many ways, this is a top-down as opposed to a bottom-up approach and has a number of attributes as it indicates a more holistic/systems outlook when looking at future risks and opportunities.

As identified in Chap. 3, which discussed the role of problem structuring methods (PSMs), scenario planners often struggle with determining what the problem is. There is often pressure to treat the problem as a puzzle and cut off chunks which have to be solved (Pidd, 1996)—leading to the dilemmas of problem-solving discussed in Chap. 3. Most problems challenged by uncertainty, complexity, and interconnectivity are "wicked" or close to being wicked. Stepping back and looking at the contextual drivers which are impacting an organisation, it helps to rapidly identify such drivers as a first stage in the process.

The advantage of using a tool like this is that the main variables are pre-determined by the acronym itself—and, as such, can speed up other idea creation activities such as brainstorming—leaving the analyst to populate the variables with appropriate criteria according to the topic being addressed.

A traditional **disadvantage** of standard PESTLE is that the analysis generated can be superficial, compounded by an unranked sequence of issues so that they appear as just a list of isolated sub-variables. Another weakness of PESTLE, and indeed SWOT, is the method's failure to offer a choice of outcomes that analysts and decision-makers can act upon. Real-world situations reflect complexity due to the various interactions of the different variables used in the model.

What I shall be presenting here is a variant which offers the analyst a much more dynamic tool and which addresses the inherent complexity of multi-variable scenarios.

The challenge for the analyst though is to populate each of the PESTLE headings with scenario-specific conditions or states. Thus, under political, there will be a need to refine and make more explicit the question that the scenario is trying to address. For example, are we talking about local, national, international, or global political issues. Social factors will also likely to be specific to any one of a sub-set of stakeholders.

Nonetheless, the PESTLE acronym does provide an initial focus from which to develop more topic-related conditions and invites the analyst to engage with factors beyond just the narrow lens of the problem of the first order scenario itself. For example, one way is to ask where the subject "pandemic" resides in the PESTLE acronym (unless you want to substitute the P—political with P—pandemic)? The answer is that it doesn't but it **does** have an impact on, and more crucially is impacted by, the acronym sectors themselves—the **context** around the pandemic.

It has to be recognised that real-world situations are much more complex due to the interactions of the different variables and their sub-components used in the PESTLE array. Using the acronym letters as just discrete arrays of conditions does not do justice to the power of the model.

Standard PESTLE analysis can be turned into something much more dynamic and meaningful for management as it addresses the inherent complexity of multi-variable scenarios. Rather than leaving the PESTLE format as just a static matrix, the approach demonstrated enables the analyst to identify much reduced sets of second and third order scenarios which are viable and thus worth exploring—filtering out much of the noise present generated by the basic PESTLE matrix.

8.2.3.2 Dynamic PESTLE: A New Approach

The process of constructing a PESTLE-based matrix allows for the creation of a problem space which identifies not only the key variables themselves but the various states (or sub-variables) within each main variable. The product of the problem space is the total number of configurations or combinations generated by the PESTLE matrix. Pair-wise analysis of each of the states within one variable is assessed for consistency with every other state in all the other variables using the MA method introduced in Chap. 7. This process reduces the original set of configurations by eliminating all those configurations in the larger set which contain inconsistent pairs. Software can then automatically compile a reduced set of **viable** solutions with no

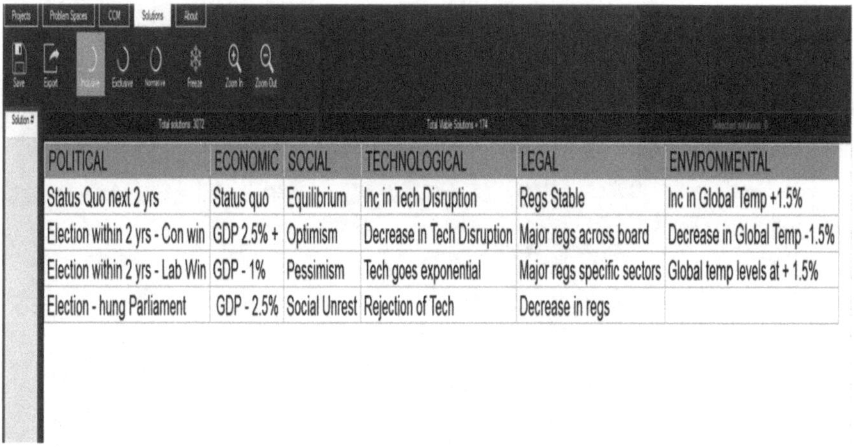

Fig. 8.2 PESTLE problem space

inconsistent pairs—i.e. they can work. Integral to the ability of identifying viable options produced by the model is the ability also to produce alternative viable configurations which in themselves can contain secondary and tertiary possible outcomes.

In our example, the analyst is looking at *"what outlier options could be considered for the UK over the next two years or so, based on a selection of political scenarios"?*

A small problem space was generated—Fig. 8.2—, totalling some 3072 different configurations (a small size). Following pair-wise analysis to reduce the original set of configurations, software compiled a reduced set of **viable** solutions, from 3072 to 174, or by 94%.

These 174 viable solutions were then triaged according to the distance principles explained in Chap. 7, earlier.

An anchor configuration reflecting current knowledge was selected, scenario 2791 (red cells)—Fig. 8.3. This "known" configuration (in effect a known-known) indicated a visible or likely outcome based on current policy analysis such that a scenario statement or narrative could read as follows:

There would be a high probability of an election yielding a hung parliament, where GDP could be under 1% causing pessimism within society, compounded by increasing disruption from new technological systems, accompanied by major regulation of specific sectors (such as Social Media), accompanied by weak action in relation to climate change due to the poor state of the economy over the next two years.

Analysis of the viable 174 scenarios identified that some 20 scenarios were distanced the maximum 6 parameter/states from the anchor configuration, representing 11.5% of the solution set. These 20 outlier scenarios, being so far distanced from the anchor, could offer intriguing perspectives not readily identifiable

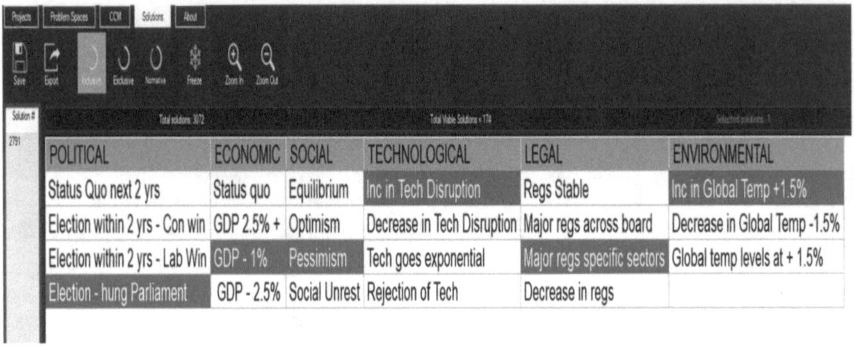

Fig. 8.3 Example of an anchor configuration

had this exercise not been carried out—interpreted here as being a low probability or occurrence/high impact event.

One of these 20 scenarios (782) was selected as being in the outlier (weak signal) zone due to the high level of variance from the anchor (current knowledge) scenario. This example of a viable configuration, substantially different from current knowledge, is shown below:

In Table 8.1, the current knowledge or anchor scenario as per Table 8.1 is "frozen" and is identified as cells with ***bold italic*** text. Outlier (solution) scenario 782 (those cells with **bold** text) is at the maximum distance from the anchor scenario in that all six variables are different from the anchor. As a VIABLE scenario (**bold** text cells), all the cells in the configuration are different from the anchor configuration (purple cells). This scenario having passed muster as a solution is very much an outlier in relation to current knowledge or policy and should be subject to further analysis. More importantly, one can ask whether the analyst would have isolated this scenario as being worthy of further analysis—its high degree of variance from the anchor scenario qualifying it as an outlier or weak signal.

In other words, this outlier indicated that a potential scenario could be characterised by the following narrative: *"There being an election within 2 years resulting in a Conservative win, with the economy remaining static and there being a decline in new disruptive technologies, whilst no additional regulation being introduced and there being a small decrease in the global temperature change due to remedial actions at a global level."*

Perhaps it is not a scenario deemed probable under current perceptions and political positions but, according to this model, possible and thus worthy of consideration.

8.2.3.3   Dynamic PESTLE: A Summary

The very flexibility of this approach thus turns the static PESTLE tool, when supported by software automating pair-wise analysis, into a much more dynamic

Table 8.1 Italicised anchor configuration (frozen)

Solution number	Political	Economic	Social	Technological	Legal	Environmental
		Total solutions = 3072	Total viable solutions = 174	Selected solutions 1		
782	Status Quo next 2 years	**Status quo**	**Equilibrium**	*Inc in Tech Disruption*	**Regs Stable**	*Inc. in Global Temp >1.5C*
	Election within 2 yrs—Con win	GDP 2.5%+	Optimism	**Decrease in Tech Disruption**	Major regs across board	**Decrease in Global Temp < 1.5C**
	Election within 2 yrs—Lab win	*GDP minus 1%*	*Pessimism*	Tech goes exponential	*Major regs in specific sectors*	Global temp levels at + 1.5C
	Election—hung Parliament	GDP minus 2.5%	Social Unrest	Rejection of Tech	Decrease in regs	

Table 8.2 Allocation of different scenarios

	Identifiable/known	Unidentifiable/unknown
Predictable/ known	**Q1. Known-known (I know what I know)** Does not apply	**Q2. Known-unknown (I know what I don't know)** Scenarios 12–14 Possible
Unpredictable/ unknown	**Q3. Unknown-known (I don't know what I know or I think I know but turns out I don't)** Scenarios 29–32 Possible Scenarios 33–34 Plausible Scenarios 43–44 Plausible *Scenarios 53–56 Highly Unlikely*	**Q4. Unknown-unknown (I don't know what I don't know)** *Scenarios 57–58 Highly Unlikely* *Scenarios 66–67 Highly Unlikely*

tool. Decision-makers and analysts are now offered a range of alternative strategic options based on different inputs AND outputs, visually, and which can be reviewed in real time.

Apart from identifying possible downstream scenarios (second, third order, and more) one can now determine where within the uncertainty profile template matrix such scenarios may reside (Table 8.2).

In Chap. 7, some 76 types of uncertainty were identified. Although initially presented as an appendix (Appendix 6) we shall re-introduce the 76 different options available.

How can the scenario profile 782, selected above in our example, be interpreted into terms of its allocation to the uncertainty file template quadrants?

The narrative description of the scenario has been expressed above but for ease of context I shall repeat the narrative again, thus:

> There being an election within 2 years resulting in a Conservative win, with the economy remaining static and there being a decline in new disruptive technologies, whilst no additional regulation being introduced and there being a small decrease in the global temperature change due to remedial actions at a global level.

We know from the model that it is viable. Although there is uncertainty as to such a specific scenario coming about, it has been visualised and thus should be seen as belonging to quadrant 2—a known-unknown. Of the 20 viable scenarios identified in the model as being different across all six configuration variables how can these be allocated within the uncertainty profile matrix? It will of course be up to the analyst and decision-maker to place these 20 viable options into some form of objective hierarchy.

As a first phase this dynamic form of PESTLE allows for the analyst to identify viable scenarios derived at secondary and tertiary levels characterised as being **low probability/high impact** (even catastrophic and existential) events of which 20 have been identified, outliers and wild cards, and even narratives seen currently as perhaps ghost technologies bordering on science fiction.

Once this first level of allocation has been performed, then other methods, such as the analytic hierarchy process (AHP—see below)), can be introduced to refine the hierarchy of viable options for further decision-based analysis.

8.2.4 Hypothesis Generation

The world of intelligence analysis has been a valuable and innovative source of methods—unfortunately little of it seems to have been adopted or absorbed by not only commercial organisations but by business school education curricula. Some of the most prolific and insightful work has been developed over the years by two former US intelligence analysts Heuer and Pherson (2010). For the purposes of looking at a method for determining how scenarios might be identified for future analysis, whether at primary secondary or tertiary levels, we shall be looking here at a number of techniques which are particularly useful when looking at exploratory scenarios (as per the previous chapter). These techniques come under the more broader term "hypotheses generation". Three approaches are reviewed in this section.

- Analysis of competing hypotheses (ACH)
- Inconsistency finder™
- Quadrant crunching

8.2.4.1 Analysis of Competing Hypotheses (ACH)

A core technique that forces analysts to challenge mind-sets is analysis of competing hypotheses (ACH), which involves the identification of a complete set of alternative explanations (presented as hypotheses), the systematic evaluation of each, and the selection of the hypothesis or hypotheses that fit best by focusing on evidence that tends to disconfirm rather than to confirm each of the hypotheses. ACH helps analysts overcome three common traps or pitfalls that can lead to intelligence failures: being overly influenced by a first impression based on incomplete date, an existing analytic line, or a single explanation; failing to generate a full set of explanations or hypotheses at the outset of a project; and relying on evidence to support one's favoured hypothesis that also happens to be consistent with alternative hypotheses and, therefore, has no diagnostic value. ACH can help overcome what is called "confirmation bias", the tendency to search for or interpret new information in a way that confirms one's preconceptions and avoids interpretations that contradict prior beliefs. These biases will be explored in more detail in Chaps. 11 and 12.

According to Heuer and Pherson (2010), ACH is appropriate for analysing where alternative explanations are needed for what has happened, is happening, or is likely to happen. It is appropriate when controversial issues require an audit trail showing how they considered and arrived at particular judgements and is well suited for dealing with tech issues such as *"For which weapons system is this part most likely to be imported?"* ACH is also useful in dealing with the potential for denial and deception (and the method was indeed originally developed for this purpose).

The technique can be used by an individual analyst but most effective with a small team that can challenge each other's evaluation of evidence. It can take time (several hours) and the introduction of a facilitator is a useful additional asset.

ACH helps analyst overcome a number of cognitive biases and intuitive traps that can lead to intelligence failures or analytic mistakes:

- Succumbing to tendency to select the first answer that appears "good enough" (satisficing).
- Failing to generate a full set of explanations or hypotheses at the outset of a project.
- Ignoring or discounting information that does not fit the preferred explanation.
- Relying on evidence to support one's favoured hypothesis that is also consistent with other hypotheses and thus has no diagnostic value in assessing the relative likelihood of the hypotheses.

ACH can help overcome confirmation bias—the tendency to search for and interpret new information in a way that conforms to one's preconceptions and avoids interpretations that contradict prior beliefs.

ACH ensures all analysts are working from the same evidence, arguments, and assumptions with each member of the team being allowed their say. Review of the ACH matrix provides a systematic basis for identifying and discussing differences between two or more analysts.

8.2.4.2   The Method of Analysis of Competing Hypotheses

ACH consists of the following 8 steps.

- Identify all possible hypotheses
- Make a list of significant evidence for/against
- Prepare a hypothesis versus evidence matrix analysing the diagnosticity of the evidence
- Refine matrix. Delete evidence and arguments that have no diagnosticity
- Draw tentative conclusions about relative likelihoods of each hypothesis. Try to disprove hypotheses
- Analyse sensitivity to critical evidential items
- Report conclusions
- Identify indicators for future observations

8.2.4.3   Other Strengths of the Method

1. *Encourages systematic analysis of multiple competing hypotheses.* As an analytic process it identifies full sets of alternative hypotheses whilst systematically evaluating both consistent and inconsistent data for each hypothesis—discarding those with high levels of inconsistency. This analysis of multiple hypotheses allows for viable, but not readily apparent, hypotheses to be assessed as opposed to the usual suspects.

2. *Creates an explicit record of the use of hypotheses and evidence that can be shared, critiqued, and experimented with by others.* This recording is important in that this part of the process allows the analysts to assess the evidence prior to making a judgement or decision.
3. *Easy to learn.* The eight-stage process as defined above is not onerous to understand.
4. *Focuses attention on disconfirming evidence—counteracting the common bias of focusing on confirming evidence.* This counteracts tendencies to rely on pre-conceived ideas and "gut feelings" as by deploying a more systematic approach to challenging evidence it helps to raise questions not previously thought of. Such a process helps being taken by surprise by an unforeseen outcome. This can occur when the topic is of a controversial nature and where sources of disagreement need to be identified.
5. *Does not require precise estimates of probabilities.* As for a number of problem structuring methods the dictum that it is often better to be approximately right rather than precisely wrong applies to the ACH method.
6. *Does not require complex explicit representations of compound hypotheses, time, space, assumptions, or processes.* ACH takes the analyst though a process of making well-reasoned analytical judgements. As such it is particularly useful for issues requiring weighing up of alternative explanations of what has happened or might happen (as an early warning system).
7. *Process benefits from computerisation of the process.* Whilst benefiting from computerisation the software is available free and can be downloaded at https://www.softpedia.com/get/Science-CAD/ACH.shtml. The only issue readers should be aware of is that the software to date is only available for download on Microsoft and not Mac.

8.2.4.4 Weaknesses

1. *Does not and cannot provide detailed and accurate probabilities.* ACH analysis can assign high weights for credibility and relevance, but may be insufficient to reflect the conclusiveness of such evidence. For example there may be circumstances when a few reports clearly support one hypothesis but are sufficient to refute all other hypotheses regardless of what other less definitive evidence may indicate. If you require mathematical accuracy in calculating probabilities for each hypothesis, other approaches may better of better use. Methods such as Bayesian belief networks (see Sect. 8.2.6 below) may require a methodologist trained in Bayesian statistics to assist in the process. Although the Bayesian probability calculations are mathematically correct, the results are still subject to a variety of subjective judgements about the evidence that go into the Bayesian calculation. ACH's strength comes from its process and takes the analyst through, but not from precise probability calculations for each hypothesis. The final judgement is made by the analyst, not by the computer.

2. *Does not provide a basis for marshalling evidence by time, location, or cause.* Evidence needs to be representative of the problem as a whole. If there is considerable evidence on a related but peripheral issue and comparatively few items of evidence on the core issue, the inconsistency or weighted inconsistency scores can be misleading. Thus, the analyst has to be aware of any unbalanced sets of evidence.

3. *Awareness is still required of behavioural factors—cognitive biases usually reflect entrenched positions.* It is unlikely that ACH will resolve an impasse between analysts with firmly entrenched views about an issue. If an analyst is unable to see alternative perspectives, the evidence will always be interpreted in a way that supports that analyst's preferred view. On the other hand, ACH can still be of value by helping to pin down the exact basis for the disagreement.

4. *Does not provide a basis for accounting for assumptions.* ACH is not appropriate for all types of decisions. It is used to analyse hypotheses about what is true or what is likely to happen. It is then left to the analyst team to identify recommended preferences. If one wants to evaluate alternative courses of action, such as alternative business strategies, or which computer to buy, this method has limited uses. A more hierarchy-based method such as AHP (see Sect. 8.2.5 below) will be of more value. This reflects the argument that decision-making under uncertainty requires the analyst to seek out a range of methods which can be linked or integrated into the decision support process—there is rarely, if ever, one method which fits all. Thus, before one can select a hierarchy of preferred options, one has to first present objectively determined viable options for the analyst to consider. Methods such as ACH (and Morphological analysis) allow for this approach.

8.2.4.5 Summary

The ACH method offers benefits for systematically considering multiple hypotheses and avoiding confirmation bias. It is easy to use and provides a basis for documenting the evidence used and the hypotheses considered. It supports a process for generating and comparing hypotheses under circumstances when accurate probabilistic scoring is not feasible (Heuer & Pherson, 2010).

8.2.4.6 Inconsistency Finder (IF) Tm

This method is a simpler form of ACH and helps focus attention on information which is inconsistent with the main hypothesis being explored. It is used whenever a set of alternative hypotheses exists or has been recently identified so that analysts need to:

- Carefully weigh the credibility of multiple explanations or alternative hypotheses explaining what has happened, is happening, or is likely to happen.
- Evaluate the validity of a large amount of data as it relates to each hypothesis.

- Challenge their current interpretation of the evidence (or interpretation of others).
- Create an audit trail.

For more details on the method I refer you to Pherson's *Handbook of Analytic Tools and Techniques* (2019).

8.2.4.7   Quadrant Crunching (QC)

Quadrant crunching (QC) is an application based on morphological analysis (MA) and was developed by Pherson and Schwartz and first published in 2008. As such it is a systematic process for identifying all potentially feasible combinations between different sets of variables. It helps analysts avoid surprise by examining multiple possible combinations of selected key variables as well as helping to identify and challenge assumptions as well as helping to discover "unknown-unknowns".

It is mainly useful when dealing with highly ambiguous situations where there is little data and the chances for surprise are great. Analysts are required to rethink an issue from a broad range of perspectives and systematically challenge all the assumptions that underlie their lead hypothesis.

By generating an extensive list of potential scenarios, decision-makers are in a better position to select those that appear most credible or deserve most attention. They can then take the necessary action to avoid or mitigate the impact of bad scenarios and help foster preferred outcomes. It will help decision-makers to identify those scenarios in quadrants 3 and 4 and transfer them to Q2 type scenarios in the uncertainty profile matrix.

8.2.4.8   The Method

The basic process is as follows:

- State your lead hypothesis or key assumptions
- Break down the lead hypothesis or key assumption into its component parts or key dimensions (aka MA)
- Identify contrary assumptions for each dimension
- Array the combinations of these contrary assumptions in a set of 2 x 2 matrices
- Generate scenarios for each quadrant
- Select the scenarios most deserving of attention
- Develop indicators that would suggest whether the selected scenarios are becoming more or less likely

A more detailed run-through based on an example has been provided by Pherson and the essence of the process is shown in Appendix 10.

A number of the methods we have introduced are excellent at identifing viable, internally consistent options. However, such options may still be numerous. Faced with an array of viable possibilities decision analysts need to form some form of prioritisation if such processes are to prove of value to management. In other words, the question needs to be asked "how can these possible options" be placed in some form of hierarchy. A group of methods do exist under the generic category of multi-criteria decision analysis (or MCDA). This guide will not cover all such methods but highlight one established approach—the analytic hierarchy process (AHP). It does have its critics although the author considers these to be of limited concern as AHP is still working close to the uncertainty domain and as such methodological purity can be sacrified in favour of a broader attempt in mitigating uncertainty.

8.2.5   The Analytic Hierarchy Process (AHP)

The method was developed in the 1970s by Thomas Saaty (2008). According to Saaty, AHP provides the process which acknowledges subjective and personal preferences of an individual or a group in making a decision. Fundamentally, the AHP works by developing priorities for alternatives and the criteria used to judge the alternatives. Software is available with probably the most well known being "expert choice" (found via expertchoice.com). Other versions are also available and a Google search yields a number of low-cost alternatives.

Wikipedia states that:

> Rather than prescribing a "correct" decision, the AHP helps decision makers find one that best suits their goal and their understanding of the problem. It provides a comprehensive and rational framework for structuring a decision problem, for representing and quantifying its elements, for relating those elements to overall goals, and for evaluating alternative solutions.

It well suited to handling intangible and fuzzy issues and where *"elements of the hierarchy can relate to any aspect of the decision problem—tangible or intangible, carefully measured or roughly estimated, well or poorly understood—anything at all that applies to the decision at hand"*.

AHP is particularly suited to group decision-making where individual experts' experiences are used to estimate the relative strengths of factors through pair-wise comparisons. Each of the respondents compares the relative importance of each pair of items using a specially designed questionnaire (generated by the software). An example of such a first level of questions addressing the question "Should we invest in this Start-up?" is shown below.

```
1.0 Goal
├─ Commercial feasibility (L: ,333)
│  ├─ Financial op (L: ,333)
│  │  ├─ Good gross margin viability (L: ,422)
│  │  ├─ Good net margin viability (L: ,081)
│  │  ├─ Short time to break-even (L: ,152)
│  │  └─ Good potential cash flow (L: ,345)
│  ├─ Investment op (L: ,333)
│  │  ├─ Cash required: good return (L: ,200)
│  │  ├─ Realistic capital structure (L: ,200)
│  │  ├─ Growth financing available (L: ,200)
│  │  ├─ Appealing risk return (L: ,200)
│  │  └─ Proven exit values (L: ,200)
│  └─ Business op (L: ,333)
│     ├─ Market (L: ,333)
│     │  ├─ Large market (L: ,250)
│     │  ├─ Good growth potential (L: ,250)
│     │  ├─ Accessibility (L: ,250)
│     │  └─ Age of market (L: ,250)
│     ├─ Product (L: ,333)
│     │  ├─ Sustainability (L: ,333)
│     │  ├─ Scalability (L: ,333)
│     │  └─ Proof of demand (L: ,333)
│     └─ Business model (L: ,333)
│        ├─ Based on existing model (L: ,250)
│        ├─ Proven model (L: ,250)
│        ├─ Growth, invest and channel strategy is aligned (L: ,250)
│        └─ Defencable USP (L: ,250)
├─ The "team" (L: ,333)
│  ├─ Strategic breadth (L: ,333)
│  │  ├─ Strategic skills/attributes (L: ,500)
│  │  └─ Strategic access (L: ,500)
│  │     ├─ Good access industry value chain (L: ,500)
│  │     └─ Good financial access (L: ,500)
│  ├─ Functional coverage (L: ,333)
│  │  ├─ Leadership/CEO/Driver (L: ,200)
│  │  ├─ Operational (L: ,200)
│  │  ├─ Marketing/sales (L: ,200)
│  │  ├─ Technical (L: ,200)
│  │  └─ Financial (L: ,200)
│  └─ Team dynamics (L: ,333)
│     ├─ Good team synergy (work well together). (L: ,333)
│     ├─ Compensation supports team dynamics (L: ,333)
│     └─ Coachability of key management (L: ,333)
└─ Technical feasibility (L: ,333)
   ├─ Stage of technical development (L: ,500)
   │  ├─ Good concept design (L: ,250)
   │  ├─ Detailed technical specs. (L: ,250)
   │  ├─ Prototype exists (L: ,250)
   │  └─ Proven capacity to scale (L: ,250)
   └─ Defensible IP (L: ,500)
      ├─ Required protection availalbe (L: ,500)
      └─ Freedom to operate (L: ,500)
```

Once the set of items being evaluated is built, the decision analyst systematically considers the various elements by comparing them using pair-wise analysis, each item being compared to another item in the array in respect to their impact on an element above them in the hierarchy and where judgement is made about the elements' relative meaning and importance. Key to the ethos of AHP is that it is human judgement that qualifies the evaluation of each pair.

The AHP software then converts these evaluations to numerical values that can be processed and compared over the entire range of the problem. In the final step of the process, numerical priorities are calculated for each of the decision alternatives.

Fundamentally, the AHP works by developing priorities for alternatives and the criteria used to judge the alternatives. First, priorities are derived for the criteria in terms of their importance to achieve the goal; then priorities are derived for the performance of the alternatives on each criterion. These priorities are derived based on pair-wise assessments using judgement. The process of prioritisation solves the problem of having to deal with different types of scales, by interpreting their significance to the values of the user or users. Finally, a weighting and adding process is used to obtain overall priorities for the alternatives as to how they contribute to the goal. With the AHP a multidimensional scaling problem is thus transformed to a unidimensional scaling problem.

A more detailed description of the process is shown in Appendix 11.

8.2.6   Bayesian Belief Networks (BBNs)

The Bayesian approach uses the degree of a person's belief that an event will occur, rather than the actual probability that the event will occur. These probabilities are known as Bayesian probabilities and are properties of the person, not the event (Kreig, 2001). The causal relationships in Bayesian belief networks allow the correlation between variables to be modelled and predictions to be made, even when direct evidence or observations are unavailable (Kreig, 2001).

Bayesian belief networks aim to provide a decision support framework for problems involving uncertainty, complexity, and probabilistic reasoning. The approach is based on conceptualising an issue of interest as a graph represented by a network of connected nodes and links. In the graph, nodes represent important domain variables, and a link from one node to another represents a dependency relationship between the corresponding variables. To provide quantitative description of the dependency links, Bayesian belief networks (BBNs) use probabilistic relations, rather than deterministic expressions. The main use of BBNs is in situations that require statistical inference—in addition to statements about the probabilities (i.e. likelihood) of events, the user knows some evidence, that is, some events that have actually been observed, and wishes to update his or her belief in the likelihood of other events, which have not as yet been observed. BBNs can use both "forward" and "backward" inference (Wooldridge, 2003).

Although the probability and Bayesian theory that forms the basis of BBNs has been around for a long time, it is only in the last few years that efficient algorithms and software tools to implement them have been developed to enable evidence propagation in networks with a reasonable number of variables. The recent explosion of interest in BBNs is due to these developments, since for the first time they can be used to solve realistic size problems.

A fuller description of BNNs is beyond the scope of the chapter. However, for a more detailed explanation of the method I would recommend that readers seek a comprehensive publication by Norman Fenton and Martin Neil, titled *"Risk Assessment and Decision Analysis with Bayesian Networks"*, published by CRC Press 2013.

Methods such as BNNs have been introduced as they are at the border where more qualitative methods addressing uncertainty start to overlap with more quantitative approaches as more data is identified. Again I should warn that although BNNs produce output in a quantitative format, such data is only to be taken as an indicator rather than a specific number—they reflect, as the title of the method indicates, a belief system rather than a precise number.

8.3 Conclusion

This chapter has attempted to make aware that scenarios are not just singular, discrete, events; most if not all main scenarios contain any number of linked downstream sub-scenarios which can be called derivatives. A number of MTTs were introduced which can support the analyst in determining what, when, and where these derivative scenarios can manifest themselves. But be aware there is no single method which can guarantee specific paths emanating from the main scenario. Suffice it to say that the major message herein for management is to be aware that any one scenario can encapsulate or even disguise any other number of scenarios. Only constant scanning for these derivative items can help mitigate unconsidered surprise.

References

50 Minutes.com. (2015, September). *PESTLE analysis: Understand and plan for your business environment: Prepare the best strategies in advance* (Management & Marketing).

Farrand, P., Hussain, F., & Hennessy, E. (2002). The efficacy of the mind map study technique. *Medical Education, 36*(5).

Fenton, N., & Neil, M. (2013). *Risk assessment and decision analysis with Bayesian networks.* published by CRC Press.

Futures Toolkit. (2017). *The futures toolkit.* UK Government Office for Science.

Heuer Jr, R. J., & Pherson, R. H. (2010). *Structured analytic techniques for intelligence analysis.* CQ Press.

Kreig, M. L. (2001). *A tutorial of Bayesian belief networks: Surveillance system division – Electronics and surveillance research laboratory* – DSTO-TN-0403.

Pherson, R. H. (2019). *Handbook of analytic tools & techniques* (5th ed.). R H Pherson, The Analyst's Bookshop.

Pherson, R. H., & Schwartz. (2008). *Handbook of analytic tools and techniques*. Pherson Associates.
Pidd, M. (1996). *Tools for thinking* (p. 40). Wiley.
Saaty, T. L. (2008). *Decision making for leaders: The analytic hierarchy process for decisions in a complex world*. RWS Publications.
Wooldridge, S. (2003). *Introduction (from Bayesian belief networks*. Australian Institute of Marine Science. Prepared for CSIRO Centre for Complex Systems Science. 1 CSIRO.

Part IV
Theoretical Underpinnings: Behaviour—
The Hidden Influencer in How We Deal
with Uncertainty

Chapter 9
Behavioural Factors: Cognitive Biases and Dissonance, Anomie, and Alienation (Or How We Humans Mess Things Up)

All may not therefore be as it would appear. We must not let our assumptions, our perceptions and "mental maps" get in the way of seeing a new, unfolding reality. . . . .It is impossible therefore to start to constructively think about a world in transition without a debate that challenges deep assumptions. Such a debate must distil fact and opinion, grounded in constructive discussion, from a mirage of convenient dreams or outdated rules. The results of this distillation process may not be totally benign, but it is better to face up to the unpleasant rather than ignore it.
Robert W. Davies "The Era of Global Transition" Palgrave Macmillan (2012).

Abstract The chapter addresses how human behaviour influences our ability to make objective decisions when faced with (perceived) uncertainty. The often unsettling nature of uncertainty allows for a variety of behavioural conditions to play out. In turn these conditions act as barriers when attempting to assess objectively the nature of uncertainty. These behavioural conditions include a whole range of cognitive biases, misapplied heuristics, cognitive dissonance, as well as social anomie (and alienation). An overall proposition of this book is that uncertainty is really a "known-unknown" and therefore can be managed. However, it is argued that the manifestation of those behavioural conditions highlighted above, such as cognitive biases, tends to drive our decision-making processes into accepting all too readily that uncertainty is an "unknown-unknown" which in turn absolves decision-makers from responsibility when things go wrong.

Keywords Cognitive bias · Misapplied heuristics · Intuitive traps · Expert opinion · Cognitive dissonance · Anomie · Alienation · Experience

9.1 Introduction: How Our Behaviour Determines How We React to Uncertainty

Throughout the earlier chapters in this book we have alluded directly and indirectly as to how individuals and social groups see, formulate, and interpret information. In this chapter, I'll be addressing in more detail those aspects of human behaviour which influence our ability to make objective decisions such as **cognitive biases, misapplied heuristics, cognitive dissonance, social anomie (and alienation), as well as those fears humans have in relation to uncertainty.**

For example, in Chap. 4 we saw how Pedbury (2019) stated that surprises come from places people are not looking at and that many organisations are focused too much on predicting the expected future, those high probability, high impact developments that could disrupt their operations. It was also highlighted that cultures exist within organisations that militate against addressing new challenges to current policy, acting as barriers to foresight.

I'm now going to turn everything we've discussed about the uncertainty profile—if not on its head—then on its side!

Let us remind ourselves as to the major components of the risk/uncertainty profile template initially developed in Chap. 2. This template reflects an attempt to establish an objective interpretation of the different profiles of uncertainty—and as discussed quadrant 3 is the main problem area—why is it so, and how can we mitigate its impact and in doing so alter our perception as to how uncertainty can be mitigated so that a more rational response be formulated?

Quadrant 3, or the "unknown-knowns" is where the most problematical interpretation of uncertainty manifests itself. This is largely due to human perception about uncertainty or rather its misconception. The challenge for management is to recognise how its own behaviour can influence how it interprets and faces up to situations containing high levels of uncertainty. More crucial is why people (including individuals, groups, management, and organisations) are all too ready to classify uncertainty as an "unknown-known" or an "unknown-unknown" when the vast majority of future events can be visualised so that they reside in quadrant 2—"known-unknowns". In this category, uncertain events can be visualised; they may happen and thus contingency plans developed—reducing the impact of surprises. As has been highlighted earlier—if we can think it—it can happen!

In essence we need to be able to transform Q3 behaviour into Q2 behaviour—and in the process eliminate or at least mitigate cognitive biases and other behavioural characteristics in order to develop hierarchy-based options as "notional probabilities". Quadrant 3 is where us humans "mess things up" or rather put barriers in place to adopting a more rational approach to uncertainty in spite of us thinking of ourselves as rational beings.

9.2   The Fallacy of the Rational Man

Conventional wisdom in classical economics is that humans are rational actors who make decisions and behave in ways that maximises advantage and usefulness whilst minimizing risk.

Much of modern thought concerning decision-making under uncertainty has strong behavioural roots. Psychology professors Daniel Kahneman and the late Amos Tversky (1982) developed the foundations of the area of research known as "cognitive bias". Their work challenges traditional economic theory, stemming from the days of Adam Smith concerning the rational man whereby people make rational choices based on self-interest. The research carried out by Kahneman and Tversky indicated that people often fail to fully analyse situations when required to make complex judgements. They found that people and organisations fall back on rules of thumb (known formally as "heuristics") as opposed to rational analysis. Moreover, such decisions are based on historical experience, fairness, or aversion to loss rather than more formal economic considerations.

Kahneman and Tversky succinctly demonstrate the impact of cognitive biases in decision-making—especially when exacerbated by the state of uncertainty at the time of making that decision. In the quotation below they highlight the relationship between the availability of data and the degree of uncertainty ascribed to a situation.

> The subjective assessment of probability resembles the subjective assessment of physical quantities such as distance or size. These judgments are all based on data of limited validity, which are processed according to heuristic rules. For example, the apparent distance of an object is determined in part by its clarity. The more sharply the object is seen, the closer it appears to be. This rule has some validity, because in any given scene the more distant objects are seen less sharply than nearer objects. However, the reliance on this rule leads to systematic errors in the estimation of distance. Specifically, distances are often overestimated when visibility is poor because the contours of objects are blurred. On the other hand, distances are often underestimated when visibility is good because the objects are seen sharply. Thus, the reliance on clarity as an indication of distance leads to common biases. Such biases are also found in the intuitive judgment of probability. (Tversky & Kahneman, 1974)

Other analysts have come to similar conclusions but from different disciplines.

9.3   The Conundrum of Bias

Any form of analysis, whether carried out by individuals or groups, can fall victim to cognitive biases and intuitive traps. Cognitive biases can be characterised as the tendency to make decisions and take action based on limited acquisition and/or processing of information or self-interest, overconfidence (hubris), or attachment to past experience.

Randolph Pherson (2019) a former CIA intelligence analyst states that:

How a person perceives information is strongly influenced by factors such as experience, education, cultural background and what that person is expected to do with that data. Our brains are trained to process information quickly which often leads to processing data incorrectly or not recognize its significance if it doesn't fit into established patterns. Such short-cuts in our thinking processes are called heuristics—experienced based techniques that quickly produce a solution that is often good enough to solve the immediate problem.

As identified earlier another term used to explain a heuristic is "rule of thumb".

Under conditions of uncertainty where there is little or no data then we increasingly fall back on heuristics in an attempt to reduce this uncertainty—**and therein lies the rub**—as it allows our biases to insert themselves into our decision-making processes. Using such "rules of thumb" when addressing problems can *"lead to cognitive biases and prevent analysts from accurately understanding reality even when they have all the data and evidence needed to form an accurate view"* (Pherson, 2019) adding that such misapplied heuristics and intuitive traps are quick to form but hard to correct and that:

After one's mind has reached closure of an issue even a substantial accumulation of contradictory evidence is unlikely to force a reappraisal—tending to ignore or dismiss outlier data as 'noise'.

It is therefore apparent that such biases manifest themselves amongst decision actors when faced with Q3—unknown-known situations—and it can be argued that much poor decision-making reflects such behaviour whereas if biases can be identified, challenged, and overcome much decision-making to mitigate uncertainty needs to be brought back to Q2 status—the "known-unknowns".

Our friends at Wikipedia identify some 188 different kinds of cognitive bias broken down into 3 main groups.

* *Decision-making, belief, and behavioural biases—119*
* *Social biases—27*
* *Memory errors and biases—42*

The area of concern in relation to decision-making under uncertain is the first one—again we see a great proliferation of approaches, in effect, topic overload—how can we manage to identify the more prominent and impactful ones.

US psychologist Dr. J Taylor (2013) points out that Kahneman and Tversky *"argue that cognitive biases can result in perceptual blindness or distortion (seeing things that aren't really there), illogical interpretation (being nonsensical), inaccurate judgements (being just plain wrong), irrationality (being out of touch with reality), and bad decisions (being stupid). The outcomes of decisions influenced by cognitive biases can range from the mundane to the lasting to the catastrophic".*

Taylor goes on to say that cognitive biases can be broadly placed in two categories. Information and ego biases. **Information** biases include the use of heuristics, or information-processing shortcuts, that produce fast and efficient, though not necessarily accurate, decisions and not paying attention nor adequately thinking through relevant information.

Ego biases include emotional motivations, such as fear, anger, or worry, and social influences such as peer pressure, the desire for acceptance, and doubt that other people can be wrong. He identifies (Taylor, 2013) 12 cognitive biases that appear to be most harmful to decision-making, notably in the business world and reflect a number of such biases as presented by Kahneman and Tversky.

Information biases include:

- Knee-jerk bias: Make fast and intuitive decisions when slow and deliberate decisions are necessary.
- Occam's razor bias: Assume the most obvious decision is the best decision.
- Silo effect: Use too narrow an approach in making a decision.
- Confirmation bias: Focus on information that affirms your beliefs and assumptions.
- Inertia bias: Think, feel, and act in ways that are familiar, comfortable, predictable, and controllable.
- Myopia bias: See and interpret the world through the narrow lens of your own experiences, baggage, beliefs, and assumptions.

Ego biases include:

- Shock-and-awe bias: Belief that our intellectual firepower alone is enough to make complex decisions.
- Overconfidence effect: Excessive confidence in our beliefs, knowledge, and abilities.
- Optimism bias: Overly optimistic, overestimating favourable outcomes and underestimating unfavourable outcomes.
- Homecoming queen/king bias: Act in ways that will increase our acceptance, liking, and popularity.
- Force field bias: Think, feel, and act in ways that reduce a perceived threat, anxiety, or fear.
- Planning fallacy: Underestimate the time and costs needed to complete a task.

Pherson (2019) makes a good attempt at identifying some key biases, misapplied heuristics, and intuitive traps. I've taken the Pherson list of cognitive biases (and misapplied heuristics and traps) as being a useful set to be aware of at the early stages of projects and attempted to reduce these to an even smaller set (15) of the most common biases to be aware of. These are identified in ***bold italics*** (Fig. 9.1).

Let's examine the highlighted (italicised) items in more detail.

Cognitive biases (selection of biases that can impede analytic thinking)

Evidence acceptance bias: Accepting data as true without assessing its credibility because it helps create a more coherent story.

Confirmation bias: Seeking only the information that is consistent with the lead hypothesis, judgement, or conclusion.

Hindsight bias: Claiming to see past events as being predictable at the time those events happened.

Key Biases, Heuristics and Traps (after Pherson)		
Biases	**Misapplied Heuristics**	**Intuitive Traps**
Evidence Acceptance Bias	*Anchoring Effect*	*Assuming a Single Solution*
Confirmation Bias	Associative Memory	Assuming Inevitability
Hindsight Bias	Availability Heuristic	*Confusing Causality & Correlation*
Mirror Imaging	*Desire for Coherence & Uncertainty Reduction*	Expecting Marginal Change
Vividness Bias	*Groupthink*	Favouring First-hand Information
	Mental Shotgun	Ignoring Base Rate Probabilities
	Premature Closure	*Ignoring Inconsistent Evidence (CD)*
	Satisficing	*Ignoring the Absence of Information*
		Judging by Emotion
		Lacking Sufficient Bins
		Misstating Probabilities
		Overestimating Probability
		Overinterpreting Small Samples
		Overrating Behavioural Factors
		Presuming Patterns
		Projecting Past Experiences
		Rejecting Evidence (CD)
		Relying on First Impressions

Fig. 9.1 Key biases

Misapplied heuristics—(when misapplied can impede analytic thinking)

Anchoring effect: Relying too heavily on one piece of information and of accepting a given value of something unknown as the starting point for generating an assessment.

Desire for coherence and uncertainty reduction: Seeing patterns in random events as **systematic** and part of a coherent world (ref CLA).

Groupthink: Occurs when a group of individuals desire conformity or harmony leading to members trying to reduce conflict and reach a consensus without critical evaluation of other viewpoints often by suppressing dissenting opinions.

Premature closure: Stopping the search for a cause when a seemingly satisfactory answer is found before sufficient information is collected and proper analysis can be performed.

Satisficing: Selecting the first answer that appears "good enough" (a form of Occam's razor).

Intuitive traps—examples of common mistakes made by practitioners)

Assuming a single solution: Thinking of only one likely (and predictable) outcome instead of acknowledging "the future is plural" and several outcomes should be considered.

Confusing causality and correlation: Inferring causality inappropriately and assuming that correlation implies causation.

Ignoring inconsistent evidence: Ignoring or discarding information that is inconsistent with what one expects to see.

Ignoring the absence of information: Not addressing the impact of the absence of information on analytic conclusions.

Over-interpreting small samples: Making conclusion based on too small sample sets.

Projecting past experiences: Assuming the same dynamic is in play when something appears to be in accord with an analyst's past experiences.

Rejecting evidence: Continuing to hold a judgement when confronted with a mounting list of contradictory experiences (cognitive dissonance).

Hubris: Arrogance born of overweening pride—usually based on erroneous information.

9.3.1 Bias and Expert Opinion

One can also challenge the reliance on "expert opinion". A Financial Times (2011) article cited how Raghuram Rajan warned of the looming financial crisis prior to 2008 but was ignored by leading central bankers. Post-crisis Rajan argued: *"Economists had all the models required to understand the credit crisis, but that the subject suffers from being segregated into increasingly narrow fields."* Which led to a dearth of generalist experts capable of connecting all the various strands. This concern about so-called expert opinion, has been most succinctly expressed by Tetlock (2005), where he explores why experts are so often wrong when predicting future events, and invariably were often no better than the informed amateur. Again, the issue of complexity is highlighted and Tetlock asks whether we are living in a world which is too complex to understand, or rather we are not using the proper tools which allow us to understand and predict social, economic, and political phenomena. Tetlock (re-cycling Isaiah Berlin's 1950s classification) breaks down experts into two main behavioural groups: "hedgehogs" who hold strong, definite views which are rarely changed and "foxes" who tend to view matters over a broader spectrum and whose opinions are often changed as new evidence becomes apparent. "Foxes" tend to work incrementally, whereas "hedgehogs" can be wrong for long periods but occasionally right for the big event. However, neither group seems significantly competent when forecasting disruptive events because it is so inherently difficult. Yet, there is still strong resistance to accepting the inaccuracy of forecasting and where the hegemony of the expert is rarely challenged. Under such circumstances we see even here that whilst many experts claim to be objective in their judgement and claim to be scrupulous when applying scientific rigour, they can be as prone as anyone to under-acknowledge or even deny biases which are part of their personal psyches. See Chap. 13 for some recent research on expert levels of accuracy.

9.3.2 Bias and the Determination of the Future

It was noted in the previous section how individual behavioural traits can lead even experts astray when attempting to determine the future whether in the form of shorter term forecast or longer term foresight predictions.

If quantitative analysis has been on the front foot in much recent (financial and economic) history—this is not due to a lack of research in the boundaries and limitations of qualitative methods. Rather that vested interests have driven much analytic research to be directed at satisfying the demands of the business and political communities, demanding high levels of perceived precision and certainty which they saw as only being achieved through a highly "mathematical" or causal approach to problem-solving. Such communities tend to be attracted to short-term solutions in response to their working within short time horizons—e.g. the next quarter's results. The short-term nature of the time horizon seduces these policy-makers into thinking that they can control events within such a short timescale—leading to silo mentalities and setting in motion a vicious myopic circle.

Makridakis and Taleb (2009) confirm the existence of these entrenched views in behavioural terms by identifying it as a resistance to accepting the inaccuracy of forecasting by inflexible decision-makers aggravated by large numbers of academics who feed off such beliefs—a pretty damning indictment of hubris compounded by myopia (aka stupidity). Our old friend "the illusion of control".

Two earlier papers by Makridakis (1982) set out to argue the inability to

> accurately predict economic and business events, and to accept such an inability, instead of illusorily relying on the predictions being correct when planning and formulating strategies" and on the other "the inability of economists to forecast forthcoming recessions that were often confirmed long after they had started .... However, the majority of academics and business people were not willing to accept these findings, and instead preferred the illusion of control, pretending that accurate forecasting was possible.

What is striking here is that this research was conducted in the early 1980s—nearly three decades before the 2008 crisis which has so revitalised our thinking about accuracy and uncertainty.

Makridakis, Taleb, and others are not alone. The over-reliance on quantitative methods has been questioned by a growing number of science trained academics (again before 2008) where:

> The mathematical modelling community believed so strongly in models that it insisted on using them even when there was no scientific basis for their application (Pilkey & Pilkey-Jarvis, 2007).

John Kay (2008) writing in the *London Financial Times*, in the wake of the 2008 Autumn financial meltdown, commented on the earlier false belief of computing being the panacea for accurate forecasting—which has since been belatedly challenged and that "*we now understand that economies are complex, dynamic, non-linear systems in which small differences to initial conditions can make large differences to final outcomes....*". Kay refers to a comment attributed to John Maynard Keynes that it is usually better to be conventionally wrong than unconventionally right—a variant of what John Vanston (2007), an American forecaster, said "*... precision and the future are incompatible terms. In essence it is far better to be approximately right than precisely wrong*".

There is a growing body of informed comment that concurs with this stance. It thus comes as no surprise that it was the Crash of 2008 that has forced analysts to re-assess the validity of, or rather, the excessive reliance on established (and largely quantitative) methods and processes. As we have noted, such clarity has still not pervaded all practitioner areas.

Apart from a significant amount of anecdotal observations, the earlier references (Makridakis & Taleb, 2009), whereby too many practitioners and academics refuse to contemplate the inaccuracy of forecasting and quantitative methods, reside not only at an individual level, but at an organisational level. This phenomenon has been termed having a "silo mentality"—where many organisations are populated by "hedgehogs" (who resolutely continue to attempt crossing the road until flattened by a vehicle appearing suddenly). Other phenomena of a similar ilk have been termed "following the herd" (Keynes' comment about being conventionally wrong rather than unconventionally right) or expressed as "no-one ever got fired for buying IBM (or hiring McKinsey)"—**in effect being constrained by orthodoxy**. Uncertainty scares people—we don't like it—so in many cases we ignore it—with often disastrous results. These individual characteristics when transposed to the organisation create inflexibility and create a real lack of foresight.

An interesting manifestation of the fragility of quantitative performance measures, when impacted by behavioural factors, has been identified by Princeton psychologist, John Darley. In 1994, Darley postulated, in what has become known as "Darley's Law", that:

> The more any quantitative performance measure is used to determine a group's or an individual's rewards and punishments, the more subject it will be to corruption pressures and the more apt it will be to distort and corrupt the action patterns and thoughts of the group or individual it is intended to monitor. ...The critical control system unleashes enormous human ingenuity. People will maximize the criteria set. However, they may do so in ways that are not anticipated by the criterion setters, in ways that destroy the validity of the criteria. The people make their numbers but the numbers no longer mean what you thought they did.

In effect Darley says that ethical problems (which we cannot quantify) are almost always inherent in systems designed to measure performance. We all know what the examples are: body count manipulation in the Vietnam War (via Robert McNamara formerly a Ford executive), the pilot in "Catch-22" who manipulates the performance measurement system by flying safe routes, sales force commission plans, and, you've guessed it—bankers' bonuses—a beautiful set of unintended consequences.

Finally, Gowing and Langdon (2017) ask "why are 'unthinkables' not thought about?" Having questioned a number of corporate and government leaders and decision-makers as to why it is so difficult to think about the unthinkable, they identified 9 recurring words and phrases, these being:

- Being overwhelmed by multiple, intense pressures
- Institutional conformity
- Wilful blindness
- Groupthink
- Risk aversion
- Fear of career limiting moves
- Reactionary mind-sets

- Denial
- Cognitive overload and dissonance

The earlier section of this chapter, which identifies a number of cognitive biases and heuristic traps, illustrates why the above items will not come as a surprise. The constraints to thinking about the unthinkable—but still possible—are largely behavioural and are barriers to the development of quality scenario narratives.

9.3.3   Bias and the Media, Bias Clusters, and "Le Defi Objectif"

Over the last few years there has been increasing attention to the role of the media in helping to develop, increase, and re-enforce a number of cognitive behaviours such as bias and dissonance in both individuals and groups—generally with negative impacts. The rapid expansion of Internet-driven social media has been a notable feature of this new century.

This growing number of media options, not just via the Internet but the profusion of cable channels targeting niche interests, increases the options available to people so that they can selectively expose themselves to particular media messages. In effect, they can control what they want to see and not want to see at a much higher level of granularity which all too often means media which is only consistent with their own point of view. Such a trend leads to a stifling of any form of objective opinion making.

Social media has increasingly been seen to be a corrosive influence on opinion forming—where bias clusters have arisen to re-inforce pre-established biases in individuals whilst acting as a barrier to alternative viewpoints which could help to "fact-check" the often highly entrenched positions of such clusters. With the tendency to seek out similar ideas with which we are more comfortable with, no longer being restricted to physical geographic communities such as a town or city—the much broader reach across geographic boundaries that social media afford strengthens the bond between individuals and groups within similar mind-sets and perspectives—ranging from a love of a particular pop group to more insidious and darker interests such as various forms of more fundamentalist political dogma and religious views.

What continues to strengthen the role and influence of bias clusters are the algorithms that social media use to re-enforce similar behaviour patterns and attitudes to the detriment and exclusion of alternative opinion to those who do not conform to our ideas lifestyles. Algorithms can be thought of as the fuel tank of search engines, social media websites, recommendation engines, online retail, online advertising, etc. There is increasing concern amongst social scientists and commentators as to the so-called neutrality of these algorithms. The term "algorithmic bias" has now entered the lexicon. Authors such a Sara Wachter-Boettcher (2017), Steffan Mau (2019), and Cathy O'Neil (2016), where they identify the foibles and dodgy coefficients of a number of algorithms which incorporate the biases of their creators—such as in credit scoring across various social and indeed racial groups.

In a recent CBC news blog Ramona Pringle, an associate professor at Ryerson University specifically addressed the issue of social media blinding us to other points of view (Pringle, 2016). In the blog she refers to research from Columbia University showing that users tend to click links that affirm their existing opinions. *"Facebook is designed to prevent you from hearing others,"* says media scholar Douglas Rushkoff. *"It creates a false sense of agreement, a 'confirmation bias' when you are only seeing stuff that agrees with you or makes the other side look completely stupid."*

In essence she confirms that the problem of much social media is that, when an individual's pre-existing opinions shape the news he or she wants to see, they are not getting an accurate picture of what is really happening. Pringle goes on to state that because people are only seeing news and media through a self-selecting group of similar minded individuals they are subjecting themselves to living in a filter bubble and not engaging with people with differing views. She quotes a study by *"Pew Research whereby 79% of social media users said they have never changed their views on a social or political issue because of something they saw on social media"*.(Pringle, 2016)

She identifies that more insidious is that it is not just a self-selected social network that creates this echo chamber but that the social network (e.g. Facebook) *"filters the news we see on the site, by suggesting media — like the ads we see — that is tailored to our preferences"*. Such points of view have recently been expounded by the Facebook whistle-blower Frances Haugen.

9.4   Cognitive Dissonance

Whilst there has been a growing interest in cognitive bias based on the work of Kahneman and Tversky—and given a boost in 2012 by the very successful publication in 2012 of Daniel Kahneman's "Thinking, Fast and Slow", there is another behavioural trait, often neglected, which the author believes is as important as cognitive bias, in explaining why humans persist in certain beliefs even when confronted by firm evidence to the contrary. This form of behaviour is called "cognitive dissonance" and there are signs that can occur at both the individual and group level.

The theory of cognitive dissonance was developed by social psychologist Leon Festinger (1957) in the 1950s. In brief cognitive dissonance is *"the mental discomfort (psychological stress) experienced by a person who holds two or more contradictory beliefs, ideas, or values. This discomfort is triggered by a situation in which a person's belief clashes with new evidence perceived by the person creating psychological conflict resulting from incongruous beliefs and attitudes held simultaneously"*. It can also be expressed as being the psychological conflict resulting from incongruous beliefs and attitudes held simultaneously.

Festinger based the theory on the belief that humans want all of their actions and beliefs to be consistent. When this not the case, a frequent occurrence, a discomfort arises. Dissonance can manifest itself in a variety of ways such as stress, anxiety, embarrassment, shame, regret, and negative self-worth.

To reduce this mental discomfort the individual seeks to create psychological consistency. This allows the afflicted person with cognitive dissonance to lessen mental stress by actions that reduce the magnitude of the dissonance. This is achieved by changing, by justifying against, or by being indifferent to the contradiction that is inducing the mental stress. In practice, people reduce the magnitude of their cognitive dissonance in four ways:

1. Change the behaviour ("I'll stop smoking.")
2. Justify the behaviour, by changing the conflicting cognition ("I only smoke once a day.")
3. Justify the behaviour by adding new cognitions ("I'll only smoke low tar filter cigarettes")
4. Ignore or deny information that conflicts with existing beliefs. (Smoking helps me relieve stress.)

One can add a fifth category whereby there are increasing trends of outright denial of the evidence and that such evidence is a plot "by the elite"—witness the denial associated with the COVID anti-vaxxers. **Conspiracy theory is now an active ingredient in the cognitive dissonance mix.**

And of course, we had (maybe still have) the highly polemicized position of the Brexit issue. Social media is causing increasing cognitive dissonance leading to many people only searching for data or evidence which re-enforces their own cognitive positions (or prejudices). In essence the theory states that people do not like to have previously held beliefs challenged. People following a given perspective, when confronted with contrary evidence, spend a great amount of effort in justifying why they should retaining the challenged perspective.

Cognitive bias does contribute to dissonance theory. Biases include justification that one does not have any biases, the bias that one is "better, more moral and nicer than average" and confirmation bias (see above list of biases).

9.4.1   Examples of Cognitive Dissonance

Apart from the example of trying to give up smoking used above other common areas where dissonance manifests itself can be found in the worlds of advertising and decision-making.

Advertisers regularly exploit the arousal of cognitive dissonance amongst their target audiences by hinting or suggesting that if you want to adopt a particular lifestyle image then why not wear this item of clothing or use this type of cosmetic or drive this model of car (years ago it used to be what type of cigarette you smoked). In other words, if you don't buy the product your self-image will be weakened in some way.

Cognitive dissonance is part of decision-making, between two or more alternatives. And of course, we can see that when the options themselves contain high levels of uncertainty then cognitive dissonance can really cause problems for the decision-maker especially when the options have positive rather than negative attributes. Which one does one select?

9.5 Anomie (and Alienation)

Back in 1970 Alvin Toffler popularised the term, "Future Shock", highlighting the negative impacts of too much change in too short a time. The reality is that most inevitable surprises arrive without much warning, if any at all—they arrive as "shocks" in spite of their inevitability and presumed contingency plans. As Mike Tyson is famously quoted as saying: *"Everyone has a plan 'till they get punched in the mouth."*

Apart from our personal biases behaviour can also be affected by how we react to what is happening around us—at the group and individual level. And when what is happening is subject to rapid change and associated levels of uncertainty we can feel a sense of alienation and purposelessness.

Emile Durkheim, a nineteenth-century French sociologist, adopted the word "anomie" to express a condition where belief systems are challenged or in conflict with what has previously been experienced, to the extent that they create a breakdown in the social bonds between an individual and the community. Durkheim developed his ideas on anomie through the study of suicide (Durkheim, 1897). He believed that one type of suicide, *anomic*, occurred following the breakdown of the social standards necessary for regulating behaviour. He posited that when a social system is in a state of anomie, where common values are no longer understood or accepted, a social vacuum exists where new values have not been established. Such a society produces a variety of negative psychological states typified by a sense of futility, lack of purpose, emotional emptiness, and despair.

In the 1930s, American sociologist Robert K Merton (1938) also studied the causes of anomie. As an example, he said that if a society heavily encouraged its members to acquire wealth but provided them with few means to do so, the stress would cause many people to violate norms. Under such circumstances the only form of regulation would be the desire for personal advantage and fear of punishment causing social behaviour to become unpredictable.

Readers may be more familiar with the term "alienation" rather than "anomie". Both anomie and alienation make an individual isolated in different forms. There are differences such that anomie can lead to a breakdown of social bonds between an individual and the society in which he or she lives due to the individual himself or herself not accepting the values or norms of that society. Alienation on the other hand occurs where the situation the individual finds himself or herself in is a result of external forces driving that individual to feel isolated or estranged. Karl Marx's interpretation of alienation was that it was the capitalist system which drove its workers into a state of alienation as they had no control over their fate.

9.6   Our Behaviour in Relation to Others: Considerations

In early 2020, and once the COVID-19 pandemic had taken hold, I wrote a blog note posted on LinkedIn posing the following question:

> Will the post pandemic "new normal" make us more aware of ourselves in relation to others?
> Such changes in behaviour will only be meaningful if we understand how others experience
> Us and We, Them—and that is no easy transformation.

With much chatter about what might be the "new normal" (or indeed "new normals") one major theme is how individuals within society may become more understanding of our own and others' foibles.

Back in the 1960s, a controversial Scottish psychiatrist, R D Laing, developed radically different views, from the contemporary orthodoxy, on how to treat mental illness especially schizophrenia. His book, *The Divided Self*, first published in 1960 was a landmark publication in the interpretation of schizophrenia—and was an early indication of a more existentialist approach to how the human mind can work. Later in the decade he published a dual tome book called *The Politics of Experience* and *The Bird of Paradise* (1967). It was the first of these papers that heavily influenced my thinking at the time (well, I was studying sociology), and has done so at frequent intervals since then. Within *The Politics of Experience* is a detailed linguistic description of how we see others and others see us.

Laing's script is not an easy read. The original core text described as "Experience as Evidence" is only 581 words long. However such is the intensity of the logic contained therein that I urge the reader to make an effort to discover this intensity. You will need to re-read it several times in order to understand its impact and how we might better relate to one another in an uncertain world. Over 50 years after it was first written the text is still key to our understanding of what is a fact. New social media-driven behaviours are driving society into increasingly fragmented opinions and behaviours.

Key extracts from the original text, along with an interpretation, highlight the complexity of fact-based evidence and how individuals experience such phenomena and their behavioural responses.

- *"Even facts become fictions without adequate ways of seeing "the facts"*: This challenges our real understanding of what is "a fact" and highlights the influence of bias when seeking to determine such facts.
- *"We can see other people's behaviour, but not their experience"* and *"I cannot experience your experience. You cannot experience my experience."*: Experience

is in effect a form of internalisation which determines our behaviour, yet humans only externalise their experience of the other person; they cannot internalise it.

- *"I see you, and you see me. I experience you, and you experience me. I see your behaviour. You see my behaviour. But I do not and never have and never will see your experience of me. Just as you cannot "see" my experience of you."* This position is an expanded version of the previous statement but re-enforces the difficulty of eradicating cognitive biases—the latter reflecting highly personal earlier experiences—unique to an individual. The best we can hope for is perhaps empathy.

- *"If, however, experience is evidence, how can one ever study the experience of the other? For the experience of the other is not evident to me, as it is not and never can be an experience of mine."*: This statement has profound implications for bias mitigation—we can only go so far in reducing biases—however this acknowledgement alone may be sufficient to reduce the worst of bias denial which is best that we can hope for, as I cannot directly experience you experiencing your experience.

- *"I do not experience your experience. But I experience you as experiencing. I experience myself as experienced by you. And I experience you as experiencing yourself as experienced by me. And so on. The study of the experience of others, is based on inferences I make, from my experience of you experiencing me, about how you are experiencing me experiencing you experiencing me ...."*: In summary, and as indicated in the previous reflection, this may be the best we can hope for. Just being aware of such limitations is a powerful defence against accepting all evidence as fact—and as Funtowicz and Ravetz (1994) postulated earlier in a post-normal world *"facts are uncertain, values in dispute, stakes high and decisions urgent".*

Extracts from page 15, 16, and 17—Chapter 1—Persons and Experience. "The Politics of Experience and The Bird of Paradise" R.D. Laing. Published by Penguin Books 1967.

References

Durkheim, E. (1897). *Le Suicide: Etude de sociologie*. Routledge.
Festinger, L. (1957). *A theory of cognitive dissonance*. Stanford University Press.
Financial Times. (2011, February 10). *Why can't economists predict disruptive events*. Gavyn Davies.
Funtowicz, S. O., & Ravetz, J. R. (1994). Uncertainty, complexity and post-normal science. *Annual Review of Environmental Toxicology and Chemistry, 13*(12).
Gowing, N., & Langdon, C. (2017). *Thinking the unthinkable*. John Catt Educational 2018 following a draft for CIMA – Chartered Institute of Management Accountants.
Kahneman, D., Slovic, P., & Tversky, A. (Eds.). (1982). *Judgment under uncertainty: Heuristics and biases*. Cambridge University Press.
Kay, J. (2008, November 26). Predictive models "Blown off course by butterflies". *Financial Times*, p. 13.

Laing, R. D.. Extract from page 15, 16 & 17 – Chapter 1 (1967). *Persons and experience. "The politics of experience and the bird of paradise"*. Published by Penguin Books.

Makridakis S, *"If we cannot forecast how can we plan?"* (Makridakis, 1981), and *"A chronology of the last six recessions"* (Makridakis, 1982).

Makridakis, S., & Taleb, N. (2009). Living in a world of low levels of predictability. *International Journal of Forecasting, 25*(4) Elsevier BV.

Mau, S. (2019). *The metric society*. Polity.

Merton, R. K. (1938). Social structure and anomie. *American Sociological Review, 3*(5).

O'Neil, C. (2016). *Weapons of math destruction*. Penguin, Random House.

Padbury, P. (2019). *An overview of the horizons foresight method using system based-scenarios and the "inner game" of foresight*. Chief Futurist, Policy Horizons, Government of Canada.

Pherson, R. H. (2019). *Handbook of analytic tools & technique* (5th ed.). Published Pherson Associates.

Pilkey, O. H., & Pilkey-Jarvis, L. (2007). *Useless arithmetic – Why environmental scientists can't predict the future*. Columbia University Press.

Pringle, R. (2016, November 14). Social media is blinding us to other points of view. *CBC News*.

Taylor, J. (2013, May). *Cognitive biases are bad for business*.

Tetlock, P. E. (2005). *Expert political judgement*. Princeton University Press.

Tversky, A., & Kahneman, D. (1974). Judgement under uncertainty: Heuristics and biases. *Science, New Series, 185*(4157), 1124–1131.

Vanston, J. H. (2007). *P40 Section 3 in "Technology forecasting – An aid to effective technology management"*. Technology Futures Inc.

Wachter-Boettcher, S. (2017). *Technically wrong*. W. Norton & Co Ltd.

Chapter 10
How to Mitigate the Impact
of the Behavioural Minefield

*We cannot fully grasp the nature and the implications of what
happened in the concentration camps if we shy away from
facing the destructive tendencies of man, the aggressive
aspect of our animal inheritance which in man has assumed a
specifically human and peculiarly destructive form
Bruno Bettelheim—The Informed Heart.*

Abstract In the previous chapter, we saw that subjectivity tends to be stronger than objectivity, which in turn impacted the efficacy of decision-making. The higher the level of uncertainty the higher the level individuals and groups rely on their biases and use of heuristics to make decisions. Here we examine a variety of approaches to counteract biases as well as confronting the challenges of digital disinformation, filter bubbles, and social media influenced echo chambers. Mitigation approaches such as improving media literacy and fact-checking are reviewed to challenge the worst of that behaviour governed by these traits and to mitigate their impact. Reference is made as to how Finland has introduced methods to mitigate the worst influence of targeted disinformation as well as a selection of ideas to reduce individual and group-based cognitive dissonance.

Keywords Counteracting bias · Digital disinformation · Fact checking · Filter bubbles · Echo chambers

10.1 Introduction

In Chap. 9, it was highlighted how various behavioural conditions can impact how effectively, or not, individuals and group make decision-based choices. Subjectivity was seen to override objectivity, impacting the efficacy of decision-making, falling back on biases when confronted with complex situations. In this chapter, we shall examine a variety of approaches to challenge the worst of behaviour governed by these traits and mitigate their impact.

10.2   Counteracting Biases

It is extremely difficult, if not nigh on impossible, to eradicate completely bias behaviour in ourselves and in others. The main defence is for individuals, analysts, and decision-makers to be, at least, aware how cognitive bias can influence decision-making—identification can help mitigate the worst effects.

Pherson (2019), a former CIA intelligence analyst, confirms that engrained mind-sets are a major contributor to analytic failures. Although recognised as a problem, past experience shows that analytic traps and mind-sets are easy to form but surprisingly difficult to change. There are a myriad of reasons why mind-sets are difficult to dislodge. Most often, time pressures lead analysts to jump to conclusions and to head down the wrong path. As more information becomes available, analysts are increasingly inclined to select that which supports their lead hypothesis and to ignore or reject information that is inconsistent. Contradictory information becomes lost in the noise.

Kahneman et al. (1982) **suggest there are three questions to ask in order to reduce the impact of cognitive biases when making decisions:**

1. Is there any reason to suspect the people making the recommendation of biases based on self-interest, overconfidence, or attachment to past experiences?
2. Have the people making the recommendation overcommitted to it and thus failure to follow up would cause some discomfort?
3. Was there groupthink or were there dissenting opinions within the decision-making team?

Taylor (2013) **identifies four practical steps to mitigate such cognitive bias:**

1. **Awareness** that such biases exist and influence decision-making. Such awareness acts as an initial buffer when faced with behaviours such as groupthink, silo thinking, and hubris. Self-reflection is key here.
2. **Collaboration** can help mitigate cognitive biases as one can observe biased behaviour easier in others than one can oneself. Self-awareness as identified in 1 above can be enhanced by such external observations in others.
3. **Continuous and iterative** inquiry is vital if one is to challenge perceptions and judgements that can be tainted by cognitive biases.
4. Though brainstorming type activities are useful introductory techniques they can hide the presence of biases especially where a dominant member pushes their particular agenda. **More structured frameworks** and processes help increase the identification of cognitive biases before they are internalised into the decision-making activity.

What Pherson calls "structured analytic techniques" can help decision-makers and analysts avoid or at least mitigate many of these biases helping them to:

- Reduce error rates
- Avoid intelligence and other analytic failures
- Embrace more collaborative work practices

- Increase accountability
- Make the analysis more transparent to other analysts and decision-makers.

All the above approaches are valid, yet in so many instances, humans remain contented to be cocooned within their entrenched biases and established thought processes—if individuals, groups, and organisations are unwilling to examine their thought processes and value systems consistently, then there is little hope that behavioural change can take place and old habits continue to contaminate objective decision analysis and decision-making.

Pherson believes diagnostic and reframing techniques can help mitigate the worst of this behaviour saying that experience shows how difficult it is to overcome the tendency to reach premature closure, embrace "groupthink", and avoid analytic traps. Overcoming mind-sets relies on employing structured forcing mechanisms that require analysts to seek out new perspectives and possibilities. Without the use of structured analytic techniques analysts are less likely to identify and challenge key assumptions, think critically about the evidence, reframe analysis, and, most importantly, avoid surprise. The techniques also impose a greater degree of transparency, consistency, and accountability. They work most robustly with the participation of a diverse set of participants bringing a variety of perspectives to the table.

Diagnostic techniques include:

- Key assumptions check: Makes explicit and questions the assumptions that guide an analyst's interpretation of evidence and the reasoning underlying any particular judgement or conclusion.
- Multiple hypothesis generation: Generates multiple alternatives for explaining an issue, activity, or event. It is done in a variety of ways, ranging from a form of structured brainstorming to the development of complex permutation trees.
- Diagnostic reasoning: Applies hypothesis testing to the evaluation of significant new information in the context of all plausible explanations. It forces analysts to challenge their existing mental mind-sets.
- Analysis of competing hypotheses (ACH): Applies Karl Popper's theory of science to intelligence analysis. It involves the weighting of the available information against a set of alternative explanations and selecting the explanation that fits best by focusing on the information that tends to disconfirm the other explanations. **Note**: *Chap. 8 introduces ACH as a key MTT in more detail.*
- Inconsistencies finder: Uses a simplified version of ACH that evaluates the relative credibility of a set of hypotheses based on the amount of disconfirming information that has been identified.
- Deception detection: Employs a set of checklists analysts can use to determine when to anticipate deception, the actual presence of Fake News deception, and what to do to avoid being deceived.
- Chronologies and timelines: Organises data on events or actions when it is important to understand the timing and sequence of relevant events or identify key gaps.

Intelligence errors, which led to the 9/11 attacks and the erroneous analysis in overstating Iraq's weapons of destruction, forced US intelligence agencies to focus on alternative forms of analysis which reduced the impact of cognitive biases via the use of "reframing techniques" including:

- Outside-in thinking: Focuses on the broader forces that can influence an issue of concern.
- Structured analogies: Applies analytic rigour to reasoning by analogy.
- High impact/low probability analysis: Warns a decision-maker of the possibility a low probability event may happen even if the evidential base for making such a conclusion is weak.
- What if? Analysis: Alerts a decision-maker to an event that could happen, or could be happening, even if it may seem unlikely at the time.
- Classic quadrant crunching: Uses key assumptions and their opposites as a starting point for systematically identifying and considering all possible relationships in a multidimensional highly complex, and usually non-quantifiable problem space.
- Pre-mortem analysis: Reduces the risk of analytic failure by identifying and analysing a potential failure before it occurs.
- Structured self-critique: Employs a checklist process to review all the possible ways an analysis could turn out to be incorrect.
- Red hat analysis: Marshalls the expertise, culture, and analytic skills required for a team to explore how an adversary or competitor would think about an issue.

The main argument here is of course the willingness of those policy-makers to avail themselves of such techniques and not fall into the trap of hubris so that alternative approaches are seen as detrimental to more ideological forms of policy development.

The diagnostic and reframing techniques described above provide a systematic and rigorous check for analysts to assure themselves that their assessment about "what is" is as accurate as possible. They are designed to uncover untested assumptions, examine alternative explanations and perspectives, and uncover hidden analytic traps. Armed with such indicators, the analyst can warn policy-makers and decision-makers of possible futures and alert them in advance, based on the evidence. Turning such messages into action is of course another issue.

None of these diagnostic or reframing techniques guarantee that all unforeseen events will be anticipated. Intelligence surprises are inevitable, but the use of these techniques will ensure a greater rigour to the analysis and reduce the chances of surprise. More important is that such application of techniques needs to be done on a regular if not continuing bases and be integrated into operational activity. If analysts continually test, probe, and indeed attack their assumptions and mind-sets, they will be more capable of knowing what they know and discovering what they did not realise they did not know. The use of these techniques helps analysts anticipate what might occur in the future and better prepare themselves to track developments that presage dramatic change. In the end, decision-makers will benefit from the more thoughtful, comprehensive analysis that results from employing these techniques (Pherson & Pyrik, 2018).

More recently and following the polarising impact of the Trump era and issues such as Brexit, Pherson (2021) turned his interest to addressing how such polarisation could be addressed. Such polarisation itself is a manifestation of ingrained cognitive biases and cognitive dissonance amongst both individuals and groups. He encourages the process of "constructive dialogues" which includes:

- Spending more time talking to each other—not arguing with each other. The focus when we speak should be **to inform, not persuade**. He continues saying:

    A good way to start a conversation is to ask where someone gets their information. If it is a different set of sources than yours then consider this a great opportunity to learn what data they are relying on to form their opinions. Later you can reflect on whether that data is valid. If it can be challenged, then send them reports or information that points out the factual errors in their data or the faults in their judgment that they can read privately without feeling challenged.

- Stop arguing about "facts" and **reframe discussions around positive narratives.**

Focus attention and energy on the future and listening to or seeking positive solutions.

- Let the parties concerned be aware that cognitive bias is extremely powerful and that **mind-sets are extraordinarily hard to change.**
- **Establish an authoritative set of objective standards** for what is appropriate and inappropriate to post on social media. This, however, may require considerable heavy lifting when it comes to lobbying various institutions and vested interests.
- **Craft your own positive personal narrative** of what needs to be done to make things better. Identify who needs to be engaged and what resources are required to make it happen. Pherson adds that you should *"Join and/or build a network connecting you with others who want to promote constructive narratives and forge fair and balanced solutions. Make sure your group is inclusive of all views on the topic. Once your "team" has agreed on a preferred, consensus outcome, construct an action plan and generate some **indicators** to track your progress"*.

In the previous chapter, we referred to how expert opinion can also be prone to bias (Tetlock, 2005). A recent academic paper entitled *"Expert biases in technology foresight. Why they are a problem and how to mitigate them"* by Bonaccorsi, Apreda, and Fantoni (2020) states that that it is extremely difficult to *"formulate foresight in new technologies by relying exclusively on quantitative methods, without the support of human experts ...."*
They continue:

    It is common knowledge in the technology foresight literature that human experts are subject to a number of biases and distortions in their judgments. It can be said that the impressive development of methodologies in the last half century is an effort to mitigate these distortions, particularly with Delphi techniques and their variants.

They go on to propose a number of newly developed techniques which are more promising for addressing the limitations of experts. However, they also observe that only a few studies have explored the role of cognitive biases recognising that Delphi techniques may mitigate some biases such as overconfidence, but not all.

A number of mitigation approaches are highlighted namely:

Mitigation by diversity—by enlarging the perspective of individual experts and combining their opinions with non-experts, the aim is that the increased diversity might mitigate cognitive biases and not be dominated by one or several individuals.

Mitigation by negation—this encourages experts to systematically consider an opposite view or counter argument. In this way framing and anchoring biases can be mitigated.

Mitigation by abstraction—it is argued here that the reasoning of experts can be deeply embedded into their specific domain knowledge. Bonaccorsi et al. state that as a result experts *"are less cognitively loaded when they reason in terms of domain knowledge, that is, in terms of known solutions to problems. On the contrary, it is very demanding to keep the reasoning active for several hours in an abstract space, in which, to make an example, drawings or calculations are not concretely available. Therefore what is needed is a strategy to alleviate the cognitive load of abstraction, helping experts to keep in their mind several, possibly conflicting, high level technological options, while exploring all potential implications"*. (Bonaccorsi et al., 2020)

As per Pherson's point of view, Bonaccorsi et al. also see post-mortem exercises are a useful format in identifying biases which can help identify what methods were most effective in reducing them. Their final call is for more research in the field of cognitive biases to be carried out in relation to expert opinion.

10.3   Digital Disinformation, Media Literacy, and Fact-checking

We have seen in the chapter on the evidence base (5) how the latest and increasing trends in the dissemination of "fake news" is a clear and present danger to rational argument and balanced objectivity. Wardle and Derakshan (2017) identified that the purveyors of disinformation tap into our biases, conscious or otherwise, and our deep-seated fears. Truth therefore needs to be more resonant if it is not to be drowned out. To re-iterate what was said in Chap. 7, if such false information is to be challenged, then our brains need to replace such falsehood with an alternative narrative. It would appear that much greater resources, neutrally funded, be made available to fact-checking organisations—since as has been identified earlier "fact-checking" costs money whereas lies are cheap. The cost of mounting a "counter-insurgency campaign" against the increasing hegemony of fake news will be a high one.

The challenge for those individuals, groups, organisations and even nations wishing to maintain and secure the veracity of their evidence bases will be to continually seek out and deploy technology-driven strategies that will counteract "bad actors"—a complex, daunting, and, probably, never-ending task.

"Fake news" is not a new phenomenon—false propaganda has been around for centuries, albeit in different guises. Wherever there is diversity of opinion, biased opinion, based on questionable sources of information, can prevail—especially when the means of communication are tightly controlled by governments and/or powerful vested interests.

Although the current and growing spate of disinformation has relied heavily on the application of technology to media-based dissemination, those same groups of technologies can also be deployed to challenge such threats and increasingly identify fake news. The challenge is to ensure that such counter platforms have a voice which is louder than the "bad actors".

Defense One (2019), an online news platform specialising in national security issues, recently stated that:

Thanks to social media, fake news can now be disseminated at breakneck pace to vast audiences that are often unable or unwilling to separate fact from fiction. Studies suggest that fake news spreads up to six times faster on social media than genuine stories, while false news stories are 70 percent more likely to be shared on Twitter. Observers call it "spam on steroids.

Pertinently the article observed:

Put another way, it is difficult to consume fake news free from the influence of personal opinion. That's where technology can help.

The article goes onto introduce two real-life approaches to combating disinformation and fake news, especially when channelled via social media. The first one goes under the name "Tanbih", a Qatari-based operation which looks at specific bits of content, searching for common propaganda techniques, including loaded language, stereotyping, and stretched facts within content and coverage. It uses AI to train users to spot usage of propaganda techniques in texts and develop critical thinking when interacting with news.

A more formalised approach has been adopted by the Finnish government in its battle against digital disinformation and where a number of commentators have referred to this template. Sources include an extensive 2019 CNN report, Defense One's online comments, and Pherson Associates' May 1921 reference in "The Analytic Insider" news sheet. In this next section, we shall examine in greater detail how the Finnish approach operates.

10.3.1 The Finnish Approach

In 2015, Finland launched a concerted campaign to advise officials help prepare its citizens identify fake news and counter narratives designed to sow division within the country, understand why it goes viral, and develop strategies to combat it. This approach was integrated into the education system curriculum so that it paid greater attention to critical thinking. Another strategy that proved highly effective was to **develop a strong, positive national narrative**, rather than trying to debunk false claims.

According to a CNN Special Report (2019), the campaign has been successful, and in 2018 in a study measuring resilience to the "post-truth" phenomenon, Finland was placed first out of some 35 countries.

Another strategy that proved highly effective was to **develop a strong, positive national narrative**, rather than trying to debunk false claims. Through its critical thinking curriculum, Finland encourages children to examine YouTube videos, social media, and news articles for factual and statistical errors. A fact-checking organisation "Faktabaari" has since 2017 adapted professional fact-checking methods for Finnish schools. A paper prepared by the Faktabaari team (2018) provides extensive detail as to the scheme's *modus operandi*.

It appears that Finland's strong position in the battle against fake news is based on a number of factors such as:

- A national narrative that places a high premium on the rule of law and belonging.
- A high education profile all helping to create an environment where media literacy can flourish.
- A high standard of living more equally spread across its population.
- A largely homogenous society free from social fragmentation.

Specific tools deployed by the Finns, especially amongst highly literate school age and higher education student cohorts, include:

- A checklist of methods used to deceive readers on social media: image and video manipulations, half-truths, intimidation, and false profiles.
- How to identify bots: look for stock photos, assess the volume of posts per day, check for inconsistent translations, and a lack of personal information.
- Exercises to examining claims found in YouTube videos and social media posts, comparing media bias in an array of different "clickbait" articles, probing how misinformation preys on readers' emotions, and even getting students to try their hand at writing fake news stories themselves (CNN Report, 2019).
- Encouraging students to think twice before liking or sharing social media and ask "who has written this?", "where has it been published", and "can I find the same information from another source?"—aka validation.

However, it is accepted that Finland has a number of advantages which makes it especially well placed to combat the tsunami of fake news and disinformation. It is a small and largely homogenous country consistently ranked at or near the top of almost every index—happiness, press freedom, gender equality, social justice, transparency, education, and literacy. This makes it difficult for external actors to find cracks within society to force open and exploit.

Even within Finland some commentators state that the social media companies themselves (Facebook, Twitter, Google, YouTube) need to be regulated as they are regularly seen as enablers of hostile actors and trolls. A journalist Jessikka Aro suggests that:

> Just like any polluting companies or factories should be and are already regulated, for polluting the air and the forests, the waters, these companies are polluting the minds of people. So, they also have to pay for it and take responsibility for it. (CNN, 2019).

Finally, even the Finns acknowledge that the battle against fake news and disinformation is a never-ending battle as "bad actors" continually seek new ways and means to contaminate the "airwaves". The battle will not be won by just the Finns of this world. Far greater international coordination between nations, the social media companies themselves, NGOs, and international regulatory bodies needs to be enacted if those bad actors who exploit cognitive biases are ever to be challenged and eventually defeated. It is one of the world's most wicked of problems!

10.4 Filter Bubbles and Echo Chambers: The Curse of the Selective Algorithm

A major criticism levelled at various social media search engines is that the algorithms used help create filter bubbles. The bubbles allow for the isolation of ideas and views belonging to an individual by selectively assuming the information a user wants to see, and then providing such information to that user according to this assumption. The website algorithms track user behaviour such as former click preferences, browsing and search history, as well as location. This means that websites will tend to present only information to that user that reflects the user's past activity. A filter bubble, therefore, can cause users to receive significantly less contact with different or contradicting viewpoints, so that the user can become intellectually isolated. It is argued that filter bubbles can lead to ideological polarisation so that users fail to receive balanced information, seeing only that information that is aimed at re-enforcing our established interests and existing worldviews. It should be said that further research needs to be carried to ascertain the full impact of how much filter bubbles actually do constrict access to alternative views.

10.4.1   A New Tool to Help Mitigate the Impact of Filter Bubbles

Je Hyun Kim,[1] a student carrying out a research project at Imperial College London and the Royal College of Art, has developed an app aimed at exploring opposing views and echo chambers in order to help mitigate the impact of polarisation caused by machine learning algorithms.

The objective of Je Hyun's project was to see if people changed their initial opinion once they are given both sides of the story. After a number of trials using the app that he developed he noticed that people did in fact hold less extreme opinions when they heard about the opposing point of view and notably for individuals who are similar in education and social/economic background as other people.

A key insight from this phase of the project was that participants were not aware of how these recommendations later influenced their opinion. To prevent individuals from having extreme opinions and to understand the other point of view (POV) of other people, the user first need to realise that their own opinion was one-sided.

By matching user A with one set of strong opinions with the opposing views of user B introduced doubt into each of the users as to their own biases, so that they started to rethink their own POV. The biggest challenge was to design a user interface that highlighted the opposing view in the most convincing way.

His research identified that this required:

- Using a personal recommendation system, as both business and users get benefit from it,

shows opposite point of view.

- The opposing view should come from someone similar in terms of social profile, age, etc.
- The ability to see directly the other user's POV
- Making the app design highly interactive.

The process is illustrated in Fig. 10.1 below

The algorithm behind the app consisted of two main parts. The first part recommends similar users. This is done by using a clustering method using unsupervised machine learning, similar to how dating apps recommend you a date. Past behaviour such as subscriptions and history will be included in the data to cluster. The second part is to find the opposing videos. By using natural language processing, keywords can be spotted. The algorithm can now find videos that aren't related to the user's keywords so that a real alternative is accessed.

The initial interface is illustrated in Fig. 10.2

---

[1]If you require further information of Je Hyun Kim's work he can be contacted at: 245656@network.rca.ac.uk. He is currently on the Innovation Design Engineering programme a joint course at Imperial College's Dyson School of Design Engineering and the Royal College of Art (RCA).

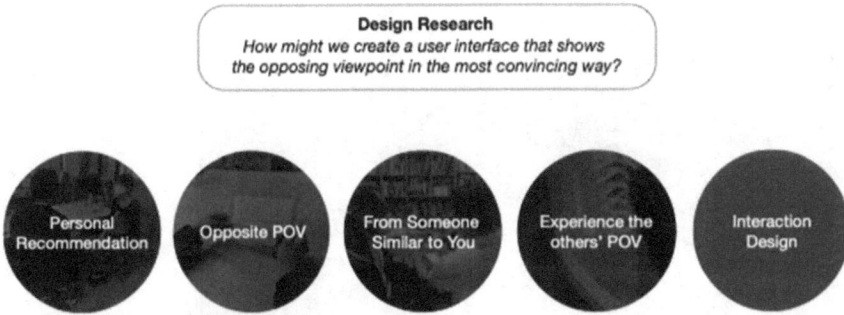

Fig. 10.1 Profile of design research

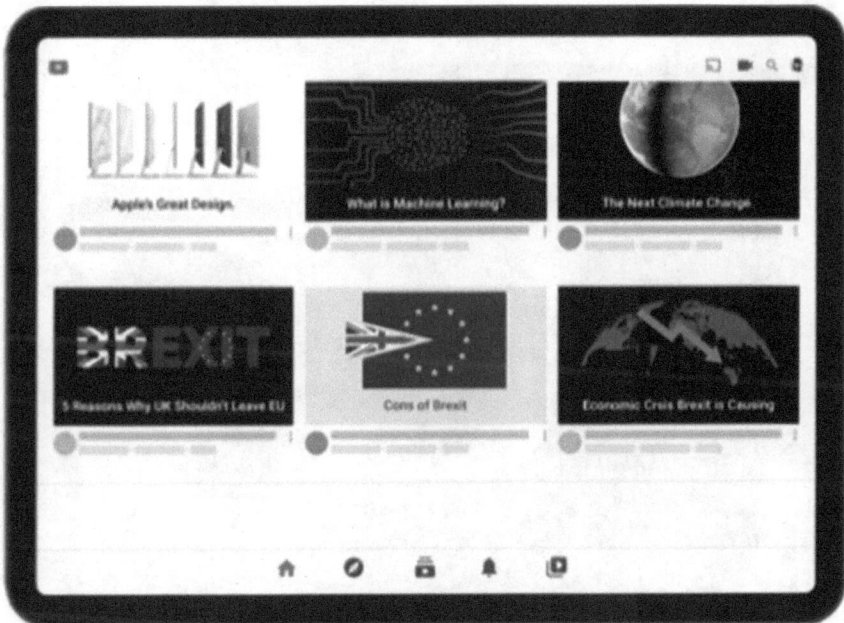

Fig. 10.2 Opening interface

The app then displays the opposing viewpoint from someone similar on the right-hand side—see Fig. 10.3 below

Then rotate the screen to experience the other user's POV as below Fig. 10.4

Fig. 10.5 shows the full interface and both pros and cons of the argument.

The app has an advantage as it is a new type of interface that can be applied to various platforms such as Netflix and Facebook. These platforms are already collecting data via machine learning algorithms to recommend contents. This data can be used and add value to the app. It can also be used in multiple environments such as on a smartphone.

Fig. 10.3 Presentation of opposing views

Fig. 10.4 Alternative point of view via screen rotation

Although JeHyun's app is only a student project it does demonstrate how the younger generation themselves, as prime users of social media, are aware of the limitations and biases it can re-inforce and seeking to mitigate the worst of such biases. This must augur well for the future and that technology itself can be used to mitigate the worst excesses of social media echo chambers. The user base itself is

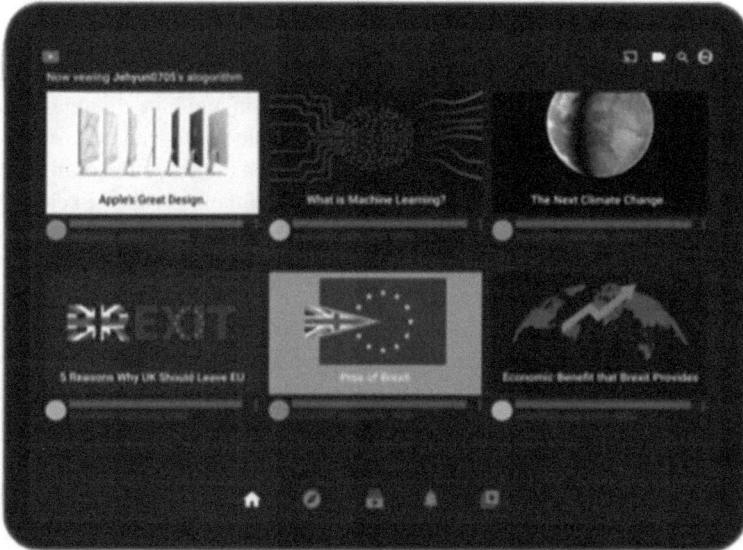

Fig. 10.5 Full array of pros and cons

becoming increasingly aware of how data can be manipulated by false premises. (Note: additional academic research is being undertaken for further product development.)

The main challenge, here of course, is how to get people to voluntarily seek out alternative views. Perhaps the best way to use such an app is as part of a recognised training programme promoting positive narratives, such as that employed in the Finnish programme.

10.5   How to Reduce Cognitive Dissonance

In a world where we are bombarded with vast volumes of data, much made up of very different points of view, it is very difficult to avoid cognitive dissonance. So, on the assumptions that an individual recognises that they are being exposed to dissonant arguments (a big assumption by the way), how can he or she reduce the mental stress of such dissonance.

The three most common approaches to mitigate such stress are:

1. Change your beliefs
2. Change your actions
3. Change the way you see your actions so as to make them less contradictory.

All this sounds quite reasonable from a logical point of view—yet we know our own biases can act as powerful barriers to allowing us to adopt such changed behaviour and perceptions.

There is very little the individual can do to confront cognitive dissonance unless he or she is aware of it in the first place (being more mindful)—and that is part of the problem—it is partly ignorance of the need for personal introspection or mindfulness and partly the stress of holding dissonant views which the individual likes to deflect or subsume in the first place. An additional barrier, of course, to reducing cognitive dissonance is that people simply don't like being told they are suffering from it in a similar way many people bridle when told they are sexist, homophobic, or racist or ageist—they prefer to seek out information that provides cognitive support for their pre-existing attitudes and beliefs and that they are acting reasonably.

Due to such a behavioural challenge, we may have to accept that it is a cognitive condition we have to live with. That may be so but there is no reason not to inform and evangelise the existence of such a mental phenomenon—a message that needs to be regularly and continuously repeated so as to increase awareness of the condition if we are to mitigate the impact of such biases.

References

Bonaccorsi, A., Apreda, R., & Fantoni, G. (2020). Expert biases in technology foresight. Why they are a problem and how to mitigate them. *Technological Forecasting & Social Change*.

CNN Report. (2019). *Finland is winning the war on fake news. What it's learned may be crucial to Western democracy*. E Kiernan

Defense One. (2019, October). https://www.defenseone.com

FactBar EDU. (2018). *Elections approach – are you ready? Fact checking for educators and future voters*. FactBar EDU.

Kahneman, D., Slovic, P., & Tversky, A. (Eds.). (1982). *Judgment under uncertainty: Heuristics and biases*. Cambridge University Press.

Pherson, R. H. (2019). *Handbook of analytic tools & technique* (5th ed.). Pherson Associates.

Pherson, R. H. (2021). *Moving toward constructive solutions: The analytic insider*.

Pherson, R. H., & Pyrik, R. (2018). *Analyst's guide to indicators*. The Analyst's Bookshop, Pherson Associates LLC.

Taylor, J. (2013). *Cognitive biases are bad for business*.

Tetlock, P. E. (2005). *Expert political judgement*. Princeton University Press.

Wardle, C., & Derakshan, H. (2017, September). *Information disorder: Toward an interdisciplinary framework for research and policy making*. Council of Europe.

Part V
Theory into Practice: Reactive and Exploratory Scenarios and Case Studies

Chapter 11
Reactive: The Covid-19 Pandemic

The quest for certainty blocks the search for meaning.
Uncertainty is the very condition to impel man to unfold his
powers—Erich Fromm

Abstract The Covid pandemic and its aftermath is a good example of an event whereby most of the responses took many of the main actors, politicians, economists, medical professionals, etc., by surprise. This was in spite of a three-day training exercise (Cygnus) by the British government in 2016, intended to determine readiness for a respiratory influenza pandemic. In reality the pandemic was an "inevitable surprise"—we know it could happen but not when and as such a detailed set of contingency plans could have mitigated the worst of its impact. The powers that be largely chose to ignore the implications of the Cygnus exercise as being too alarming—a classic case of not thinking about the unthinkable. The chapter looks at a number of future options identified by various experts post event—among them being derivative impacts not specifically health related. The method of red teaming is identified as a useful foresight approach to challenge established perspectives and assumptions.

Keywords Reactive scenario · Red Teams

11.1 Introduction

So much has been written about the Covid-19 pandemic within the last two years that this example will not seek to offer specific foresight observations or policy recommendations, but rather present a simple structured route that could have been followed during the first stages of the pandemic back in early 2020. In July 2021, I carried out a basic search on Google referencing the term Covid-19. It yielded nearly 4.6 billion items of which the vast majority would have been added since January 2020—a classic reactive response. It also needs to be understood that I am not an expert in any of the medical disciplines that have been involved in the process of analysing and attempting to resolve the health and medical related problems that the pandemic has brought about.

The pandemic though, is a classic example of a reaction to an event which seemed to take many of the main actors, politicians, economists, even elements of the medical profession, policy makers, etc., by surprise.

First of all, it was NOT a black swan event—numerous academics and thought leaders such as Bill Gates had given notice in prior years of not only the possibility of a global pandemic but the probability of one occurring. Indeed in the UK, supplies of PPE (personal protection equipment) had been set aside—the problem was that many of these supplies had not been replenished and much PPE was out of date at the time when it was needed. In reality the Covid pandemic outbreak was an "inevitable surprise"—a quadrant 2 event in the Uncertainty profile matrix—we know something like this can and will happen, we just do not know when. As such suitable contingency plans should have been in place at least during the early phases of the outbreak.

Back in 2016, the World Economic Forum produced a report (2016) on global disease outbreaks stating:

> The recent Ebola crisis will not be the last serious epidemic the world faces; indeed, public health outbreaks are likely to become ever more complex and challenging. Despite progress in some aspects of public health over the past two decades, endemic infectious diseases remain a major problem, and new or resurging infections, the spread of drug resistance and the rise in non-communicable diseases all pose enormous challenges to often fragile health systems.

The report goes on to highlight that:

> A recent study led by the University of Cambridge identified 20 known infectious diseases that have re-emerged or spread geographically, including dengue, chikungunya, typhoid, West Nile, artemisinin-resistant malaria and the plague (Coburn et al., 2013). Other known threats—such as influenza (i.e. H1N1 Swine Flu), MERS-Cov, and Ebola—continue to raise fears, especially when they take hold in densely populated areas and when treatment and prevention measures are not necessarily available. Even when known infectious diseases can be mitigated by existing treatments or vaccines, we face the risk of emerging resistant strains, mutating viruses, or a pandemic that is so large it renders response supplies inadequate.

Late in 2016, the British government and health authorities held "Exercise Cygnus",[1] a three-day training exercise intended to determine readiness for a respiratory influenza pandemic. Cygnus aimed to test coordination between hospitals, health authorities, and those tasked with tracking the disease and central government. The results of the report on the exercise were alarming with indications of the health services and supporting agencies being completely overwhelmed. Indeed the results were considered initially as being so alarming that they were deemed too sensitive for release to the public. The report only became public after the pandemic had taken hold **and** only after it had been leaked to "The Guardian"

---

[1] Exercise Cygnus was a three-day simulation exercise carried out by NHS England in October 2016 to estimate the impact of a hypothetical H2N2 influenza pandemic on the UK. It aimed to identify strengths and weaknesses within the United Kingdom health system and emergency response chain by putting it under significant strain, providing insight on the country's resilience and any future ameliorations required.

newspaper in May 2020. The complete 57-page report was not officially released by the Department of Health and Social Care until 23 October 2020!

11.2 Scenario Proposals in Reaction to the Pandemic Event

As already mentioned above much has been written post the commencement of the pandemic. In this chapter, I have selected just a few comments from acknowledged foresight specialists which at least highlight some of the implications of the pandemic beyond just medical and health considerations—taking into account secondary and tertiary possible outcomes. Although the pandemic is an example of a largely reactive response to an event which has already manifested itself, this does not absolve decision makers from exploring any secondary and tertiary impacts from the event itself.

In a briefing note by a group of researchers early in the pandemic, at consulting firm McKinsey and Company (2020) two main scenarios were outlined which explored how the interplay between the virus and society's response might unfold and the implications on the economy. The two scenario choices were

1. The impact of a delayed recovery
2. A prolonged contraction

In the delayed recovery scenario two levels were explored:

- Epidemiology—where the researchers provided an overview of current knowledge about the pandemic itself—in effect a reactive response to epidemiological data.
- Economic impact—here relatively short-term (up to two years) observations were made about the implications that the pandemic might bring about for the global economies and business sectors for the coming two quarters.

The second scenario used the same base of epidemiological impacts as the first case but looked at a different economic scenario component whereby the assumption was made for a prolonged contraction.

It can be argued that scenarios were limited in their choice of variables emanating from the pandemic outbreak with only economic and business considerations being addressed—albeit the two presented cases did explore the problem from two different time frames (short and longer term). The team argued that addressing the *"near term is essential, but don't lose focus on the longer term (which might be worse)"*. They did acknowledge that whilst immediate and effective response is vital the coronavirus crisis is a story with an unclear ending.

What is encouraging however, is that the McKinsey team realised that the situation was rapidly evolving with multiple uncertainties indicating that continual, iterative work was required over the duration of the pandemic. In essence this required decision makers to finally adopt a more exploratory approach rather than just reactive.

11.2.1 Not Just Health

Also in March of 2020, a team of academics led by Arjen Boin et al. (2020) of Leiden University in the Netherlands proposed a number of challenges facing leaders during the pandemic. The team took a more holistic approach to potential challenges rather than specific sectors or disciplines. As such, the offering is multi-faceted and not restricted to just the health and medical perspectives.

Boin confirms that *"the COVID-19 pandemic has become the ultimate stress test for communities, countries and the world. It falls into the 'once in a lifetime' category, but the dynamics and challenges it will entail have been studied for years by researchers investigating 'super wicked problems', 'transboundary crises' and 'mega crises'"*.

With time at a premium senior decision makers (in the political, public service, and major corporate sectors) have to perform "in the face of exceptional threats, gaps and flaws in the available data, and high levels of uncertainty about how any interventions will play out".

Key to Boin et al's argument is the need to identify key current and future leadership challenges, along with a number of recommendations so as to navigate a highly complex and evolving landscape. Their observations are worth summarising as follows.

11.2.1.1 Challenge 1: Detecting Incoming Issues in a Fast-Changing Situation

The speed and scale the COVID threat have surprised most, if not all, governments. By the time it became an "official" crisis, the virus and its impact were already cascading across national borders and economic sectors from health to tourism and hospitality.

Recommendation: Now in new territory, where the normal rules of problem emergence and problem definition no longer apply. Leaders will have to grasp quickly the evolving nature of the crisis to stay ahead of the curve. Timing and framing are everything.

11.2.1.2 Challenge 2: Making Sense of a Dynamic Threat with Limited Information

Problem of understanding the speed, scope, and consequences of COVID. There are numerous variables and not enough information. Seemingly dramatic predictions are based on modelling efforts that make use of disputed input variables leading result, navigating in semi-darkness.

Recommendation: Be aware of what happens in other countries but recognise that threat trajectories and success measures do not automatically translate into valid prescriptions for different environments. Deep uncertainty is the essence of the crisis. Accept major limitations to your information flow rather than waiting for better conditions for decision-making to emerge.

11.2.1.3   Challenge 3: Making Life-or-Death Decisions

The COVID-19 crisis brings all the dilemmas that crisis experts fear most: choosing between who will live and die; weighing how much economic damage we will take to save the lives for a select category of fellow citizens; balancing unpopular measures against the necessity of legitimacy.

Recommendation: Avoid the temptation of heroic leadership—the historic model of the ultimate decision that demands the ultimate sacrifice. Stick with the limited hard data that is available whilst realising that experts will not take all values into consideration.

11.2.1.4   Challenge 4: The Art of Strategic Coordination

In a global crisis such as the pandemic, many organisations—public and private, will need to work together, as the effectiveness of the overall response is dependent on them co-operating and coordinating their different responses.

Recommendation: Explore responses across sectors and across (geographic) boundaries. Integration with the key stakeholders is key. Office-driven or agency-centric command and control are overrated.

11.2.1.5   Challenge 5: Keep Worried Publics and Wary Workers
On Side

Crisis communication "best practice" needs to be identified and consistently deployed with the need for clear, timely, and repeated messaging and actionable advice, delivered by credible sources. Yet often the quality of communication can be the Achilles heel of crisis response, being "behind the curve" or offer ambiguous messaging. In the UK we have indeed seen evidence of this in relation to discussions as whether new lockdown measure should be introduced. Leaders often fail to convince, be disconnected from people's experiences, overly cautious to avoid panic leading to a failure to communicate the whole truth.

Recommendation: If you get it wrong, rumours and intensifying criticism will soon let you know. Be aware of such social dynamics and do not let it get to that point.

What is informative about Boin's arguments is that whilst accepting that a crisis has already manifested itself, decision makers need to be made aware of unfolding uncertainties—and that a whole plethora of stratagems need to be deployed in order to respond in the most effective way to such a complex and dynamic series of events.

Presented in this way we can see how the three core axes of the approach expounded in this book, scenarios, behavioural factors, and the deconstructed components, in an environment characterised by high levels of uncertainty, allow decision makers to better formulate their responses even when in react mode.

Other informed commentators have also addressed derivative components beyond just responding to the "medical and health" implications of the pandemic. Researchers at Chatham House, an internationally renowned think tank identified in a February 2021 report (Hakmeh et al., 2021) that *"The COVID-19 pandemic has underscored that tech governance must be based on human-centric values that protect the rights of individuals but also work towards a collective good"*. In addition the report also recognised that:

> The COVID-19 pandemic has put many of these aspects into sharp relief. The unprecedented digital adoption has shown how important and indispensable digital technologies are, and for the millions of people who have transitioned at speed into a more "virtual" way of living, the benefits as well as the risks abound. Reaching a sound approach to tech policy has been made all the more complex by the pandemic.

Whilst basing its findings as a reaction to an event, the Society of International Futures (SOIF) published in January 2021 a report called *"The long pandemic after the Covid 19 crisis"* where it attempts to take a longer term view as to how the pandemic might pan out. In addition much of its findings address, what can be termed secondary and tertiary issues, rather than just concentrating on purely health, medical, and epidemiological factors of the event itself.

A number of contextual factors were included in the report, namely:

- *After the health crisis is over*—highlighting what happens next after adjustment to the short-run health aspects short after adjustment to the pandemic. It observes that in many areas of society the pandemic has simply revealed existing weaknesses and made visible issues that are large, predictable, and ignored. Again the quadrant three syndrome.
- *Different speeds*—whilst the health crisis is likely to persist, possibly at a lower level, for another 1–2 years the economic impacts are likely to last for 5–10 years, given the scale of the immediate economic shock. Interestingly enough it identifies that the psychological crisis is likely to last a generation, given the impact of COVID-19 deaths, the experience of lockdown, and household anxiety about finances and the future. As has been reinforced by arguments in part 3 on behaviour, the human factor is ignored by decision makers at their peril.
- *The health crisis*—naturally enough one cannot ignore the main driver of the event—the pandemic. The report identifies that the coronavirus may continue to mutate. While vaccine development has been an international scientific success, it will likely take two years or more to manufacture and deliver billions of doses globally. With international travel returning to some form of normality such a lag exposes travellers to new forms of infection—which in turn they bring back to a territory deemed clear.
- *The economic crisis*—SOIF advances the view that whatever the government response, some industries will not recover, and nor will some businesses. The

IMF anticipates a significant output gap and a slow recovery over the next few years.

- *The psychological crisis*—the report offers an interesting perspective on how people may have been affected by the pandemic stating that *"For many, the medium term health effects are likely to be psychological. If young people have escaped the worst of the physical impacts of COVID-19, they may get the worst of the mental health impacts. The data on generations that come into the labour market in times of high unemployment suggest that their earnings never recover, so their lifetime outcomes are worse. Further, the experience makes them more adverse to risk"*. As highlighted in the section on different speeds SOIF is to be praised for identifying the impact of behavioural factors—which intercede across most of the derivative scenarios.

The SOIF document looked at the more downstream (or derivative) effects of the pandemic such as:

- the impact on the labour market
- the relationship between an ongoing financial crisis and social equality (or inequality)
- increased pressure to regulate "big tech"
- that the psychological and social psychology impacts of the pandemic are likely to be long term
- the destabilising influence of a more multi-polar world accentuated by the pandemic
- ongoing failure of global leadership to resolve not only a more evenly spread roll-out of vaccination (what hope for climate change—a much more wicked problem)
- not forgetting the impact on health and care services themselves in addition to epidemiological issues.

The SOIF analysis suggests a number of clear features and which correlate largely with the author's own conclusions.

- These issues, and many of the second-order effects of COVID-19, are not risks or uncertainties. Instead, they are predictable surprises. Within the uncertainty profile matrix most of the outcomes can and should be allocated to Quadrant 2—the known-unknown.
- Many of the impacts are interconnected and create feedback loops and other amplifying effects. As we have seen such complexity and interconnectivity confound decision makers with appeals for "black swan" status when we really know they belong in quadrant 2 (as in above).
- And, as with the pandemic—widely anticipated by epidemiologists, zoologists, and risk analysts—optimism bias leads us to assume that the unthinkable probably will not happen—that is if we even think about it in the first place.

11.3   Reacting to the Experts

One of the main observations about the pandemic itself is how effective the experts are. Unfortunately with experts there is a tendency to minimise their effectiveness when they are right but to use them as scapegoats when they are wrong—the latter behaviour manifested by politicians, tabloid journalists, and the general public alike. With Covid much of role or rather accuracy of experts has concentrated, naturally enough on epidemiological factors such as contagion rates, deaths, etc., rather than secondary and tertiary impacts. As we have seen in the case of the expert examples (McKinsey, Boin, and SOIF) provided above, all of whom look at impacts beyond just the reactive response to the medical and health drivers, one has to ask how much of this more in-depth awareness of derivative impacts is being taken on board by policy makers and decision strategists at all levels? One can assume that expert opinion will increasingly be listened too if it can be proved that such advice is generally correct AND that awareness of such accuracy is broadcast more widely in the media.

A very recent research study funded by the Winton Centre for Risk and Evidence Communication based at Cambridge University asked this very question in a paper titled "How well did experts and laypeople forecast the size of the COVID-19 pandemic"? (Recchia et al., 2021).

The researchers conducted a survey in April 2020 of 140 UK experts and 2086 UK laypersons and where all were asked to make four quantitative predictions about the impact of COVID-19 by 31 Dec 2020. Overall the findings showed that experts exhibited greater accuracy and calibration than laypersons. According to the survey it nevertheless showed that experts substantially underestimated the ultimate extent of the pandemic, and that experts should consider broadening the range of scenarios they consider plausible. The results indicated that *"predictions of the public were even more inaccurate and poorly calibrated, suggesting that an important role remains for expert predictions as long as experts acknowledge their uncertainty"*.

The researchers go on to point out that before making conclusions about expert predictions, it is critical to compare them to nonexpert predictions. Acknowledging that if *"expert predictions are disregarded by the public, nonexpert predictions are liable to drive behaviour in their stead"*.

A key observation from the study was that experts showed a certain amount of overconfidence in their predictions (out of the four intervals that experts expected outcomes to fall within 75% of the time, fewer than half of actual outcomes fell within these intervals on average).

On the other hand, nonexpert predictions were less accurate than expert predictions, and that nonexperts were more overconfident than experts in their predictions. They summarise the results as follows:

> ...although our findings on expert accuracy and overconfidence may read as a cautionary tale against taking expert predictions at face value, it is critical to highlight that we could do worse: we could believe the predictions of people who are not experts. We have arguably witnessed many examples of the latter approach being taken by individuals across the globe,

sometimes with dire results. Focusing solely on poor expert performance may simply make nonexperts more adamant about their own preconceptions—not a good thing if they are already even more inaccurate and more overconfident than the experts, as our results suggest.

This would indicate that our discussion in Chaps. 9 and 10, relating to behavioural factors shows that issues such as inherent biases and cognitive dissonance are very much in evidence even in responses to a reactive event such as the pandemic. The report authors conclude however that: *"The ultimate message may be that 'the experts have much to learn, but they also have much to teach'"*.

11.4 A Note on MTTs

In an ideal world one would hope that we should be better prepared to avoid too the worst effects of having to react to scenarios such as COVID-19. As has been argued hereto in this book the vast majority, if not all events, can be identified to a greater or lesser extent—the variety of MTTs which can help us to improve decision-making when faced with complex scenarios is already in existence. The great challenge lies at the behavioural level—the willingness to move beyond just seeing discrete, linear outcomes to events. Acceptance that what is termed "Uncertainty" consists of varying degrees of "Inevitable Surprises" and can thus be foreseen and accommodated.

There is one method that I should like to introduce readers, but which has largely been deployed by defence and military organisations but rarely seen in the corporate world.

11.4.1 Red Teaming

Red Teaming can be defined as the art of applying independent structured critical thinking and culturally sensitised alternative thinking from a variety of perspectives, to challenge assumptions and fully explore alternative outcomes, in order to reduce risks and increase opportunities. The process should:

- identify strengths, weaknesses, opportunities, and threats, hitherto unthought-of; challenge assumptions
- propose alternative strategies
- test a plan in a simulated adversarial engagement
- and ultimately lead to improved decision-making and more effective outcomes

The benefits of red teaming include: broader understanding of the operational environment, filling gaps in understanding, identifying vulnerabilities and opportunities, reducing risks and threats, avoiding groupthink, mirror imaging, cultural miss-steps, and tunnel vision. It can reveal how outside influences, adaptive adversaries, and competitors could counter plans, concepts, and capabilities as well as identifying desired or undesired second- and third-order effects and unforeseen consequences.

The main premise of the red team is to "think like your enemy" and to do so, red team participants need to be fully immersed into the behaviour, cultures, and thought process of the opposition. In essence it is a more structured way to "think the unthinkable", moving out of one's comfort zone and avoiding groupthink and other cognitive biases which might influence decision makers.

A variety of publications exist which introduce red teaming in more detail. These publications are generally published by military type organisations or agencies but as mentioned above can readily be deployed in the commercial and general organisational settings. I refer readers to those documents in the footnote below[2,3,4]

References

Boin, A., McConell, A., & Hart, P. (2020, March). Leading in a crisis: strategic crisis leadership during the COVID-19 pandemic. *A Boin, (Leiden University), A McConnell, (University of Sydney), P 't Hart (Utrecht University/ANZSOG)*, The Mandarin.

Coburn, A., Chang, M., Sullivan, M., Bowman, G., & Ruffle, S. (2013). *"Disease outbreak: Human pandemic". Cambridge Risk Framework: Profile of a Macro-Catastrophe Threat Type*. (Centre for Risk Studies Working Paper 201303.31). University of Cambridge Judge Business School.

Craven, M., Liu, L., & Mysore, M., & Wilson, M. (2020, March). *Briefing note on Covid scenarios*. McKinsey and Company.

Hakmeh, J., Taylor, E., Peters, A., & Ignatidou, S. (2021). *The COVID-19 pandemic and trends in technology: Transformation in governance and society, Research Paper*. Royal Institute of International Affairs. https://www.chathamhouse.org/2021/02/covid-19-pandemic-and-trends-technology

Recchia, G., Freeman, A., & Spiegelhalter, D. (2021, May 5). *How well did experts and laypeople forecast the size of the COVID-19 pandemic?* PLoS One.

SOIF. (2021, January). *The long pandemic: after the COVID-19 crises*. SOIF (School of International Futures).

World Economic Forum. (2016). *Global Disease Outbreaks – Risk of Infectious Disease Outbreaks: Analysis*. World Economic Forum.

---

[2]"A GUIDE TO RED TEAMING DCDC GUIDANCE NOTE", Assistant Chief of the Defence Staff (Development, Concepts, and Doctrine) The Development, Concepts and Doctrine Centre Ministry of Defence, February 2010.

[3]"The Applied Critical Thinking Handbook (formerly the Red Team Handbook)", University of Foreign Military and Cultural Studies TRISA (TRADOC G2 Intelligence Support Activity), Ft Leavenworth, Kansas, USA, January 2015.

[4]"NATO ALTERNATIVE ANALYSIS (AltA) HANDBOOK", NATO/OTAN, April 2017.

Chapter 12
An Exploratory Scenario Case Study: Social Mobility and Inequality

"Many problems are too 'messy' to be addressed effectively by the standard management scientist's toolkit of mathematically-based techniques. Such problems are typically characterised by complexity, a high degree of uncertainty and ignorance, and multiple subjectivity. Structuring them into a form in which they can be addressed is at least as challenging as formally solving them"—*Professor Sally Brailsford, Southampton University.*

Abstract This chapter adopts an exploratory approach for the issue of social mobility. Whilst the topic is known any scenarios developed cannot truly be classified as reactive as the inherent complexity of the subject allows for the researcher to be highly innovative and exploratory when seeking out alternative strategic options. This case study deploys two decision support methods in combination, mind maps and strategic options analysis (using MA) to build a number of exploratory and viable scenarios to bring about greater clarity and focus for the decision maker and ultimately better benefit those underestimated groups. Much of the published commentary on social mobility takes a traditional, linear, and left-brain view—with associated recommendations and actions that only marginally benefit the target underestimated group. More diverse thinking is required along with richer models that allow transformative actions and insights to be considered when addressing social mobility.

Keywords Social mobility · Mind map · Solution space

A note on the contributing author Dowshan Humzah:

In order to enhance the quality of the specific topic under consideration, the author has engaged the services of a contributing author and subject matter expert from the respective field (for the example in this chapter). On the topic of social mobility and inequality, subject matter expert input and this section has been provided by **Dowshan Humzah** whose profile is summarised in the authors' section.

B. Garvey et al., *Uncertainty Deconstructed*, Science, Technology and Innovation Studies, https://doi.org/10.1007/978-3-031-08007-4_12

12.1 Introduction

An exploratory approach is reflected when addressing the issue of social mobility—being governed by essentially qualitative arguments (of course, quantitative elements can be introduced when specific is available to support more qualitative observations and judgements). Of additional interest is the use of two decision support methods in combination, mind maps and strategic options analysis (using principles of morphological analysis).

12.2 The Problem Statement

> We still live in a country where an individual's future potential is mostly defined by the circumstances of their birth and early years—especially parental income, family wealth, and associated privileges.[1]

The UK, on the whole, still remains a deeply divided society—not just according to gender, race, disability, age, or any other protected characteristic, but more so between the "haves" and the "have-nots" based on inherited privilege, money, and opportunity. Improving social mobility is one of the major interventions that can help address this divide and bridge the gap.

In terms of a specific focus question requiring analysis one could ask: *"How can we get to grips with the complexities of social mobility"? In turn this may allow us to answer more succinctly whether social mobility is increasing or decreasing.*

12.3 Social Mobility Background

> Privilege, preference and opportunity have been passed down the generations in the UK—and have pretty much trumped fairness, equity and hard-graft. Some would say mediocrity over meritocracy.

We can define social mobility as how much the circumstances of your birth and early years determine your future place in society: the probability that those born into underestimated[2] circumstances can work their way to the top based on hard-graft and access to opportunity—and equally have those born of privilege can fall out of it.

---

[1] Quote from Dowshan Humzah taken from The Lack of Social Mobility in the UK (article published 2018).

[2] Dowshan Humzah has been using the term "underestimated" for a number of years in various articles especially on social mobility. Media and politician generally refer to this audience being disadvantaged and under-privileged—which does not feel captures the insights and positive aspects of that audience.

Social mobility in the UK is amongst the lowest of comparable developed nations—lagging most of northern and western Europe, Australasia, Canada and now East Asia. Denmark is seen as the world leader in social mobility. This is evidenced on the narrower income gap between the top 20% and bottom 20%. This has been achieved by a combination of high taxes at the top income end and significant transfer payments at the lower income end. However, it should be pointed out that this is economic social mobility and Denmark still has challenges regarding opportunity and aspiration for all.

The need for a richly experienced and diverse population, organisations representative of all segments of society, together thriving fairly and openly has many benefits in today's challenging world. It is not just a matter of being fair and equal; it is also about competitive advantage at national and international levels.

In a speech at the Centre for American Policy in 2013, President Obama said that social inequality is one of the defining challenges of our time. Globally, a combination of rising inequality and declining social mobility is bad for society—be it social integration, social cohesion, happiness or economic prosperity. This has been further magnified post the Covid-19 pandemic that has disproportionately affected and shone a light on the challenges faced by underestimated communities.

Furthermore, Obama stated that if we are to take on the problems of growing inequality and try to improve upward social mobility for all people, then we have to move on from the false notion that this is an issue exclusively of minority concern. In addition, we have to reject a politics that suggests any efforts to address social mobility in any meaningful way somehow pits "deserving" richer, privileged, upper and middle classes against "undeserving" poorer, underestimated, and lower classes.

12.4 Why We Are Doing This?

Social mobility exhibits the characteristics of a "wicked problem" (see Chap. 4) as even the problem statement is difficult to define. Is the statement too broad or too narrow? Is a lack of social mobility caused by high levels of social inequality or does social inequality cause low levels of social mobility? It is complex in its nature and outcomes are uncertain due to the long-term implications of potential solutions. The complexity itself is driven by the interconnectivity of the variables contained within the broader topic. In addition, there is copious research, lots of ideas, much commentary and political jostling—all adding to a very highly dispersed body of knowledge and accepted beliefs. However, much of this is focused on the causes of social inequality. Detailed and costed solutions brought together under one umbrella and based on the prevailing environment are lacking.

In the UK, there is much available research—primarily from the UK Government's Social Mobility Commission; a variety of think tanks and organisations such as Social Mobility Foundation, Sutton Trust, Business in the Community, Resolution Foundation, Rowntree Foundation; as well as leading world-renowned academics[3] and other sources. However, much of this is focused on the causes and challenges of social mobility—and lacking transformative actions to remedy the situation. In addition, the presentation is wordy—normally pages and pages of text and graphs with little clarity and cut-through. An added challenge is that much of the commentary is not written through the eyes and lived experience of those from underestimated communities.

It is evident that there is a need to develop something more simplistic and dynamic whilst acknowledging that the "wickedness" of the issue pushes it towards the volatile, uncertain, complex, and ambiguous (VUCA). I began my approach and journey using strategic options analysis with input from the author of this book, by adapting a mind map covering social mobility, developed in conjunction with other subject matter experts holding diverse views. The aim of which was to provide a holistic and clear view of the challenges, potential solutions, and the interrelationships. In essence, mind maps were used to capture as much of the data as simply as possible on one side of a piece of paper (covering hindrances to social mobility and drivers to improve it). Moreover, it highlighted as wide a range as possible of the component parts when addressing the issue of social mobility with all its complexity and interconnectivity. Unless such a holistic view is taken then there is a risk of problems as highlighted earlier by Michael Pidd in Chap. 4:

> One of the greatest mistakes that can be made when dealing with a mess is to carve off part of the mess, treat it as a problem and then solve it as a puzzle—ignoring its links with other aspects of the mess.

This mind map is shown in its entirety in Fig. 12.1 below.

We accept that many of the items within the map are difficult to read due to the publishing format constraints. A PDF which can be enlarged is obtainable from Dowshan Humzah or the author of this book.

12.5   Core Issues

The level of complexity and numerous variables needed to be incorporated into the mind map called for a number of conditions to be addressed.

1. Multiple and diverse stakeholder standpoints to challenge and improve the original mind map—as well helping to further simplify and scope the scale of the problem as defined by volatility, uncertainty, complexity, and ambiguity (VUCA—for more details, see Chap. 3).

---

[3] There are too many to mention. However, the work of Professor Jane Waldfogel at The LSE and Columbia University and Professor Robert Putnam at Harvard is illuminating, bold and focuses on the second-order challenges.

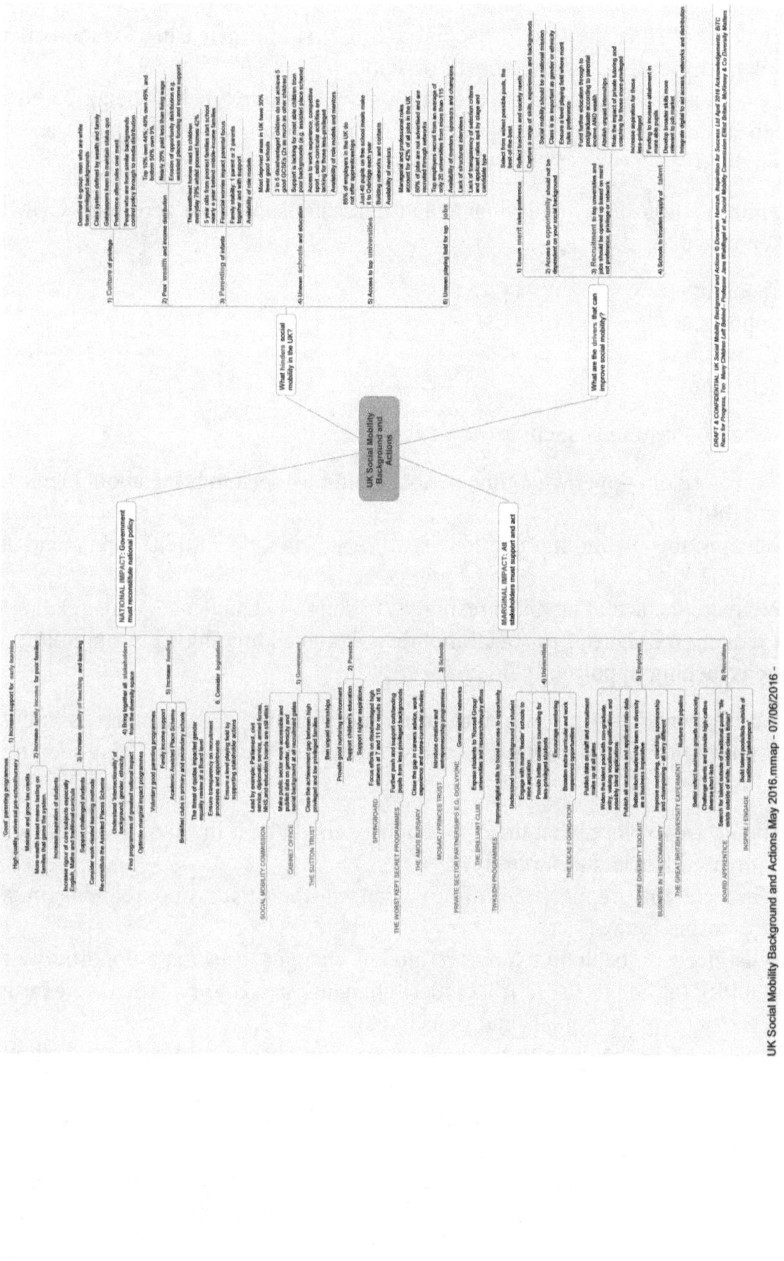

Fig. 12.1 Full social mobility mind map

2. The deployment of some "decision support technology" via the introduction of a methodology which makes it more manageable and facilitates the process to arrive at a set of potential, yet viable, solutions (strategic options analysis).
3. In relation to the core focus question (see Sect. 14.2 above), *"How can we get to grips with the complexities of social mobility?"*, it is essential to include a number of additional variables or parameters such as:

    • Enquire whether the trend of social mobility is up (increasing for the better), down (decreasing for the worse), or static.
    • How should we differentiate the various social groups such as being based on education, parental background, income band, wealth that can be inherited, etc.?

4. The introduction of a qualifying model characterised by an acronym, COMB, broken down as:

    • Capability
    • Opportunity
    • Motivation
    • Behaviour

5. Contextual constraints such as (non-exclusive):

    • Time horizon—over what time period should we seek to bring about increased mobility?
    • What is the prevailing political sentiment (rhetoric or real intent and for whom)?
    • What are the actual physical resources to support change and goals relating to a reduction in barrier to social mobility—such as funding for programmes or areas lacking opportunity?

6. "What if" scenarios—this introduces the concept of the scenario being essentially exploratory in nature, albeit off a base which is reacting to an existing identified social issue.

    • Should we explore what the consequences might be if the situation gets worse (increased barriers to mobility)?
    • What are the implications of no change—the status quo remains in the foreseeable future?
    • What needs to be done to achieve modest changes to increase opportunity for mobility (although the term "modest changes" needs to be articulated further in terms of specific goals and objectives)?
    • What needs to be done to bring about a major change (radical or transformative) in social mobility? Again definition of "major" needs to be articulated?
    • What might be the circumstances that could bring about further political and social polarisation.
    • What needs to be done to bring about a fairer society with real opportunity for all (if such a condition is deemed to be a key national policy objective)?

12.6   What to Do?

The first phase of structuring the problem was developed from the mind map and reflected in the four main branches spreading from the central core. This allows us to define a number of problem spaces (i.e. key parameters which characterise the issues within the problem). In addition to the key variables being ascertained, we need to determine the interaction between each of these variables to identify those which are consistent with each other in order to help define the potential solutions. As with "wicked problems" their wickedness is enhanced not only by the number of variables and sub-variables but by their interconnectivity.

However, it is not necessary to formulate an immediate solution (as there may be many—some better, some worse). It is a good practice to deploy an iterative approach to mitigate the risk of selecting a poor set of solutions (with negative unintended consequences) and which could help to engage fully with a wide a range of stakeholders as possible so as to reduce input bias.

The original mind map (Fig. 12.1) consisted of 4 core areas or branches. For the purposes of this exercise (which demonstrates the application of an options analysis method to a complex, emotive, and socially resonant problem today) one of these topic areas (National Impact) was used to bring this to life and identify potential viable solutions to be considered by government and decision makers.

Again, for the purposes of this exercise, we accepted the first iteration of the mind map as given, and this was used to define the problem space. However, circumstances change and the mind maps can be amended or specific items moved to reflect the evolving environment which requires any method used to be flexible enough to allow iterations. There is also the need to account for major disruptions such as the global pandemic, increased digital disruption, and growing inequality.

The mind map was a useful format to collate and show the relationships between the data; however, in any decision-making environment additional aspects of the problem may be required. In this case, we have included the usual suspects such as operational constraints: money, time, and current political landscape as defined by the government and its power. Of course, these constraints and the detail can and may need to be better defined by experts in the field and from government.

The next part of this chapter looks at how one of the core sectors (or branches) within the map was used as input to a Strategic Options Analysis exercise (see Chap. 8 section 8.12, for more background as to the method).

12.7   Summary Process Workflow Using Strategic Options Analysis

12.7.1   Basic Process

It is important to emphasise that strategic options analysis is a methodological process—not solely dependent on software in bringing about reduced configuration solutions. Operational and behavioural realities demand that the methodology address such concerns if it is to have value for practitioners.

A summary of the programme (broken down into a 10-step process) is illustrated below with a three-phase summary process being shown in Appendix 13.

12.7.2   Breakdown of the Process Phases Applied to Social Mobility

1. **Define the problem to be addressed**. Present in the form of a focus question (this is not set in stone and may change through the process). For example: "Is social mobility increasing or decreasing"?
2. **Identify the major stakeholders with an interest and expertise relating to the problem.** Stakeholders should represent as wide a constituency as possible (i.e. not all from the same discipline—stretched positions to avoid groupthink). Stakeholders should also have similar levels of responsibility and accountability within their respective organisations. Stakeholders can be a mix of internal and external personnel.
3. **Use the focus question as an anchor statement to build a structure such as a mind map.** This can help to create a simple, holistic, and system overview of main issues and parameters. This is also a useful first stage in the problem structuring exercise. It is possible that the mind map exercise can be complex with a large number of problem defining parameters. In the example of social mobility this part of the process helped to actual define what we mean by social mobility; what the drivers are and the possible solutions. A workshop is a preferred way to draw out insights from the major stakeholders, generate and validate the structure. Appendix 13 presents a sample social mobility workshop schedule—for reference only. The preferred number of stakeholder members in the workshop team (excluding a neutral facilitator) is between 6 and 12. This would include representatives from: a Government commission (Social Mobility Commission); central government; local government; civil society groups; commercial organisations; education sector (school and university); academic expert (research lead/authority); wild cards (such as a behavioural scientist or consumer expert); and the target/affected underestimated audience. The output may take a number of forms but can be simply and elegantly captured as a mind map with the right facilitator.

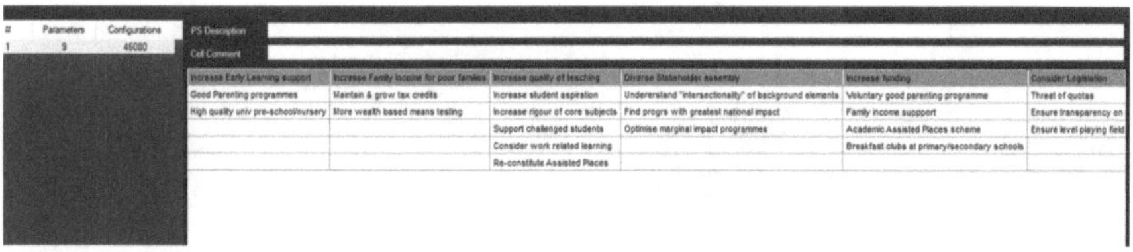

Fig. 12.2 Populating the problem space via the 6 solution parameters and states for social mobility

4. **Extract a subset from the output (mind map) and transcribe into a matrix format.** This allows the user to create a "Problem Space" (PS). Figure 12.2 shows a PS with 6 parameters (aka main variables) where each parameter is described in terms of a series of discrete states or dimensions (aka sub-variables or second-level variables). In our example, we have isolated the top left-hand branch (National Impact) for further detailed analysis using the strategic options analysis method. The main headings of the problem space are thus the next level down in the branch structure, e.g. Early Learning, and the third branching as the conditions under each of the second-level variables.

This matrix can be described as representing the problem space and is made up of 720 different configurations (i.e. the product of all states: $2 \times 2 \times 5 \times 3 \times 4 \times 3$).

5. **Decide if additional parameters such as constraints or outcomes need to be added** (e.g. Timing, Money, and Resource)? If yes, then add to the initial PS matrix as below Table 12.1. A smaller workshop may be required to check and validate the detailed PS as the software starts to do its work and we prepare to move to the phase.

The software allows each parameter and parameter state to be described as a form of audit trail, for example, what is meant by "current political priority". The additional three constraint variables expand the original mind map branches or configurations from 720 to 46,080.

6. **Confirm final review–does the problem space reflect the views of ALL stakeholders?** Is there a high level of consensus that the PS encapsulates the problem being addressed? If not, then revisit and adjust accordingly. Sign-off is by the stakeholder team and depending on how the outputs will be used by their stakeholders/seniors/board.

The problem space (PS) transposed into the options analysis software for social mobility—due to space conditions only a partial tableau is shown (3 constraint variables out of frame) as the full nine variable frame cannot be shown for print out conditions (Table 12.2).

According to this PS tableau some 46,080 different configurations have been identified—such a large number needs to be reduced to a viable option for decision purposes.

Table 12.1 Adding constraints to the problem space, given the realities of implementation for social mobility

NATIONAL IMPACT: Government must reconstitute national policy						OPN Constraints		
Increase support **Early Learning**	Increase **Family Income** for poor families	Increase **quality of teaching &** learning	Bring together all stakeholders from **diversity** space	Increase **funding**	Consider **legislation**	**Money**	**Time**	**Curr political**
Good parenting programmes	Maintain & grow tax credits	Increase aspiration of students	Understand "intersectionality" of background, gender, ethnicity	Voluntary good parenting programme	Threat of quotas impacted gender equality review at a Board	<1 bn	< 2 years	Cat A
High-quality, universal pre-school/nursery	More wealth based means testing on families	Increase rigour of core subjects esp, English,	Find programmes of greatest national impact	Family income support	Ensure transparency on recruitment processes	1–3 bn	2–5 years	Cat B
		Support challenged students	Optimise marginal impact programmes	Academic Assisted Places Scheme	Ensure a level playing filed by supporting	3–5 bn	5–10 years	Cat C
		Consider work-related learning methods		Breakfast clubs in primary & secondary schools		5+	10+	Desirable but back burner
		Re-constitute the Assisted						

Table 12.2 Social mobility problem space

#	Parameters	Configurations	PS Description	Cell Comment	Increase Early Learning support	Increase Family Income for poor families	Increase quality of teaching	Diverse Stakeholder assembly	Increase funding	Consider Legislation
1	9	46080			Good Parenting programmes	Maintain & grow tax credits	Increase student aspiration	Understand "intersectionality" of background elements	Voluntary good parenting programme	Threat of quotas
					High quality univ pre-school/ nursery	More wealth based means testing	Increase rigour of core subjects	Find programmes with greatest national impact	Family income support	Ensure transparency on
							Support challenged students	Optimise marginal impact programmes	Academic Assisted Places scheme	Ensure level playing field
							Consider work related learning		Breakfast clubs at primary/secondary schools	
							Re-constitute Assisted Places			

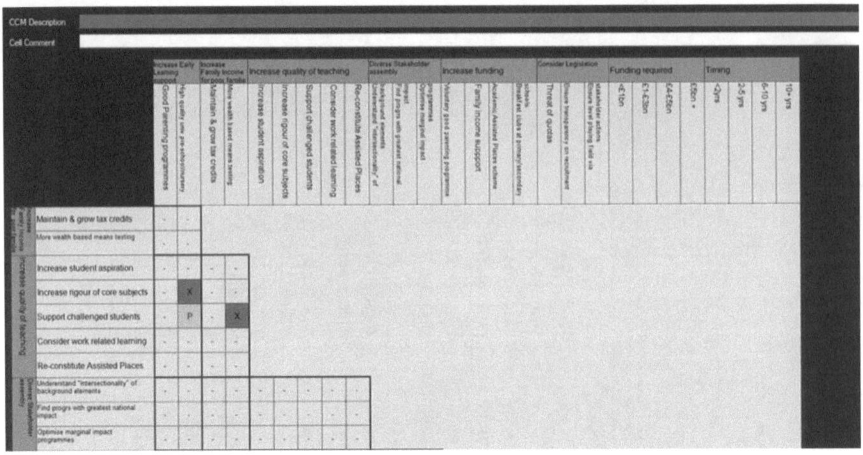

Fig. 12.3 The PS transposed into the options analysis software for social mobility (partial view)

7. **Use the strategic options analysis software (based on MA) to convert the PS matrix to the "Pair-wise analysis matrix"** whereby the PS matrix is transposed to a "tableau" where each parameter and their respective states (descriptors) can be analysed in relation to every other state in every other parameter. An additional workshop session will be required to run the analysis across steps 7 and 8 (Fig. 12.3).

The result shows the paired cells; those which are red with a cross are paired cells deemed inconsistent, whilst blank cells are deemed consistent.

8. **Perform analysis via a detailed evaluation of the relationship between each of the pairs in the CCM.** Decisions are audited via an audit recorder which can be aggregated post exercise.
9. **Once the pair-wise assessment within the CCM is completed then click the "Compile" button.** The model algorithm then discards all configurations with one of more inconsistent pairs and generates a "Solution Space" made up of only those configurations which are totally consistent. If the PS has been properly constructed, then it is expected that over 95% of the PS configurations are discarded so that the remaining 5% represent possible viable options. A smaller workshop will be required to evaluate and feedback on the solution space.
10. **The solution space represents visually and dynamically all the potential options which work.** This "filtered" selection can then be further evaluated for preference, comfortable in the knowledge that these options are compatible. Examples are shown in Figs. 12.4 and 12.5.

The selected profile based on the red cells as input would indicate a narrative as follows. A potential viable option would be composed of the combination of features.

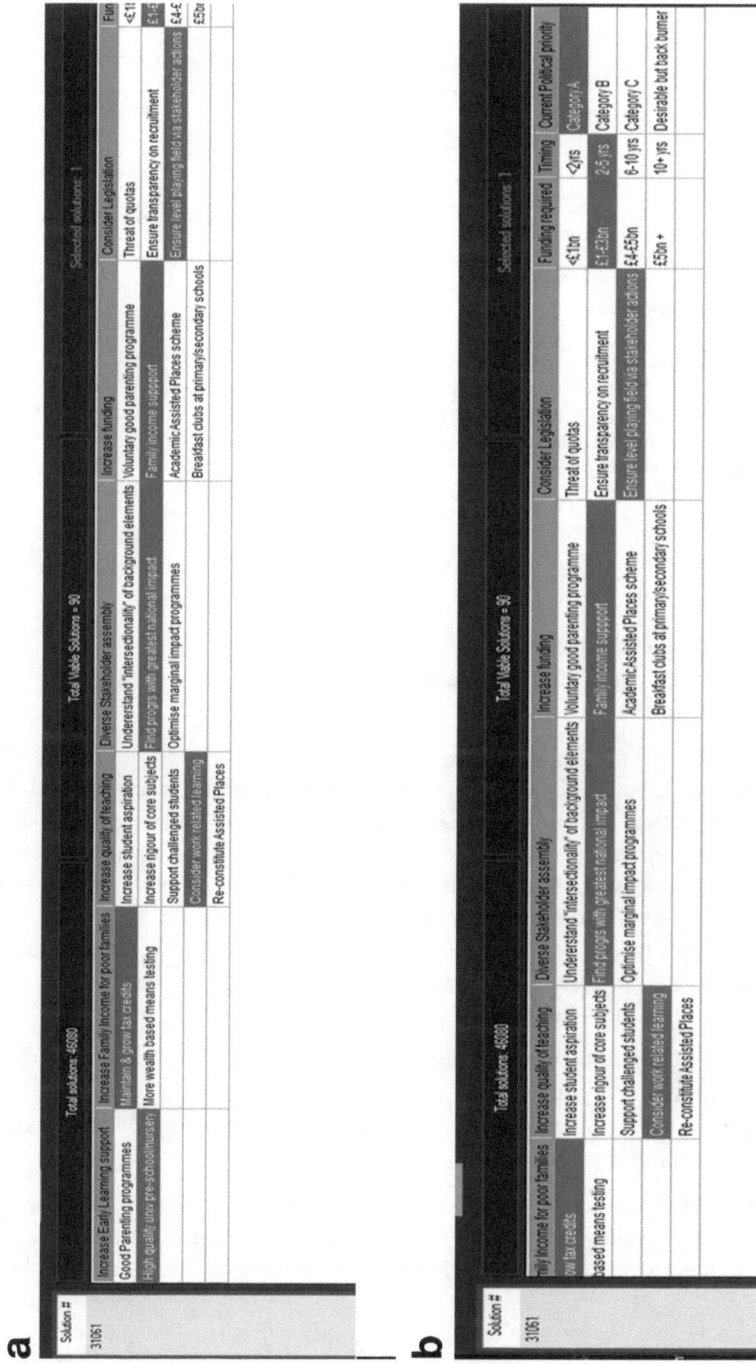

Fig. 12.4 (a & b): This graphic shows 1 of 90 scenarios in the solution space—red (or shaded) indicates inputs

			Total Solutions = 46080	Total Viable Solutions = 90	Selected Solutions 6	
Solution Number	Increase Early learning Support	Increase family income for poor families	Increase quality of teaching	Diverse Stakeholder assembly	Increase Funding	Consider Legislation
24037	Good Parenting programmes	Maintain & grow tax credits	Increase student aspirations	Understand "intersectionality" of backround elements	Voluntary goodparenting programme	Threat of quotas
24038	High quality universal pre-school nursery	More wealth based means testing	Increase rigour of core subjects	Find progs with greatest national impact	Family Income support	Ensure transparency on recruitment
24101			Support challenged students	Optimise marginal impact programmes	Academic assisted places scheme	Ensure level playing field via stakeholder actions
24102			Consider work related learning		Breakfast clubs at primary/secondary schools	
24165			Re-constitute assisted places			
24166						

Fig. 12.5 Criteria selection

High quality universal pre-school/nursery type education should be provided whilst increasing transfer payments such as family tax/universal credits. Programmes should be selected based on their ability for major impact at a national level. The resources required to realise such a scenario include moving such actions up to the top of the political agenda whilst requiring up to £3 billion in financial input so the programme could be achieved within a 2 to 5 year time frame.

Figure 12.5 above shows that when the inputs (cells in **bold** type) are based on three criteria, namely:

- High-quality preschool education
- An increase in family tax credits, and
- An increase in student aspirations

Outputs are shown as **shaded** cells.

Then six viable options based on a number of output conditions become available for further selection and review. The six variants are listed down the left-hand column of the graphic. It is then up to the stakeholders how to present and release the results of the analysis. However, there is rich content and insight from the model that can be used for a variety of purposes.

In the example below, the model allows us to identify the profiles of a number of outcomes (blue) when certain input constraints are selected. By selecting a combination of the following input criteria:

- Required funding of between £4-5bn
- Delivery within 2 5 years
- Operating in a political environment when the issue is deemed to be of secondary political importance

Up to six different scenario profiles are seen to be viable. These can be shown individually by selecting on each of the options in the left-hand column. Note that due to printing constraints the schedules are shown as two separate sheets (Fig. 12.6).

Please note that the results and interpretations presented here are purely for process illustration purposes. In an officially commissioned exercise with a team

	Total Solutions = 46080		Total Viable Solutions = 90	Selected Solutions 6		
Solution Number	Increase Early learning Support	Increase family income for poor families	Increase quality of teaching	Diverse Stakeholder assembly	Increase Funding	Consider Legislation
24038	Good Parenting programmes	Maintain & grow tax credits	Increase student aspirations	Understand "intersectionality" of backround elements	Voluntary goodparenting programme	Threat of quotas
24102	High quality universal pre-school nursery	More wealth based means testing	Increase rigour of core subjects	Find progs with greatest national impact	Family Income support	Ensure transparency on recruitment
24166			Support challenged students	Optimise marginal impact programmes	Academic assisted places scheme	Ensure level playing field via stakeholder actions
30950			Consider work related learning		Breakfast clubs at primary/secondary schools	
31014			Re-constitute assisted places			
31078						

	Total Solutions = 46080		Total Viable Solutions = 90	Selected Solutions 6			
Solution Number	Increase quality of teaching	Diverse Stakeholder assembly	Increase Funding	Consider Legislation	Funding Required	Timing	Current Political Priority
24038	Increase student aspirations	Understand "intersectionality" of backround elements	Voluntary goodparenting programme	Threat of quotas	<£1bn	< 2 years	Category A
24102	Increase rigour of core subjects	Find progs with greatest national impact	Family Income support	Ensure transparency on recruitment	£1-3 bn	2-5 years	Category B
24166	Support challenged students	Optimise marginal impact programmes	Academic assisted places scheme	Ensure level playing field via stakeholder actions	£4-5 bn	6-10 years	Category C
30950	Consider work related learning		Breakfast clubs at primary/secondary schools		£5 bn +	10+ years	Desirable but back burner
31014	Re-constitute assisted places						
31078							

Fig. 12.6 (a & b): Input drivers (constraints) are shown in **bold type under the last three variables in the lower matrix**—with outputs shown as shaded cells in both matrices

of stakeholders as identified earlier in the chapter then one should expect a number of different variances in output from those shown here.

12.8 Conclusion

For the purposes of this chapter, it is not the aim to present a set of outcomes which could be used as specific policy formulation positions or to transform the environment for those from underestimated backgrounds to progress and succeed on as equitable terms as possible. Indeed the topic of social mobility is large and complex enough for a research driven publication in its own right.

The objective here was to demonstrate how such a complex and ambiguous topic can use methods such as mind maps and strategic options analysis to build exploratory scenarios consisting of a number of viable options so as to bring about greater clarity and focus for the decision maker and ultimately better benefit those underestimated groups.

Much of the published commentary on social mobility takes a traditional, linear, and left-brain view—with associated recommendations and actions that do not or only marginally benefit the target underestimated group. It is clear that more diverse thinking is required along with richer models that allow transformative actions to be considered and insight from those who are underestimated suffering from a lack of social mobility.

In general, humans care very deeply about areas such as inequality and fairness; yet there are hard to define and attribute hard measures to. As a result, problems such as social mobility are framed poorly and measurement is misguided. We often hear management and strategy consultants' maxim or cliché: "What gets measured gets managed..." On its own, it is both wrong and a misquote. The full quote is: *"What gets measured gets managed even when it's pointless to measure and manage it, and even if it harms the purpose of the organisation to do so"* (Caulkin, 1956).

So not everything that matters can be measured—and not everything that we can measure matters. This is particularly relevant here when we need lived experience and insight from affected groups, cognitive diversity and more of a creative, oblique, and right-brain approach.

The approach and methods such as mind maps and strategic options analysis better allow us to frame problems and consider a wide range of solutions from the traditional to the oblique, especially in times of challenge, uncertainty, and ambiguity. As a result, the solution space is expanded and more impactful ways forward can be considered as opposed to persistent misdirected efforts.[4]

Reference

From Simon Caulkin summarising V F Ridgway's paper 'Dysfunctional Consequences of Performance Measurements' in Administrative Science Quarterly 1956.

---

[4]This captures the concept of "creative consultancy" as developed by Dowshan Humzah which is thinking differently to get transformative results. This is helped by using psychology and creativity, in addition to metrics, to expand possibility and the solution space—moving from a traditional, linear, left-brain approach to a more creative, oblique, and right-brain approach. This is more relevant and impactful in our current disruptive times characterised by volatility, uncertainty, complexity, and ambiguity.

Chapter 13
Achieving Net Zero—The Small Island Developing States (SIDS) Initiative: An Exploratory Investment Decision Support Framework to Help Address Uncertainty

Small Island Developing States (SIDS) stand at a critical juncture on their paths to sustainable development. Economic growth, human development, and vulnerability indicators point to specific challenges facing SIDS and suggest that new development solutions and approaches are needed to chart the course to prosperity for their people and their environments—OECD.

The next frontier of development for SIDS is the oceans, which will be the key to food, energy and water security, and fuel innovation—Arvin Boolell, Mauritius Foreign Minister.

Small Island Developing States (SIDS) know too well the costs of the climate crisis in both lives and livelihoods. For us, Irma, Maria, Dorian, and Harold are not just names. These hurricanes in the Caribbean and Pacific have wiped out the entire annual GDP of nations hit and, in some cases, left islands totally uninhabitable. Stemming climate change is not a desire, it is a necessity—Gaston Browne—Prime Minister of Antigua and Barbuda—Chair of the Alliance of Small Island States—Financial Times, 6 September 2021

Abstract The plight of small islands states has gone unnoticed for a long time. Only in the last decade, largely through their own endeavours has the international community started to take notice. This chapter presents a system approach providing a generic solution for achieving net zero in the Small Island Development States (SIDS) initiative. The components of the system architecture are described with introduction of the SIDS Net Zero Climate Strategy. In defining a potential investment structure, as part of the strategy plan, a cube format is introduced, providing a multidimension multi-variable methodology, tested in 200+ cases over a seven year period. The system architecture also defines the need for a robust decision support framework. A number of proven approaches are reviewed for decision-making on climate change strategies under deep uncertainty, as to be expected for future initiatives such as achieving net zero in SIDS. *"Initiative"* is defined as a focused strategy on a challenging problem, using a multidimension multi-variable matrix, capable of delivering a strategy and an investment model identifying the required financial instruments.

© The Author(s), under exclusive license to Springer Nature Switzerland AG 2022   233
B. Garvey et al., *Uncertainty Deconstructed*, Science, Technology and Innovation
Studies, https://doi.org/10.1007/978-3-031-08007-4_13

Keywords Climate neutrality · Net zero · Sustainability · Investment model · Decision-making under deep uncertainty (DMDU) · Strategic options analysis

13.1 Introduction

As in Chap. 12, this chapter's material has largely been contributed by an expert in the case study topic, in this case, climate impacted sustainability issues. On this topic a subject matter expert input has been provided by Storm Le Roux, whose profile is also summarised in the authors' section.

A sense of urgency is slowly sweeping across the world, with a growing consensus and understanding of the challenges accompanying the widely used concept "climate change". Although the concept is not always fully understood, the effects however are increasingly observed on a worldwide basis, such as floods, hurricanes, and wild fires, affecting the everyday lives of people, previously unaffected.

Global warming has been a regular topic of discussion, especially since the publication of the Stern report on 30 October 2006, in meetings of world leaders at events such as COP (Conference of the parties) under UN auspices. Developing countries have continuously called for financial assistance for protection against potentially disastrous effects of climate change.

Without presenting a detailed analysis it would be correct to state that world leaders have been slow to respond with political leadership towards taking constructive action on suitable investment structures. We have seen growing action in recent years by activist groups calling on world leaders to wake up.

What has also become clear is that governments alone are not in a position to provide the required funding and that the time has come for the private finance domain to also step up to the plate. This chapter seeks to introduce a financing framework using exploratory scenario principles (in effect a strategy development tool), to mitigate the inherent uncertainties surrounding the broader issue of climate change.

13.2 Towards a Climate Neutral Strategy

The race against climate change, whether by mitigation or resilient adaptation, given the accompanying uncertainty and applicable industry, can only effectively be executed by using a suitable climate neutrality strategy. In addition, a suitable timeline has to be decided on whether being 2, 5, 10, 20, or 50 years.

Addressing the challenge of developing a suitable climate neutral strategy for any party under discussion (whether a policy maker such as government, a corporate, or a private individual) one suggested approach is the application of a strategy development tool to a case study for an initiative currently in progress. As the project details cannot be disclosed, it will be considered on a generic basis.

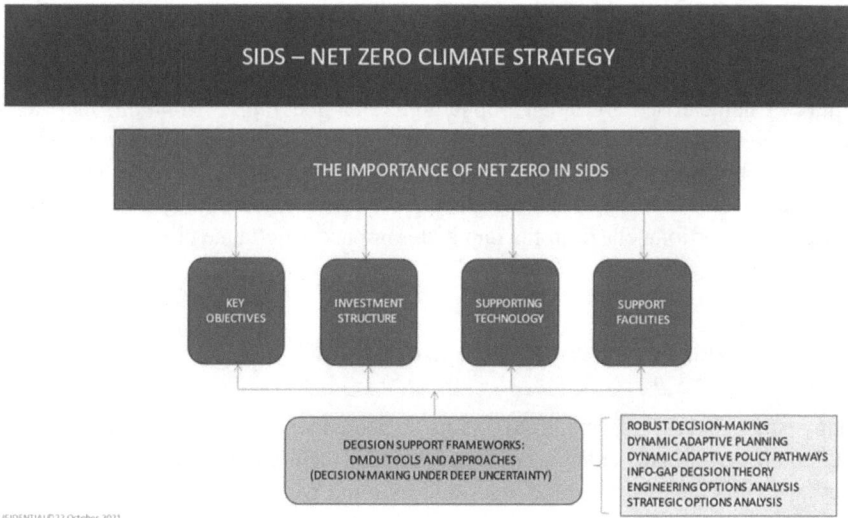

Fig. 13.1 Overall strategic framework

The initiative under consideration is the development of a Net Zero climate strategy, delivering a set of objectives, within a 10-year time frame for a typical SIDS (Small Island Developing States), for which the system architecture is as depicted in Fig. 13.1 and listed below:

- Achieve overall NET ZERO status (i.e. climate neutrality);
- Develop a set of key objectives, and managed by the relevant stakeholders;
- Establish a suitable funding structure through which investment funds will be channelled in
   order to achieve the desired impact;
- Obtain applicable technologies in support of strategic objectives;
- Ensure that the necessary support functions are in place in order to ensure desired delivery;
- Define a Decision Support System, as part of the overall structure, in order to achieve
   adaptation and resilience under deep uncertainty;

13.3   The Importance of Net Zero in SIDS

The contemporary challenge posed by climate change is of global concern. The destructive impacts have, and will, touch all nations and populations. Yet, although climate change affects all, it does not affect all equally. Nor are the capacities to respond to the challenges in equal distribution. The small states and territories of the world are some of those most affected and at risk, in particular those under the grouping small island developing states (SIDS). These are a distinct set of small islands and low-lying coastal countries and territories, recognised by the international community as facing specific social, economic, and environmental vulnerabilities. Characterised by small populations and geographic isolation, they also contend with resource constraints that affect their ability to effectively protect against such vulnerabilities. With SIDS combined population of around 65 million, contributing less than 1% of global greenhouse gas emissions, they have, and will, suffer disproportionately from the damaging impacts of climate change.

13.3.1 What Is Different for Small States?

Many small states, especially SIDS, have been identified as being particularly vulnerable to climate change. With populations centred largely in costal zones they are vulnerable to sea-level rises and extreme weather events; these environmental vulnerabilities combine with a particular set of social and economic factors to make small states some of the world's most affected by climate change.

Examples are:

- Most small states are close to sea-level and vulnerable to sea-level rises—some are at risk of going entirely underwater;
- Already the most disaster-prone states, this is made worse with increased intensity of extreme weather from climate change;
- Small and often dispersed populations mean small domestic markets, limiting economies of scale;
- Overdependence on imported fossil fuels and limited progress transitioning to alternative energy;
- Access to and management of uncontaminated freshwater and management of land to control waste and contamination.

13.4 Key Objectives (+ Vision and Mission)

Key objectives of the SIDS initiative strategy:

- Decide on an appropriate strategy for the SIDS initiative
- Continue promoting global awareness regarding the continued vulnerability of SIDS with regard to climate change
- Develop a bankable investment plan, delineating and delivering a portfolio of bankable financial solutions leading to the implementation of a suitable action plan
- Plan for resilient adaptation including allowing the possibility of mass migration with dignity.

These objectives are supported by a preliminary vision statement for the SIDS initiative thus:

Deliver a resilient climate change adaptation plan for SIDS globally, ensuring sustainable human well-being, environmental integrity and economic effectiveness for all its people.

The overall mission statement proposed is *"introducing a delivery platform in partnership with suitable interested stakeholders, delivering the stated vision and key objectives"*.

13.5   The Investment Structure

13.5.1   Investment Opportunities

A sustainability CUBE developed by the chapter author is used to deliver a portfolio of investment opportunities, jointly constituting an investment model for the initiative. The sustainability Cube consists of six core dimensions, with an unlimited number of variables in each dimension.

Taking a systems approach to the focus area, a small island in this case, our objective is to divide the focus area into elements, using relevant frameworks, for creating the required CUBE dimensions. Each element, formed from the cross-over of the frameworks, is then evaluated for its revenue generation capability and hence attracting investment (Fig. 13.2).

The dimensions are distinguished as (1) Input dimension (2) One or more reference dimensions, and (3) Output dimension.

In the SIDS CUBE the Input dimension is created using the 17 SDGs (UN Sustainable Development Goals) with special reference to SDG 14—Life under Water, with ten targets (sub-goals) listed in Box 13.1 below, and SDG 11—Sustainable Cities and Communities—in Box 13.2 below.

Fig. 13.2 Sustainability cube

Box 13.1 SDG 14 TARGETS—LIFE UNDER WATER

14.1 PROTECT AND RESTORE ECOSYSTEMS
14.2 REDUCE OCEAN ACIDIFICATION
14.3 REDUCE MARINE POLLUTION
14.4 SUSTAINABLE FISHING
14.5 CONSERVE COASTAL AND MARINE AREAS
14.6 END SUBSIDIES CONTRIBUTING TO OVERFISHING
14.7 INCREASE THE ECONOMIC BENEFITS FROM SUSTAINABLE
USE OF MARINE RESOURCES
14.A INCREASE SCIENTIFIC KNOWLEDGE, RESEARCH, AND
TECHNOLOGY FOR OCEAN HEALTH
14.B SUPPORT SMALL-SCALE FISHERS
14.C IMPLEMENT AND ENFORCE INTERNATIONAL SEA LAW

Box 13.2 SDG 11 TARGETS—SUSTAINABLE CITIES AND COMMUNITIES

11.1 SAFE AND AFFORDABLE HOUSING;
11.2 AFFORDABLE AND SUSTAINABLE TRANSPORT SYSTEMS;
11.3 INCLUSIVE AND SUSTAINABLE URBANISATION;
11.4 PROTECT THE WORLD'S CULTURAL AND NATURAL
HERITAGE;
11.5 REDUCE THE ADVERSE EFFECTS OF NATURAL DISASTERS;
11.6 REDUCE THE ENVIRONMENTAL IMPACT OF CITIES;
11.7 PROVIDE ACCESS TO SAFE AND INCLUSIVE GREEN AND
PUBLIC SPACES;
11A STRONG NATIONAL AND REGIONAL DEVELOPMENT
PLANNING;
11B IMPLEMENT POLICIES FOR INCLUSION, RESORCE EFFI-
CIENCY, AND DISASTER RISK REDUCTION;
11C SUPPORT LEAST DEVELOPED COUNTRIES IN SUSTAINABLE
AND RESILIENT BUILDING.

The first SIDS CUBE reference dimension is created using a Climate Neutrality Framework developed by SCNiiC, consisting of the following ten variables, each of which provides a platform on which to obtain net zero climate neutrality:

Water, energy, health, agriculture, biodiversity, waste, industry, buildings, transport and forestry.

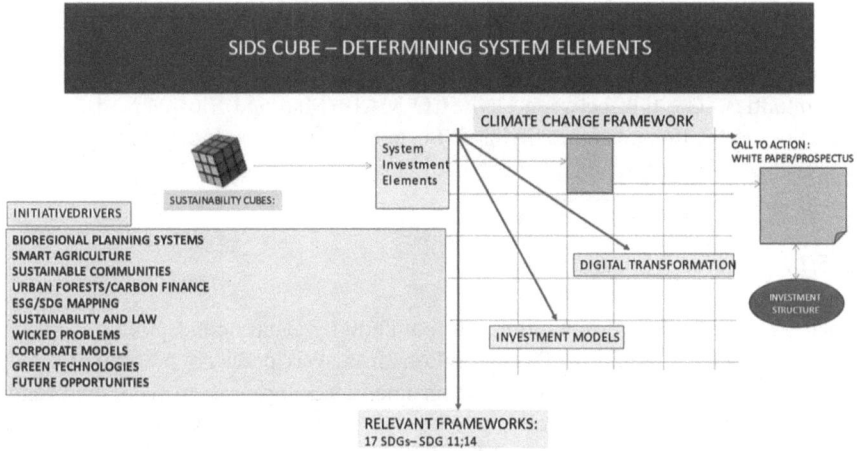

Fig. 13.3 System elements

The second SIDS CUBE reference dimension is created from a Digital Platform also developed by SCNiiC, providing fourteen advanced technologies, each considered for its contribution towards enhancing climate neutrality of the CUBE element under consideration. The fourteen technologies are listed in Sect. 13.6 below.

The SIDS CUBE Output Dimension generates INVESTMENT MODELS, which are schematically indicated in Fig. 13.3, and results from the elements created. The evaluation of each such element results in a mini-whitepaper (or prospectus), the combination of which creates an investment portfolio, to be presented to the applicable investment structure.

13.5.2 Initiative Drivers

As indicated in Fig. 13.3, ten drivers are presented for consideration in the development of the SIDS Initiative. These ten drivers result from the experience gained in the development of a range of sustainability initiatives over a period of twenty years. The next section explains these ten drivers in more detail.

13.5.2.1 Driver 1 Bioregional Planning Systems

Bioregionalism is a philosophy that suggests that political, cultural, and economic systems are more sustainable and just if they are organised around naturally defined areas called bioregions. Bioregional planning is the process of facilitating decision-making to carry out land development with the consideration given to the natural environment, social, political, economic, and governance factors and provides a holistic framework to achieve sustainable outcomes. A major goal of environmental planning is to create sustainable communities, which aim to conserve and protect undeveloped land, a subject area further explored in Village 21 Sustainability Communities. The link between UNESCO MAB (Man and Biosphere) Biosphere Reserves and Climate Neutrality and Sustainability is explored with particular reference to UN Sustainable Development Goals.

13.5.2.2 Driver 2 Smart Agriculture

Smart agriculture refers to two different but complementary concepts, i.e. climate-smart and digital agriculture. Two definitions from Wikipedia are presented:

Climate-smart agriculture (CSA) is an integrated approach to managing landscapes to help adapt agricultural methods, livestock, and crops to the ongoing human-induced climate change and, where possible, counteract it by reducing greenhouse gas emissions, at the same time taking into account the growing world population to ensure food security. Thus, the emphasis is not simply on sustainable agriculture, but also on increasing agricultural productivity. "CSA is in line with FAO's vision for Sustainable Food and Agriculture and supports FAO's goal to make agriculture, forestry and fisheries more productive and more sustainable". CSA has three main pillars—increasing agricultural productivity and incomes; adapting and building resilience to climate change; and reducing and/or removing greenhouse gas emissions.

Digital agriculture refers to tools that digitally collect, store, analyse, and share electronic data and/or information along the agricultural value chain. Other definitions, such as those from the United Nations Project Breakthrough, Cornell University, and Purdue University, also emphasise the role of digital technology in the optimisation of food systems.

Sometimes known as "smart farming" or "e-agriculture", digital agriculture includes (but is not limited to) precision agriculture. Unlike precision agriculture, digital agriculture impacts the entire agri-food value chain—before, during, and after on-farm production. Therefore, on-farm technologies like yield mapping, GPS guidance systems, and variable-rate application fall under the domain of precision agriculture and digital agriculture. On the other hand, digital technologies involved in e-commerce platforms, e-extension services, warehouse receipt systems, blockchain enabled food traceability systems, tractor rental apps, etc., fall under the umbrella of digital agriculture but not precision agriculture.

An important development explored in this chapter is that of Vertical Farming, the practice of growing crops in vertically stacked layers. It often incorporates controlled-environment agriculture, which aims to optimise plant growth, and soilless farming techniques such as hydroponics, aquaponics, and aeroponics.

13.5.2.3   Driver 3 (Village 21) Sustainability Communities

A sustainability community takes into account, and addresses, multiple human needs, not just one at the exclusion of all others. It manages its human, natural, and financial capital to meet current needs while ensuring that adequate resources are available for future generations. The design of typical communities takes on different shapes, dependent on local circumstances. In this regard it is closely related to considerations related to bioregional planning.

Village 21 as a concept considers various frameworks, e.g. climate neutrality and digital transformation, with special reference to twenty-first century technologies.

13.5.2.4   Driver 4 Carbon Finance/Urban Forests

The 3R-C concept is explained by the different methods of reducing, removing, or retaining carbon in the environment and atmosphere.

Wikipedia defines carbon finance as a branch of environmental finance that covers financial tools such as carbon emission trading to reduce the impact of greenhouse gases (GHG) on the environment by giving carbon emissions a price.

Financial risks and opportunities impact corporate balance sheets, and market-based instruments are capable of transferring environmental risk and achieving environmental objectives. Issues regarding climate change and GHG emissions must be addressed as part of strategic management decision-making.

The general term is applied to investments in GHG emission reduction projects and the creation (origination) of financial instruments that are tradeable on the carbon market. It has been forecast that urban areas across the world will have expanded by more than 2.5 billion people by 2050. The scale and speed of urbanisation has created significant environmental and health problems for urban dwellers. These problems are often made worse by a lack of contact with the natural world.

According to Alan Simson, Professor of Landscape Architecture and Urban Forestry, Leeds Beckett University: *"These problems are often made worse by a lack of contact with the natural world. it is only through re-establishing contact with the natural world, particularly trees, that cities will be able to function, be viable and able to support their populations. The creation of urban forests will make cities worth living in, able to function and support their populations".*

13.5.2.5   Driver 5 ESG/SDG Mapping Applications

In this section, the transformational relationship between ESG (Environmental, Social, and Governance) and SDG (Sustainable Development Goals) frameworks is explored in a number of applications. Investopedia defines ESG criteria as a set of standards for a company's operations that socially conscious investors use to screen potential investments.

Environmental criteria consider how a company performs as a steward of nature. Social criteria examine how it manages relationships with employees, suppliers, customers, and the communities where it operates. Governance deals with a company's leadership, executive pay, audits, internal controls, and shareholder rights.

The SDGs or Global Goals are a collection of 17 interlinked global goals designed to be a *"blueprint to achieve a better and more sustainable future for all"* (United Nations). The SDGs were set up in 2015 by the United Nations General Assembly and are intended to be achieved by the year 2030, with the following mission statement "A blueprint to achieve a better and more sustainable future for all by 2030".

13.5.2.6   Driver 6 Sustainability and Law

"Sustainability law" encompasses a variety of inter-related disciplines, the common theme of which is the constitutions imperative of securing "ecologically sustainable development and use of natural resources while promoting justifiable economic and social development"—IMBEWE Sustainability Law practice, Johannesburg, South Africa.

The sustainability challenges we face today are greater than any we have previously confronted. Each year we are losing over 5 million hectares of forest, and an estimated 10,000 distinct species. Climate change is accelerating and will have sweeping impacts on marine and terrestrial ecosystems as well as weather patterns. Land, air, freshwater, and marine pollution further threatens conditions in the natural environment. These challenges translate into direct impacts on human well-being. Poverty, hunger, water scarcity, lack of sanitation, and violent conflict can all be linked to environmental problems.

Law is a necessary part of the solution to sustainability challenges. It is not the whole solution—that encompasses a complex system of social, economic, and political processes and relationships—but it is an essential component. To achieve sustainability goals, appropriate and well-implemented legal frameworks and tools must be in place. And, importantly, they must be effective. It is not enough that laws are enacted, or even that they are fully implemented—they must work. And to ensure that laws work, we must first understand what makes law effective. What factors contribute to its design, implementation, outcome, and ultimate impact? And what can we do to improve it?

13.5.2.7   Driver 7 Wicked Problems

The complexity of the sustainability problem is daunting. The multiple interdependencies and the varying levels of uncertainty, not to mention the multitude of stakeholders with conflicting short- and long-term interests, make responding to the sustainability challenge extraordinarily difficult. The temporal and spatial reach of the needed changes reach every aspect of society.

These kinds of thorny public-policy dilemmas have an evocative name: they are often called "wicked problems". A wicked problem is one that is reflexive, meaning that each attempt to create a solution actually changes the way the problem is understood and perceived. In other words, coming up with new possible solutions causes the very definition of the problem to change. Moreover, wicked problems lack a definite formulation, have no clear set of possible solutions, and offer no obvious means of determining whether or not the problem has been resolved.

Sustainability is a particularly wicked problem, in part because of the lack of an institutional framework capable of developing, implementing, and coordinating the responses necessary to address the problem. As a result, sustainability, like climate change, can be characterised as a "super wicked problem". See Chap. 4 for a more detailed description of Wicked Problems.

13.5.2.8 Driver 8 Corporate Models

We cannot solve our problems with the same mindset we used to create them. Albert Einstein

Einstein's wisdom has never been truer than it is today, where we are experiencing, on a daily basis, huge leaps forward in technological development. With the progress made, it is inevitable that there will be social challenges which will require totally new ways of thinking and corresponding business models. We must all take our responsibility for the development of this new thinking, not only in society but also in business, if we are to create a world which will remain habitable for future generations.

The time has come for a new corporate ethic. Sustainability understanding is growing and becoming an essential component of the business strategy of modern companies. This required understanding, Sustainable Entrepreneurship, translates as the entrepreneurial contribution to sustainable action. In simplified terms, Sustainable Entrepreneurship is about solving the problems of our era, linking these with profitable business strategies, and producing added value for society and business alike by doing so. Sustainability has the potential to function as an engine of growth, profit, and innovation. For many companies, it represents a huge chance to generate clear competitive advantage in the market. It is a guiding principle, an entirely new way of living, and a lifestyle movement which views sustainability not as something to reject, but as a means of creating added value. Is Corporate Social Responsibility (CSR) a New Global Business Language?

13.5.2.9 Driver 9 Green Technologies

Not a day passes for me without seeing the many ways in which digital technology can advance peace, human rights and sustainable development for all. António Guterres, Secretary-General, United Nations

Environmental technology, green technology, or clean technology is the application of one or more of environmental science, green chemistry, environmental monitoring, and electronic devices to monitor, model, and conserve the natural environment and resources and to curb the negative impacts of human involvement—again as defined by Wikipedia.

Research and Markets, arguably the world largest research store, introduces their 2020 report—"Green Technology and Sustainability Market Research Report" with the following statement: *"Due to the rising awareness about the harmful effects of greenhouse gas emission on the environment, the need for low-carbon electricity is increasing, which is driving the global green technology and sustainability market. Governments and utility firms around the world are focusing on generate power from renewable sources like the sun, wind, and water, to reduce the carbon footprint. By employing artificial intelligence (AI), the created energy can be stored for cloudy days, when the photovoltaic (PV) panels cannot function. Thus, with an increase in the renewable power capacity and integration of advanced systems to store the energy, the green technology and sustainability market is growing. Compared to $8.3 billion in 2019, the industry is predicted to generate revenue of $57.8 billion in 2030. Green Buildings to be the largest application area till 2030".*

13.5.2.10 Driver 10 Future Opportunities (Focus Areas)

One immediate example is Sustainability in Sport—Creation of Sport Villages.

A further and most important example is Climate Justice while developing towards a Net Zero Climate.

It is expected that during the development of the SIDS initiative further focus areas, of importance in SIDS sustainable development, whilst aiming at climate adaptation, will be identified.

13.6 Supporting Technologies

The fourteen technology based components (variables) currently in this framework (also referred to as Digital Transformation Platform) are, in no particular order:

Artificial Intelligence, Blockchain, IoT (Internet of Things), Intelligent Sensors, Digital Twinning, Cybersecurity and Cloud Management, Big Data Analytics, Virtual Reality/Augmented Reality, UAVs (Unmanned Aerial Vehicles), Robotics,

5G Networks, 3D-printing, BIM (Building Information Modelling), and GIS (Geographic Information Systems).

In the use of CUBES in strategy development over several years, these advanced technologies have been found to provide a robust reference framework. A justification for this choice is not provided but will be forthcoming in the development of the SIDS Initiative.

13.7 Support Facilities

In support of the SIDS Initiative, the required facilities are provided by SCNiiC through a portfolio of Support Tools and a range of Methodologies, developed over a period of twenty years during a search for robust solutions in sustainability finance. It is important to be reminded that our end goal in delivering sustainable solutions to achieve a net zero environment is our ability to be able to finance that delivery.

13.7.1 Support Tools

13.7.1.1 Sustainability Toolbox

The Toolbox aims at providing appropriate assistance (tools) in all kinds of applications, addressing the subject "sustainability finance" holistically, specifically progressing investments from addressing highly qualitative challenges to highly quantitative solutions, delivering the required impact. Toolbox extracts are normally SCNiiC internally applied in various consulting opportunities but can be made available to other parties on request. The content of the Toolbox has mostly been developed internally, but rather than "re-inventing the wheel" a considerable number of additional solutions have been obtained externally.

13.7.1.2 Crypto Basket

The crypto basket is currently an internal investment pilot study in operation since September 2020, in which a selection of crypto coin investments is combined with a portfolio of SDG investments, on a predetermined ratio. The aim is to apply the basket in support of risk adjustment, where the non-crypto component of the basket will allow long-term qualitative investments with no or low return, as to be found in certain SDG investments.

13.7.1.3 Sustainability Wrap

As a financial instrument, the Sustainability Wrap addresses the global challenge nexus of urbanisation, climate change, and sustainability through the design and delivery of sustainability-smart communities, being defined as either an eco-district, precinct, or city of any size. According to the ODI (Overseas Development Institute—a 60-year-old London based think tank) by 2050, 6.5 billion people will live in urban centres—two-thirds of the projected world population. We believe that the construction of housing alone is insufficient for the creation of a sustainable community. What is required is a self-funding "sustainability wrap" comprising a range of development themes, each combined with one or more SDGs, effectively creating an investment model. The combined revenue generated through each of the resulting investment models constitutes the "wrap" applied in discretionary projects towards the well-being of occupants and their natural environment, without an additional call on the project finance. Relevant consulting exercises are available, to create in appropriate applications, a detailed design template: including housing, sustainable infrastructure, urban master planning, a portfolio of fourteen investment models (jointly providing the WRAP), and a portfolio of sustainability products.

13.7.2   Methodologies

13.7.2.1   Unlocking Intellectual Capital

Investopedia defines Intellectual Capital (IC) as the value of a company's employee knowledge, skills, business training, or any proprietary information that may provide the company with a competitive advantage. It is a mission of the chapter's author to assist clients in unlocking of IC in their operations, with a specific focus on the three focus areas of sustainability, climate neutrality, and natural capital. The unlocking process is to be followed by establishing a suitable growth strategy. Clients vary from relatively small SMEs to large corporates. In the latter, one approach is to identify smaller functional units within the organisation, to be subsequently treated as if a SME. Considering the three listed focus areas, the process proposed could be considered as the "Unlocking of green capital" referring to the capability and capacity in the organisation to contribute applicable solutions to these focus areas. Intellectual capital is considered an asset, broadly defined as the collection of all informational resources a company has at its disposal to drive profits, gain new customers, create new products, or otherwise improve the business. It is the sum of employee expertise, organisational processes, and other intangibles that contribute to a company's bottom line. Over the last two decades, the term Intellectual Capital (IC) has become synonymous with the knowledge economy, whereby the intangible resources of organisations are linked to the development of value. The strategic framework outlined is to provide a methodology for the unlocking of Intellectual Capital with specific focus on a green economy.

13.7.2.2 Decision-Making Under Deep Uncertainty

A recent comment in a conference paper (Garvey, 2021) by the book's author and referred to in the preface and introductory chapter of this book, underlines the wider concerns when addressing uncertainty.

The term "unknown – unknowns" is now ubiquitous, albeit the vast majority of future uncertain events do not fall into this category. However, it has been used to absolve decision makers from criticism post event, whereas poor foresight is the prime culprit. Since the start of the twenty-first century, there is increasing talk about uncertainty—particularly in political, economic, and social circles—not surprising really, as in the two first decades we have seen waves of events that appear to have taken many people by surprise, including politicians, experts, academics, the media, the so-called informed pundits, let alone the rest of us. "Uncertainty" is no longer a conceptual slogan but a reality we are living through. Events from 9/11, Covid 19 to the drip-drip-drip of climate change, have elevated the term "uncertainty" much more into the public domain. Or rather the term is exhorted to justify (often in reaction to inadequate responses to earlier events by decision makers) poor performance post event. In other words, the term is too often applied retrospectively to an event that has already occurred so that the impossibilities of yesterday have morphed into today's challenge: "it is one thing to be caught out by a wholly novel threat, and quite another to be toppled by something we knew about all along".

A framework for supporting management to address uncertainty has been developed by specialists within the SCNiiC team. The framework dissects the main elements of uncertainty so as to inform management and policy makers where the core drivers lie and to reveal how uncertainty can be better recognised and mitigated. Information relating to uncertainty is highly dispersed with all sorts of different inputs and interpretations.

In the following section (13.8), an extensive overview is provided on Decision Support Systems, enabling decision-making under deep uncertainty.

13.8 Decision Support Systems: Decision-Making Under Deep Uncertainty (DMDU)

13.8.1 Introduction

In reviewing decision support systems, constituting an important component to decision-making under deep uncertainty, we are making use of the book "Decision making under deep uncertainty—From theory to practice".

Editors—Vincent A.W.J.Machau, Warren E. Walker, Pieter J.T.M. Bloemen, and Steven W. Popper (2019).

The complete book is freely available as a pdf file and can be downloaded from:

https://www.google.co.uk/books/edition/Decision_Making_under_Deep_Uncer
tainty/gkuQDwAAQBAJ?hl=en&gbpv=0

This open access book focuses on both the theory and practice associated with the tools and approaches for decision-making in the face of deep uncertainty. It explores approaches and tools supporting the design of strategic plans under deep uncertainty, and their testing in the real world, including barriers and enablers for their use in practice. The book broadens traditional approaches.

Strategic planning for the future has to involve anticipating changes. When these changes are characterised by a high degree of uncertainty, the resulting situation is considered to be "deeply uncertain"—a situation in which the parties to a decision cannot agree upon *"(1) the appropriate models to describe the interactions among a system's variables, (2) the probability distributions to represent uncertainty about key variables and parameters in the models, and/or (3) how to value the desirability of alternative outcomes"* (Lempert et al., 2003).

13.8.2   An Overview of DMDU Tools and Approaches

Five approaches presented here in the book, in summary form, are:

- *Robust Decision-making* (RDM) (Lempert, 2019): RDM is a set of concepts, processes, and enabling tools that use computation, not to make better predictions, but to yield better decisions under conditions of deep uncertainty. RDM combines decision analysis, assumption-based planning, scenarios, and exploratory modelling to stress test strategies over myriad plausible paths into the future and then to identify policy-relevant scenarios and robust adaptive strategies.

RDM analytic tools are often embedded in a decision support process called "deliberation with analysis" that promotes learning and consensus-building among stakeholders. Note that this interpretation of Robustness is somewhat different from Robustness Analysis as expounded by Rosenhead—see Chap. 3 and Appendix 2.

- Dynamic Adaptive Planning (DAP) (Walker et al., 2019): DAP focuses on implementation of an initial plan prior to the resolution of all major uncertainties, with the plan being adapted over time based on new knowledge. DAP specifies the development of a monitoring programme and responses when specific trigger values are reached. Hence, DAP makes adaptation over time explicit at the outset of plan formulation. DAP occurs in two phases: (1) the design phase, in which the dynamic adaptive plan, monitoring programme, and various pre- and post-implementation actions are designed and (2) the implementation phase, in which the plan and the monitoring programme are implemented and contingent actions are taken, if necessary.
- Dynamic Adaptive Policy Pathways (DAPP) (Haasnoot et al., 2019): DAPP considers the timing of actions explicitly in its approach. It produces an overview of alternative routes into the future. The alternative routes are based on

Adaptation Tipping Points (ATPs). An ATP focuses on "under what conditions will a given plan fail".

- Info-Gap Decision Theory (IG) (Ben-Haim, 2019): An information gap is defined as the disparity between what is known and what needs to be known in order to make a reliable and responsible decision. IG is a non-probabilistic decision theory that seeks to optimise robustness to failure (or opportunity for wind fall) under deep uncertainty.

It starts with a set of alternative actions and evaluates the actions computationally (using a local robustness model). It can, therefore, be considered as a computational support tool, although it could also be categorised as an approach for robust decision-making.

- Engineering Options Analysis (EOA) (de Neufville & Smet, 2019): EOA refers to the process of assigning economic value to technical flexibility. It consists of a set of procedures for calculating the value of an option (i.e. the elements of a system that provide flexibility) and is based on Real Options Analysis. The interested reader would be appreciate the fact that the availability of options embody the idea of flexibility and would be interested in the variety of papers produced by Richard de Neufville, a Professor of long standing at MIT. Of further interest, with particular reference to infrastructure related decisions under uncertainty, are two books:

Flexibility in Engineering Design—Richard de Neufville and Stefan Scholtes, The MIT Press; and Flexibility and Real Estate Valuation under uncertainty—Richard de Neufville, Wiley Blackwell.

13.8.3   Strategic Options Analysis (SOA)

In Chap. 7 of the main body of the book there is a detailed description of SOA also known as Morphological Analysis (MA). In this section, a shortened summary of the method is presented by way of continuity with other decision support systems.

Morphological analysis (MA) belongs to a broader set of methods in the decision support area known as Problem Structuring Methods (PSMs)—methods which were highlighted in Chap. 3.

MA can be defined as being (Heuer & Pherson 2011):

> . . . ..is a method for systematically structuring and examining all the possible relationships in a multidimensional, highly complex, usually non-quantifiable problem space. The basic idea is to identify a set of variables and then look at all the possible combinations of these variables. . . . . .and reduces the chance that events will play out in a way that the analyst has not previously imagined and considered.

In a morphological model, there is no pre-defined driver or independent variable (or parameter). Any variable, or set of variables or discrete conditions within the main variable—can be designated as a driver. It is this ability to define any combination of conditions as an input or output that gives morphological models such flexibility. Thus, given a certain set of conditions—what is inferred with respect to other conditions in the model? This "what if" functionality makes MA an extremely powerful tool, and when combined with software, allows researchers to explore viable alternatives in real time from very large configurations of variables and conditions (also known as the Problem Space).

This flexibility in determining what the main variables and parameters to a problem are, makes MA a particularly useful tool for developing Exploratory scenarios whilst encouraging high levels of objectivity.

MA fits our criteria for modelling uncertainty, especially when dealing with large amounts of intangible data and can be updated and modified in real time, especially where it incorporates strong facilitation with "stretched" teams of multi-disciplinary experts.

Operating at the fuzzier end of the uncertainty/risk spectrum, a central feature of morphological analysis is the flexibility it provides to parameterize a problem complex, acting as scene setter for other decision support methods. In this case, the results of a morphological model can provide input for the development of other (possibly more complex) models such as those highlighted above.

It should be pointed out that the term Strategic Options Analysis (SOA) is a perfectly acceptable substitute for Morphological Analysis (MA) in the context of this publication.

13.9   Conclusions

The plight of small islands states has gone unnoticed for a long time. It is only in the last decade, largely through their own endeavours that the international community have started to take notice.

At the time of writing this chapter, COP 26 is approaching the end of the first week of the conference. We are aware of a strong small island delegation present in Glasgow and are awaiting further pronouncements.

SIDS offer a particular challenge to the implementation of suitable deliverable adaptation solutions, e.g. relative geographic remoteness, technological sophistication, and the availability of finance. The broad initiative outline presented in this chapter has been in various phases of development since its inception in 2009 in the Maldives. In the meantime major solutions have become available in sustainability finance along with maturation in advanced digital solutions, all these to be jointly and collectively integrated into the initiative investment model.

We have one major objective, i.e. to enable a compelling SIDS focused bankable investment model to facilitate the flow of net zero adaptation finance.

We are treating the SIDS initiative effectively as a "wicked" problem, with full respect for associated risk not allowing short-term solutions that could lead to longer term disruptive unintended consequences.

References

Ben-Haim, Y. (2019). *Info-Gap Decision Theory chapter 5 in Decision Making Under Deep Uncertainty*. Springer.

de Neufville, R., & Smet, K. (2019). Engineering Options Analysis, chapter 6. In R. de Neufville & K. Smet (Eds.), *Decision Making Under Deep Uncertainty*. Springer.

Garvey, B. (2021, August). *Re-assessing How Uncertainty Should Be Treated To Mitigate Risk: A Management Template*. Paper accepted for SSIM Conference Taiwan.

Haasnoot, M., Warren, A., & Kwakkel, J. H. (2019). *Dynamic Adaptive Policy Pathways chapter 4 in Decision Making Under Deep Uncertainty*. Springer.

Heuer, R. J., Jr., & Pherson, R. H. (2011). *Structured Analytic Techniques for Intelligence Analysis*. CQ Press.

Lempert, R. J. (2019). *Robust Decision Making chapter 2 in Decision Making Under Deep Uncertainty*. Springer.

Lempert, R. J., Popper, W., & Bankes, S. C. (2003). *Shaping the next one hundred years: New methods for quantitative, long-term policy analysis.*, (MR-1626-RPC). RAND.

Machau, V. A. W. J., Walker, W. E., Bloemen, P. J. T. M., & Popper, S. W. (Eds.). (2019). *Decision making under deep uncertainty – From theory to practice*. Springer.

Walker, W. E., Marchau, V. A. W. J., & Kwakkel, J. H. (2019). *Dynamic Adaptive Planning chapter 3 in Decision Making Under Deep Uncertainty*. Springer.

Chapter 14
Concluding Comments

> Uncertainty, as a concept we can relate to, only exists in our
> mind. Everything else is possible even if we think it isn't!
> *Author comment 2021*

So what have we—yes even me—learned on this journey to better know and understand the nature and complexities of uncertainty?

It seems logical that in order to understand something as fuzzy and complex and "uncertain" as Uncertainty, a good starting point would be to **deconstruct** it. I started this book by illustrating graphically the three main axes of Uncertainty thus (Fig. 14.1):

This first level of deconstruction into three parts allowed for the interrogation to proceed by asking the following key questions:

- What are the main **structural components** that make up the conditions under which uncertainty operates?
- What **scenario** lenses can be used when exploring uncertainty?
- What **behavioural factors** do we need to consider when analysing the human responses to uncertainty?

In addition, various methods, tools, and techniques (MTTs) were introduced to bring users closer to achieving outcomes, qualitative and quantitative, and to help improve the quality of decision-making whilst mitigating the worst of negative unintended consequences.

14.1 Main Structural Components

Uncertainty is less about the totally unknown but more about thinking about the components that make up uncertainty (hence how deconstruction helps us to understand the topic with its inherent complexity and interconnectivity).

The deconstruction process generated a further series of questions which need to be asked by the decision analyst.

Fig. 14.1 Uncertainty
deconstructed

Structural Components

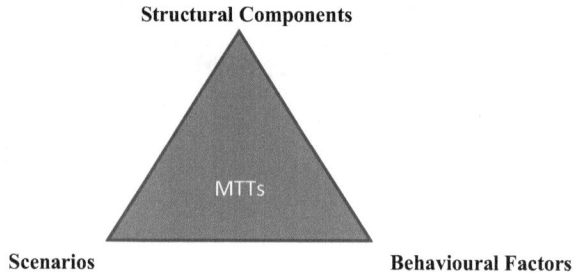

Scenarios   **Behavioural Factors**

Table 14.1 Basic uncertainty
profile

	Known	Unknown
Known	Known-Known	Known-Unknowns
Unknown	*Unknown-Knowns*	Unknown-Unknowns

- **Where along the uncertainty/risk spectrum does the issue reside?** The less data (whether numerical or not) that is available the more the analyst will need to look at qualitative as opposed to quantitative methods
- **What is the nature of the problem**—the more uncertain, the more "wicked" it is likely to be and vice versa?
- **What time horizons should you be looking at**—not too short—how far into the distance?
- **What is the evidence base?** How reliable is the evidence and data we are using— even information from the recent past may be suspect—how strong is the evidence and what sort of confidence does it give us when projecting into the future? Does the evidence allow us to make linear or exponential or cyclical projections?
- **How should we qualify or visualise the future?** What sort of confidence levels should we apply when qualifying uncertainty, as being probable, or possible?

In the Introduction a basic framework or schema was presented which highlighted the various dimensions and interrelationships of uncertainty and, of course, risk and indeed certainty (Table 14.1).

Here the various forms of uncertainty, as articulated by a range of academics, practitioners, and thought leaders (including the former governor of the Bank of England and the late Donald Rumsfeld) were synthesised into the above schema. The schema forms the main thread of how we can explain different types of uncertainty and how we respond to it.

14.2 Scenarios

Scenarios were introduced as being a known and proven vehicle for visualising different forms of the future. Two main scenario lenses were identified—the reactive and the exploratory. Such lenses are not discrete and indeed a third variant composed of a hybrid of the two was also included. Apart from the danger of reacting to just one specific event we need to move beyond the immediate impact of the primary event to secondary/tertiary impacts and outcomes—what might be called "derivative" events? On the other hand, should we spend more time on scanning the horizon and not just wait for something to happen—explore the future? And where we are reacting to an event, how far should we seek out and explore secondary and tertiary outcomes?

The matrix below illustrates the range and scope of the scenario based approach discussed in the book (Table 14.2).

The main emphasis of this section is that management and decision makers need to move away from being in respond mode to major events (i.e. as a reaction to an event) but increase their exploratory approaches so as not to be caught out by a whole range of "possible" events that can and should have been foreseen. The greater the warning, or rather awareness of the possibility of certain future events happening, then the better contingency and adaptive planning processes can help mitigate the worst impacts of future surprises with negative outcomes. This can also help formulate innovative responses to various weak signals and outlier events as well as creating an environment where real innovation (technological, social, economic, etc), can take place—avoiding the risk of being left behind at a time of rapid change. **The more exploratory the approach the more likely that unintended consequences of actions, good and bad, can be flagged up sooner rather than later.**

However, many of our responses to future events and possible scenarios are largely dependent on our ability to visualise futures which do not follow predictable and linear paths and accepting that the past may not be like the future—even in the short term. Many responses are essentially behavioural in origin. This is why the third axis which explores how we humans handle uncertainty, or, regularly, fails to handle it, through a variety of cognitive factors, is crucial to our understanding of uncertainty so as to mitigate its worst effects.

Table 14.2 Scenario alternatives

Type "Derivative"	Reactive	Exploratory	Hybrid
Primary			
Secondary			
Tertiary			
Other downstream			

14.3   Behavioural Factors

How do we humans react to uncertainty?

As this study progressed it became apparent that a wide range of behavioural and cognitive factors largely determined how we identify and confront uncertainty. Rather than seeing behavioural factors as the third axis at the base of the pyramid, the realisation emerged that their influence led to the inversion of the original pyramid, i.e., so that behavioural factors largely determine how we confront uncertainty. In essence, when addressing uncertainty, behavioural factors can considered to be the principal driver in confronting Uncertainty, not just post event but pre-event. So my viewpoint about positioning Uncertainty was transformed to look more like this (Fig. 14.2).

As already mentioned a common thread throughout the study has been to refer to an advance form of the basic known/unknown schema. In Chap. 2, this basic schema was expanded to present "The Uncertainty Profile Template" (UPT). Each of the UPT quadrants was then populated with additional items describing further each quadrant's profile and characteristics bounded by whether events were either identifiable or unidentifiable as well as being predictable or unpredictable. All these elements were brought together and described in Chap. 2 and illustrated in Fig. 14.3:

14.4   A Different Perspective on How We Treat Uncertainty

Yes, uncertainty is complex, but this very acknowledgement of complexity, including bedfellows such interconnectivity, non-linearity, asymmetry, exponentiality, and all the lovely messy components introduced in part 1 of this book, is too often used as an excuse to absolve ourselves of the responsibility of looking deeper into the topic. In effect we fall back on convenient heuristic devices and cognitive biases and dissonance to justify a failure to acknowledge that what is termed "uncertain" are not "black swans" or unknown-unknowns, but with more judicious forms of due diligence, actual possibilities.

The author has determined that **uncertainties be treated as known-unknowns or inevitable surprises.** As such, rough probabilities may be attached to such events

Fig. 14.2 Enhancing the   **Behavioural Factors**   Scenarios
behavioural

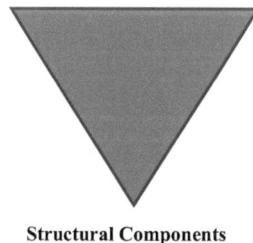

Structural Components

Profiling uncertainty: a multi-faceted problem?

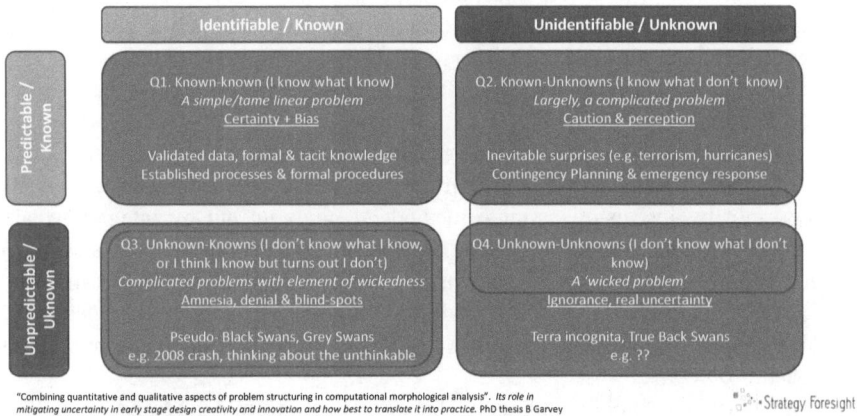

Fig. 14.3   The uncertainty profile

for contingency planning purposes so as to mitigate negative effects or accelerate positive effects. Whilst the term "if we can think it—it can happen" is relevant to this quadrant, the challenge for practitioners is how to position such events into some form of hierarchy—and what criteria should we select for establishing such a hierarchy? Criteria selection again leads us into that territory which can be impacted by behavioural factors. So awareness of such cognitive biases and behaviours is crucial to the selection of such variables and crucially, their ranking. Uncertainty is highly dynamic and so in turn the search process must be ongoing and not restricted to discrete planning cycles. This would indicate that semi-quantitative methods such as AHP and more quantitative methods be introduced once a broad range of viable options have been identified, such as Bayesian Belief Networks (BBNs) and Fuzzy Logic[1] principles as developed by Lotfi Zadeh.

This book has indicated that there exist different types of Uncertainty. The trouble is that all too often we allow ourselves to be seduced by the term—leading to a fatalistic acceptance that we can do little to mitigate its impact through interpreting Uncertainty as an unknown-unknown. The author's view is that this position is erroneous (if not dangerous).

I have argued that the three major types of uncertainty, (excluding Q1 the known-knowns), as presented in the Uncertainty Profile Template—quadrants 2, 3, and 4, should really be reduced to just one category—Q2, known-unknowns or "inevitable surprises". Unknown-unknowns (Q4) are truly beyond the ability of homo sapiens to comprehend what this might be, so why bother spending time on them? Quadrant 3, the unknown-knowns only exists to demonstrate our cognitive limitations—from a whole gamut of individual and group biases, silo thinking, group-think, denial, blind spots, short-term thinking, amnesia, and intellectual myopia as

---

[1] Zadeh and Kacprzyk (1992).

well as cognitive dissonance. If we can overcome or at least mitigate the effects of Q3 behaviour, then what is left is just the known-unknown in Q2! This requires not only a change in perception about uncertainty by individuals and groups but a constant awareness of how easy it is to fall back onto subjective opinions which in turn can act as a barrier to the exploration of ideas, especially those outside our comfort zone.

In addition, both practitioners and academics much be willing to broaden their knowledge and awareness of decision support methods, techniques, and tools (MTTs)—not by just using a single method *ad nauseam* but by integrating and mixing and matching a wide range of MTTs that are already available. This needs to be tempered by the awareness that there is no one single method or group of methods which can be adapted to "solve" all conditions where uncertainty exists. Such is the complexity of uncertainty that the best we can hope for is some degree of mitigation in impact of outcome.

Uncertainty is a "blob" continually shape-shifting and mutating and moving in erratic patterns. One can conclude that it is our understanding of its structure and component parts that defines how we address uncertainty. Awareness of our behavioural shortcomings would indicate that—unknown-unknowns and more importantly "unknown-knowns" do not really exist—but just show a lack of imagination. Anything is possible. Science fiction writers have taken us to the outer boundaries of what the brain can conceive—it really is quite amazing what we humans can visualise. Barriers to handling uncertainty are not so much lack of methods or even information but lack of acceptance to move out of our comfort zones and a plethora of cognitive barriers which prevent us from thinking about the unthinkable—so we get stuck too often in quadrant 3—treating unforeseen events as "Unknown-knowns".

Apart from the behavioural barriers to our understanding and acceptance of uncertainty, real constraints do exist of course, which compromise the efficacy of decision-making under uncertainty, namely time, money, and scale of investigation, availability of hard and soft data, if any at all—all interlinked. These are real substantive threats to the decision-making process.

The role of management when faced with uncertainty is to see such uncertainty as residing in Quadrant 2—and identify "inevitable surprises". Once identified objective analysis needs to attempt to place issues into some form of hierarchy. All this has to be done against a background of real constraints—but it would be dangerous to allow such constraints to dictate the evidence base—it being crucial that wherever possible the evidence (and even the lack of it) drives policy rather than the other way round.

This requires a very different balancing act by management—sufficient resources need to be allocated to address uncertainty whilst acknowledging the ever present impact of behavioural factors in decision-making. Bringing Uncertainty to the fore our management thinking requires major organisational transformation and above all not be hived off to a specialist uncertainty department. Uncertainty affects every aspect of an organisation and the evidence would indicate that the origins of uncertainty are increasing. Our perspective about future events needs to change so that decision makers can reduce incidences of "not seeing it coming"!

Reference

Zadeh, L., & Kacprzyk, J. (Eds.). (1992). *Fuzzy logic for the management of uncertainty.* John Wiley & Sons Inc.

Appendices

Appendix 1 Robustness Analysis: Rosenhead's Summary

Rosenhead's own description of the method (apart from the more detailed descriptions and process in Chap. 8 of the 2001 book "Rational Analysis for a Problematic World Revisited) was best summarised in a EWG-MCDA Newsletter dated Autumn 2002. Here is an edited version of that paper.

Robustness Analysis is a way of supporting decision-making when there is radical uncertainty about the future. It addresses the seeming paradox—how can we be rational in taking decisions today if the most important fact that we know about future conditions is that they are unknowable? It resolves the paradox by assessing initial decisions in terms of the attractive future options that they keep open.

Principles of Robustness Analysis

Robustness analysis is applicable when:

(i) *uncertainty is a factor that obstructs confident decision—which has been discussed above; and*
(ii) *decisions must be or can be staged—that is, the commitments made at the first point of decision do not necessarily define completely the future state of the system. There will be one or more future opportunities to modify or further define it.*

A simple statement of the robustness criterion is that, other things being equal, an initial commitment should be preferred if the proportion of desirable future situations that can still be reached once that decision has been implemented is high. Put still more simply, i t is a good thing to keep your options open. That is the intuitively sensible proposition that underlies robustness analysis.

Specifying a Problem Situation for Robustness Analysis

The first set of elements which must be specified are

- *a set of alternative initial commitments to be considered*
- *(normally) a set of "futures" representative of possible environments of the system*
- *a set of relevant possible configurations of the system which the decisions will modify.*

The three elements above need to be complemented by information of the following types:

- *assessments of the compatibility of each commitment-configuration pair*
- *evaluation of the performance of each configuration in each future.*

If these two stages need to rely extensively on elicitation rather than on computation, there is a clear danger of combinatorial escalation rendering the process infeasible. Groups are not good at rapid and repeated but thoughtful evaluations of the kind that are required. There is therefore a strong argument for keeping the dimensions of the problem formulation as small as possible; and it may be necessary for the group to delegate the first attempt at one or both of these stages to one of its members, working with a consultant.

Analysing for Robustness

The robustness of a commitment is the ratio of the number of acceptably performing configurations with which that commitment is compatible, to the total number of acceptably performing configurations.

Clearly, this limits robustness scores to the range (0, 1). A robustness score of zero indicates that no acceptable options are kept open, while a robustness of unity means that they all are.

Each commitment now has a robustness score for each future, since a configuration's performance will vary across future contexts. Commitments can thus be assessed for the spread of flexibility they offer both within and across futures. This process will rarely identify a dominant commitment, but it will usually eliminate non-contenders, and focus discussion on just a small number of relatively attractive alternatives. It may also concentrate attention on those futures which are most crucial to the choice between these alternatives.

Some Comments

It may be noted that this procedure depends on identifying alternative futures which the system under consideration may confront. It is a fair criticism that since the future is infinitely devious, we cannot know that any of our identified futures will capture the key aspects of the future that actually happens. Evidently the elicitation process should endeavour to reduce this risk, for example, by selecting a broad range of contrasting possible future environments. However, the approach does not, cannot, require that this eventual future is actually identified with certainty.

Consider an initial commitment which is the first step to an "optimum" solution in a single predicted future. It will maintain flexibility at best only by accident. By contrast, a robust commitment will maintain flexibility over a wide range of conceivable futures. The value of this in a future which may be outside the range of those considered cannot be rigorously demonstrated. However, it is at least highly plausible that this diversity of options is more likely to include routes to one or more future configurations that will perform acceptably in the eventual future context. In any case, the principle advantage of robustness analysis lies more in its process than in its product.

Applications of Robustness

"Practical uses of robustness analysis have included; brewery location, chemical plant expansion, hospital location, regional health planning, oil field development, personal educational and career planning".

Rosenhead himself recognises that the method, based on multiple variables and large-scale matrices, can create a combinatorial explosion, so that the number of outcomes can become unmanageable. This has not doubt inhibited the method's dissemination and usage, similar to that experienced by users of the Morphological Analysis method. Broader acceptance of the approach would greatly benefit from the availability of a computerised version to "crank through" the numerous configurations and options that the method can generate, so as to arrive at a smaller set of viable options that the decision maker can work with.

Appendix 2 Causal Layered Analysis (CLA): After Inayatullah

Method Process

Identify the critical issues or trends of a problem that are contentious or critical to better understand.

Phase 1—Apply the CLA method thus by brainstorming participants ideas on:

1. Litany: map current responses and views about the issue—at this level people are describing their reaction to the issue as they "feel" it.
2. Social causes: identify what is causing the issue to develop—this level identifies the trends and drivers shaping the issue as it appears to participants—these drivers are usually accepted and not questioned at this level.
3. Discourse/worldview: ask whose worldview is shaping the issue, whose voice is being heard, and whose is not.
4. Myth/metaphor: identify stories and myths that underpin the dominant and minority world views to demonstrate the depth of thinking that is generating the issues we see today.

Phase 2—Look at each criterion in turn.

5. Then conduct a group discussion about the exercise making sure you capture the myths and metaphors that arise.
6. The next stage is to re-build that thinking by exploring a new metaphor that can inform thinking and start to shape the issue in a shared way.
7. Now take one of the myths or metaphors and reverse the order of the criteria working up the list in a secondary round of brainstorming sessions to finally create a new litany of happenings and a potentially new alternative future.
8. Capture your most exciting idea and biggest fear.
9. Determine the fixed elements (almost certain hard trends) that will inform your strategic response: slow-changing phenomena, e.g., demographic shifts, constrained situations, e.g., resource limits, in the pipeline, e.g. ageing of baby boomers, inevitable collisions, e.g. climate change arguments.
10. Capture critical variables, i.e. uncertainties, soft trends, and potential surprises. Both these and the fixed elements will be key to creating scenarios and examining potential future paradigm shifts.
11. Capture unique insight into new ways of seeing that can be utilised by the organisation.

Phase 3—Concluding Interrogation

- What conclusions can we draw from the exercise(s)?
- How might the future be different?
- What certainties/uncertainties are implied in the conclusions?
- How does A affect B?
- What is likely to remain the same or change significantly?
- What are the likely outcomes?
- What and who will likely shape our future?
- Where could we be most affected by change?
- What might we do about it?
- What do not we know that we need to know?
- What should we do now, today?
- Why do we care?

- When should we aim to meet on this?
- Develop next steps and determine if any further research required

Appendices 3 to 7

Due to the amount of detail provided in Appendices 3–7 in Chap. 7 **"Scenarios— What are they, why are they useful and how can we best use them"?** the information is best referenced by a link to the author's website at https://www. strategyforesight.co.uk/learning

Once on the landing page called "Insights"—scroll down page to section just before "Multimedia" to open the detailed schedules for Chap. 7 Appendices 3–7.

Appendix 3. Mini Scenario Outcome Options

Appendix 4. Complete Solution Sets

Appendix 5. Most Impactful Scenarios

Appendix 6. 64 Preferable and Undesirable Scenarios

Appendix 7. Allocation of Options to Uncertainty Matrix Quadrants

Appendix 8 Morphological Analysis/Morphological Distance (MA/MD) Case Study

The case study addressed the focus question: *"What possible configurations can the design of an apartment block take, which ensures cross-ventilation and sufficient daylight"*.

Proof of Concept Case Study 1 Integrating MA and MD

Summary

A case study conducted on Apartment Typology illustrates the 99.9% reduction of an initial problem consisting of 155,520 configurations to a mere 213 internally consistent options. The 10-dimensional problem space was initially reduced by deploying Morphological Analysis methods then refined further using Morphological Distance principles. The final 213 solutions post Morphological Distance were found to be distanced 4-5 parameters away from existing, state-of-the-art, solutions. Finally, these solutions, termed as the Terra Incognita, were processed by a visual algorithmic editor and output as tri-dimensional CAD models which in turn can easily be evaluated and analysed by the designer.

The focus question was stated as follows: "What possible configurations can the design of an apartment block take, which ensures cross-ventilation and sufficient

daylight". The question was chosen in anticipation that it could be easily translated in parametric geometry terms and to show that additional focus questions (e.g. energy usage or glare analysis) could be used applying the same methodological approach.

For this case, *Grasshopper*®—a plugin for the modelling software *Rhinoceros*®, was used due to its popularity amongst the parametric modelling community, its intuitive use, and the authors' familiarity with the language. Grasshopper is a node-based editor which has a large number of built-in functions and available plugins but also allows for user-defined components.

Parametric modelling was chosen as a visual tool for the analysis of configurations for two main reasons: Firstly, since all configurations are guaranteed to be internally consistent (post CCA) the designer has no way of identifying which configurations are truly creative just by looking at the text output and manually visualising all 213 configurations as tri-dimensional models. To do this would be overly time-consuming.

The problem space developed from the focus question is represented as follows:

Table A.1 shows the full problem space with the apartment block being well defined by ten parameters with between two-five states each It is important to note that apartment blocks are almost always multi-purpose or at least combine several of these possible configurations. In this study, possible configurations will later be placed in context alongside other similar apartment cells in order to provide the designer with a way of evaluating the configuration.

The parameters give a **problem space** consisting **of 155,520 configurations** $(3 \times 3 \times 3 \times 5 \times 4 \times 4 \times 3 \times 4 \times 3 \times 2)$

The MA Process: Cross Consistency Assessment Analysis

Following pair-wise analysis, conducted by the authors and an external subject specialist, 32 inconsistent pairs were identified which reflect contradictions in all three constraint categories. These are: Logical contradictions (i.e. pairs which cannot logically co-exist) which included pairs such as "Studio-Duplex", Empirical contradictions (i.e. pairs which are not permitted by building regulations) included pairs such as "Single Perpendicular-Natural Ventilation", whereas Normative or Ethical constraints (i.e. pairs which would pass building regulations but are bad practice to produce and sell) included pairs such as "Double Loaded Horizontal–Excellent Daylight".

Post CCA compilation, the **solution space** was reduced to 8,472 internally consistent pairs (a 94.6% reduction). This was reduced further to **2412 configurations** when using *Natural Ventilation and Excellent/Satisfactory Daylight* as inputs (in essence excluding poor daylight and the need for mechanical ventilation).

Table A.1 Problem space

Building orientation	Building height	Building shape	Building access	Number of bedrooms	Aspect	Type	Private open spaces	Lighting	Ventilation
E-W	Low rise	Block	Single Loaded Horizontal	Studio	Single perpendicular	One	Cantilever	Excellent	Natural
N-S	4-6 storeys	Courtyard block	Double loaded horizontal	1 bed	Single parallel	Duplex	Recessed	Satisfactory	Mechanical
Mixed	High rise	Open block	Skip-stop single	2 bed	Double	Mezzanine	Semi-recessed	Poor	
			Skip-stop double	3+ bed	Corner		None		

Morphological Distance Analysis

The number of selected solutions scenes (2412) is still a substantial total, hence the need to refine further via MD triage. The results of the MD triage exercise are shown in Table A.2 and show that, 213 configurations were identified as being 4–5 configurations apart from existing solutions, within the specified TI zone, and as such, worth further analysis.

Results and Discussion

The text-based scenes in the TI zone were fed into Grasshopper® which converted them to tri-dimensional models. It was considered that for comparison purposes, the use of such graphics would be easier to understand by designers more familiar to such visual representations.

In keeping up with standard architectural typology and literature, the following parameters were used: Building orientation, height, shape, access, Number of bedrooms, Apartment aspect, type, private open spaces, lighting, and ventilation. A more detailed, schematic representation of all the parameters is given in Figure X.

This case provides, firstly, a more detailed description of the parametric modelling in identifying *Terra Incognita* solutions (i.e. those outcomes majorly different from current state-of-the-art solutions) and thus of greater interest for those designers seeking alternative options. Secondly, extensive graphics generated from the configuration strings, and converted to images using *Grasshopper*® (a plugin for modelling software *Rhinoceros*®), are provided in this paper. These graphics are used to illustrate how the scene descriptions were translated into meaningful inputs for the algorithm components processed by *Grasshopper*®.

Methodology and Rationale

Parametric modelling was chosen as a visual tool for the analysis of configurations for two main reasons: Firstly, since all configurations are guaranteed to be internally consistent, the designer has no way of identifying which configurations are truly creative just by looking at the text output and manually visualising all 213 configurations as tri-dimensional models is likely to be more time-consuming and meaningless.

More importantly though, for a reason which stems from one of the core principles of Morphological Analysis, it systematically avoids designer bias. For example, according to Morphological Analysis, one of the parameters which fully describes the design of a car might be "*Number of wheels*", with possible states ranging from one to five or more wheels. If, following pair-wise analysis, such states are deemed to be internally consistent, there appears to be no reason—other than institutional memory and design bias—that a car needs to run on four wheels. Even if

Table A.2 Morphological Neighbourhoods

State of the art	Perimeter zone			Terra incognita		Total
	1 Configuration Away	2 Configurations Away	3 Configurations Away	4 Configurations Away	5+ Configurations Away	
98	438	927	736	*202*	*11*	**2412**

modelling each configuration manually made sense time-wise, it is likely to sub-consciously suffer from the designer's bias. Algorithmic modelling of the *Terra Incognita* configurations, post CCA and subject to MD triage, on the other hand, has the possibility of surprising the designer and lead to truly creative solutions.

The Solution Space Post Cross Consistency Assessment

The solution space scenes shown below indicate how a priori there can exist no solutions with "single perpendicular" aspect apartments as they provide inadequate daylight. In Table A.3 below the two right hand cells (red in e-version—grey in print version)

Morphological Distance Analysis

The two scenarios selected produced 2412 solution scenes (972 + 1440) and which were then subject to MD triage. It was first necessary to identify which configurations are in use today and be classified as "State of the Art" (aka Occupied Territory).

Due to time considerations, the authors forewent the use of bibliometric and census data to identify the OT configurations and elected to base their judgement upon 5 case studies carried out in the "Good Solutions Guide for Apartments". Despite the low number of case studies, their multi-purpose nature yielded 98 different configurations which were deemed as being sufficient considering the large size of the solution space (10th dimensional space) and thus the diminishing returns with additional OT (SoA) configurations.

The results of the MD triage exercise are shown in Table A.2and suggest 213 configurations were identified as being 4–5 configurations apart from existing solutions, within the specified TI zone, and as such worth analysing.

Table A.2 as above.

Parametric Modelling of Terra Incognita *Solutions*

It is readily understood from the problem space that certain parameters, namely *Orientation, Height, Shape, and Access,* refer to the entire building whereas others, such as *Number of bedrooms, Aspect, Type, and Private Open Spaces,* refer to the particular apartment in question. Due to this difference in scale and other factors concerning Grasshopper's sequential logic, the parametrisation needed to occur with a specified order. A detailed description of walk-through logic is provided in the full paper which can be obtained on request from the author at (garvey@strategyforesight.org).

Table A.3 The Solution Space Post Cross Consistency Assessment

Cross Consistency Matrix CCM Wizard Solution Matrix

□ Inclusive □ Frozen Solution

Building orientation	Building height	Building shape	Building access	Number of bedrooms	Aspect	Storeys	Private open spaces	972 Lighting	972 Ventilation
E-W	Low rise	Block	Single loaded horizontal	Studio	Single perpendicular	One	Cantilever	Excellent	Natural
N-S	4–6 storeys	Courtyard block	Double loaded horizontal	1 bed	Single parallel	Duplex	Recessed	Satisfactory	Mechanical
Mixed	High rise	Open block	Skip-stop single	2 bed	Double	Mezzanine	Semi-recessed	Poor	
			Skip-stop double	3+ bed	Corner		None		
			Vertical						

Results and Discussion

Figure A.1 illustrates representative examples of the tri-dimensional models generated by the algorithm. The models were easy to analyse visually and as such identify
subtleties. For instance, in order for configuration 5(vi) to have vertical access **and**
double aspect apartments, the elevators need to be wide enough to allow entrance to
all apartments (alternatively additional towers could be used).

The table below shows the original configuration scene components prior to
translation into Grasshopper and from which the tri-dimensional graphics in
Fig. A.1 were generated.

Table A.4 Configuration descriptions list relating to Fig. A.1.

Conclusions

Of great interest to designers is that large problem spaces containing multi-variable
inputs by the designer can not only be majorly reduced using the MA method but be
further refined using MD triage to help identify viable design options significantly

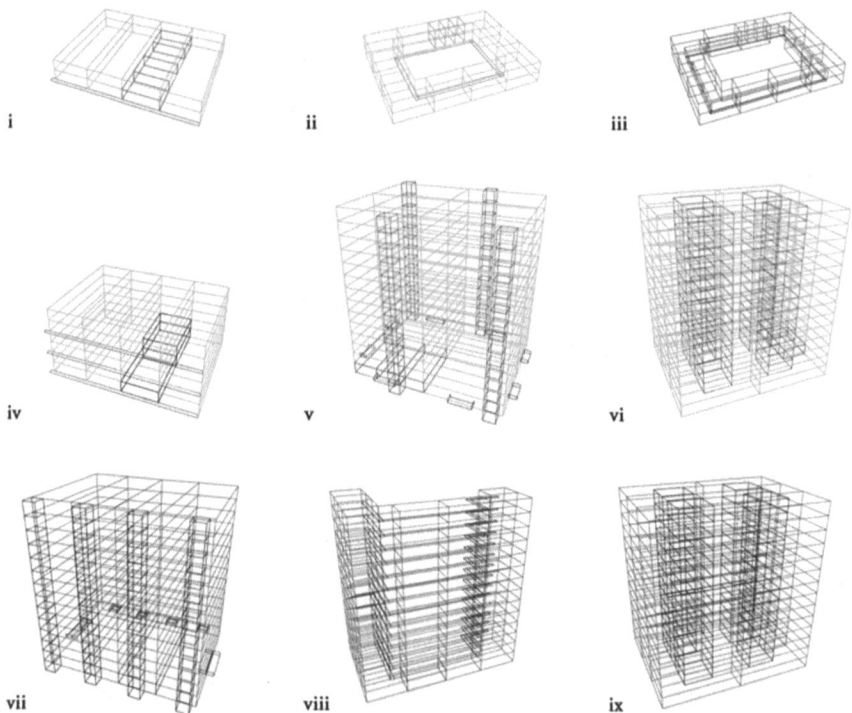

Figure A.1 Wire diagram options

Table A.4 Configuration descriptions list

#	Building orientation	Building height	Building Shape	Building access	Number of bedrooms	Apartment aspect	Apartment type	Private open spaces	Lighting	Ventilation
i	EW	Low rise	Block	Skip-stop single	3+	Double	One	None	Excellent	Natural
ii	Mixed	Low rise	Courtyard block	Skip-stop single	2	Double	Duplex	None	Excellent	Natural
iii	Mixed	Low rise	Courtyard block	Skip-stop double	2	Double	Duplex	None	Satisfactory	Natural
iv	EW	4–6 storeys	Block	Skip-stop single	1	Double	Mezzanine	None	Excellent	Natural
v	EW	High rise	Block	Vertical	2	Corner	One	Cantilever	Excellent	Natural
vi	**Mixed**	**High rise**	**Courtyard block**	**Vertical**	**Studio**	**Single parallel**	**One**	**None**	**Excellent**	**Natural**
vii	EW	High rise	Block	Vertical	Studio	Double	One	Semi-recessed	Satisfactory	Natural
viii	Mixed	High rise	Open block	Single loaded horizontal	Studio	Single parallel	One	None	Satisfactory	Natural
ix	Mixed	High rise	Courtyard block	Vertical	Studio	Single parallel	One	None	Satisfactory	Natural

removed from standard state-of the-art designs. Those options deemed to occupy the *Terra Incognita* zone are thus more likely to offer innovative, non-standard insights for designers seeking alternative outcomes. In our proof of concept study, a problem space of over 155K potential options was reduced by 95% to generate 8472 internally consistent solutions. Two scenario sets—using both lighting and daylight parameters as the key inputs, reduced solutions even further to 2412 configurations (a 98.45% reduction). Finally, by applying MD principles, some 213 (a 99.87% reduction) configurations were identified as being significantly different from current designs to be worth investigating further. These 213 configurations were subsequently processed to provide the designer with tri-dimensional graphics of the set which facilitated the visual representation for the designer.

The paper thus succeeds in outlining a way of translating the text-based output of the Morphological Distance analysis to a set of tri-dimensional models which can be analysed and further manipulated by the designer. The configurations produced were not evaluated by the authors with respect to their aesthetic value as that falls outside the scope of the paper.

Appendix 9: Distance Examples in Creative Design & PESTLE

This example comes from architectural design and addressed the question: "What possible configurations can the design of an apartment block take, which ensures cross-ventilation and sufficient daylight". See previous appendix for more details.

The methodology helped to design new options for Apartment Typology. A 10-parameter problem space, composed of 155,520 configurations was initially reduced by deploying basic MA from which solutions were then reduced further using MD triage principles. The two-stage process generated a 99.9% reduction of the initial (155k configuration) problem space, to a mere 213 internally consistent options classified as being in the Outlier zone. Such was the remoteness from current knowledge that these 213 options qualify as representing weak signal configurations.

The final 213 solutions post MD were found to be distanced 4–5 parameters away from Current Knowledge solutions (from a 10-parameter configuration set). Finally, these Outlier solutions were processed by a visual algorithmic editor and output as tri-dimensional CAD models which in turn could be easily evaluated and analysed by the architect/designer to reveal interesting, difficult to identify, design alternatives. Appendix 3 gives a detailed work through of this case study.

Case 2: A second example applied MA/MD to a PESTLE variable format, looking at what outlier options could be considered for the UK over the next two years or so, based on a selection of political scenarios. A small problem space was generated, totalling some 3072 different configurations. Following pair-wise analysis to reduce the original set of configurations, software compiled a reduced set of viable solutions, from 3072 to 174, or by 95%. These 174 viable solutions were then triaged according to distance principles.

An anchor configuration reflecting current knowledge was selected (scenario 2791). The set of Outlier/weak signals configurations was determined to contain 2 or less parameter/states which matched the configuration profile of the anchor set. Alternatively, at least 4 of the 6 sub-variables in the configuration were different from the anchor set. Analysis of the viable 174 scenarios identified that some 20 scenarios were distanced the maximum 6 parameter/states from the anchor configuration, representing 11.5% of the solution set. Another 42 scenarios, or 24%, were identified as being 5 parameter/states distanced from the anchor. These 20 outlier scenarios, being so far distanced from the anchor, could offer intriguing perspectives not readily identifiable had this exercise not been carried out.

Appendix 10 Quadrant Crunching

QC requires the analyst to break down the lead hypothesis into its component parts, identifying the key assumptions that underlie the lead hypothesis or dimensions that focus on Who, What, When, Where, Why, and How? (the 5 Hs + H). Once articulated, the analyst should generate at least two examples of contrary dimensions. The various contrary dimensions are then arrayed in sets of 2 × 2 matrices. If four dimensions are identified for a particular topic, the technique would generate six different 2 × 2 combinations of these four dimensions (AB,AC,AD,BC,BD, and CD). Each of these pairs would be represented as a 2 × 2 matrix with four quadrants. Different scenarios would be generated for each quadrant in each matrix. If two stories are imagined for each quadrant in each of these 2 × 2 matrices, a total of 48 different ways the situation could evolve will have been generated. Similarly, if six drivers are identified, the technique will generate as many as 120 different stories to consider (Table A.5).

The last step in the process is to develop lists of indicators for each scenario in order to track whether a particular scenario is beginning to emerge.

The example used here has been taken from the chapter 5.7 Quadrant Crunching in Richards Heuer's and Randolph Pherson's book "Structured Analytic Techniques for Intelligence Analysis" (CQ Press 2011). The example used by Heuer and

Table A.5 Creating a set of stories

Number of dimensions	Number of matrices generated	Number of scenario categories (4 per matrix)	Number of scenarios (up to 2 per quadrant
3	3	12	24
4	6	24	48
5	10	40	80
6	15	60	120

Table A.6 Flipping Assumptions

Key assumption	Contrary assumption	Contrary dimensions
Single attack	Multiple attacks	• Simultaneous • Cascading
Contamination	Other strategies	• Denial of service • Water as a weapon
Drinking water	Waste water	• Treatment plants • Sewage pipes
Outsider	Insider	• Staff employees • Contractors/visitors
Major casualties	Minor casualties	• Terrorise population • Disrupt economy

Table A.7 Sample matrices

Multiple attacks/ insider	Multiple attacks/ insider	Multiple attacks/minor casualties	Multiple attacks/minor casualties
• Simultaneous • Staff employee	• *Simultaneous* • *Contractor or visitor*	• Simultaneous • Spark terror	• *Simultaneous* • *Disrupt economy*
• Cascading • Staff employee	• *Cascading* • *Contractor or visitor*	**• Cascading • Spark terror**	• *Cascading* • *Disrupt economy*

Pherson explores the question "How might terrorists attack our domestic water system?"

1. State the conventional wisdom for the most likely way the attack might be launched, e.g. Al-Qaeda or affiliates will contaminate the domestic water supply causing mass casualties.
2. Break down the statement into its component parts, e.g. statement makes four key assumptions (a) a single attack, (b) involving drinking water, (c) conducted by an outside attacker, (d) that causes large number of casualties.
3. Posit a contrary assumption for each key assumption, e.g. what if there are multiple attacks?
4. Identify at least two dimensions of that contrary assumption, e.g. different ways a multiple attack could be launched (e.g. Twin Towers and Pentagon)
5. Repeat process for each of the key dimensions (Table A.6).

• Array pairs of contrary dimensions int sets of 2 × 2 matrices. In this case, ten different 2 × 2 matrices would be created. Two of the ten matrices are shown below (Table A.7).

• For each cell in each matrix, generate one to three examples of how terrorists might launch an attack. In some cases, such a scenario might already have been imagined. In other quadrants, there may be no credible scenario. But several of

Table A.8 Selecting scenarios (3 of ten 2 × 2 matrices)

Multiple/ insider	Multiple/ insider	Multiple/ casualties	Multiple/ casualties	Insider/ casualties	Insider/ casualties
Story 1	Story 2	Story 5	Story 6	Story 9	*Story 10*
Story 3	*Story 4*	*Story 7*	Story 8	***Story 11***	Story 12

*Scenarios deserving the most attention **Nightmare Scenario***

the quadrants will usually stretch the analyst' thinking, pushing them to think about the dynamic in new and different ways.
- Review all the scenarios generated; using a pre-established set of criteria, select those most deserving of attention. In this example, possible criteria might be those scenarios that are most likely to:

(a) Cause the most damage; have the most impact
(b) Be the hardest to detect or prevent
(c) Pose the greatest challenge for consequence management

- This process is illustrated below (Table A.8)

- Here three stories were selected as the most likely scenarios. Story 1 became Scenario A, Stories 4 and 7 were combined to form Scenario B and Story ten became Scenario C. Story eleven should also be considered as a wild card or nightmare scenario.
- Consider what decision makers might do to prevent bad scenarios from happening, mitigate their impact, and deal with their consequences.
- Generate a list of key indicators to help assess which, if any, of these scenarios is beginning to emerge.

Appendix 11 Analytic Hierarchy Process: AHP

See Figs. A.2, A.3, A.4, A.5, A.6, A.7, A.8, A.9, A.10, A.11, and A.12.

Analytic Hierarchy Process is a decision making method for prioritising alternatives when multiple criteria must be considered

- Developed by Thomas Saaty in the 70's for rational decision support for complex decision situations with multiple criteria

- Why? Observed the lack of practical, systematic, approach for priority setting and decision making by groups

- Crucial decision situations, forecasts or resource allocations involve too many dimensions for humans to synthesize intuitively

Figure A.2 Introduction

Analytic Hierarchy Process

Figure A11.2

"100 Question" framework is a bespoke facilitation tool which maps the entire investment landscape and assesses multiple outcomes, intended and unintended

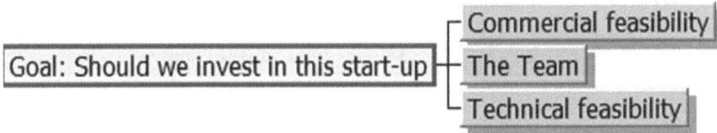

Goal: Should we invest in this start-up — Commercial feasibility / The Team / Technical feasibility

1) Four levels for deep drilling down
2) Over 100 questions on the fourth level
3) Over 70 cross-tiered evaluative pairwise comparisons
4) "Programmable" to include bias of any investor / group / organization

Figure A.3 Question Framework

Tool Hierarchy

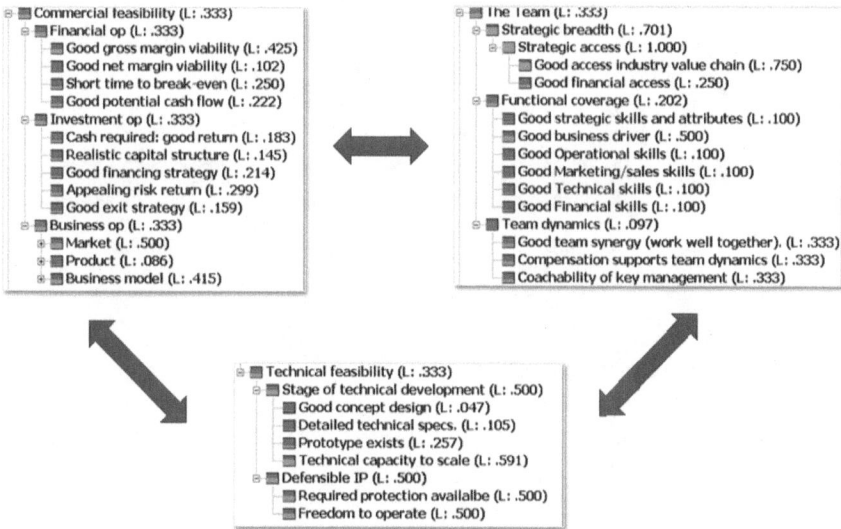

Figure A.4 Tool Hierarchy

Analytic Hierarchy Process is a method for organizing and supporting decision-making processes (such as choice, ranking, prioritization, resource allocation) based on the multi-criteria evaluation (e.g. price, quality, time, experience) of alternatives (e.g. projects, investments, vendors).

1) Constructs a decision-making problem in hierarchies as goal, criteria, sub-criteria and decision alternatives

2) Performs pairwise comparisons measuring relative importance of elements at each level

3) Evaluates alternatives at the lowest level to make the best decision among multiple alternatives

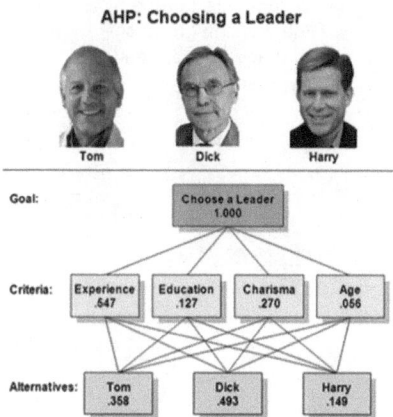

Figure A.5 Choosing a Leader

People deal with complexity by decomposing the problem into hierarchy of common clusters of criteria, sub-clusters of criteria etc.

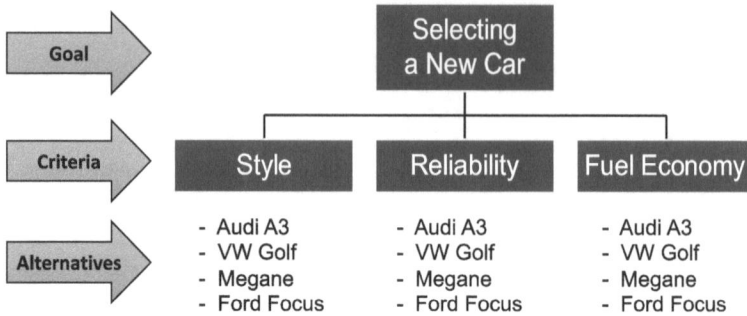

Figure A.6 Decomposing the problem

It is simpler to make comparative judgements between two factors using a ratio scale

	Style	Reliability	Economy
Style	1:1	1:2	1:3
Reliability	2:1	1:1	4:1
Economy	1:3	1:4	1:1

Given uncertainty or incomplete data, relative weights are agreed by the working group or managerial team and led by a facilitator

Ratio	Description
1	Equally preferred
3	Moderately preferred
5	Strongly preferred
7	Very strongly preferred
9	Extremely strongly preferred

Figure A.7 Ratio Scale

As an illustration, ranking the priorities of the criteria can be done by a simple method

				Criteria weights	PRIORITY
Style	0.30	0.29	0.06	0.22	2
Reliability	0.60	0.57	0.75	0.64	1
Economy	0.10	0.14	0.19	0.14	3
SUM	3.33	1.75	5.33	100%	

1. Sum elements in each column
2. Divide each value by the column sum
3. Compute the row averages

Figure A.8 Ranking

Repeat process with each decision alternatives: style, reliability and fuel economy

STYLE	Audi A3	VW Golf	Peugeot 205	Ford Focus	Normalised
Audi A3	1:1	1:4	4:1	1:6	0.12
VW Golf	4:1	1:1	4:1	1:4	0.25
Megane	1:4	1:4	1:1	1:5	0.06
Ford Focus	6:1	4:1	5:1	1:1	0.58

FUEL ECONOMY	Miles per gallon	Normalised
Audi A3	45	0.26
VW Golf	50	0.28
Megane	42	0.24
Ford Focus	39	0.22

Qualitative judgements **and** Quantitative measures can be incorporated in the same decision matrix

Figure A.9 Decision Alternatives

Combine the hierarchy.....

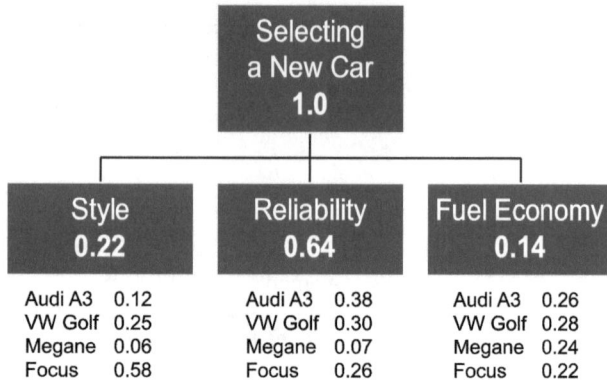

```
                      Selecting
                      a New Car
                         1.0

        Style             Reliability          Fuel Economy
        0.22                 0.64                   0.14

   Audi A3  0.12       Audi A3  0.38         Audi A3  0.26
   VW Golf  0.25       VW Golf  0.30         VW Golf  0.28
   Megane   0.06       Megane   0.07         Megane   0.24
   Focus    0.58       Focus    0.26         Focus    0.22
```

Figure A.10 Combining the Hierarchy

The correct method requires dedicated software to facilitate the calculation of ...

- Eigen Vector
  - mathematical function used in prioritising elements with different sizes and scale in a matrix

- Consistency ratio
  - a measure how consistent the judgements have been relative to large samples of purely *random* judgements
  - Should be less than 10%

Figure A.11 Software

To recap....

The Process

1. Deconstruct problem into a hierarchy – facilitation
2. Make pairwise comparison and establish priorities of elements in the hierarchy
3. Synthesise the results (to obtain the <u>overall ranking</u> of alternatives w.r.t. goal)
4. Evaluate consistency of judgements

The rationale

- For multi-attribute modelling
  - i.e. 'and' rather than 'or'
- Allows group decision making where stakeholders can use experience, data and knowledge to address uncertainty
- Manages organisational conflicts of 'messy' problems

Figure A.12 Summary

Appendix 12: Strategic Options Analysis and Social Mobility Case Study

See Fig. A.13.

Phase 1 *Generate the entire Problem Space* *(Steps 1-6)*	• Identification of the main problem being addressed • Selecting an expert team representing the key stakeholders • Determining a focus question which encapsulates the problem • Facilitating the expert team to generate a problem space made up of the key parameters of the problem and then the states/dimensions within each of the parameters • *The first steps here may require external facilitation and stakeholder management to finely structure the problem – before programming the software to generate the Problem Space which reflects the total number of possible configurations to be addressed.*
Phase 2 *Perform Cross Consistency Assessment* *(Steps 7-8)*	• This phase involves a form of cross impact analysis where the Problem Space is transposed[2] and each state within a parameter is assessed for consistency against every other state within the other parameters (i.e. can these two states logically co-exist). If they cannot, then every configuration where such an inconsistent pair exists is discarded.
Phase 3 *Generate the Solution Space for decision support* *(Steps 9-10)*	• Supporting software compiles those configurations only where all pairs within a configuration are consistent with each other. This process can eliminate over 95% of the original Problem Space to produce a set of viable internally consistent solutions. These solutions are presented as 'what-if' scenarios where any dimension in a parameter can be an input or an output.

Fig. A.13 Social Mobility Case Study

Appendix 13 Social Mobility Workshop: Sample Schedule

1. Terms of reference:

   – Background.

      Why are we doing this—re social mobility complexity challenges. Copious
         research, lots of ideas—but a lack of costed/detailed actions brought
         together under one umbrella.
      Rationale on mind map, source data/reports, and contributors/validators.
      Holistic and simple view of challenges and potential solutions.

   – Core Issues

      Context above highlighted complexity, multiple variables, the need for
         multiple/diverse stakeholder standpoints.
      Simplify and scope the scale of the problem (as defined by its complexity
         and uncertainties).
      Attempt to introduce a methodology which makes it more manageable and
         facilitates the process to arrive at a set of potential, yet viable, solutions.

   – The Problem—initial statement

      We still live in a country where your future potential is more defined by the
         circumstances of your birth (more than anything else).
      Furthermore, there are indications that this gap is becoming wider leading
         to a more polarised and unequal society.

2. Holistic understanding of the topic—Mind Map (inc. rationale for development)

   a. Done above

3. Highlight issue of the multi-variable nature of the topic, the scale, and
   manageability.

   a. Done above and illustrated by mind map

4. What to do?

   – Phase 1:

      The first phase of structuring the problem was developed from mind map.
         This allows us to define a number of problem spaces (a number of key
         parameters which characterise the issues within the problem).
      In addition to the key variables being ascertained, we need to determine the
         interaction between each of these variables to identify those which are
         consistent with each other to help define the potential solutions.
      It is not necessary to an immediate solution (as there may be many—some
         better, some worse), but develop an iterative approach to mitigate the
         risk of selecting a poor set of solutions (with negative unintended
         consequences) and to engage fully with a wide range of stakeholders
         as possible so as to reduce input bias.

5. Revisit the Mind map and convert to a Strategic Options Model model—for a "straw-man" work through.

- The original mind map consisted of 3/4 core topic areas. For the purposes of this exercise (which demonstrates the application of an options analysis method to a complex, emotive, and socially resonant problem today), one of these topic areas (National Impact) was used to bring this to life and identify potential viable solutions to be considered by government and decision makers.
- For the purposes of this exercise, we have accepted the first iteration of the mind map as given, and this was used to define the problem space.

  However, we recognise that circumstances change and the mind maps can be amended or specific items moved to reflect changing environment which requires any method used to be flexible enough to allow iterations.

  The mind map was a useful format to collate and show the relationships between the data; however in any decision-making environment additional aspects of the problem may be required.

  In our case example we have added the "usual suspects" as operational constraints: money, time, and current political landscape as defined by the government and its power. However, these constraints and the detail need to be defined by experts in the field and government.

Glossary

Analysis of Competing Hypotheses (ACH) ACH is a tool to aid judgment on important issues requiring careful weighing of alternative explanations or conclusions. It helps an analyst overcome, or at least minimise, some of the cognitive limitations that make intelligence analysis so difficult to achieve. It is a surprisingly effective, proven process that helps analysts avoid common analytic pitfalls. Because of its thoroughness, it is particularly appropriate for controversial issues when analysts want to leave an audit trail to show what they considered and how they arrived at their judgment. ACH is an eight-step procedure grounded in basic insights from cognitive psychology, decision analysis, and the scientific method. The steps are 1. Identify possible hypotheses, 2. Make a list of significant evidence for/against 3. Prepare a Hypothesis versus Evidence matrix, 4. Refine matrix. Delete evidence and arguments that have no diagnosticity, 5. Draw tentative conclusions about relative likelihoods. Try to disprove hypotheses, 6. Analyse sensitivity to critical evidential items, 7. Report conclusions, and 8. Identify milestones for future observations.

Analytic Hierarchy Process (AHP) In a structured and traceable manner, to support a process of choosing the best among a number of well-defined alternatives, in relation to a well-defined hierarchy of goals and goal criteria. The Process allows one to construct hierarchies or feedback networks, then makes judgments or performs measurements on pairs of elements with respect to deriving ratio scales that are then synthesised throughout the structure to select the best alternative. AHP provides the objective mathematics to process the subjective and personal preferences of an individual or a group in making a decision. AHP works by developing priorities for alternatives and the criteria used to judge the alternatives. Usually the criteria, whose choice is at the mercy of the understanding of the decision maker (irrelevant criteria are those that are not included in the hierarchy), are measured on different scales, such as weight and length, or are even intangible for which no scales yet exist.

Bayesian Belief Networks (BBN) Bayesian Belief Networks are an emerging modelling approach of artificial intelligence (AI) research that aim to provide a decision support framework for problems involving uncertainty, complexity, and probabilistic reasoning. The approach is based on conceptualising a model domain (or system) of interest as a graph (i.e. network) of connected nodes and linkages. In the graph, nodes represent important domain variables, and a link from one node to another represents a dependency relationship between the corresponding variables. To provide quantitative description of the dependency links, Bayesian Belief Networks (BBNs) utilise probabilistic relations, rather than deterministic expressions. The main use of BBNs is in situations that require statistical inference—in addition to statements about the probabilities (i.e. likelihood) of events, the user knows some evidence, that is, some events that have actually been observed, and wishes to update his/her belief in the likelihood of other events, which have not as yet been observed. Given the node-link structure for the model domain, BBNs use probability calculus and Bayes theorem to efficiently propagate the evidence throughout the network, thereby updating the strength of belief in the occurrence of the unobserved events. BBNs can use both "forward" and "backward" inference.

BCG Matrix A business strategy model. The Boston Consulting Groups matrix also known as the Product Portfolio Matrix. Classic 2×2 matrix presenting High and Low options for businesses assessing Market Growth and Relative Market Share. The 4 quadrants generated identify Stars (High Market Growth and High Relative Market Share), Cash Cows (LMG and High RMS), Question Marks (HMG and LRMS), and Dogs (LMG and Low RMS).

Brainstorming This technique could be applied individually but it should be better applied in group (which must be heterogeneous and free from inhibitions/restraints). The technique does not need specific requirements and, in particular, the working group does not require preliminary training. A single session of brainstorming produces more good ideas than a traditional discussion, requiring short time. Sometimes brainstorming sessions give only simple hints for future ideas, especially working with complex problems. Moreover, since these sessions are not structured, results may vary a lot depending on people involved. Limitations include: faulty operation: lack of adhesion with procedures based on experience, overrated expectation: sometimes people forget that miracles do not happen that often, the group can suffer by domination of one or more strong individuals who push their agenda/ideas to the detriment of other members.

Causal Layered Analysis (CLA) As a method, its utility is not in predicting the future but in creating transformative spaces for the creation of alternative futures. It is also likely to be useful in developing more effective—deeper, inclusive, longer term—policy. Causal layered analysis consists of four levels: the litany, social causes, discourse/worldview, and myth/metaphor. The first level is the litany—the official unquestioned view of reality. The second level is the social causation level, the systemic perspective. The data of the litany is explained and questioned at this second level. The third level is the discourse/worldview.

Deeper, unconsciously held ideological, worldview and discursive assumptions are unpacked at this level. As well, how different stakeholders construct the litany and system is explored. The fourth level is the myth/metaphor, the unconscious emotive dimensions of the issue. The challenge is to conduct research that moves up and down these layers of analysis and thus is inclusive of different ways of knowing.

Collaborative Methods Aim to increase the success of groups of people or teams as they engage in collaborative problem solving, ideally to establish a consensus. The method used may employ the services of a facilitator to assist in the establishment of objectivity and balance. It is particularly useful where team members are dispersed geographically and where operationally it is difficult to assemble in one location for any period of time.

Complexity Is a function of structure and uncertainty, where there are multiple and inter-dependent information sources and which are uncertain. An increasing number of links combined with high uncertainty creates a system which is extremely difficult to comprehend manage.

Configuration An arrangement of component parts or elements in a particular form, figure, or combination. In some methods such as Morphological Analysis, it is used to describe one unique string of cells composed of an individual states from each of the different parameters in the string.

Creativity Is a phenomenon whereby something new and somehow valuable is formed. The created item may be intangible or a physical object (Wikipedia).

Cross Consistency Assessment (CCA) The activity of carrying out pair-wise analysis of cells where one state in a parameter is judged to able to co-exist (logically, empirically, or even normatively) with another state from another parameter. Both consistent and inconsistent states are identified.

Cross Consistency Matrix (CCM) The physical framework for carrying out a CCA exercise made up of pair-wise cells.

Data Analytics The identification, interpretation, and presentation of meaningful patterns in data especially when confronted by large, often unrelated sets of data (Big Data). It relies on the integrated application of statistics, computer programming, and operations research to quantify performance. Also just called Analytics.

Decision Support A body of models, tools, and processes which help to mitigate risk and imbue greater clarity in relation to decision-making. It is less interested initially in solving a problem as opposed to structuring it—so the appropriate methods can be applied.

Decision Support Method (DSM) A generic term for a wide range of methods and tools to assist decision-making.

Decision Support System (DSS) Is composed of various methods across the risk and uncertainty spectrum which progressively allows for such risk to be mitigated.

Delphi Delphi can be used to help bring to the surface and judge components of messy issues. Its main disadvantage being its high administrative overhead;

however, the method has been successfully incorporated in some computerised problem solving systems. Between 2 and 5 consecutive questionnaires to a group of perhaps 15–25 people (occasionally up to 100) selected either as experts in the matter being investigated or as people directly concerned in some issue. Nominate the Panel; assuming they are experts and busy people, it is likely that they will require reassurance that there are advantages to their accepting the considerable commitment involved. The process requires the adjudicator to: 1. Develop, send out, and get back the opening questionnaire; one or two broad open-ended questions are sent out initially and responses are preferred in the form of a list of separate sentences or short paragraphs rather than continuous text. 2. Repeat for a second questionnaire. This subsequent document is created in light of the responses to the initial questionnaire. The responses to the first questionnaire are collated into a single anonymous list. The respondents are then asked to rate every item in the list (e.g. on a five-point scale of importance, priority, feasibility, relevance, validity…) and finally to include any additional items suggested by the combined listing. A brief Delphi might end at this point; however, a more extended Delphi may profit from additional rounds. Alternatively, the items rated above a certain threshold could be printed on separate cards, with a request for each panel member to sort the cards into related clusters. When the Delphi method is used to address a single, well-defined, problem (such as its original use in estimating likely damage levels from nuclear war) the outcome may be easily summarised. However, when used to surface and prioritise concerns, the output can be quite large (a panel of 20 can easily generate 15–20 concerns each—perhaps 2–300 distinct items) so as in any form of brainstorming some type of convergent post-Delphi analysis may be needed.

Dynamic Adaptive Planning (DAP) DAP focuses on implementation of an initial plan prior to the resolution of all major uncertainties, with the plan being adapted over time based on new knowledge. DAP specifies the development of a monitoring programme and responses when specific trigger values are reached. Hence, DAP makes adaptation over time explicit at the outset of plan formulation. DAP occurs in two phases: (1) the design phase, in which the dynamic adaptive plan, monitoring programme, and various pre- and post-implementation actions are designed and (2) the implementation phase, in which the plan and the monitoring programme are implemented and contingent actions are taken, if necessary.

Dynamic Adaptive Policy Pathways (DAPP) DAPP considers the timing of actions explicitly in its approach. It produces an overview of alternative routes into the future. The alternative routes are based on Adaptation Tipping Points (ATPs). An ATP focuses on "under what conditions will a given plan fail".

Engineering Options Analysis (EOA) EOA refers to the process of assigning economic value to technical flexibility. It consists of a set of procedures for calculating the value of an option (i.e. the elements of a system that provide flexibility) and is based on Real Options Analysis.

Ideation A key part of the creative process of generating, developing, and innovating new ideas.

Impact Analysis Also called high impact/low probability analysis (HI/LP) and provides decision makers with early warning that an apparent unlikely event might occur. It is a useful accompaniment to weak signal analysis. HI/LP allows analysts to explore consequences of an event especially one not deemed like by conventional wisdom (or trend analysis). Emphasis is not on what will happen but what could happen. Not to be confused with What If analysis which assumes something has happened—HI/LP looks for potential outliers.

Info-Gap Decision Theory (IG) An information gap is defined as the disparity between what is known and what needs to be known in order to make a reliable and responsible decision. IG is a non-probabilistic decision theory that seeks to optimise robustness to failure (or opportunity for wind fall) under deep uncertainty. It starts with a set of alternative actions and evaluates the actions computationally (using a local robustness model). It can, therefore, be considered as a computational support tool, although it could also be categorized as an approach for robust decision-making.

Innovation The process of translating an idea or invention into a good or service that creates value for users, and ideally meets a specific need. It has also been referred to as being applied creativity.

Key Assumptions Check Assumption Testing examines other people's opinions and assumptions to ensure they are consistent. The process will embrace Stakeholder Identification, Identification of Factions or interests, if necessary group stakeholders into factions, "points of view" or "interests", Group Formation, Assumption Surfacing, in each sub-group, discuss each stakeholder reasons (assumptions) and prioritises them, Assumption Testing, members of the sub-groups debate if these assumptions were reversed and it made no difference should we ignore it and finally Assumption Ranking, members of the sub-group rank their assumptions: Results can be exhibited as a 2×2 matrix of High/Low potential versus Likely/Unlikely occurrence.

Long-Term Planning Analysis (LTPA) According to the RAND Corporation Long-Term Policy Analysis helps policy makers "whose actions may have significant implications decades into the future make systematic, well-informed decisions. LTPA is an important example of a class of problems requiring decision-making under conditions of deep uncertainty—that is, where analysts do not know, or the parties to a decision cannot agree on, (1) the appropriate conceptual models that describe the relationships among the key driving forces that will shape the long-term future, (2) the probability distributions used to represent uncertainty about key variables and parameters in the mathematical representations of these conceptual models, and/or (3) how to value the desirability of alternative outcomes. In particular, the long-term future may be dominated by factors that are very different from the current drivers and hard to imagine based on today's experiences. Meaningful LTPA must confront this potential for surprise" (2003). In effect this interpretation comes very close to that defined by a "wicked problem".

Mess A term ascribed to Russell Ackoff and akin to the term "wicked problem". Ackoff and Rittel & Webber developed their ideas on messes and wicked problems contemporaneously.

Method A series of specific and defined steps to reach a certain outcome or objective.

Methodology Often wrongly used when what is meant is a method (see above). Methodology is the study of how research is done and the principles determining how methods and tools are deployed and why they are being used and interpreted.

Methods, Tools, and Techniques (MTTs) A general reference to all devices used in problem structuring and problem solving—can be qualitative and/or quantitative.

Mind Maps Mind Maps provide an effective method of taking notes. They show not only facts, but also the overall structure of a subject and the relative importance of individual parts of it. Mind Maps help individuals to associate ideas and make connections that might not otherwise make. A Mind Map is a powerful graphic technique which provides a universal key to unlock the potential of the brain. It harnesses the full range of cortical skills—word, image, number, logic, rhythm, colour, and spatial awareness—in a single, uniquely powerful manner. Mind Maps hold information in a format that your mind will find easy to remember and quick to review. In fact, they abandon the list format of conventional note taking, doing this in favour of a two-dimensional structure. The maps support representation and creativity because they let the reader have an overall point of view of the topic by a single look.

Morphological Analysis or MA A key PSM is a method for systematically structuring and examining the total set of possible relationships in a multidimensional, usually non-quantifiable, problem space. Such problems are not only complex but exacerbated by high levels of interconnectivity. Each set of configurations generated can be considered as a bundle of attributes. By identifying all the variables relating to the problem, all possible combinations of these variables (configurations) are examined. Through a reductive process, whereby inconsistent individual pairs of variable are filtered out with the help of software, computing only those configurations where all variables are consistent with one another, a final set of viable solutions can be compiled for further analysis. MA allows for all ideas to be considered as a first stage in the analysis process and as such is an exploratory method par excellence. Practically, MA provides management and policy makers with the ability to identify informed and innovative options when confronted with complex problems, particularly under conditions of uncertainty and compounded by high levels of interconnectivity.

Morphological Distance (MD) A solution configuration reduction process to help identify those internally consistent configurations which are at variance with those configurations deemed state of the art, and thus likely to offer innovate options for further assessment.

Morphological matrix Also called a matrix of alternatives. It decomposes the key parameters of a problem and then lists potential solutions for each dimension or state.

Pair-wise analysis A process whereby two separate states or entities are compared with each other—usually to identify if they compatible or not. Intermediary states of concurrence can act as additional filters in the assessment—such as empirical or normative.

Parameter Is a characteristic, feature, or measurable factor that helps define a particular system. It is an important element when evaluating the depth and breadth of a situation especially problematic ones.

PESTLE Is an acronym which in its expanded form denotes P for Political, E for Economic, S for Social, T for Technological, L for Legal, and E for Environmental (although sometimes the term Ethical is substituted for Environmental). It is used as a tool by organisations to track the environment they are operating in. In some ways, it is the external version of SWOT. The output from a PESTLE analysis is often used as an input for other business management tools such as SWOT analysis, risk assessment, or a Business Model Canvas. There are many variations of this framework, which examine different combinations of external factors, specific to particular industries. Examples include: PEST, STEEPLE, STEER, and STEEP. The framework: encourages strategic thinking and helps you evaluate how your strategy fits into the broader environment, provides an overview of the crucial external influences on the organisation, allows decision makers to make more decisive and knowledgeable decisions.

Pre-mortem Analysis Aim is to reduce risk of surprise and which might lead to a post-mortem analysis of what went wrong. Helps to identify potential causes of error previously overlooked. Poses questions such as: Did we consider alternative hypotheses? Did external influences affect the outcome? Did deception go undetected? Were our sources or key evidence unreliable? Was any contradictory evidence ignored? Did the absence of information mislead us? Were our key assumptions valid?

Problem Space The total combination of parameters, and separate states within parameters, that have been determined to characterise and simultaneously addressing the key variables that make up the problem. It is the starting point of analysis to which reductive processes are applied in order to generate a viable solution space.

Problem Structuring Method (PSM) PSMs include methods such as Soft Systems Methodology (SSM), Strategic Choice Approach, and Robustness Analysis. PSM's are important in that they allow analysts to frame and position complex problems, identifying interrelated sub-components, rather than first considering the multitude of issues and positions inherent in such problems as part of a larger system.

Puzzle A conundrum to which there is only one answer. Ackoff defined the term as being the simplest form of problem solving due to its linear nature.

Qualitative Reflects the subjective quality of a thing or phenomenon, such as feel, taste, expertise, image, leadership, reputation, and are abstract, not requiring measurement because the reality they represent can only be approximated (Business Dictionary).

Quantitative Associated with an objective quality of a thing or phenomenon that is measurable and verifiable, such as lightness or heaviness, softness or hardness, and thickness or thinness (Business Dictionary).

Red Teaming Red Teaming is the art of applying independent structured critical thinking and culturally sensitised alternative thinking from a variety of perspectives, to challenge assumptions and fully explore alternative outcomes, in order to reduce risks and increase opportunities. Red teaming should: identify strengths, weaknesses, opportunities, and threats, hitherto unthought-of; challenge assumptions; propose alternative strategies; test a plan in a simulated adversarial engagement; and ultimately lead to improved decision-making and more effective outcomes. The benefits of red teaming include: broader understanding of the Operational Environment, filling gaps in understanding, identifying vulnerabilities and opportunities, reducing risks and threats, avoiding group think, mirror imaging, cultural miss-steps, and tunnel vision. It can reveal how outside influences, adaptive adversaries, and competitors could counter plans, concepts, and capabilities as well as identifying desired or undesired second- and third-order effects and unforeseen consequences.

Risk Indicates that partial information (often involving metrics), is available and generally, is probabilistic, so that when future events or activities occur they do so with some measure of probability. Alternatively, risk can be defined as the probability or threat of a damage, injury, liability, loss or negative occurrence, caused by external or internal vulnerabilities, and may be neutralised through premeditated action (risk management). A risk is not an uncertainty, a peril (cause of loss), or a hazard.

Robust Decision-making (RDM) RDM is a set of concepts, processes, and enabling tools that use computation, not to make better predictions, but to yield better decisions under conditions of deep uncertainty. RDM combines decision analysis, assumption-based planning, scenarios, and exploratory modelling to stress test strategies over myriad plausible paths into the future and then to identify policy-relevant scenarios and robust adaptive strategies. RDM analytic tools are often embedded in a decision support process called "deliberation with analysis" that promotes learning and consensus building among stakeholders. Note that this interpretation of Robustness is somewhat different from Robustness Analysis (see below).

Robustness Analysis Robustness Analysis is a way of supporting decision-making when there is radical uncertainty about the future. It addresses the seeming paradox—how can we be rational in taking decisions today if the most important fact that we know about future conditions is that they are unknowable? It resolves the paradox by assessing initial decisions in terms of the attractive future options that they keep open. Robustness analysis is applicable when uncertainty is a factor that obstructs confident decision and when decisions must be or can be staged. That is, the commitments made at the first point of decision do not necessarily define completely the future state of the system. There will be one or more future opportunities to modify or further define it. A simple statement of the robustness criterion is that, other things being equal, an initial commitment should be preferred if the proportion of desirable future situations that can still be reached once that decision has been implemented is high. Put still more simply, it is a good thing to keep your options open. What counts as a desirable future situation? How do we count them? How do we identify which of them are kept open?

Role Playing Analysts assume the roles of main stakeholders who are subject of their analysis and act out their responses to developments. It is a less intense form of red teaming. Used to improve understanding of what might happen when two or more people or organisations interact. Shows how each side might react to positions by the other side.

Scenario A possible series of future events based on variable input assumptions for each "scene".

Scenario Planning A possible series of future events based on variable input assumptions for each "scene". Scenarios are different quality models of "plausible futures". They give a deeper understanding both of the potential environments in which an organisation might have to operate and of what an organisation might have to do today. On the basis of this information, you can make some predictions about the future and then you can apply them to possible future scenarios which are based upon the present time. Scenario Building helps you to identify a range of potential opportunities that can make organisational planning and decisions more flexible. This technique can be easily implemented and work group members are neither required to be experts in any specific matter, nor to cooperate too close. Scenario building can especially help you to foresee the technological developments of a given organisational area.

Simulation Gaming In simple terms, a simulation is a recreation of a real-world situation, designed to explore key elements of that situation. It is a simplification of a process that allows participants to experience that process. A simulation game has elements like score, performance rating, conflict, and payoff and simulates a real-world situation for decision-making or alternative evaluation. These multi-variable learning tools allow the player to experience cooperation and teamwork without the risk of expensive mistakes. Simulation games follow the widely accepted "learning by doing" philosophy.

SODA SODA (Strategic Options Development and Analysis) is a methodology for helping someone understand the various viewpoints of a problem area. Whilst the detail of any projects is tailored to the specific problem, the general steps are; Planning meetings: Client interviews: Development of causal maps: Check-back interviews: Merging the maps: Presentation: Interpret the map in terms of goals, strategies, and tactics: The completed, agreed, map can be used to determine the high-level goals, medium-level strategies, low-level tactics, and operational targets. Action selection, allocation, and implementation: Now that the goals, strategies, and targets have been determined, these need to be allocated to people for implementation.

Solution Space In MA it is those configurations, which have been deemed to be internally consistent across all its various states and parameters. It is derived by identifying inconsistencies in the CCA process and subtracting only those configurations that are internally consistent from the original problem space array of configurations.

Stakeholder Analysis Is the process of assessing a system and potential changes to it as they relate to relevant and interested parties (stakeholders). This information is used to assess how the interests of those stakeholders should be addressed in a project plan, policy, or programme. A stakeholder analysis of an issue consists of weighing and balancing all of the competing demands on an organisation by each of those who have a claim on it, in order to arrive at the organisation's obligation in a particular case. A stakeholder analysis does not preclude the interests of the stakeholders overriding the interests of the other stakeholders affected, but it ensures that all affected will be considered. Stakeholder analysis is frequently used during the preparation phase of a project to assess the attitudes of the stakeholders regarding the potential changes.

Strategic Choice Approach (SCA) Strategic choice is viewed as an ongoing process in which the planned management of uncertainty plays a crucial role. It focuses on decisions to be made in a particular planning situation, whatever their timescale and whatever their substance. It also highlights the subtle judgements involved in agreeing how to handle the uncertainties which surround the decision to be addressed—whether these be technical, political, or procedural. The approach is an incremental one, rather than one which looks towards an end product of a comprehensive strategy at some future point in time and consists of 4 basic principles: Shaping, Designing, Comparing, and Choosing.

Strategic Options Analysis (SOA) A generalised version (more user friendly term) of Morphological Analysis (MA).

SWOT Strengths, Weaknesses, Opportunities, and Threats: a classic but dated analysis tool. This technique does not require any particular training. It is also already well known among organisations. SWOT analysis is used to analyse the competition context and product strategies in particular. It deals with the impact of the main internal factors (i.e.: organisational structure, culture, competences, partnership networks, etc.) and the main external factors (i.e.: technology level in the sector, competitors' position, etc.) which define a firm's or an organisation's market position, in order to develop a competitive strategy.

Systems Dynamics System dynamics is an aspect of systems theory as a method to understand the dynamic behaviour of complex systems. System dynamics (SD) is an approach to understanding the nonlinear behaviour of complex systems over time using stocks, flows, internal feedback loops, table functions, and time delays. The basis of the method is the recognition that the structure of any system, the many circular, interlocking, sometimes time-delayed relationships among its components, is often just as important in determining its behaviour as the individual components themselves. Examples are chaos theory and social dynamics. SD can be seen as a discipline in its own right rather than just a method or model.

Technological Forecasting Also simply known as (TF) is concerned with the investigation of new technologies and trends. It is a combination of creative thinking, expert views, and alternative scenarios as input to the strategic planning process.

Tool A MTT—a specific and tangible device to address a unitary problem (such as a post-it note for use in a brainstorming exercise).

Uncertainty and Risk Often used interchangeably but essentially different: Uncertainty implies incomplete information where some or all of the relevant information to a problem is unavailable. Risk indicates only partial information (usually metrics), is available, and is probabilistic so that when future events or activities occur they do so with some measure of probability. Whilst Risk can be quantified, Uncertainty cannot, as it is not measurable but both can be modelled.

Variable "A characteristic, number, or quantity that increases or decreases over time, or takes different values in different situations" (Business Dictionary). The term can be substituted for parameter for purposes of morphological modelling.

Weak Signal Analysis "Weak signals" reside within the domain of the uncertain. Identification can help organisations deal with discontinuities and strategic surprises based in the assumption that discontinuities do not emerge without warning. Weak signals are first symptoms or early signals of a change telling about a strengthening trend and bringing information that is not yet seen . . .and can reveal threats and opportunities for an organisation. They could also be defined wild cards that change the development and are unpredictable when turning up. Weak signals are events below the surface, overlooked, but that may be signs of big evolution.

Wicked Problem A "wicked problem" is one that is difficult or impossible to solve because of incomplete, contradictory, and changing requirements that are often difficult to recognise. Typically, the problem is viewed from different perspectives from different stakeholders, is highly dynamic and complex with inherent uncertainties.

Bibliography and Resources

Main List of Bibliographical Sources Used in Book

Ackoff, R. (1961). *Progress in operations research*. Wiley.

Ackoff, R. (1974a). *Redesigning the future*. Wiley-Interscience.

Ackoff, R. L. (1974b). *Redesigning the future*. Wiley-Interscience.

Alexander, M. A. (2002). The Kondratiev cycle. *Writers Club Press*.

Ansoff, H. I. (1975). Managing strategic surprise by response to weak signals. *California Management Review Winter, XVIII*(2).

Ayres, R. U. (1969). *Technological forecasting and long range planning* (pp. 72–93). McGraw-Hill, Inc. Ch.5, Morphological Analysis.

Azhar, A. (2021). *Exponential*. Random House.

Beer, S. (1984). The viable system model: Its provenance, development, methodology and pathology. *Journal of the Operational Research Society, 35*, 7–26.

Ben-Haim, Y. (2019). Info-Gap Decision Theory chapter 5. In *Decision making under deep uncertainty*. Springer.

Bennett, N., & Lemoine, G. L. (2014). What VUCA really means for you. *Harvard Business Review Magazine*.

Boin, A., McConell, A., & Hart, P. (2020, March). *Leading in a crisis: Strategic crisis leadership during the COVID-19 pandemic*. A Boin, (Leiden University), A McConnell, (University of Sydney), P 't Hart (Utrecht University/ANZSOG), The Mandarin.

Bonaccorsi, A., Apreda, R., & Fantoni, G. (2020). Expert biases in technology foresight. Why they are a problem and how to mitigate them. *Technological Forecasting & Social Change*.

Bostrom, N., & Circkovic, M. M. (2008). *Global catastrophic risks*. Oxford University Press.

Bowman, C. (1995). Strategy workshops and top-team commitment to strategic change. *Journal of Managerial Psychology, 10*(8), 4–12.

Camillus, J. (2008). Strategy as a wicked problem. *Harvard Business Review*.

Cass/Airmic. (2011, July). *Roads to Ruin – "a study of major risk events"*. Cass Business School/Airmic.

Ceeney, N. (2010, February). *The National Archives – "Challenges and opportunities going forward for information and knowledge management across government" at "The Future of Evidence"*. Foresight Horizon Scanning Centre – Government Office for Science.

CNN report – "Finland is winning the war on fake news. What it's learned may be crucial to Western democracy" E Kiernan, 2019.

Coburn, A., Chang, M., Sullivan, M., Bowman, G., & Ruffle, S. (2013). *"Disease outbreak: Human pandemic". Cambridge risk framework: Profile of a macro-catastrophe threat type.* (Centre for Risk Studies Working Paper 201303.31). University of Cambridge Judge Business School.

Conklin, J. (2006). Dialogue mapping: Building shared understanding of wicked problems. *John Wiley & Sons Ltd.*

Connell, N.. Evaluating soft OR: some reflections on an apparently "unsuccessful" implementation using Soft Systems Methodology (SSM).

Courtney, H. G., Kirkland, J., & Viguerie, S. P. (2000). Four levels of uncertainty (Strategy under Uncertainty). *McKinsey & Company.*

Craven, M., Liu, L., Mysore, M., & Wilson, M. (2020). Briefing note on Covid scenarios. *McKinsey and Company,* (March 2020).

Curry, A., & Schultz, W. (2009). Roads less travelled: different methods, different futures. *Journal of Futures Studies.*

Dator, J. A. (2002). *Advancing futures.* Praeger.

de Neufville, R., & Smet, K. (2019). *Engineering options analysis. Chapter 6, in Decision Making Under Deep Uncertainty.* Springer.

Defense One – October 2019. https://www.defenseone.com

Durkheim E. (1897) Le Suicide: Etude de sociologie. .

EIU. (2011). *The complexity challenge – How businesses are bearing up.* The Economist Intelligence Unit.

FactBar EDU. (2018). Elections approach – are you ready? Fact checking for educators and future voters. FactBar EDU

Fenton, N., & Neil, M. (2013). *Risk assessment and decision analysis with Bayesian networks.* CRC Press.

Festinger, L. (1957). *A theory of cognitive dissonance.* Stanford University Press.

Financial Times, Why can't economists predict disruptive events. Gavyn Davies, February 10th 2011.

French Simon. (Ed.) (2018). *Decision support tools for complex decisions under uncertainty*: Published by the Analysis Under Uncertainty for Decision Makers Network (AU4DM).

Friedman, T. (2014, November 22). *Stampeding Black Elephants.* New York Times.

From Simon Caulkin summarising V F Ridgway's paper 'Dysfunctional Consequences of Performance Measurements' in Administrative Science Quarterly 1956.

Funtowicz S.O & Ravetz J.R (1994, May). *Uncertainty, complexity and post-normal science.* Annual Review of Environmental Toxicology and Chemistry Vol 13, No 12. Pergamon.

Future Today Institute. (2020, January). *2020 Tech Trends Report* (13th edn.). The Future Today Institute

Futures Toolkit. (2017, November). *"The Futures Toolkit": UK Government Office for Science.*

Gallasch, G., Jordans, J., & Ivanova, K. (2017). *"Application of Field Anomaly Relaxation to Battlefield Casualties and Treatment: A Formal Approach to Consolidating Large Morphological Spaces" Paper in "Data and Decision Sciences in Action".* Springer.

Gartner Glossary. (2021). Dark Data.

Garvey, B., & Childs, P. R. N. (2013, February 15). *Applying Problem Structuring Methods to the Design Process for Safety Helmets.* In Proceedings of the 1st International Conference on Helmet Performance and Design, London.

Garvey, B. (2016, October). *Combining qualitative and qualitative aspects of problem structuring in computational morphological analysis* (PhD Thesis Dyson School of Design Engineering). Imperial College London.

Garvey, B. (2021, August). *Re-assessing How Uncertainty Should Be Treated To Mitigate Risk: A Management Template.* Paper accepted for SSIM Conference Taiwan.

Garvey, B., Childs, P. R. N., & Varnarvides, G. (2013). *"Using Morphological Distance to Refine Morphological Analysis Solutions"* B Garvey (Imperial College London), P R N Childs

(Imperial College London), G Varnarvides (Massachusetts Institute of Technology). Unpublished paper London.

Garvey, B., & Childs, P. R. N. (2016). *Design as an unstructured problem: New methods to help reduce uncertainty – A Practitioner Perspective: Impact of Design Research on Industrial Practice*. Springer International.

Goldstein, M. (2011). *Uncertainty analysis for computer models*. Durham University.

Gowing, N., & Langdon, C. (2017). *Thinking the Unthinkable – a new imperative for leadership in the digital age: An interim report*. Published by CIMA London.

Grint, K. (1997). *Fuzzy management: Contemporary ideas and practices at work*. Oxford University Press.

Liu, H.-Y., Lauta, K., & Maas, M. (2020). Apocalypse now? *Journal of International Humanitarian Legal Studies, 11*.

Haasnoot, M., Warren, A., & Kwakkel, J. H. (2019). *"Dynamic Adaptive Policy Pathways" chapter 4 in "Decision Making Under Deep Uncertainty"*. Springer.

Hakmeh, J., Taylor, E., Peters, A., & Ignatidou, S. (2021). *The COVID-19 pandemic and trends in technology: Transformation in governance and society, Research Paper*. Royal Institute of International Affairs. https://www.chathamhouse.org/2021/02/covid-19-pandemic-and-trends-technology

Hand, D. J. (2020). *Dark data – why what you don't know matters*. Princeton University Press.

Harrysson, M., Metayer, E., & Sarrazin, H. (2014). The strength of 'weak signals'. *McKinsey Quarterly*.

Henchey, N. (1978). Making sense of future studies. *Alternatives, 7*, 104–111.

Heuer, R. J., Jr., & Pherson, R. H. (2011). *Structured analytic techniques for intelligence analysis*. CQ Press.

Hiltunen, E. (2008). Good sources of weak signals: A global study of where futurists look for weak signals, Journal of Futures Studies, *12*(4), 21–44.

Ho, P. (2017, April 7). *Hunting Black Swans & Taming Black Elephants: Governance in a Complex World*. IPS-Nathan Lectures, Singapore.

Hubbard, D. W. (2007). *How to measure anything – Finding the value of intangibles in business*. Wiley.

Imperial College TechForesight. (2018, January). *Table of disruptive technologies*. .

Inayatullah, S. (Ed.), (2004). *The Causal Layered Analysis (CLA) Reader - Theory and Case Studies of an Integrative and Transformative Methodology* Edited by Sohail Inayatullah - Published by Tamkang University Press Graduate Institute of Futures Studies, Taipei, Taiwan 251 2004. (Document can be downloaded from the web as a Pdf).

Jantsch, E. (1967). *Technological forecasting in perspective* (pp. 29–34). OECD.

Kahn, H., & Wiener, A. J. (1967). *The year 2000 – A framework for speculation on the next thirty-three years*. Macmillan.

Kahn, H. (1962). *Thinking about the unthinkable*. Horizon Press.

Kahneman, D., Slovic, P., & Tversky, A. (Eds.). (1982). *Judgment under uncertainty: Heuristics and biases*. Cambridge University Press.

Kay, J. (2008, November 26). *Predictive models "Blown off course by butterflies*. Financial Times P13.

King, M., & Kay, J. (2020). *Radical uncertainty – Decision-making for an unknowable future*. The Bridge Press.

Knight Frank. (1921). *Risk, Uncertainty, and Profit*.

Kreig, M.L. (2001). *A Tutorial of Bayesian Belief Networks*. Surveillance System Division – Electronics and Surveillance Research laboratory – DSTO-TN-0403.

Kunz, W., & Rittel, H. (1970). *Issues as elements of information systems* (Working Paper No.131). Heidelberg-Berkeley.

Kuosa, T., & Stucki, M. (2020a, December 8). Futures Intelligence: Types of Futures Knowledge. *Futures Platform*.

Kuosa, T., & Stucki, M. (2020b, December). Trends – they are everywhere. *The Futures Platform*.

Kuosa, T., & Stucki, M. (2020c, December 8). Futures intelligence: Types of futures knowledge. *Futures Platform*.

Kuosa, T. (2012). *The evolution of strategic foresight*. Alternative Futures Finland.

Kurzweil, R. (1999). *The age of spiritual machines - How we will live, work and think in the new age of intelligent machines*. Texere.

Laing, R. D. (1967). *Extract from page 15, 16 & 17 – Chapter 1 – Persons and Experience. The politics of experience and the bird of paradise*. Penguin Books.

Lempert, R. J. (2019). *Robust decision making chapter 2 in Decision making under deep uncertainty*. Springer.

Lempert, R. J., Popper, W., & Bankes, S. C. (2003). *Shaping the Next One Hundred Years: New Methods for Quantitative, Long-Term Policy Analysis*. MR-1626-RPC, RAND.

Levin, K., Cashore, B., Auld, G., & Bernstein, S.Introduced the distinction between "wicked problems" and "super wicked problems" in a 2007 conference paper, followed by a 2012 journal article in *Policy Sciences*. Problems.

List, D. (2004). *Multiple pasts, converging presents, and alternative futures. Futures 36*. Elsevier.

Lorenz, E. (1993). *The essence of chaos*. University of Washington.

Lum, R. (2016, March). *4 Steps to the Future: A Quick and Clean Guide to Creating Foresight*. Vision Foresight Strategy.

Machau, V. A. W. J., Walker, W. E., Bloemen, P. J. T. M., & Popper, S. W. (Eds.). (2019). *Decision making under deep uncertainty – From theory to practice*. Springer.

Majaro, S. (1988). *The creative gap: Managing ideas for profit*. Longman. Ch. 8.

Makridakis, S., & Taleb, N. (2009, October-December). Living in a world of low levels of predictability. *International Journal of Forecasting, 25*(4) Elsevier BV.

Makridakis, S. (1982). *If we cannot forecast how can we plan? (Makridakis, 1981), and "A chronology of the last six recessions"* Makridakis.

Marchau, V., Walker, W., Bloeman, P., & Popper, S. (Eds.). (2019). *Decision making under deep uncertainty - From theory to practice*. Springer.

Marczyk, J. (2009). *A new theory of risk and rating*. Editrice UNI Service.

Marsh, D. *A robust approach to military research programme planning*. Smith System Engineering Ltd.

Mau, S. (2019). *The metric society*. Polity.

Merton, R. K. (1938, October). Social structure and Anomie. *American Sociological Review, 3*(5).

Mitchell, M. (2009). *Complexity: A guided tour*. Oxford University Press.

Mohammad, A., & Sykes, R. (2012). Black swans turn grey – The transformation of risk. *PWC*.

Nelson, H. G., & Stolterman, E. (2012). In H. G. Nelson & E. Stolterman (Eds.), *The design way* (2nd ed.). MIT Press.

Nelson, R. R. (1974). *Intellectualizing about the Moon-Ghetto Metaphor*. Policy Sciences 5 (pp. 375–414). Elsevier Scientific Publishing Amsterdam.

O'Neil, C. (2016). *Weapons of math destruction*. Penguin, Random House.

Ord, T. (2020). *The precipice – Existential risk and the future of humanity*. Bloomsbury Publishing.

Ormerod, R. (2001, October). *Viewpoint: The success and failure of methodologies – a comment on Connell (2001): Evaluating soft OR*. The Journal of Operational Research Society. Palgrave.

Ota, S., & Maki-Teeri, M. (2021, February). *"Science Fiction", from Futures Platform – Wild Cards and Science Fiction* Free Imagination.

Padbury, P. (2019). *An Overview of the Horizons Foresight Method Using system based-scenarios and the "inner game" of foresight. Chief Futurist, Policy Horizons*. Government of Canada.

Pherson, R. H., & Pyrik, R. (2018). *Analyst's Guide to Indicators. The Analyst's Bookshop*. Pherson Associates LLC.

Pherson, R. H., & Schwartz, A. (2008). *Handbook of analytic tools and techniques*. Pherson Associates.

Pherson, R. H. (2019). *Handbook of analytic tools & techniques* (5th ed.). R H Pherson, The Analyst's Bookshop.

Pherson, R.H. (2021, May). *Moving toward constructive solutions*. The Analytic Insider

Pidd, M. (1996). *Tools for thinking* (p. 40). Wiley.

Pilkey, O. H., & Pilkey-Jarvis, L. (2007). *Useless arithmetic – Why environmental scientists can't predict the future*. Columbia University Press.

Poli, R. (2018). A note on the classification of future- related methods. *European Journal of Futures Research, 6*, 15.

Pringle, R. (2016, November 14). Social Media is blinding us to other points of view. *CBC News*.

PWC. (2012, January). *Black Swans Turn Grey – the transformation of risk*.

Rajan, A. (2017, January). *Fake News: Too important to ignore*. BBC News Item.

Recchia, G., Freeman, A., & Spiegelhalter, D. (2021, May 5). How well did experts and laypeople forecast the size of the COVID-19 pandemic? *Plos One*.

Ringland, G., Lustig, P., Phaal, R., Duckworth, M., & Yapp, C. (2012). In G. Ringland, P. Lustig, R. Phaal, M. Duckworth, & C. Yapp (Eds.), *Here be Dragons*. The Choir Press.

Ritchey, T. (2006). Problem structuring using computer-aided morphological analysis. *Journal of the Operational Research Society, 57*, 792–801.

Ritchey, T. (December 2002). *Modelling complex socio-technical systems using morphological analysis*. Adapted from Address to the Swedish Parliamentary IT Commission.

Ritchey, T. (2011). *Wicked problems and social messes: Decision support modelling with morphological analysis*. Springer.

Rittel, H., & Webber, M. (1973). *Dilemmas in a general theory of planning. Policy Sciences*. (Vol. 4, pp. 155–169). Elsevier Scientific Publishing Company Inc.

Rosenhead, J., & Mingers, J. (2001). *A new paradigm of analysis in rational analysis for a problematic world revisited* (2nd ed.). John Wiley.

Rumsfeld, D. (2002, February 12). *Department of Defense news briefing*.

Saaty, T. L. (2008). *Decision making for leaders: The analytic hierarchy process for decisions in a complex world*. RWS Publications.

Sandal, G. (2021, February 16). Future of Truth in the Information Age? *The Futures Platform*.

Schwartz, P. (2003, June). *Inevitable surprises – Thinking ahead in a time of turbulence*. Gotham Books (Penguin Group – USA).

Scott, R., Nicholas Bloom, B., & Davis, S. J. (2015, October). *Measuring Economic Policy Uncertain* (Working Paper 21633). National Bureau of Economic Research, 1050 Massachusetts Avenue. http://www.nber.org/papers/w21633.

Shell. (2005). *Shell Global Scenarios to 2025*. Pub Shell.

Siegel, E. (2017). *Star trek treknology – The science of star trek from tricorders to warp drive*. Voyageur Press.

Simon, A. H. (1977). *The new science of management decision*. Prentice-Hall.

SOIF. (2021, January). *The long pandemic: After the COVID-19 crises*. SOIF (School of International Futures).

Stanley Robinson, K. (2020). The Ministry for the Future. *Orbit*.

Stern, N. (2009). The global deal – Climate change and the creation of a new era of progress and prosperity. *The Bodley Head*.

Taleb, N. N. (2007). *The Black Swan*. Allen Lane.

Taylor J, Cognitive Biases are Bad for Business –May 2013

Tetlock, P. E. (2005). *Expert Political Judgement*. Princeton University Press.

The Global Risks Report. (2021). *16th Edition, is published by the World Economic Forum*. Strategic Partners Marsh McLennan SK Group Zurich Insurance Group.

Thom, R. (1972). *Structural Stability and Morphogenesis*. W.A Benjamin.

Toffler, A. (1970). *Future Shock*. The Bodley Head.

Treverton, G. (2010). Addressing complexities in homeland security. In L. K. Johnson (Ed.), *The Oxford handbook of national security intelligence*. Oxford University Press.

Tversky, A., & Kahneman, D. (1974, September 27). Judgement under uncertainty: Heuristics and biases. *Science, New Series, 185*(4157).

Uncertainty Toolkit for Analysts in Government. https://analystsuncertaintytoolkit.github.io/UncertaintyWeb/index.html

van der Heijden, K. (1996). *Scenarios – The Art of Strategic Conversation*. John Wiley & Sons.

van Notten, P., Philip, W., Rotmans, J., van Asselt, M., & Rothman, D. (2003). *An updated scenario typology. Futures, 35*. Pergamon / Elsevier.

Vanston, J. H. (2007). *P40 Section 3 in "Technology forecasting – An aid to effective technology management"*. Technology Futures Inc.

Voigt, C., Unnterfrauner, E., & Kieslinger, B., (2011). *Identifying Weak Signals in Expert Discussions of Technology Enhanced Learning*. Centre for Social Innovation, Linke Wienzeile 246, 1150 Vienna, Austria. eChallenges e-2011 Conference Proceedings Paul Cunningham and Miriam Cunningham (Eds) IIMC International Information Management Corporation, 2011. ISBN: 978-1-905824-27-4.

Voros, J. (2001, December). *A primer on futures studies, foresight and the use of scenarios*. Swinburne University of Technology. The Foresight Bulletin, No 6, Swinburne University of Technology.

Voros, J. (1994). *The Futures Cone, use and history*. 2017 (Source: Adapted from Voros (2003, 2017), which was based on Hancock and Bezold.

Wachter-Boettcher, S. (2017). *Technically wrong*. W. Norton & Co Ltd.

Walker, W. E., Marchau, V. A. W. J., & Kwakkel, J. H. (2019). *"Dynamic Adaptive Planning" chapter 3 in Decision Making Under Deep Uncertainty*. Springer.

Wardle, C., & Derakshan, H. (2017, September). *Information Disorder: Toward an interdisciplinary framework for research and policy making*. Council of Europe.

Wooldridge, S. (2003). *Introduction (from Bayesian Belief Networks)*. Australian Institute of Marine Science Prepared for CSIRO Centre for Complex Systems Science 1 CSIRO.

World Economic Forum. (2016). *Global disease outbreaks – Risk of infectious disease outbreaks: Analysis*. World Economic Forum.

Wucker, M. (2016). *The Grey Rhino*. St Martin's Press.

Yritys, A.-M. (2014, October 18). Identifying weak signals before they become strong trends. *Change Management, Futurology, Global Economics*.

Zwicky, F. (1969). *Discovery, invention, research: Through the morphological approach*. Macmillan.

Zwicky, F. (1948). Morphological astronomy. *The Observatory, 68*(845), 121–143.

Zwicky, F. (1947). Morphology and nomenclature of jet engines. *Aeronautical Engineering Review, 6*(6), 49–50.

Zwicky, F. (1962). *Morphology of propulsive power*. Society of Morphological Research.

Zwicky, F. (1967, May 22–24). *The morphological approach to discovery, invention, research and construction from new methods of thought and procedure. Contributions to the symposium of methodologies*. Springer.

Additional Resources

The Futures Platform: https://www.futuresplatform.com/ (Finland)
Shaping Tomorrow: https://www.shapingtomorrow.com (UK)
The Future Institute: https://thefuturesinstitute.org (USA)
SITRA: https://www.sitra.fi/en/ (Finland)
"sciFutures.com"
www.strategyforesight.org
https://insyt.today